Classroom Management

Classroom Management

Sound Theory and Effective Practice,
Third Edition

Robert T. Tauber

Bergin & Garvey
Westport, Connecticut
London

Library of Congress Cataloging-in-Publication Data

Tauber, Robert T.
    Classroom management : sound theory and effective practice / by
Robert T. Tauber.—3rd ed.
        p. cm.
    Rev. ed. of: Classroom management from A to Z. c1990.
    Includes bibliographical references (p.   ) and indexes.
    ISBN 0–89789–618–1 (alk. paper).—ISBN 0–89789–619–X (pbk. :
alk. paper)
        1. Classroom management—United States.   2. School discipline—
United States.   I. Tauber, Robert T. Classroom management from A
to Z. II. Title.
LB3011.T38   1999
371.102'4—dc21   99–12711

British Library Cataloguing in Publication Data is available.

Library of Congress Catalog Card Number: 99–12711
ISBN: 0–89789–618–1
        0–89789–619–X (pbk.)

First published in 1999

Bergin & Garvey, 88 Post Road West, Westport, CT 06881
An imprint of Greenwood Publishing Group, Inc.
www.greenwood.com

Printed in the United States of America

The paper used in this book complies with the
Permanent Paper Standard issued by the National
Information Standards Organization (Z39.48–1984).

10 9 8 7 6 5 4 3 2

Copyright Acknowledgments

The author and the publisher gratefully acknowledge permission for use of the following
material:

Line drawings of B. F. Skinner, Carl R. Rogers, James C. Dobson, Marlene and Lee Canter,
Fredric H. Jones, Rudolf Dreikurs, William Glasser, and Thomas Gordon are used with
permission by the artist, Patrick R. Sharbaugh, and with permission of *Distance Education*,
The Pennsylvania State University.

Contents

Preface   xiii

PART I   INTRODUCTION AND FRAMEWORKS   1

Chapter 1   Introduction: Some Straight Talk on Discipline   3

Objectives   3
Discipline: A Real Problem?   3
What Is Your Philosophy of Discipline?   4
Teacher Evaluations   5
Little New in the Discipline World   7
Hula Hoops, Pet Rocks, and Rubik's Cubes   8
Playing the Odds   8
Omission and Commission   9
Effective Teaching Must Be Present   9
Water Seeks Its Own Level   11
Courses in Classroom Management   11
Where Do Teachers Develop Competency in Classroom
        Management?   12
Read More on Classroom Management   13
Effective Discipline: Simply Common Sense?   14
Doctor, Doctor, I Have This Pain!   14
Summary   15

**Chapter 2   Theoretical Frameworks for Selecting a
                    Discipline Model**   17

Objectives   17
Discipline Models: Their Origin   17
A Schools of Thought Framework: Wolfgang and Glickman   19
A Social Bases of Power Framework: French and Raven   21
A Behaviorist-Humanist Framework: Skinner versus Rogers   28
A Keeping It Simple Framework: Lewis   35
Why Not an Eclectic Approach?: A Few Final Arguments   35
Using a Discipline Model That "Works"   38
Test Yourself   39

**PART II   "TRIED AND TRUE" MODELS OF CLASSROOM
                  MANAGEMENT**   41

Chapter 3   James Dobson: A Place for Punishment   43

Objectives   44
*Where Does Dobson's Model Fall within the Four Theoretical
        Frameworks Discussed in Chapter 2?*   44
Introduction   44
Virtues of Punishment   46
First-Day Approaches of Two Teachers   48
Others Who Support Punishment   49
Guidelines for Administering Punishment   51
Challenges to Punishment   54
Organizations Favoring the Abolishment of Corporal Punishment   56
The Demographics of Punishment   57
Center for the Study of Corporal Punishment in Schools   58
*What Parents Can Do If Their School District Uses
        Corporal Punishment*   59
Selected Research on Dobson's "A Place for Punishment" Model   61
Learning More about Dobson's "A Place for Punishment" Model   64
Test Yourself   64
Ask Yourself: Is This Model for You?   65

**Chapter 4   Lee and Marlene Canter: Assertive Discipline: A
                    "Take-Charge" Approach to Classroom
                    Management**   67

Objectives   67

Where Does the Canters' Model Fall within the Four Theoretical
Frameworks Discussed in Chapter 2?   68
"C" for Controversy; "C" for Canter   68
A "Take-Charge" Attitude: Becoming the Alpha *Male*   69
Response Styles   70
Response Styles in Action   72
Rules and a Discipline Plan   73
Positive Recognition: A Canter Emphasis   75
Several Other Assertive Discipline Tactics   76
Delivering Your Assertive Message Assertively   78
I-Messages: The Canter Way   79
Does Assertive Discipline Work?   80
Punished by Rewards   81
Selected Research on the Canters' Assertive Discipline Model 83
Learning More about the Canters' Assertive Discipline Model 87
Test Yourself   87
Ask Yourself: Is This Model for You?   88

Chapter 5   Fredric H. Jones: Positive Discipline   **89**

Objectives   89
Where Does Jones' Model Fall within the Four Theoretical
Frameworks Discussed in Chapter 2?   90
From Theory to Practice   90
Layer Cake Approach   90
Classroom Structure   91
Limit Setting   93
Responsibility Training (Including PATs)   99
The Backup System   103
Positive Classroom Instruction   103
Selected Research on Jones' Positive Discipline Model   104
Learning More about Jones' Positive Discipline Model   106
Test Yourself   106
Ask Yourself: Is This Model for You?   107

Chapter 6   Rudolf Dreikurs: Social Discipline   **109**

Objectives   109
Where Does Dreikurs' Model Fall within the Four Theoretical
Frameworks Discussed in Chapter 2?   110
Kids Are People, Too   110
Clues to a Child's Goal for Misbehaving   112

Alternative Behaviors for Teachers   115
Natural, Logical, and Contrived Consequences   118
Encouragement or *Praise*   121
Praise versus Encouragement Research—An Eye-Opener!   123
Delivering Encouragement Messages   125
Selected Research on Dreikurs' Social Discipline Model   127
Learning More about Dreikurs' Social Discipline Model   129
Test Yourself   130
Ask Yourself: Is This Model for You?   131

**Chapter 7   William Glasser: Reality Therapy, Choice Theory,
                and Quality Schools   133**

Objectives   133
*Where Does Glasser's Model Fall within the Four Theoretical
    Frameworks Discussed in Chapter 2?*   134
Introduction   134
Schools without Failure   135
Elements of Reality Therapy   135
School Must Be a Good Place   136
Forming Rules   137
Steps in Reality Therapy   138
Choice Theory in the Classroom   142
Learning: The Key for Meeting All Basic Human Needs   146
The Quality School: Managing Students without Coercion   148
*Selected Research on Glasser's Reality Therapy, Choice Theory,
    and Quality Schools Model*   150
*Learning More about Glasser's Reality Therapy, Choice Theory,
    and Quality Schools Model*   152
Test Yourself   154
Ask Yourself: Is This Model for You?   155

Chapter 8   Thomas Gordon: Teacher Effectiveness Training   157

Objectives   157
*Where Does Gordon's Model Fall within the Four Theoretical
    Frameworks Discussed in Chapter 2?*   158
Two Common Problems   158
T.E.T.: Some Background   158
The T.E.T. Rectangle   159
Practice with "Other Owns the Problem" Situations   161
Roadblocks to Communication   162

Alternatives to Roadblocks — 164
I-messages: When You Own a Problem — 167
Differences Between a Canter and a Gordon I-message — 170
Conflict Resolution — 171
Don't Keep T.E.T. a Secret — 172
Selected Research on Gordon's Teacher Effectiveness Training Model — 173
Learning More about Gordon's Teacher Effectiveness Training Model — 175
Test Yourself — 175
Ask Yourself: Is This Model for You? — 176
Time to Choose One of the Six "Tried and True" Discipline Models — 177

PART III THEORIES AND PRACTICES RELATING TO MORE EFFECTIVE CLASSROOM MANAGEMENT 179

Chapter 9 Other Noted Authors: What They Have to Say about Discipline 181

Objectives — 181
Linda Albert: Cooperative Discipline — 182
Stephen G. Barkley: Project T.E.A.C.H. — 184
Richard Curwin and Allen Mendler: Discipline with Dignity — 186
Forrest Gathercoal: Judicious Discipline — 188
Haim G. Ginott: Communication Discipline — 190
Herb Grossman: Multicultural Discipline — 191
Madeline Hunter: Enhancing Teaching (Preventative Discipline) — 194
Larry Koenig: Smart Discipline — 196
Jacob S. Kounin: Withitness (*and more*) Discipline — 197
Jane Nelsen: Positive Discipline (*not the same as Jones'* Positive Discipline *model*) — 200
William A. Rogers (Australian Author): Decisive Discipline — 202
Michael Valentine: A Family-Systems Approach Adapted to Schools — 205
Harry K. Wong: The First Days of School — 208
Test Yourself — 210

Chapter 10 Ideas for Preventing Problem Behaviors 211

Objectives — 211
Teachers as Pygmalions: Good or Bad, What We Expect We Generally Get! — 212
Changing Teachers' Attitudes Toward Punishment — 221
Acting Lessons for Teachers: Using Performance Skills in the Classroom — 224
Test Yourself — 231

Chapter 11   Some Surprising Ideas about Discipline   233

Objectives   233
The Negative Side of Praise   234
The Positive Side of Negative Reinforcement   241
Defusing Power Struggles: Alternatives to "Fighting Back" or "Giving In" 247
Test Yourself   252

**Chapter 12   "A" Through "Z" Suggestions for More Effective
                Classroom Management**   253

Objectives   253
A Through Z Suggestions   253
   "A" for Act; Don't Just React   256
   "A" for Assign Responsibility   257
   "B" for Back Away   258
   "C" for Calm and Businesslike   259
   "C" for Catch Students Being Good   260
   "C" for Individual or Private Correction   261
   "D" for Make a Deal with a Fellow Teacher   262
   "E" for Prepare an Emergency Plan   263
   "E" for Enforce; Don't Negotiate   264
   "E" for Eye Messages   265
   "F" for Friendly versus Friends   266
   "G" for Don't Hold a Grudge   267
   "I" for Identify Specific Misbehaviors   267
   "J" for Judge and Jury   268
   "M" for Mr. or Miss   269
   "N" for Learn Their Names   270
   "N" for Personal Needs: Yours and Theirs   271
   "O" for Organized   272
   "O" for Overprepare   273
   "P" for Don't Take It Personally   273
   "P" for Premack Principle (Grandma's Rule)   274
   "P" for Punctuality   275
   "R" for Return Assignments and Tests Quickly   277
   "S" for Secure Their Attention—First!   277
   "S" for Surprise Them, or "How Did You Know That?"   278
   "T" for Say "Thank You"   279
   "T" for Threats and Warnings   280
   "U" for Be Up   281
   "V" for Visibility (and At Times Invisibility)   282

"W" for Wait-Time   283
"W" for "We," Not "You"   283
"X" for Exemplify Desired Behavior; Don't Be a Hypocrite   284
Test Yourself   285

Chapter 13   Violence in Today's Schools   287

Objectives   287
The Increasing Problem of School Violence   287
Origins of School Violence   288
What Is the School's Responsibility?   289
Preventing School Violence   290
What Is the Teacher's Responsibility?   292
Recognizing Warning Signs   293
A Team Approach to Intervention   293
Using a CAT   294
An Individual Approach to Intervention   295
Conclusion   296
Selected Internet Resources   296
Test Yourself   297

Chapter 14   Educational Resources Information Center (ERIC)   299

Objectives   299
Introduction   299
Discipline Topics of Interest to Teachers   300
What Is ERIC?   301
Access to ERIC   301
Resources in Education   301
Current Index to Journals in Education   303
Thesaurus of ERIC Descriptors   303
Computer-Search Capability   304
ERIC on the Internet   304
Warning! Prepare a "Shopping List"   305
Publish, Who Me?   305
Conclusion   306
ERIC Clearinghouses   306
Test Yourself   310

References   311

Author Index   329

Subject Index   335

Preface

Educators need to balance discipline theory with its practice in the classroom. This is especially important in today's educational arena where increased demands for teacher accountability exist. *Classroom Management: Sound Theory and Effective Practice* is designed for those who are new to teaching or who have had little course work in discipline and do not have the time to read numerous theory-based articles and books. Among those most likely to benefit from this book are the following:

- College students taking part in early off-campus field experiences. Such activities are increasingly being required by state and regional certification boards. It is never too soon to begin reading and studying classroom management theory and practice.

- College students taking an educational psychology course in which the primary textbook (like most) devotes, at best, a single chapter to discipline.

- Student teachers who are taking part in a semester-long practicum for which effective classroom management skills, and the theories behind them, are a must—not a luxury.

- First- and second-year classroom teachers who, like their student teacher counterparts, need effective discipline techniques for success—perhaps even survival.

- Seasoned teachers who may not have had sufficient course work (and most have not) in classroom management or who simply wish to review the area of discipline.

- Students enrolled in a classroom management course or seminar.

- Faculty and administrative mentors who wish to offer constructive suggestions regarding discipline that are based upon sound pedagogical theory.

Part I, titled "Introduction and Frameworks," consists of two chapters. The first chapter offers some up-front, straight talk on discipline. It argues that discipline, as a means to an end, is necessary to "keep the learning act afloat." Chapter 2 presents several theoretical, but very readable, frameworks within which each of the six "Tried and True" Models of Classroom Management described in Part II can be pigeonholed.

Part II, titled "Tried and True" Models of Discipline, presents six classroom discipline models, one per chapter, that have stood the test of time. All of the models work! The key to effective discipline is deciding which model will work best for you. The models, arranged from the most to the least interventionist in nature, include:

- James Dobson: A Place for Punishment
- Lee and Marlene Canter: Assertive Discipline
- Fredric H. Jones: Positive Discipline
- Rudolf Dreikurs: Social Discipline
- William Glasser: Reality Therapy, Choice Theory, and Quality Schools
- Thomas Gordon: Teacher Effectiveness Training

Part III investigates further the "Theories and Practices Relating to More Effective Classroom Management." Chapter 9 summarizes what other recognized authors have to say on the subject of classroom management. Chapter 10 explores several topics specifically designed to prevent problem behaviors from occurring in the first place. Chapter 11 presents some surprising (and sometimes controversial) ideas about discipline. Chapter 12 offers a series of specific "A through Z" suggestions that teachers can use immediately to more effectively handle classroom discipline. Chapter 13 deals with the increasing problem of school violence. Finally, Chapter 14 presents the Educational Resources Information Center (ERIC), a resource for unlocking additional information on any and all topics in education—including discipline!

Many people have provided help toward the development of this book. I would like to thank my educational psychology students who, through their many hours of off-campus field experience in local schools, have contributed questions and comments to help me add focus to the theory and practice of classroom management. I want to thank each of the authors of the six discipline models highlighted in this second edition. All of them, or their representatives, were extremely helpful in supplying resource materials and reviewing drafts of chapters.

Extra special thanks are offered to Mrs. Wendy Eidenmuller who willingly read and marked drafts of this book. Without her dedication, this book would not have been possible. I want to thank my wife, my colleague, and my best friend, Cecelia S. Tauber, for her unwavering support and encouragement in this, and all, projects. Finally, I want to acknowledge my son, David, and my daughter, Rebecca, for being part of my life.

PART I

INTRODUCTION
AND FRAMEWORKS

CHAPTER 1
Introduction:
Some Straight Talk on Discipline

OBJECTIVES

This chapter will help you, among other things, to:

- Define the extent to which discipline is, as well as perceived as, a major problem in today's schools.
- Defend the philosophy, models, strategies sequence.
- Recognize classroom management skills as an integral part of instructional evaluation.
- Defend the use of discipline models that have stood the test of time.
- Acknowledge that effective teaching is a prerequisite to effective discipline.
- Accept the need for ongoing study in the area of classroom management.
- Challenge the belief that discipline is nothing more than common sense.

DISCIPLINE: A REAL PROBLEM?

The annual Gallup Poll of the public's attitudes toward public schools, published each September in *Phi Delta Kappan*, has for almost three decades identified lack of discipline as one of the biggest problems in public schools. In fact, the journal has singled out lack of discipline as the number one problem more often than any other. Classroom management strategies, a more palatable name for "discipline," clearly need some attention!

Charles (1981, p. 13) points out the harsh realities of classrooms:

> Discipline, class control, classroom management—by whatever name you call it—keeping order in the classroom is a teacher's greatest concern. You may not like that fact; you may wish it weren't true. But it is. That's a given in the daily life of teachers. Discipline is so crucial, so basic to everything else in the classroom, that most educators agree: it is the one thing that makes or breaks teachers.

Wang, Haertel, and Walberg (1994) confirm Charles' statement when they report in their article, "What helps student learn?," that when data from both research analyses and surveys from experts are combined, classroom management tops a list of twenty-eight categories that most influence learning. Thus, for many educators, Charles' statement is as true today as it was almost two decades ago when it was written.

The United States is, of course, not alone in its recognition of the importance to teachers of having sound theory and using effective practices when it comes to classroom management. Lord Elton's upsetting report in Great Britain on discipline in schools states that, "teachers group management skills are probably the single most important factor in achieving good standards of classroom behaviour" (*Discipline in Schools: Report of the Committee of Enquiry*, 1989, p. 70). This report argues, further, that discipline skills can be taught, but that training in this critical area is inadequate.

As a concern of both new and experienced teachers, discipline is not a recent phenomenon. A sampling of more than fifty years of discipline articles repeatedly cites classroom management as a major worry of educators. Our experienced colleagues report that the ability to govern is the first essential of success in teaching. For instance, 25 percent of the teachers who fail do so primarily because of troubles growing out of discipline (Brown, E. J., 1949). Reinforcing this view, Schubert (1954) reports that one of the most perplexing problems facing many teachers in our schools today—particularly beginning teachers—is maintaining control in the classroom. Discipline has been, and continues to be, a problem for many teachers. But does it have to be a problem in the future? No!

WHAT IS YOUR PHILOSOPHY OF DISCIPLINE?

It has been my experience that principals regularly ask at least two questions of those applying for teaching jobs: "What is your philosophy of discipline?" and "What is your philosophy of education?" Actually, the latter is a prerequisite for the former. Although those asking the questions are often

Figure 1.1
Philosophy, Models(s), Strategies Sequence

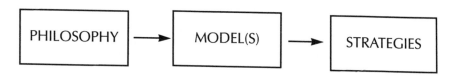

thankful that they don't have to answer them, the questions are fair ones to ask. As a parent, I would be deeply disturbed if teachers disciplined my children without any guiding philosophy.

I am not sure whether those asking about your philosophy are really interested in receiving an answer or in simply seeing how you respond under pressure while trying to answer. After all, who is going to say anything other than something suggesting respect for "individual student differences," helping all students reach their "full potential," promoting students' "self-discipline," recognizing "multicultural factors," and the like?

Selecting a philosophy of discipline is a necessary prerequisite to choosing a discipline model—one consistent with that philosophy. Strategies of classroom management, then, flow from a chosen model. This sequence, as shown above in Figure 1.1, Philosophy, Model(s), Strategies Sequence, helps guarantee a congruence among the three factors.

For teachers who are having discipline problems, the temptation exists to grab any strategy that works. A sailor from a sinking ship who cannot swim wants only to be thrown a flotation ring; he does not want to be taught the theory behind swimming. Hopefully, you are not in an analogous position. Instead, you have the luxury to examine and begin to form a philosophy of education, study available classroom management models, and select a model or models consistent with your fundamental beliefs. Once you select a model, it will dictate the day-to-day discipline strategies you implement.

After you synthesize your philosophy of how children learn, grow, and develop, you may want to turn around and question the questioners, interview the interviewers. Ask them to clarify what their philosophy of education and/or philosophy of discipline is. See if it agrees with yours. Whatever your philosophy, you will be happier operating in an environment that reflects your beliefs.

TEACHER EVALUATIONS

Your competency as a disciplinarian will be judged not only during the interview process but throughout your career. The connection between per-

Figure 1.2
Sample Instructional Evaluation Form

INSTRUCTIONAL EVALUATION FORM

Name of Teacher _____ Date _____

Name of Observer _____ Room # _____

Title of Observer _____ Enrollment _____

Observation Length _____

Subject Observed _____

Instructions to Observer.

Consider this teacher in relation to the following teacher dimensions. Check the appropriate box using the following scale:

5 = Extremely competent
4 = Very competent
3 = Competent
2 = Less than competent
1 = Much less than competent
0 = No basis for judgment

Teacher Dimensions	5	4	3	2	1	0
MANAGEMENT OF STUDENT CONDUCT: Rule explication and monitoring, quality of desists, reference to discipline model, and movement smoothness.						
PLANNING: Content coverage, utilization of instructional materials, goal focusing, and diagnosis.						
INSTRUCTIONAL ORGANIZATION AND DEVELOPMENT: Efficient use of time, review of subject matter, lesson development, teacher treatment of student talk, and management of seatwork/homework.						
PRESENTATION OF SUBJECT MATTER: Presentation of conceptual, explanatory. academic rule, and value knowledge.						
VERBAL AND NONVERBAL COMMUNICATION: Control of discourse, emphasis task attraction speech, and body language.						

Additional Comments (Use additional paper, if necessary)

_____

_____

I have had an opportunity to discuss this observation with the observer.
Signed:_____ Date:_____

ceived teacher competency and successful classroom management has existed for more than 150 years. Bettencourt (1982, p. 51), in his description of Concord, Massachusetts, schools of the 1840s, cites that teacher competency was based on a single theme, discipline: "The loss of governance over a class was the highest form of incompetence, taking precedence over poor reading and inadequate moral development."

Most states require that principals or other designated administrators/ supervisors formally evaluate your teaching by sitting in on your classes. Typically, a form such as the one shown in Figure 1.2, Sample Instructional Evaluation Form, is used to collect data. Such forms usually include a question on classroom management. It is clear from the categories of questions included on such a teacher evaluation form that both content expertise and pedagogical expertise will be—in fact, should be—evaluated. Your competence in the eyes of others will be judged by your ability to perform in each of the questioned areas. Your competence in your own eyes will similarly be judged. To be forewarned is to be forearmed. Consider yourself forewarned regarding the importance the profession ascribes to a teacher's ability to manage (i.e., discipline) his or her classroom.

LITTLE NEW IN THE DISCIPLINE WORLD

Little brand new information has been generated on classroom management in recent years. For example, Overman's (1979) article on effective student management presents the work of Gordon, Dreikurs, and Glasser. Wolfgang and Glickman's standard-setting book *Solving Discipline Problems* (1980, 1986) devotes whole chapters to these same authors. McDaniel's "Developing the Skills of Humanistic Discipline" (1984), Cangelosi's *Classroom Management Strategies* (1988), and Charles' *Building Classroom Discipline* (1996) list these same authors among seven highlighted models of discipline. You would be hard pressed to find an article or book on discipline that did not rehash materials presented elsewhere over the past thirty years or more.

As further evidence that little is new with respect to discipline, one might look at the number of articles published over the years in respected journals having a primary interest in discipline. For instance, *NASSP Bulletin* is the official publication of the National Association of Secondary School Principals. Its readers (school administrators) certainly have a vested interest in establishing and maintaining classroom as well as schoolwide discipline. Yet, an examination of their yearly *Subject Index* for the past two decades reveals that, overall, less and less is being published on the subject of discipline. The number of *NASSP Bulletin* articles indexed under "Discipline" for 1977 through 1981 is seventy-six; the number indexed for 1982 through 1986 is twenty-three; the number indexed for 1987 through 1991 is thirty-four (one issue had eleven articles); and the number indexed for 1992 through 1996 is just sixteen. For 1997 there are only two articles indexed under the subject "Discipline."

Having recently served a six-month-long sabbatical at the University of Melbourne studying classroom management Down Under, I can attest that little is "new." For instance, Maurice Balson of Monash University is an elder statesman of classroom management in Australia. Until his recent retirement, he was in constant demand to conduct workshops and to teach classes on discipline. His book *Understanding Classroom Behaviour* (1992) primarily presents the early 1970s work of Rudolf Dreikurs, as well as the 1970s and 1980s work of William Glasser.

My previous yearlong sabbatical at the University of Durham, England, also revealed that little is original in the field of discipline. For example, while examining the training program headmasters had designed for deputy headmasters, the major component on classroom management was Thomas Gordon's *T.E.T.: Teacher Effectiveness Training* (1974). Note, more than two decades later, C. M. Charles, a respected classroom management author, describes the Gordon model of discipline as "NEW!" in his most recent edition of his discipline book. While observing typical primary and secondary classes, it was clear to me that the ideas of popular discipline gurus here in the United States have been transported overseas.

Because so little is new in the world of classroom management, it is worthwhile to study the literature on discipline, even if the information appears to be dated. It is unlikely that, once you spend the energy and time to learn what is currently available on classroom management, such information will become dated. Study it now! Learn it now! Practice it now! I foresee little truly new coming along to take its place.

HULA HOOPS, PET ROCKS, AND RUBIK'S CUBES

As Americans, we often find ourselves in a disposable world—diapers, soft drink containers, cigarette lighters, and the latest fads. Hula hoops, pet rocks, and Rubik's Cubes all hit the market, were big (if short-lived) successes, and then disappeared, only to be replaced by the next year's new fad. This situation probably is okay in the world of business where new products—cars, fashions, toys—are expected each year.

Unfortunately, that same thinking is not okay when it comes to theories of classroom management. One should not simply dispose of last year's workable discipline theory and expect that a new one, just because it is new, will be equally effective. It doesn't work that way.

Only a limited number of theories of effective classroom management are available for our use. It makes no sense to dispose of a theory as long as it is working. Unlike foods that spoil, effective classroom management theory and practice do not carry expiration dates.

I suggest that educators hold on for dear life to any effective theory of classroom management that works. Don't give up a theory just because it has an earlier publication date. Don't give up successful theories of classroom management until you know for sure that you have a replacement theory that, when put into practice, is just as, or more, effective.

PLAYING THE ODDS

In education we play the odds. Although we might wish for theories that work for all children, at all times, and in all situations; this just does not happen. Instead, we try to use theories that work for *most* children *most* of the time in *most* situations. Our goal is to increase the odds that the theories we use will work. "The fact is that in classroom management there are few absolutes, no panaceas, and none who can evidence a 'failsafe' system" (Hansen, 1979, p. 41). This is real life—the life teachers live in.

So it is with theories and techniques of classroom management. No theory or technique works with all children all the time in all situations. But some theories and techniques work better than others. We should use these theories for what they can do for us. What about the students upon whom our theories do not work? Unfortunately, these exceptions will always exist. Fortunately, they exist in very small numbers. According to Curwin and Mendler (1988a), an 80–15–5 principle exists in classrooms. Eighty percent of the students rarely break the rules; 15 percent break the rules on an occasional basis; and 5 percent often break the rules. If you are using classroom management theories and techniques that are successful for *most* children *most* of the time in *most* situations, then the majority of students are more often "on task" and, as such, demand less of your time and attention. You can now direct your efforts to either working with the "exceptions" or identifying and enlisting the aid of others who can offer the help you can't offer.

You need to recognize what you can and cannot do for the child. Be aware of your network of fellow professionals. Use them. Do what you are able to do effectively and then, if necessary, refer (or seek additional help for) those students you cannot help. This is not a sign of weakness on your part; it is the professional thing to do.

OMISSION AND COMMISSION

Effective classroom management is influenced just as much by things you don't do as it is by things you do. The words "you don't do" and "you do" clearly point out that you have control over the situation. Teacher behaviors don't occur all by themselves. You can decide to omit certain behaviors that, more often than not, precipitate or worsen discipline problems. You also can decide to commit certain behaviors that, more often than not, lead to effective discipline. Sins of omission are just as unforgivable in a professional as sins of commission. They are also just as ineffective.

EFFECTIVE TEACHING MUST BE PRESENT

No classroom management technique will be effective for long if effective teaching is absent. I cannot stress this point strongly enough. Classroom management models, and their accompanying strategies, are not substitutes for good teaching. Effective teaching, perhaps the "most difficult job of all in our society" (Glasser, 1990, p. 14), is actually a preventative discipline measure that keeps students so involved and interested that they are not inclined to cause problems.

For instance, the often-made teacher statement, "When you are able to act in an acceptable manner, you will no longer have to stand outside in the hallway," assumes that what is going on in your class is more interesting and exciting than remaining in the hallway. If ineffective teaching is taking place in the classroom, then the student will not feel that he or she is missing anything by staying in the hall. Hence, your discipline efforts have no impact.

Be on the lookout for more effective teaching methods and more exciting curricula. Recognize that different students may have different learning styles. To the degree that you are able, try to accommodate these styles. Survey school district material and personnel resources. Do the same thing at the regional, state, and national level. Check with your professional association, such as, if you are an English teacher, the National Council of Teachers of English (NCTE). Query the Educational Resources Information Center (ERIC) clearinghouse (see chapter on ERIC) that best represents your subject area. Contact colleges and universities for ideas.

Excited, as well as well informed, faculty are more effective teachers; excited students have neither the time nor the inclination to misbehave. At the same time, though, good teaching will not prevent all classroom management problems. Every classroom management model that I am aware of includes some sort of backup system for the inevitable discipline problems. To that end, even effective teachers must be ready with appropriate strategies of classroom management to "keep the learning act afloat."

As in medicine, an "ounce of prevention is worth a pound of cure." If many (certainly not all) discipline problems can be prevented through effective, stimulating, and interesting teaching, then one would be foolish not to provide such teaching. Be an effective teacher—first and foremost.

Jones, the author of one of the discipline models highlighted in this book, reinforces the need for effective teaching through his dual (1987) publications *Positive Classroom Discipline* and *Positive Classroom Instruction*. His book on classroom instruction, at 250 pages, is three-fourths as long as his book on classroom discipline, suggesting the importance of instruction in any overall classroom management plan.

Is effective teaching all that is needed? No. You must understand that children have a personal history and experience that goes beyond your influence. In the real world, these children cannot simply leave their out-of-school problems at the school's front door in the morning and collect them at day's end. Students' problems will accompany them to your classroom. Skills to manage students, all kinds of students with all kinds of problems, are essential to even the most effective teacher.

WATER SEEKS ITS OWN LEVEL

Picture a scorching hot day. You have been out for a long dusty walk in the hills and are dying of thirst. A cold, clear, sparkling mountain spring flows just ahead. You rush to the water's edge, grab your trusty tin cup (cold water always seems colder in a metal cup), and scoop up the thirst-quenching liquid. What does this have to do with discipline? Well, note that when you scooped up a cup full of water, no lasting hole was left in the spring. "Of course not," you say. "Water seeks its own level and quickly fills the temporary void created by my tin cup." No matter how many cupfuls you scoop out, other water seems to flow in to replace what you removed.

In discipline, though, this does not happen. Discipline problems that have been *effectively handled* are not readily replaced with still other discipline problems. Although the replacement water may appear to be endless, discipline problems are not endless—really! Jones (1979) reports that 80 percent of classroom discipline problems involve students "talking" (such as whispering to a friend), while another 15 percent involve students "moving" about the room (such as sharpening pencils). This leaves only 5 percent for all other discipline problems combined. Therefore, if we could effectively handle students' "talking" and "moving," we would have made a big, nonrefillable hole in the discipline problem.

COURSES IN CLASSROOM MANAGEMENT

Few teacher education programs have available, and still fewer programs mandate, specific courses in classroom management for their students. I am not alone in holding this view. Hyman and D'Alessandro (1984, p. 42) conclude, "Few U.S. educators have received formal training in the theory, research, and practice of school discipline." McDaniel (1984, p. 71) offers further support for this view:

> Most teachers enter the profession, and persevere in it, with little or no training in school discipline techniques. This is indeed strange when discipline problems are so frequently cited as the greatest dilemma facing public schools. . . . Few states mention behavior management in certification regulations. . . . Few colleges or universities require (or even provide) courses in classroom discipline for regular classroom teachers.

Circumstances are no better for in-service teachers. According to Hansen (1979, p. 41), "A perplexing dilemma for classroom teachers is their uncertain preparation for handling discipline problems." Citing an earlier comprehensive review of the literature, Plax, Kearney, and Tucker (1986, p. 32) report that "beginning elementary and secondary teachers perceive classroom management as their most serious problem." The not-so-surprising effect upon teachers is "that disruptive student behavior is a major factor contributing to teacher stress and job dissatisfaction" (Jones, 1984, p. 60). Informal surveys conducted when I present discipline-oriented workshops confirms the continued lack of teacher preparation in the area of classroom management.

The situation probably will not get any better in the immediate future given the public's mood that teachers in training require, if anything, more content courses, not more pedagogy courses. Today's "blue-ribbon" committees' proposals for strengthening teacher education programs clearly carry the message that teachers need more preparation, but that additional preparation ought not to include more education courses (see the National Commission on Educational Excellence, *A Nation at Risk: The Imperative for Education Reform 1983*, which has influenced public opinion since its publication). In fact, many of these reports suggest we already offer too much in the way of education-type courses. If the additional recommendations suggesting that teachers should obtain a liberal arts degree in a content area first and then return for fifth-year teacher-training courses should be implemented, then there will be little room for classroom management courses.

Where then will teachers in training learn classroom management skills? Although it is common for educational psychology courses (required of most education majors) to use textbooks that devote at least one chapter to classroom management, this amount of attention probably isn't enough.

WHERE DO TEACHERS DEVELOP COMPETENCY IN CLASSROOM MANAGEMENT?

Richardson (1985) studied teachers' perceptions of their own classroom management behavior. His research shows that teachers attribute that behavior's development to actual experiences on the job, subsequent years on the job, and student teaching—in that order of importance. Unfortunately, learning while doing seems to be the norm. Coursework while in college, what little there is of it, is perceived to be less of a factor in the development of classroom management competency.

It must be a lonely, as well as a threatening, situation for new teachers who must learn classroom management skills on the job. To whom can new teachers turn? Administrators rarely discuss discipline with teachers in specific terms, and curriculum supervisors, as well as fellow teachers, are also judged to be of little help. Although in-service training holds the potential for helping both new and experienced teachers develop classroom management competencies, too often these efforts suffer from "a prevalence of competing approaches, lack of continuing reinforcement, practice and coaching" (Duke & Jones, 1984, p. 30).

Just as it is the case that today's education graduates have had little in the way of training or education concerning classroom management techniques, so it is also true for past graduates—today's senior teachers and administrators. You may get lucky and find a mentor who can pass on pedagogically sound, well-researched, effective, fair, and constitutionally legal strategies of discipline—all of which are consistent with your philosophy of education. But what if you don't? What I hope you don't get from these people are statements such as, "Well, this worked for me, why don't you try it?"

READ MORE ON CLASSROOM MANAGEMENT

One important part of being a professional is regularly turning to a recognized body of knowledge to solve problems. Chances are that, as professionals, teachers have invested a good deal of their lives acquiring the knowledge and skills that make up that recognized knowledge base. That knowledge base deserves to be regularly used and, on a continuing basis, updated. People who seek professional treatment—whether they be students, patients, or clients—deserve, at a minimum, knowledge-based responses.

For instance, I hope medical doctors, as professionals, regularly turn to such a knowledge base—especially when they are treating my illnesses. We all know or have heard of the horrors that can occur when such knowledge is ignored or misapplied. Skyrocketing malpractice insurance is a clear sign that the public will no longer blindly trust health professionals. Surely, educators do not think they are immune from similar public challenges. Let's not wait until we, as teachers, have to purchase malpractice insurance. Let's regularly use the best knowledge bases, including those in discipline, available to us. Effective disciplinarians are secure in the belief that they are using techniques that can be defended. All teachers should be prepared to be held accountable—to be ready to explain to any student, parent, fellow teacher, principal, or school board member what they are doing and why. The "why" part of this responsibility can only be justified by referring to a recognized body of knowledge. This is a sign of a *professional!*

Make it a regular part of your professional development to read more, more often, on classroom management. Just as you might remind your students that learning is a lifelong endeavor, I remind you that classroom management is not something that can be totally presented between the covers of a single book—even this one. What is presented in this book will certainly get you started in the right direction and, hopefully, should whet your appetite for still more *sound theory* and *effective practices* of discipline.

EFFECTIVE DISCIPLINE: SIMPLY COMMON SENSE?

Many teachers, and even more of the general public, believe that what teachers do in their profession is nothing more than common sense. This is simply not true. For instance, common sense might tell you that if a student is repeatedly out of his seat, then the teacher should remind him each and every time that he should be sitting down. Yet, assuming the child's motive is to gain attention, a far more effective teacher response is to ignore the child's out-of-seat behavior, praise others who are in their seats, and, when it occurs (even out of exhaustion), praise the misbehaving child when he is sitting down. Which teacher response do you believe works better? Only the latter set of responses has a basis in that "recognized body of knowledge" referred to earlier. Common sense also told us the world was flat, man could not fly, women were suited only for motherhood, and . . . well, you get the message.

Does common sense have a place in education? Sure it does, as long as it has a recognizable foundation in the research literature. It is not uncommon for experienced teachers to dismiss what they do as common sense when, in fact, it should more correctly be described as second nature. They have been using a technique for so long that they may have forgotten its origin. Unfortunately, experienced, as well as inexperienced, teachers use techniques that have become second nature to them that cannot be supported by the research literature.

A recognized body of knowledge in any field, including education, is really an effort to unravel nature's mysteries and, therefore, should not be in conflict with common sense. Nature's truths, once unraveled and understood, will be about as much common sense as they are ever going to get.

DOCTOR, DOCTOR, I HAVE THIS PAIN!

We are probably all familiar with the temptation to get some free advice from medical doctors if we happen to run into them at a party. Come to think of it, I catch myself trying to get free advice from lawyers, accountants, bricklayers, and septic tank installers when I see them at informal gatherings. It is no different for authors of books on classroom management. You probably have a specific child in mind that you would like to ask about. Your question might begin, "I have this second grader who does such and such. What should I do with him?" Keep that child in mind as you read this book. Read it with a purpose. Continually ask yourself how you could apply this material with your children in your unique set of circumstances. Do it, it works!

SUMMARY

Even the best teachers will experience discipline problems now and again—discipline is an unavoidable and critical part of classroom management. Jones (1979, p. 27) states it best when he says, "In the end, there is no alternative to effective discipline. Discipline is either done poorly, or it is done well. When done poorly, the process often becomes punitive or is abandoned altogether. When done well, however, it can be low key, supportive, and almost invisible." Ineffective disciplinarians make it look hard and get few results. Effective disciplinarians make it look easy, as if they really are not doing anything at all. You can enhance your effectiveness through increased knowledge (i.e., sound theory) and skills (i.e., effective practices). This book should help.

CHAPTER 2

Theoretical Frameworks for Selecting a Discipline Model

OBJECTIVES

This chapter will help you, among other things, to:

- Identify and explain four theoretical frameworks for evaluating "tried and true" discipline models.
- Accept the need for using theoretical frameworks as the basis for selecting a discipline model.
- Compare and contrast Wolfgang and Glickman's interventionist versus non-interventionist positions as a basis for selecting a discipline model.
- Compare and contrast French and Raven's five social bases of power as a basis for selecting a discipline model.
- Compare and contrast Skinner and Rogers' behaviorist versus humanist positions as a basis for selecting a discipline model.
- Compare and contrast Lewis' control versus influence positions as a basis for selecting a discipline model.
- Explain why eclecticism, a smorgasbord approach to discipline, is inappropriate.

DISCIPLINE MODELS: THEIR ORIGIN

The six "tried and true" discipline models in Part II of this book flow from one or more broad, all-encompassing theoretical frameworks. Such frameworks, several examples of which are presented in this chapter, provide a wider, balanced view of the beliefs and options within the study of discipline that exist for use by new, as well as seasoned, practitioners.

Everything, including models of classroom management, should have an origin that can be traced. Educators, as well as other professionals, rely upon access to such organized knowledge bases. The four theoretical frameworks presented in this chapter are designed to act as advanced organizers (e.g., Ausubel, 1980), providing artificial mental structures or scaffolds onto which individual discipline models and the information and skills contained within them can be hung.

The frameworks vary in their number of subcategories, from French and Raven's five social bases of power to Lewis' three (control, manage, and influence). They also vary in philosophical positions as revealed clearly in the Skinner-Rogers dichotomy. What these frameworks have in common is their recognition that individual classroom management models are better understood when viewed in comparison to one another.

Understanding where specific discipline models fit within a larger framework will assist you in selecting and defending a preferred model. It will help you become more accountable—better able to explain *why* you have adopted a particular model and *why* you have not adopted still other models. The specific classroom model you select should be consistent with your beliefs about how one person (a teacher) should interact with another (a child). Your organized set of beliefs regarding discipline, in reality, will represent your philosophy of discipline.

Your philosophy of discipline will prompt you to adopt, even champion, some models of classroom management while shunning others. Certain models will "feel" right, but others will not. The model that you select, a reflection of your own philosophy, will guide you in your decision making concerning classroom management-related situations. Using a model that you have selected, and that you believe in, sets the stage for your discipline system, not you, to take the strain associated with effective classroom management. Isn't this how you would prefer things to work? I hope so.

Although a recent issue of *NEA Today* (1998) says that "When it comes to discipline issues, there's no one right answer" (Dear Dr. Discipline, p. 6), there should be a *right answer* for you. The *right answer* will be your using a classroom management model that you believe in—one that reflects your fundamental beliefs on how fellow human beings (including children) should be treated!

For those schools that have a mentoring program to assist newer teachers, one might question why particular mentors are chosen. Are they, in their own right, recognized to be effective teachers? Do they have lots of seniority and thus are entitled to this position? Were they the only faculty to volunteer? The fact is that giving "assistance is easier when recommendations are based on a theoretical framework" (Trumble & Thurston, 1976). Therefore, mentors should be chosen because they possess knowledge of such theoretical frameworks and, when offering advice to newer teachers, can cite particular frameworks—chapter and verse. Note how much better this is than simply saying to a newer teacher, "Well, this is what worked for me, why don't you try it?" This chapter contains four theoretical frameworks that can help teachers place discipline advice, suggestions, and recommendations into some sort of pedagogical perspective.

Each of the classroom management frameworks presented in this chapter purports to best categorize, usually in the form of some sort of hierarchy, classroom management models. The specific frameworks discussed include those developed by Wolfgang and Glickman, French and Raven, Skinner and Rogers, and Lewis. These frameworks provide the "theory" behind each of the discipline models presented in Part II. The models themselves provide the basis for the effective "practice" of disciplining. A good balance is required between "sound theory" and "effective practice." One is little good without the other.

A SCHOOLS OF THOUGHT FRAMEWORK: WOLFGANG AND GLICKMAN

Interventionist <— Interactionalist —> Noninterventionist

Possibly fearful that the word *philosophy* would scare away readers, Wolfgang and Glickman (1980, 1986) substituted the generic term *school of thought* as the basis for their framework. What is your school of thought regarding how students learn, develop, and grow? What is your school of thought regarding discipline? As shown in Figure 2.1, teachers are either interventionists, interactionalists, or noninterventionists at heart. Although each school of thought comes complete with classroom management models that get the job done—establishing and maintaining discipline—each represents its own unique set of beliefs.

Interventionists believe that children develop according to environmental conditions. As a classroom teacher, you are one of those conditions. A teacher's job is to control the environment by implementing a logical system (the teacher's, of course) of conditioning. "By accepting a position as a teacher, a person has not only the right but an 'obligation' to modify student behavior" (Axelrod, 1977, p. 158). To do less would be inconsistent with an interventionist's perception of the role of a teacher.

Interventionists are proponents of the carrot-and-stick approach.

Figure 2.1
Wolfgang and Glickman's Teacher Behavior Continuum

Interventionist ———— Interactionalist ———— Noninterventionst
(cT)   (Ct)
c = child low in power   C = Child high in power
T = Teacher high in power   t = teacher low in power

Dispensing rewards and punishments are the tools these teachers use to get otherwise unmoving and unmotivated students moving and motivated. A student's behavior must be modified, be shaped. Interventionists would argue that this directing of a student's actions is being done for the student's own good.

Consistent with this theory, the teacher is seen in the forefront—he or she wields the power. Children are seen in the background, wielding little, if any, power. The less power students have, the easier it will be for teachers to intervene. Skinner (1972, p. 205) describes a desired powerless state for children when he posits, "It is the autonomous inner man who is abolished, and that is a step forward." Canter's *Assertive Discipline* (1976, 1992) and *Succeeding with Difficult Students* (1993), Dobson's *Dare to Discipline* (1970, 1992), and Skinner's thinking (numerous citations) fall within the interventionist category.

At the other extreme, noninterventionists believe in providing a supportive, facilitating environment for students. A faith exists that the student possesses an internal motivation that, if simply nurtured (not controlled), will blossom. Like the flower that requires only nurturing water, soil, and sunlight to bloom, so too the capacity for a child's growth is dependent upon that child, not a controlling teacher. A student is viewed as having power over his or her own destiny. By contrast, the teacher, better called "director" or "facilitator," is no longer in the forefront—no longer a power wielder.

Don't students have to be motivated by teachers? Isn't it natural for students to avoid learning, and the work associated with it, if they can get away with it? Won't chaos develop in the absence of adult direction? Noninterventionists think not. They simply point out the natural desire to learn that exists among the very young when everything about the world is motivating—chemistry, biology, geology, math, history, computers, language, reading. Just try putting an infant to bed when, despite near exhaustion, there is so much of the world to discover. What happens to children's curiosity about knowledge as they make their way through many school systems?

Lest the reader jump to the wrong conclusions, noninterventionism is not a synonym for a hands-off or laissez-faire approach. Noninterventionists have complete classroom management models designed to handle every situation interventionists (and their models) must handle. The concepts in Gordon's (1970, 1974, 1977) several books and Rogers' *Freedom to Learn* (1969) fit in the noninterventionist category.

Between these two extremes are interactionalists. They believe that conflicts cannot be resolved without shared responsibility, without full participation in decision making by all the participants in a conflict. It takes two to tango! It takes two to cause a problem, and it takes two to solve it. Both share a desire to resolve the problem; both share equally the available power. What is important to interactionalists is not how many conflicts occur, but how those conflicts are resolved so that relationships remain intact, both parties save face, and both feel their needs have been met.

Democracy, with institution-imposed limits, operates. Interactionalists believe that all human beings choose their behaviors—to cheat or not cheat, to hit or not hit a fellow student, to study or not study. With this recognition comes an expectation of greater responsibility for one's actions. Interactionalists, where possible, provide students with choices. When students are called upon to make choices, much (not all) of the responsibility for their behavior is transferred to their shoulders. See Glasser's (1969, 1986, 1990) several books, Dreikurs and Cassel's *Discipline without Tears* (1972), and Balson's *Understanding Classroom Behaviour* (1992).

Whatever your philosophy, you will be happier operating in an environment that reflects your school of thought. Later you will be asked to place the six "tried and true" classroom models that will be described in Part II into Wolfgang and Glickman's Schools of Thought framework.

A SOCIAL BASES OF POWER FRAMEWORK: FRENCH AND RAVEN

Coercive <— Reward — Legitimate — Referent —> Expert

A school is a study in group dynamics, a study of how one person (such as a teacher) exerts power over another person (such as a student). According to Glasser (1986), although exerting power is a basic human need, it carries a cultural taint that does not seem to extend to the other human psychological needs such as loving and belonging. Regardless of cultural bias, the seeking of power itself is neither good nor bad.

Almost forty years ago, French and Raven (1960) identified five specific bases of social power that can be used by educators to influence students.

Table 2.1
Hypothetical Weighted French and Raven's Power Distributions

35%	45%	10%	5%	5%
Coercive Power	Reward Power	Legitimate Power	Referent Power	Expert Power

5%	5%	15%	55%	20%
Coercive Power	Reward Power	Legitimate Power	Referent Power	Expert Power

Social power is exercised in all human contacts. These five bases are *coercive, reward, legitimate, referent,* and *expert* power. Together, they represent 100 percent of the power that we have available to wield over others and for others to wield over us. Although we will discuss these power bases individually, in real classrooms they all operate at the same time.

Depending upon your beliefs regarding classroom management, the best you can do is attempt to use some power bases more often than others and attempt to use the remaining ones less often. Thus, your own French and Raven Social Bases of Power Distribution may correspond to the one shown at the top of Table 2.1, Hypothetical Weighted French and Raven's Power Distributions, while that of a colleague may correspond to the one at the bottom.

Coercive Power

Because students perceive teachers to be in a position to mete out punishment, students allow teachers to dictate their behavior. But how much is really known about the effects of punishment on behavior? How many educators know how to use punishment effectively as a basis for social power? How do students handle punishment?

Students cope with repeated punishment in a variety of ways, including rebelling, retaliating (if not at the teacher, at a weaker classmate), lying, cheating, conforming, apple polishing, submitting, and withdrawing (either mentally or physically) from learning. These coping mechanisms, however, are only outward signs of the student's inner anger, frustration, embarrassment, feelings of unworthiness, fear, and vindictiveness.

Should teachers avoid using coercive power? That is a personal, or perhaps district-mandated, decision. What I can say, however, is that if teachers continue to rely upon coercive power, they have a responsibility to learn enough about it to use it effectively—recognizing both its strengths and limitations.

Reward Power

Students allow teachers to exert power over them because they perceive that the teacher is in a position to pass out or withhold desired rewards. An entire supporting vocabulary surrounding reward power has been developed including words such as *stimulus, response, cueing, satiation, consequence,* and *schedules of reinforcement.*

Some see the dispensing of rewards as providing an incentive; others see it as offering a bribe. What one teacher sees as creating dependent students—working/behaving only for the reward—others see as preparation for the world of work. What one educator sees as training students in the same way we train our pet dog, another sees as the only way to maintain order in schools. Clearly, reward power, like coercive power, is more complicated than it appears at first glance.

Manipulation: The Common Element

Coercive power and reward power share the common element of manipulation. These two power bases do, in fact, work. But how long do they work? The surprising answer lies in the words *allow* and *perceive.* These power bases are allowed to work only as long as the students perceive that the teacher controls desired rewards or dreaded punishments. The instant student perceptions change, the teacher's power changes.

For the elementary child who no longer wants scratch-and-sniff stickers, the teacher handing them out has lost power. For the student who decides that he no longer needs a teacher's written recommendation, the teacher who has been withholding it as a condition for improved classroom behavior has lost power. For the student who decides that she doesn't really mind detention, the teacher assigning it has lost power. And so it goes. Students have the ultimate power over the power used on them. This is a scary realization for proponents of these two power bases.

Overlooked Bases of Social Power and Influence

Although you have probably had some coursework dealing with coercive and reward power, you have probably never taken a course that focused upon the three remaining power bases—legitimate, referent, and expert. Yet these three power bases have a far greater potential to influence student behavior than do coercive and reward power.

Legitimate Power

Students perceive that a teacher has the right to prescribe behavior.

Legitimate power operates on the basis that people accept the social structure of institutions—homes, churches, the military, schools. Inherent in this structure is a hierarchy of power. Students recognize and respect the teacher's position.

Teachers should be aware of their legitimate power—their legitimate authority—and use it to assert a leadership role in the classroom. A teacher, hired by the school board and delegated the responsibility for seeing that conditions for learning are present, might announce, "I have contracted with the district to teach. I have an obligation to live up to the terms of that contract. Any disciplinary infractions that interfere with my efforts to teach cannot be tolerated."

Administrators could assist teachers by carrying this message of legitimate power throughout the building. They could stress in their contacts with school personnel, parents, and community leaders that within the school's social structure, teachers have been delegated the legitimate power to do what is necessary to keep the "learning act afloat."

Teachers, of course, must do their part too. They must avoid overstepping the boundaries of their legitimate power. The position of "teacher" may give one the right to assign homework or direct student behavior within the classroom. It does not give one the right, generally, to comment on students' hair length, choice of clothes or friends, or dictate student behavior off school property and after school hours. To do so invites the statement, "Just because you are the teacher, that doesn't give you. . . ."

Referent Power

In cases of referent power, probably the most powerful of the five social bases, students identify with the teacher. They respect and are attracted to the teacher personally. The greater the attraction, the broader the range of referent power. For instance, a teacher may have referent power within a math classroom and, because of the strong sense of identification the students feel for the teacher, he or she also is able to exert influence over them outside the classroom—at a pep rally, in the cafeteria, during hall duty, at a local shopping center, and so on.

What creates this attraction, this feeling of oneness? Those teachers who possess referent power care about their students, and they *show* it in their actions. They are fair in their dealings with students, sacrificing neither their own convictions nor the students' rights. They do not solve problems for students but instead respect the students enough to take the posture of facilitator, leaving the responsibility for change with the students. They do more listening than talking. They communicate with students without seeing communication as a sign of weakness.

Teachers, both pre- and in-service, need assistance in developing their referent power. Referent power can be learned; it is not simply some innate charisma that either you have or you don't. Thomas Gordon's (1974) *T.E.T.: Teacher Effectiveness Training*, also available as *L.E.T.: Leader Effectiveness Training* (1977) for administrators, is a good place to start. Gordon's communication model combines theory and practice. It provides concrete skills for teachers to show them how to act as facilitators in the problem-solving process, to confront students and influence them to modify their behavior willingly, to substitute a no-lose for a win-lose conflict resolution technique, and more.

Expert Power

Finally, we come to French and Raven's expert power. With expert power, students perceive that the teacher has special knowledge or expertise; they respect the teacher professionally. Take a student who enrolls in machine shop in a district's vocational-technical high school. Here, discipline problems are almost nonexistent. The apprentice finds himself or herself in the presence of the "master" and behaves accordingly.

For most teachers, though, this source of power and influence lies dormant—unexploited. Students and too often colleagues, administrators, school board members, and parents are unaware of teachers' expertise. Why is this so? In part, it is because teaching is seen as a helping profession in which teachers are expected to be humble, to get on with the job, to put others' interests first, and to avoid the limelight. Teachers, unlike professionals in other fields (such as medicine), are uncomfortable tooting their own horns or advertising their own expertise. But at what cost?

How are teachers affected by this lack of recognition of their expertise? Even the most basic understanding of Rosenthal and Jacobson's (1968) self-fulfilling prophecy reveals that the expectations of others can have a definite effect, to the extent that teachers will live up or down to these expectations of others.

Imagine the effect on students if efforts were made schoolwide and community-wide to illuminate the real expertise of a district's faculty. The effect would be that teachers would then have another long-lasting social base of power to use in establishing and maintaining discipline (Tauber, 1992). Because referent power and expert power are so rarely consciously used by teachers, specific suggestions for incorporating these power bases follow.

Building Referent Power

- Use more self-disclosure. Tell pupils how the concepts and principles in the course have impacted upon your life. This helps students see how they apply in their own lives. Thus a sense of common identity is developed.

- Associate with students in nonteaching ways, but keep it professional. Advise a club, coach a sport, participate in a run for charity; such activities give you and the students greater common experiences to draw upon later in class. At the same time, maintain a position of maturity, and do not act as a peer.

- Be fair in the attention you give to all students. Spend time in face-to-face positive interactions with all students, not just with the ones you feel are the most "ideal." Too often the "ideal" students are those just like yourself!

- Be accepting, yet not patronizing; recognize students' interests, yet avoid frequent tangents from the academic tasks at hand; show loyalty and trust, yet not at the expense of students' welfare.

- When disciplining, discipline the student's behavior, not the student: there is a difference. Students may not know that difference, but they will feel it. Although many youngsters equate a criticism of their behavior as criticism of them as human beings, disciplining in a calm and businesslike manner (not "taking it personal") and disciplining with dignity (so that you both save face) can help students differentiate between the two.

- Read the book, *T.E.T.: Teacher Effectiveness Training* (1974), by Thomas Gordon. (Note: Gordon's model is presented in Chapter 8 of this book.) Begin using the skills of active listening when students let you know they have a problem; send "I-messages" when you know you have a problem; try conflict resolution (working for a win/win solution) when you both acknowledge you share a problem. Better still, take a P.E.T. or T.E.T. course.

- Be a good role model. Students are more likely to do as you do, not as you say—so do it right! A plus when you use referent power is that students want to "get even" with you, doing unto you as you have done unto them, in order to earn your respect!

From my sabbaticals served abroad, I have observed that the British (as well as the Australians) *may* have an advantage when it comes to promoting referent power—in my opinion, the most effectual power base available. Pastoral care (a concept less common in American schools) has faculty, staff, and administration willingly attending to a student's total needs, at home or school, personal or academic. Such a posture on the part of educators helps to create a sense of common purpose between students and teachers—a main ingredient of referent power. This sense of oneness is heightened through school uniforms (complete with the school's coat-of-arms) and daily opening exercises that take place in a student/staff-filled auditorium. In the United States uniforms are rare, and opening exercises take place over an impersonal public address system.

Building Expert Power

- Demonstrate expertise by being thoroughly prepared. It is not possible to know all there is to know about any subject, but be well versed and willing to say you do not know when you do not know.

- Practice what you preach. Education is a lifelong endeavor—it should not stop. As professionals, our expert power can be enhanced if we continue to take courses and attend, as well as conduct, workshops, seminars and in-service sessions. Let the students know you are keeping up to date.

- Be an informed consumer of the literature in your subject area and in your professional craft, pedagogy. Obviously, you are reading this book, so you are keeping up with the pedagogical research and practice of classroom management. Do the same with your specific subject matter.

- Where possible, teach students how to locate answers on their own. That builds independence; giving answers on a silver platter reinforces dependence. The greatest compliment to your expert power is when your student equals, or outshines, you, the master.

- Tactfully make students and parents aware of your formal education and professional accomplishments. Perhaps, in the school's entrance foyer some of the display cases full of sports trophies (evidence of student expertise) can be emptied and filled with evidence of teacher expertise—degrees, diplomas, awards. Unlike doctors and lawyers, teachers are too humble when it comes to revealing their expertise. Paper credentials do not guarantee good teaching, but they form expectations in the minds of others. It is then up to teachers to fulfill them.

- Recognize student expertise and incorporate it into class presentations, discussions, and work set. Knowing more about one's students (which is also referent power) is the first step. Computer whiz-kids are often well known, but other children too may have expertise based on travel, hobbies, sports and part-time jobs. True experts recognize and utilize the expertise of others.

Conclusion

Five social bases of power exist. Each can be or has been used in every social context imaginable—home, industry, and school. It has been argued that teachers have overused and ineffectively used two of the power bases (coercive and reward), while overlooking the potential of the remaining three (Tauber, 1986a, 1986b). This observation holds true across several countries.

Whatever your philosophy, you will be happier operating in an environment that reflects your school of thought. Later you will be asked to place the six "tried and true" classroom models that will be described in Part II into French and Raven's Social Bases of Power framework.

A BEHAVIORIST-HUMANIST FRAMEWORK: SKINNER VERSUS ROGERS

Behaviorism <————————————————————————> Humanism

Of the frameworks for discipline models presented in this chapter, none has a more scholarly basis than this one. Burrhus Frederic Skinner's and Carl Ransom Rogers' works go far beyond a simple framework for classifying and organizing popular discipline models. Their respective works address the fundamental issue of *how* humans learn. Classroom discipline is simply a small, though important, part of what human beings must learn. Hence, the views of both Skinner and Rogers apply to classroom management.

Skinner's and Rogers' theories of how human beings learn represent two extremes; they describe opposite ends of a learning continuum. These two opposing views of human nature can be traced back to Skinner's *Science and Human Behavior* (1953) and Rogers' *Client-Centered Therapy* (1953). This behaviorism-humanism dichotomy finds its roots in the ancient past, continues in the present, and is predicted to have an impact on psychology and education in the future (Alonzo, LaCagnina & Olsen, 1977; Bordin, 1981; Krasner, 1978; Milhollan & Forisha, 1972). Their views represent two opposing views of human nature.

Skinner was a prolific writer. His fundamental views of learning are offered in numerous publications over a four-decade period. One needs only to type his name into ERIC (see chapter 13) or some other information retrieval system to locate countless citations written by or about him and his views to begin to appreciate his impact on the American scene. Skinner has had a profound influence on the theory and practice of child rearing, teaching, worker-manager relations, and military training. Among his publications are books such as *Walden II* (1948), *Verbal Behavior* (1957), and *Beyond Freedom and Dignity* (1971), and articles such as "The Science of Learning and the Art of Teaching" (1954) and "The Free and Happy Student" (1973).

Some classroom management books include Skinner as simply another author of a specific classroom management model called "Neo-Skinnerian" (Charles, 1996) in the same vein as they include other recognized authors of discipline models (such as the Canters, Dreikurs, and Glasser). I believe a more appropriate presentation of Skinner's work is to offer it as the *basis* of

B. F. Skinner

C. R. Rogers

several classroom management models, including those popularized by Dobson, the Canters, and Jones.

Whether applying his operant conditioning principles to pigeons, pets, or people, Skinner believes that "by carefully constructing certain 'contingencies of reinforcement,' it is possible to change behavior quickly and to maintain it in strength for long periods of time" (Skinner, 1986, p. 106). Constructing contingencies of reinforcement is exactly what is recommended in Dobson's *Dare to Discipline* (1970, 1992), the Canters' *Assertive Discipline* (1976, 1992), and, to a lesser degree, in Jones' *Positive Classroom Discipline* (1987).

Cultural practices, whether across an entire society or within a single classroom, are aided by the use of language or verbal behavior that can greatly increase the ability of individuals to take advice from others, learn rules, and follow instructions (Bower, 1986). Effective classroom disciplinarians regularly use such verbal behavior when interacting with students to define good and bad behaviors—reinforcing the former while extinguishing the latter. These teachers consciously set about modifying student behavior.

Skinner contends that one does not learn by doing alone but instead learns as the result of the consequences that follow what one does. Hence, to teach (to discipline) is to arrange such consequences (Skinner, 1986). "It is the teacher's function to contrive conditions under which students learn" (Skinner, 1973, p. 15). Arranging such consequences or conditions, and doing so immediately and in sufficient quantity and frequency, is as important to the designer of programmed learning machines and Las Vegas gambling devices as it is to parents trying to teach their children right from wrong and to teachers trying to create a necessary learning climate in the classroom. Gamblers, children, and students all pay attention when doing so has reinforcing consequences.

Teachers cannot, Skinner argues, abrogate their responsibility to control these consequences. If teachers do not consciously control them, the environment—for example, peers, media, and the real world—will. Students freed from teachers' control simply come under the control of other environmental conditions. Whether in scholarship or self-discipline, freedom is an illusion.

With reference to two frameworks already presented in this chapter, Skinner would be classified as an interventionist by Wolfgang and Glickman, and he would make heavy use of reward power, but surprisingly little use of coercive power, in French and Raven's Social Bases of Power. Skinner is, in the proudest tradition, a behaviorist.

Rogers, too, was a prolific writer. As with Skinner, one needs only to type Rogers' name into most any information retrieval system to locate countless citations written by or about him and his views. Among his writings are *Client-Centered Therapy: Its Current Practices, Implications, and Theory* (1951), *Freedom to Learn* (1969), and *On Becoming a Person: A Therapist's View of Psychotherapy* (1961)—according to Kilpatrick (1985), "the Bible" on Rogers. Almost single-handedly, Rogers initiated the humanistic education field and thereby changed the counseling profession (Kirschenbaum, 1991). From skilled high school and elementary school guidance counselors to highly trained clinical psychologists, Rogerian counseling serves as the primary recognized technique for helping clients, including students, help themselves.

"Reflective counseling," or mirroring back to a client (student) what he or she has just said, often sounds, when taken out of context, hilariously funny or extremely irritating (like talking to a tape recorder). Yet, when used by those skilled in such techniques, these facilitators often help clients help themselves become better able to confront tomorrow's problems. The picture of students demonstrating self-discipline moves from just a goal to a reality.

For Rogers, and also Abraham Maslow (*Toward a Psychology of Being,* 1968), students are driven inwardly to perfect themselves outwardly. They possess an inner desire to become the best person they are capable of becoming—to "self-actualize." For Rogers, humans are endowed with an actualizing tendency to grow, develop, and create. To ignore the learner's need to self-actualize will produce only inconsequential learning (Rogers, 1977). (Note: Rogers and Maslow were founders of the American Association of Humanistic Psychology.)

The role of teachers, then, is to help facilitate this natural-growth motivation in children. Teachers will have to give away some of their power to empower students. Nowhere is this more evident than in a Montessori classroom where adults are in the background and children are in the foreground, where intrinsic rather than extrinsic motivation is used. Children create themselves through purposeful activity by using their unusual sensitivity and mental powers for absorbing and learning from a prepared environment rather than from an all-knowing teacher. How this is accomplished best with respect to classroom discipline is presented in chapter 8, which describes Thomas Gordon's *T.E.T.: Teacher Effectiveness Training* (1974) model.

No author of classroom management books that I am aware of offers a Carl Rogers' model of classroom management. Yet his theories do serve as the primary basis of at least one major discipline model—Gordon's *T.E.T.: Teacher Effectiveness Training* (1974). And it is no wonder because Rogers was Gordon's master's thesis advisor in graduate school at Ohio State University! They later were colleagues at the University of Chicago.

Both Skinner and Rogers apparently value the concept of student freedom. Where they differ is in how students exercise this freedom. Skinner argues that the struggle for personal freedom in education can be helped best by teachers striving to improve their control of students rather than abandoning it (Skinner, 1973). For Rogers, discipline (control) should not be imposed, but self-discipline, in a "Rousseau-like commitment to natural inner forces of creativity and self-determination" (Bordin, 1981, p. 30), should prevail. Qualities of empathy, genuineness, respect, honesty, and helpfulness should be consciously developed in both teachers and students.

An hypothetical exchange between a behaviorist and a humanist is presented by Kramlinger and Huberty (1990) in the publication, *Training & Development Journal.* The exchange highlights the advantages of each approach, describes the principles of application for both, and addresses the levels of performance expected from workers under each system. The transfer from the workplace to the classroom is obvious.

Which Are You: A Skinnerian or a Rogerian?

One way to help determine whether you are basically a Skinnerian or a Rogerian when it comes to classroom management is to complete the following Exercise 2.1—Skinner-Rogers Terminology. No one can be a perfect Skinnerian or a perfect Rogerian, but one can aspire to one view or the other—and act the part. Particular beliefs and actions reflect one view, while other beliefs and actions characterize the other view. Like the statement, "If it looks, feels, and smells like an elephant, then it probably it is an elephant."

Exercise 2.1
Skinner-Rogers Terminology

Pretend that you are about to have an altercation with a student. The words below represent a number of possible attitudes and/or actions that one might feel appropriate to hold and/or apply in such an encounter.

Directions:

Circle the six or seven terms that best reflect your beliefs regarding the discipline of children. Select the terms that you believe in; ignore the terms that you do not believe in. There are no right or wrong answers. Be prepared for something very surprising to emerge as a result of completing this exercise!

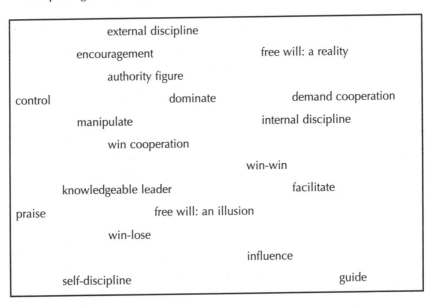

If you "believe in one view's beliefs and effortlessly act in ways that reflect that view's beliefs, then you are probably—heart and soul—committed to that belief." What are some of the words that can be used to reflect one view or the other—Skinnerian or Rogerian?

Interpreting the Exercise

How many of you circled "win-win"? If you did, then what I think you are saying is that in an altercation, or some other problem situation, it is desirable for both you and the other person to come out "winners"—in other words, both of you get your needs met. In fact, not only do you believe that it is desirable, you believe that it is possible. After all, you like to win, don't you? And, one would expect that the other person, too, would like to win. Wouldn't it be nice if you could both win?

How many of you circled "win-lose"? This would suggest that in your experience when there is an altercation, just like in major league sports, someone has to win and someone has to lose. And, if you can have it your way, you would prefer winning and not losing. Unfortunately, the other person probably feels the same way. Some teachers and parents practice "win-lose" with their children and rationalize their actions with the belief that they are actually doing the children some good: they are teaching the children a good lesson in life. Perhaps yes; perhaps no. Perhaps the lesson they are teaching is an unintended lesson—that is "I lost this time, but I'll try a lot harder to make sure that I do not lose next time."

How many of you circled *both* "win-win" and "win-lose"? Few if any people circle both. To do so would be illogical. How could you hold a fundamental belief (i.e., personal philosophy) of "win-win" and at the same time hold a fundamental belief of "win-lose"? For the quantitative philosophers among the readers, holding both a "win-win" and a "win-lose" set of beliefs about how to treat other people would fail a Venn Diagram test. At this point, most people who complete this exercise accept that a "win-win" and a "win-lose" attitude toward problem-solving situations are diametrically opposed to each other. They understand, although they may not like it, that they really should choose one position or the other as representative of their fundamental beliefs.

In case it is not obvious already, Skinner, and the discipline models that flow from his beliefs, live, eat, sleep, endorse, and embrace a "win-lose" attitude—one where the adult knows best and is only making you (i.e., the child) lose because he or she somehow knows what is best for you. When I quiz workshop attendees as to how many of them have their lives completely in order, no one raises a hand. Yet, Skinnerians, with their "win-lose" attitude, believe that although they may not know what is good for themselves, they sure do know what is good for others. How do you feel when someone does something that results in your losing and then that person announces, "I only did it for your own good." Does the hair on the back of your neck stand up? Do you feel like saying, "Hey, it's my life; let me make my own decisions"? Rogers, and discipline models that flow from his beliefs, would live, eat, sleep, endorse, and embrace a "win-win" attitude and, hopefully, acquire the skills to make it happen.

I promised you a surprise and here it comes. How many of you circled the term "praise"? Those of you who did apparently see the value of delivering, as well as receiving, praise. When this question is asked in my workshops, most hands are raised. How many of you circled the term "encouragement"? When this question is asked of workshop participants, lots of hands are raised. How many of you circled both "praise" and "encouragement"? Once again, when this question is asked of workshop attendees, many hands go up. At this point I announce that they have committed a "no-no." They have made an illogical response. Selecting both "praise" and "encouragement" once again fails the Venn Diagram test of logic.

"How so?" you might ask. Skinner, and the discipline models that flow from his beliefs, live, eat, sleep, endorse, and embrace the use of "praise." Rogerians, and the discipline models that reflect Rogers' fundamental beliefs, would not touch "praise" with a ten-foot pole! Instead, Rogers, and discipline models that flow from his beliefs, would live, eat, sleep, endorse, and embrace the use of "encouragement." As surprising as it may seem, praise and encouragement are not synonymous. If you don't believe it, look up both words in a dictionary. Further, praise is not an effective vehicle for encouraging someone.

Chapter 6 (Dreikurs' Social Discipline Model) and Chapter 11 (Some Surprising Ideas about Discipline) provide more information on the differences between praise and encouragement. Encouragement is not a synonym for praise. Further, praise is not a tool to encourage. Suffice to say, praise is praise, and encouragement is encouragement. Skinnerians rely heavily upon the use of praise (and rewards); Rogerians rely heavily upon the use of encouragement. Once again a clear dichotomy exists between Skinnerian and Rogerian beliefs and parent/teacher actions that reflect these respective beliefs.

Finally, how many of you circled one of the terms that deal with "free will"? No circled term highlights the dichotomy between Skinnerian and Rogerian fundamental beliefs (i.e., philosophy) more than does this one. Those of you who circled the term "free will: a reality," apparently believe that mankind (including children) possesses at least some degree of it. Those of you who did not circle the term, or who circled the term "free will: an illusion," believe otherwise. Skinner believes that there is no such thing as free will. Human beings just pretend that free will exists, so that they can feel more important than the rest of the animal kingdom. Rogers, on the other hand, believes that free will within human beings does exist, and, thus, discipline models must take its existence into consideration. Like being pregnant, you either are or you are not, there is no in-between; either you believe in free will or you do not, there is no in-between. You must choose one side or the other of this Skinnerian-Rogerian dichotomy. Hence, you should choose a discipline model from one side or the other of this same dichotomy. It would be illogical, as well as less workable, to do otherwise.

One way to appreciate the differences between Skinner and Rogers is to examine the representative terminology—the jargon—that typifies both views. Such a listing of terminology is shown in Table 2.2.

"Skinner reduces the science of human behavior to responses to environmental contingencies. Rogers rejects this outward orientation, emphasizing man's self-determined potential for creative action" (Bordin, 1981, p. 29). The dichotomy, at least for Skinner and Rogers, is clear.

Whatever your philosophy, you will be happier operating in an environment that reflects your school of thought. Later you will be asked to place the six "tried and true" classroom models that will be described in Part II into a Skinner versus Rogers' Behaviorist-Humanist framework.

A KEEPING IT SIMPLE FRAMEWORK: LEWIS

Control <——————— Manage ———————> Influence

While on sabbatical in Melbourne investigating classroom management in Australian schools, I attended several University of Melbourne lectures on discipline. One lecture presented by Ramon Lewis, a senior lecturer in education at La Trobe University (outside of Melbourne), captured my attention—especially because of the categories' simplicity. Upon summarizing his lecture, he grouped the available models on classroom management into three obvious categories. The models either tried to *control, manage,* or *influence* (Lewis, 1991). There it was, right in front of me. It was that simple. A more detailed description of his ideas appears in the book, *The Discipline Dilemma: Control, Management, and Influence* (Lewis, 1997).

Whatever your philosophy, you will be happier, and more effective, operating in an environment that reflects your school of thought. Later you will be asked to place the six "tried and true" classroom models that will be described in Part II into Lewis' Keeping it Simple framework.

WHY NOT AN ECLECTIC APPROACH?:
A FEW FINAL ARGUMENTS

Each time I conduct a workshop on discipline theory and practice, I find that initially participants resist the recommendation that they select a single discipline model that best reflects their fundamental beliefs (i.e., philosophy), become trained in that model, and practice it with skill and a sense of commitment. They ask, "Why can't we use an eclectic approach—a skill from one model for Susie, a skill from another model for Sam, and still

Table 2.11
Skinner versus Rogers: Representative Terminology

SKINNER	ROGERS
Authority figure	Knowledgeable leader
Control	Influence
Pressure	Stimulation
Demand Cooperation	Winning cooperation
Praise	Encouragement
Dominate	Guide
Win-lose	Win-win
External discipline	Self-discipline
Free will: An illusion	Free will: A reality
Lack of trust	Trust
Manipulator	Facilitator
Environmental contingencies	Actualization

another skill from another model for Juan?"

More than a handful of classroom management authors, too, believe that teachers should use an eclectic approach to discipline. I disagree. What follows is one author's points in favor of eclecticism (Morris, 1996), followed immediately by my rebuttals.

"Individually none of these . . . discipline models appears to be adequate for today's classrooms—mainly because they were developed around presumptive, ideal classroom characteristics."

Tauber's rebuttal: Select, learn, and use a model that works *most* of the time with *most* students in *most* situations. It should be the *exception*, then, rather than the *rule*, when practices other than those recommended in a teacher's chosen model should be used! Don't be tempted to too easily give up on using the model that reflects your fundamental beliefs (i.e., your philosophy) and that you have learned and believe in, even when the going gets tough—and it occasionally will!

"Another internal weakness in the models is their lack of acknowledgment of how teachers must vary their discipline procedures and approaches based on the unique classroom dynamics of each class period."

Tauber's rebuttal: This suggests that different discipline models and/or portions of different models would be used for "each class," maybe even for "each child." Translated into actual practice, we could have perhaps thirty individual six-year-old first graders or 180 ninth grade junior high students all dictating what discipline model and/or techniques teachers will use with each and every one of them. Not only is this probably impossible to do, this is absurd; it is the "tail wagging the dog." Shouldn't it be the other way around? Shouldn't teachers, the trained professionals in the classroom, decide the discipline model they use—one that they strongly believe in?

"I am convinced my practical disciplining in the classroom necessitates a blending from these . . . theories."

Tauber's rebuttal: Most teachers don't have the time and energy to learn *one* discipline model well, let alone learn *several* discipline models well! Let me repeat this point. Most teachers don't have the time and energy to learn *one* discipline model well, let alone learn *several* discipline models well! Is this not the case in your situation? Without learning all models well, teachers would be ill prepared to do any effective "blending." Unfortunately, this smorgasbord approach to discipline is deceptively attractive both to teachers and parents.

"Thus, teachers must remain flexible, innovative, and consistent in disciplining their students in the classroom."

Tauber's rebuttal: How is picking and choosing discipline strategies from many discipline models, some very different in fundamental beliefs about how to treat fellow human beings, being "consistent"? I agree that it may be possible to combine features of models that are close together philosophically (i.e., Jones & Canters; Glasser & Gordon). Unfortunately many educators who advocate an eclectic approach want to use strategies from discipline models that are philosophically opposed to each other (i.e., Canters and Glasser).

A more scholarly argument against eclectic approaches to problem-solving situations (i.e., classroom discipline) was outlined by Henle (1957). Below are listed several of Henle's major arguments against eclecticism or smorgasbord approaches to problem solving. Read them and see if you agree or disagree that they have merit even today, four decades after they were published.

- Not only does the eclectic lose prematurely the advantages of controversy, he may to some extent give up the advantages of theory as well. (p. 300)

- [E]clectics have to a large extent succeeded in resolving conflicts in psychology by ignoring differences and obscuring the issues. (p. 302)

- It seems to the present writer that reconciliations can be reached in psychology only by focusing on the existing differences, examining them, and carrying on research to settle issues. If this is eclecticism, it is eclecticism after the fact rather than the prevailing eclecticism before the fact. (p. 303)

- Since competing theories on any particular issue in psychology today—or competing psychological systems—each tend to be plausible and to be supported by evidence, it is unlikely that any one will win a clear victory over the others. (p. 303)

- The eclectics are, of course, right in maintaining that where a genuine controversy exists in psychology, and where evidence seems to support both sides, there is likely to be some truth to both positions. But they (eclectics) solve their problem too soon. Existing theories cannot be made more comprehensive by adding divergent ones together. (p. 304)

- [E]clectics tend to resolve conflicts in psychology by glossing over real differences and obscuring the issues. Such solutions achieve harmony at the price of specific theory in the area of controversy, and thus sacrifice fruitlessness in the discovery of new fact. (p. 304)

USING A DISCIPLINE MODEL THAT "WORKS"

If part of the argument in favor of eclecticism is that teachers must be free to "use what works," the fact is that all six of the discipline models presented in this book "work"—work with *most* kids, *most* of the time, and in *most* situations. After all, these "tried and true" classroom management models have had decades of testing and refinement. If all of the models work, then using alone the fact that a given model works is an insufficient justification for choosing that model over any others. A classroom management model should be chosen, and then learned, studied, practiced, and used because, and only because, it reflects one's fundamental views (i.e., philosophy) about how fellow human beings should be treated.

Having to make a choice of a single discipline model (or at least a choice of ones that are philosophically aligned) is not an easy thing to do, but I believe it is a necessary thing to do. Either a discipline system is designed to make students more obedient or more personally satisfied; either a discipline system is designed to have students be in charge of their destiny or be acted upon by powerful external forces (Blumenfeld-Jones, 1996). Goldberg and Wilgosh highlight the nature of the two philosophical views by looking at the importance of meeting students' needs. The Canters (Skinnerians) emphasize teachers' rights in meeting their professional needs over the importance of students meeting their needs. Dreikurs (a Rogerian) emphasizes students satisfying their personal-social needs as essential for discipline "which he defines as the development of intelligent inner control" (Goldberg & Wilgosh, 1990, p. 41). Freiberg (1997) contrasts these opposing philosophies by labeling students as "tourists" in a Skinnerian classroom and as "citizens" in a Rogerian classroom. In the former, the student is "just passing through"; in the latter, the student is "taking responsibility for self, others, and the classroom environment."

Swaim, perhaps, sums it up best when he concludes, "The main conclusion is that both Skinner's and Rogers' models have their merits, but an educator cannot value both of them equally without creating an inconsistency within his professional practice" (Swaim, 1974, p. 48). It is hard, perhaps impossible, for a teacher to operate effectively from both ends of a philosophical dichotomy. Having said all of this, recently I ran across a tattered paperback titled *Humanizing Classroom Discipline: A Behavioral Approach* (Dollar, 1972). Although this title sounds like an oxymoron to me, an article by Madeline Hunter (1977), while she was still a school principal, wrote that the Humanism/Behaviorism argument was simply "a silly squabble" (p. 98). Is it? You decide.

TEST YOURSELF

This is a sampling of the kinds of factual and open-ended questions that you should be able to answer after having read this chapter.

1. Contrast Wolfgang and Glickman's terms of interventionist and noninterventionist.

2. Which of Wolfgang and Glickman's terms, interventionist or noninterventionist, best describes how you *have been* parented and taught? Which describes how you *would like* to parent and teach?

3. Explain how Wolfgang and Glickman's noninterventionism approach to discipline is not simply a laissez-faire approach?

4. Identify French and Raven's five Social Bases of Power *and* indicate which three are argued to be overlooked.

5. Which of French and Raven's Social Bases of Power have been argued to be overused and ineffectively used? Why?

6. Explain how legitimate power is a "positional" power, while referent power and expert power are "personal" powers.

7. Which of French and Raven's Social Bases of Power might one expect to last for a life-time? Why?

8. Contrast the positions of B. F. Skinner and Carl R. Rogers as they relate to motivating people to learn and work.

9. Hypothesize why, in the Skinner/Rogers Exercise, most respondents did not select win/win and win/lose, but did select encouragement and praise.

10. Do you believe that human beings possess "free will," and, if so, how might that fact help you decide which fundamental set of beliefs—Skinner's or Rogers'—to embrace?

11. How could two individuals, Skinner and Rogers, who were respected scholars, prolific writers, and at heart, accomplished scientists, have such different views on how to treat fellow human beings?

12. Although when asked how they would like to be treated—"controlled" or "influenced"—most respondents selected "influenced," many respondents still saw a need for "controlling" others. Why?

13. Is it possible for an educator to hold conflicting fundamental sets of beliefs, learn a number of discipline models well, and then draw from these models in an eclectic fashion to discipline students? Why or why not?

14. What is wrong with choosing a discipline model on the basis of the argument that "it works?"

15. Defend your position on eclecticism as it relates to using discipline models that reflect fundamentally different sets of beliefs.

PART II

"TRIED AND TRUE" MODELS OF CLASSROOM MANAGEMENT

Part II, consisting of chapters 3 through 8, presents six popular classroom management models. These models are "tried and true"—they have been on the American and world scenes for two decades or more. The classroom management models are presented in a sequence from those most interventionist in nature to those most noninterventionist in nature—from those that purport to control to those that purport to influence. You should note clear differences between discipline models at opposite ends of the interventionist-noninterventionist or control-influence continuum—for example, Dobson's A Place for Punishment model and the Canters' Assertive Discipline model versus Gordon's Teacher Effectiveness Training model. You will observe fewer clear differences between discipline models adjacent to each other.

The differences between the opposite ends of the control-influence continuum are reflected in the theme of a recent Robert Redford movie, *The Horse Whisperer*, where nontraditional ways are used to train wild horses. For years it was believed that you had to dominate, as well as break the will of, a wild horse in order to make it obey and cooperate. In *The Horse Whisperer*, the horse trainer talks to and uses mutual trust and respect to bond with the wild horse in order to gain its cooperation willingly.

Several of these classroom models (the Canters', Dreikurs', Glasser's, and Gordon's) have been widely used for in-service and, to some extent, pre-service training. Surprisingly, though, in a comprehensive survey by Emmer and Aussiker of 120 school districts in the United States and Canada, "only a few of the school districts reported evaluation research on the models, in spite of their widespread use" (1990, p. 133). One wonders upon what basis school district administrators and staff choose which discipline programs to adopt.

Those with some psychology background may wish to attempt to determine the psychological theories upon which each classroom management model is based. After all, psychology can be defined as the scientific study of (mis)behavior—what discipline is all about.

Read and study all of the models—not just those that at first glance seem most attractive. Read them with an open, yet critical, mind. Take nothing at face value. Learn more about each model by reviewing the suggested readings offered at the end of each chapter. Read the original sources—for example, Gordon's *T.E.T.: Teacher Effectiveness Training* (1974) or the Canters' *Assertive Discipline* (1992).

Compare and contrast these classroom management models. Think about which were used on you when you were a student in grade school or high school. Think about how you and your peers responded to teachers when they used these models. Consider which model(s) you personally like and dislike. Ponder why this is the case.

Discuss with other readers their likes and dislikes. Challenge theirs; defend yours. If you don't practice defending your choice of a discipline model now, I guarantee that you will have to do it sometime soon in your teaching career—probably during a job interview! Better to do it now!

CHAPTER 3

James Dobson:
A Place for Punishment

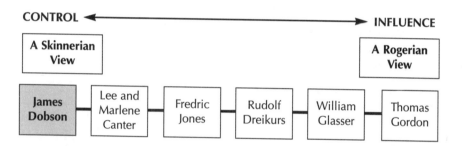

CONTROL ◄——————————————————————► INFLUENCE

| A Skinnerian View | | | | | A Rogerian View |

| James Dobson | Lee and Marlene Canter | Fredric Jones | Rudolf Dreikurs | William Glasser | Thomas Gordon |

James C. Dobson (1936–) holds a Ph.D. in child development and, prior to establishing the nonprofit organization Focus on the Family, was associate clinical professor of pediatrics at the University of Southern California School of Medicine. Focus on the Family employs more than one thousand three hundred people and receives up to twelve thousand calls, e-mails, and letters every day (Gerson, 1998). His organization receives so much mail that it has its own ZIP code. Dr. Dobson's syndicated radio programs, concentrating upon parenting and related issues, are heard on many radio stations. His book *Dare to Discipline* (1970), reissued as *The New Dare to Discipline* (1992), has sold more than three million copies. In addition to the *Focus on the Family* magazine, his organization publishes the magazine *Teachers in Focus*. Dr. Dobson also has been heavily involved in governmental activities related to the family and to child-rearing. He is an outspoken critic of permissive parenting. Dobson's support and council were sought by virtually all of the 1996 Republican presidential candidates and, most recently, he has appeared on the cover of *U.S. News & World Report* (May 4, 1998) where, within the article inside, his conservative power over politics is highlighted.

OBJECTIVES

This chapter will help you, among other things, to:

- Classify, using the theoretical frameworks presented in chapter 2, James Dobson's A Place for Punishment model.
- Explain the popularity of Dobson's views regarding the use of punishment.
- Identify guidelines for using punishment.
- Identify the common challenges to the use of punishment.
- Identify organizations that call for the abolishment of punishment.
- Explain the demographics of punishment.
- Explore whether Dobson's A Place for Punishment model is for you.

WHERE DOES DOBSON'S MODEL FALL WITHIN THE FOUR THEORETICAL FRAMEWORKS DISCUSSED IN CHAPTER 2?

Now is an opportunity for you to apply what you have learned in chapter 2, "Theoretical Frameworks for Classifying Discipline Models." Dobson's A Place for Punishment model clearly finds a place in French and Raven's Social Bases of Power framework under "coercion." It finds a home in Wolfgang and Glickman's Schools of Thought framework as the most extreme "interventionist" strategy. With its emphasis upon the use of punishment, Dobson's position is aligned with the Skinnerian side of the Skinner-Rogers' dichotomy although, in reality, Skinner believed that one could more effectively condition animals (including children) solely through the use of rewards. In Lewis' Keeping It Simple framework, punishment is equated with "control."

INTRODUCTION

Within the field of discipline, more has been written on the topic of punishment and its variations (especially corporal punishment) than on any other single topic. Much of what has been written says that the use of punishment should be reduced, if not stopped, no matter its goal—retribution, deterrence, or reform. Yet punishment, whether corporal (such as spanking, shaking, choking, excessive exercise, disrobement, or confinement in an uncomfortable place) or nonphysical (such as verbal beratement, neglect, loss of privileges, detention, and suspension), has not stopped, and in some schools, has not been significantly reduced.

Does the public generally support less punishment? No one realistically expects a ground swell to ban all forms of punishment—sequences supplied to reduce the likelihood of a behavior's occurring in the future. Besides, such an all-encompassing ban would be unenforceable. What about public support for less corporal punishment? "As of May, 1992, only 21 states . . . and the District of Columbia had bans on corporal punishment" (Orentlicher, 1992, p. 3205). What does the future hold? In spring 1992, Michigan and Kentucky revoked their prohibition on corporal punishment. The Office of Civil Rights reports that more than 1.5 million students are physically punished every year. These are probably conservative estimates.

What is the mood of the American public? Referring to the Patterson, New Jersey, high school principal who made himself famous by using a bullhorn, wielding a baseball bat, and expelling 10 percent of his students during the first week on the job, William J. Bennett, former Secretary of Education under President Reagan, once said, "Sometimes you need Mr. Chips, and sometimes you need Dirty Harry" (Hyman, 1989, p. 20). In his portrayal of Joe Clark in the film *Lean on Me*, Morgan Freeman brought Clark's take-charge approach to the motion picture screen. The American public loved it. Make my day!

May teachers legally punish children? According to Zirkel and Gluckman (1988, p. 105), in Ingraham v. Wright, "the Supreme Court clearly settled the question insofar as the Eighth Amendment's cruel and unusual punishment clause and the Fourteenth Amendment's right of procedural due process." The Court held that corporal punishment by public school personnel does not violate these two rights "so long as state law provides for subsequent redress against unwarranted or excessive punishment through tort suits or criminal prosecution" (Sendor, 1987, p. 32). The key words here are *unwarranted* and *excessive*.

Liberals such as A. S. Neill of *Summerhill* fame may claim that "thousands of teachers do their work splendidly without having to introduce fear of punishment. The others are incompetent misfits who ought to be driven out of the profession" (Neill, 1968, p. 124). Actions, though, speak louder than words. The sole fact that punishment is so pervasive in our society (home, school, military, correction facilities) makes it worthy of study.

The term *punishment* carries with it a cultural or traditional stigma that does not exist in the scientific community. Dobson, as we will see below, disagrees. Technically, *punishment* is simply a word used to describe a consequence that, when supplied, reduces behavior. In daily practice, though, the word is emotionally laden. For many adults there is a blur between punishment for the sake of punishment (retribution, eye-for-an-eye) and punishment for the sake of therapy (behavior reduction). Further, punishment is "tainted by an association with brutality, child-battering, and control achieved by sheer force" (Walters & Grusec, 1977, p. 2).

VIRTUES OF PUNISHMENT

What are the virtues of punishment? There must be some, otherwise its popularity would not have persisted for so long both in homes and schools. A review of articles indexed in *Psychological Abstracts* from 1980 to 1989 reveals more than five hundred citations dealing with punishment. This is twice the number cited for positive reinforcement (Tauber, 1990). A more recent examination by the author of *PsycINFO* from 1988 to 1998 reveals 329 titles containing the words "positive reinforcement" and 732 titles containing the word "punishment." Once again a two-to-one ratio favoring the topic of punishment exists. Still another literature review by the author, this time of *ERIC* (Educational Resources Information Center), for the period 1983 through 1998, reveals four times as many articles with the words "corporal punishment" in the title as with the words "positive reinforcement." Clearly, authors like to write, and editors like to publish, articles that deal with punishment rather than with positive reinforcement. Perhaps editors are just giving readers what they want.

Standing out as a champion for the use of punishment in child-rearing (home or school) is James Dobson. His views, having a strong biblical foundation, are outlined in his book *The New Dare to Discipline* (1992)—first published in 1970 as *Dare to Discipline*. The Bible is often quoted to provide the rationale for punishment. Solomon's familiar admonition, "Spare the rod and spoil the child," has a biblical basis in Proverbs where we read, "Withhold not correction from the child: for if thou beatest him with the rod, he shall not die. If you beat him with a rod, you will save his life from hell" (23:13–14).

Chastisement by rod, according to Dobson, is the primary biblically ordained response to a child's challenge to authority—woodshed therapy in action. "He who spares the rod hates his son, but he who loves him is diligent to discipline him" (Prov. 13:24). Spanking is not some harebrained idea man invented for disciplining children. Spanking is not optional, and it is not old-fashioned. Dobson argues that "some strong-willed children absolutely demand to be spanked, and their wishes should be granted" (1978, p. 61). Spanking, according to Lessen (1979), is God's idea—it is an expression of love. One could almost be convinced that one is doing a child a favor by beating him.

An acceptance of the doctrine of biblical literalism thus sets the stage for some adults' enthusiastic support for corporal punishment (Ellison &

Sherkat, 1993). "Add to these biblical sanctions the traditional Christian concept of children born into sin, and it becomes clear why it was thought that God sanctioned the molding of children's character through severe punishment" (Cryan, 1987, p. 148). "If the punishment is of the right kind, it not only takes effect physically, but through physical terror and pain, it awakens and sharpens the consciousness that there is a moral power over us . . . a law which cannot be broken" (Christenson, 1970, p. 100). There seems to be a lingering belief that harsh punishment is necessary for children to develop as decent human beings (Webster et al., 1988).

What reaction does Dobson have to those scientific principles of child-rearing that may appear to challenge a literal interpretation of the Bible? "The principles of good discipline cannot be ascertained by scientific inquiry" (Dobson, 1970, p. 13). Dobson believes that child development authorities have muddied the water with permissive philosophies that contradict the very nature of children. For educators, who as professionals have been told to consult a recognized body of knowledge (i.e., the scientific literature) before making decisions, Dobson's assertion is disturbing. Further, Dobson's ignoring of scientific inquiry seems at odds with his recommendation: "The wise parent must understand the physical and emotional characteristics of each stage in childhood, and then fit the discipline to a boy's or girl's individual needs" (Dobson, 1978, pp. 38–39). How do parents, then, acquire this wisdom? By trial and error? One hopes not.

Dobson believes that parents (and presumably teachers) should do their best to influence a child's choices. "My entire book, you see, is a product of the biblical orientation to human nature. We are not typically kind and loving and generous and yielded to God. Our tendency is toward selfishness and stubbornness and sin. We are all, in effect, 'strong-willed children' as we stand before God" (Dobson, 1978, pp. 174–175). Strong-willed children need strong parents and teachers to shape that will. There is no doubt that Dobson's heart is in the right place when it comes to advising parents and teachers on how to discipline. This point should never be suspect.

Discipline should be part of a child's early experiences, both at home and at school. While at home, children should learn to yield to the loving authority of their parents. Dobson is not simply advocating that parents become dictators. He points out that any rule enforcement by adults must be accompanied by relationship building, otherwise, rebellion may ensue (Gerson, 1998). By doing so, the child learns to submit to other forms of authority—teachers, principal, police, employers—that will confront him later in his life. At school, discipline should begin with the crucial interaction between a primary or elementary teacher and his or her students. These contacts help form the attitudes toward authority the child will carry into junior and senior high school. How teachers approach their classes, especially on the first day, can make all the difference in the world.

FIRST-DAY APPROACHES OF TWO TEACHERS

Dobson (1992) describes the first-day approaches of two teachers: one, Miss Peach, condemned to a long year of frustration and student behavioral problems; another, Miss Justice, destined for a productive and satisfying year for both teacher and students. On the first day, Miss Peach conveys the message, "We are going to have a fun, fun year; you are going to love me—and a long string of other peachy stuff." The first student's challenge (and there will be a first) to Miss Peach's authority is ignored. The unsaid message is clear: "Miss Peach is a pushover." The challenges increase in number and intensity. It soon is called lack of control.

In contrast, Miss Justice conveys her first-day message, "This is going to be a good year. . . . Your parents have given me the responsibility of teaching you some very important things this year. . . . That's why I can't let one or two show-offs keep me from doing my job. Now, if you want to try and disrupt what we're here to do, I can tell you it will be a miserable year for you. I have many ways to make you uncomfortable, and I will not hesitate to use them. Any questions? Good, let's get back to work" (Dobson, 1992, p. 142). The inevitable first student challenge is made. Miss Justice "socks it to him." Everyone gets the message: "Miss Justice means business."

Dobson has observed that students at all levels prefer and respect, even love, more strict teachers. First, when a class is out of control, particularly at the elementary level, the children are afraid of one another. Without adult control, who controls the bullies? Who protects the less able and less strong? No one did in *Lord of the Flies*, and the results were painful. Second, children love justice. Children admire the teacher who can enforce an equitable system of rules. Third, undisciplined classrooms reek of chaos. They are nerve-racking, tiring, and irritating (Dobson, 1970, p. 125).

Freedom of choice and democracy have little place in Dobson's model. Choice would only encourage rebellion against authority, egocentric conduct, and further disposition toward selfishness (Dobson, 1978, pp. 17–18). Democratic conceptions of adult-child relations are irresponsible because they encourage the abrogation of crucial parental and teacher authority (Dobson, 1978). Adherence to adult-imposed standards is an important part of discipline. Clearly, Dobson's advice to parents, "When that nose-to-nose confrontation occurs between generations, it is *extremely* [italicized by Dobson] important for the adult to win decisively and confidently" (Dobson, 1978, p. 32), typifies a win-lose model of discipline.

It is important to note that Dobson does not simply favor administering punishment. He recommends that parents and teachers represent the two sides of God—loving compassion and decisive justice—to their youngsters. "God is loving, merciful, and forgiving. At the same time, however, because God's punishment of sin is understood as inevitable and consistent, it is vitally important for parental discipline to embody these characteristics" (Ellison & Sherkat, 1993, p. 134). The "loving compassion" side of this approach cannot—must not—be overlooked.

One way to clarify what one means is to contrast it with something just the opposite. In *The Strong-Willed Child* (1978), Dobson does this in a chapter titled "An Evaluation of Parent Effectiveness Training (P.E.T.)," Thomas Gordon's noninterventionist discipline model presented later in this book. For instance, Dobson "wishes" that Gordon's assessment of human nature were accurate, "that the tendency to lie is not natural in youngsters. It is a learned response" (Gordon, 1970, p. 179). He argues, however, that it contradicts scripture: "The heart is deceitful above all things, and desperately wicked; who can know it?" (Jeremiah I 7:9). Hence, strong-willed adult interventionist responses are required.

In summary, Dobson sees three major flaws in Gordon's model: (1) his failure to understand the proper role of authority in the home, (2) his belief that children are born innately good and then learn to do wrong, and (3) his lack of resolve regarding the parent's duty to instill spiritual principles in a child during his or her most teachable years (Dobson, 1978, p. 177). Humanistic thinking—the concept that children are basically good and if left to themselves will grow into fulfilled adults—hinders discipline (Lessen, 1979). These fundamental differences in beliefs dictate drastically different adult strategies of child management at home or school.

The difference between Dobson, an interventionist, and Gordon, a noninterventionist, is revealed in their views about what motivates children. "To say that children have an innate love of learning is as muddle-headed as to say that children have an innate love of baseball. Some do. Some don't" (Dobson, 1992, p. 135; Dobson, 1996, p. 1). Gordon would disagree, at least with Dobson's beliefs about whether or not children have an innate love of learning. These differences in beliefs influence the design of their respective classroom management models. Prodding, even punishment, has a place in Dobson's model; it has no place in Gordon's model.

OTHERS WHO SUPPORT PUNISHMENT

Although Dobson may appear to be extreme in his legitimization of punishment, he has, in fact, plenty of company. Walters and Grusec (1977,

p. 115), for instance, state that "a large body of research, all of it carried out
with children, suggests that punishment for incorrect behavior leads to
faster learning than does reinforcement for correct behavior, and a combination of reinforcement and punishment is no better than punishment
alone." Just the opposite recommendation is offered by Rich (1983, p.
298), who states, "It is desirable to combine punishment with positive
statements. . . . While the undesirable behavior is weakened, it is important
to teach correct behavior."

In a study of the real world of education, Rutter and his colleagues (1979,
p. 186) state in *Fifteen Thousand Hours* that "obviously a certain amount of
firm disapproval, and also punishment, is necessary in the control of disruptive behaviour." Also representing the real world, Paul Armstrong, then pres-
ident-elect of the West Virginia Association of Elementary School Principals,
believes that corporal punishment is needed as an option with students who
do not respond to other methods of discipline. Armstrong (1984) argues
that although corporal punishment is banned in police stations and prisons,
schools are different because they have "professional educators who are
trained to deal with children and can be trusted to use the paddle" (p. 79).

In a well-documented article in *Education and Urban Society*, Bauer and
others (1990) comment on whether or not corporal punishment is effective.
They answer, "Yes, at least under certain conditions. . . . It can serve as a useful behavioral management instrument for suppressing undesirable behaviors" (p. 288). Rich (1991, p. 184) concludes his recent article "Should
Students Be Punished?" by stating that "in certain cases punishment may
help restore classroom order; it may promote discipline and early moral
development by teaching students to obey rules and follow instructions."
Skiba and Deno (1991) claim that research data "have consistently contra-
dicted assertions that punishment is ineffective" (p. 299) and that "contingent negative consequences, in fact, have been shown to be more effective in
reducing behavior than a variety of other procedures" (p. 300).

In his recent book, *The American Family*, Dan Quayle endorses control
and punishment as a way to shape children's behavior and secure their
respect and obedience (*U.S. News & World Report*, 1996). He and the families he surveys in his book reject the advice of so-called child-rearing experts
who document the pitfalls surrounding the use of spanking.

Three specific advantages of corporal punishment are outlined by Vockell
(1991): (1) It is very likely to be perceived by the recipient as unpleasant
(and therefore punishing), (2) it can be administered quickly and life can
return to more productive activities, and (3) its meaning is clear and easily
communicated. According to Vockell (p. 282), "The judicious use of corporal punishment will not necessarily thwart the development of self-disci-

pline." Like it or not, some researchers have built a theoretically-based case for the use of punishment.

More often, though, trends in approval of corporal punishment are revealed in general surveys of attitudes toward spanking. For instance, Straus, Gelles, and Steinmetz (1980) found that 77 percent of parents surveyed believed that spanking a twelve-year-old who misbehaved was both normal and necessary. Another parent survey found that 84 percent agreed that a good hard spanking is sometimes necessary (Lehman, 1989).

GUIDELINES FOR ADMINISTERING PUNISHMENT

If you feel you must punish students, do it effectively. The literature is replete with guidelines regarding procedures for supplying punishment, especially corporal punishment. Read them. Follow them. If you must err, do so on the side of caution. I could cite specific guidelines for how to punish properly, especially physical punishment. Although many such descriptions are available (McDaniel, 1980; Vockell, 1991), to provide them may leave you with a false sense of security that if you simply follow the guidelines, you are protected.

Instead, I have chosen to present Essex's (1989) ten costly mistakes one should avoid when administering corporal punishment:

1. Administer corporal punishment for offenses that clearly do not warrant such force.
2. Neglect to inform students ahead of time that specific infractions will result in punishment (physical or otherwise).
3. Overlook student characteristics such as age and physical or emotional state.
4. Fail to use a reasonable instrument.
5. Deny any, or even minimal, prior due process.
6. Fail to have an appropriate witness present.
7. Administer punishment with malice or anger.
8. Use excessive force or exercise poor judgment.
9. Ignore alternative options and/or administer punishment over a student's or parent's objection.
10. Fail to follow district or state policy.

Note that all of the warnings start with a verb, something someone can choose to do or not to do. In each case, the educator must make such choices and then be prepared to be held accountable for those choices. Make the right choices!

The guideline of using a "reasonable instrument" bears a comment. What is a reasonable instrument? One's hand? Dobson says no. "The hand should be seen by the child as an object of love rather than an instrument of punishment" (1978, p. 46). Neutral objects, though, such as a switch, a belt, or a paddle would be acceptable. One wonders what Dobson's reaction would be to the application of today's technology to the supplying of corporal punishment. In a newspaper article titled "Man Pleads Guilty to Shocking Sons with Dog Collar" (*Erie Daily Times*, 1996, p. 9A), a parent admitted to shocking his two sons with an electrically powered dog collar when they disobeyed. Some people are appalled by this. Are you? Is an electrically powered dog collar a reasonable, neutral instrument? In principle, an electric shock, a swat with a paddle, or a barrage of belittling and embarrassing comments have one thing in common: they all are designed to hurt! And hurt they do. All three are used successfully in training household pets. Why not children? Is this so outrageous?

Dobson's own magazine, *Focus on the Family. Newsletter of Focus on the Family: With Dr. James Dobson*, offers guidelines for administering disciplinary spankings. Two of these guidelines merit comments. One guideline, "Spanking should always be a planned action, not a reaction, and should follow a deliberate procedure" (Trumbull, 1998, p. 4), seems to fly in the face of a basic principle of operant conditioning whereby consequences are supposed to follow immediately after the behavior in question has occurred, and appears to challenge directly Dobson's own recommendation of "it is important to spank *immediately* [Dobson's italics] after the offense, or not at all" (1978, p. 47). A second guideline, "Spanking should never cause physical (or I assume, psychological) injury" (Turnbull, 1998, p. 4), suggests that parents and teachers are capable of remaining calm, cool, and collected, in the emotional heat that often accompanies the testing of wills between children and adults. This is a lot to ask of anyone; I know.

When my two children were infants and it was my time for the 2:00 A.M. feeding, my son David took his bottle and went back to sleep immediately. With my daughter Rebecca, it was another story. She seemed to sense it was me and not her mother giving her the bottle and that now was the time for her to test her strong will with her dad. I remember being dead tired, worried about how I would make my early morning class, and wanting to just get back into my nice warm bed. I recall giving her some very healthy "squeezes" to the point, later, of wondering whether I came close to squeezing the breath right out of her. What scared me then, and scares me now, was that I already was in my early thirties, had a Ph.D., a secure job, a sound marriage, a supportive mate, two incomes, and a promising future and, yet, I almost "went over the edge." If I came that close to causing my daughter physical injury, and I had all the advantages listed above, I can't begin to imagine how parents (or just one parent) without all of these advantages cope!

Skinner's research offers two more guidelines regarding punishment. First, punishing only serious infractions encourages students to misbehave just about up to that point. "Continual, gentle, nonemotional, clearly directed punishment lessens the emotional overtones that accompany much punishment" (Sylwester, 1970, p. 72). Second, the imaginative teacher should take advantage of the period of suppressed response that typically follows punishment to encourage and strengthen desired behaviors (Sylwester, 1970). Dobson, too, suggests using this period of time to reassure and teach.

One of the 1997/1998 guidelines for administering corporal punishment for a nearby school district reads, "A maximum of three swats with a paddle is permitted." This guideline raises a number of questions. Where in the scientific literature is the fact that administering three swats is acceptable, yet delivering four or more swats is unacceptable? How hard should the swats be? I am a six foot one and one-half inch male who weighs 210 pounds. My wife, also a teacher, is five foot and weighs about 105 pounds. Now, whose swat are we talking about, mine or hers? It surely would make a difference to the child who is being paddled.

Another corporal punishment guideline of this same school district states that "reasonable force" may be used but under no circumstances may that reasonable force cause "bodily injury." What training, if any, do teachers, or for that matter parents, have in order to decide what is reasonable force and at what point such force may or may not cause bodily injury?

Still one more guideline of another school district's policy states that "Corporal punishment should be used infrequently and as a last resort." Dobson, though, says otherwise. "A spanking is to be reserved for use in response to willful defiance, *whenever it occurs* [Dobson's italics]. Period!" (Dobson, 1978, p. 36). Dobson says that to wait and then paddle later often results in the parent or the teacher being perceived by the child as nagging, in other words, using less effective techniques over and over again such as screaming, reminding, and hand-wringing. All of which don't work.

While much of the discussion in this chapter centers upon physical or corporal punishment, similar cases could be made for forms of psychological punishment—that is, humiliation, embarrassment, and fear. Where is it written just how much humiliation, embarrassment, and fear can be administered so that a teacher or parent doesn't exceed the equivalent of this school district's "three swat" policy? Yet, many of these other forms of punishment can hurt more, and hurt longer, than corporal punishment. They just do not leave the obvious swelling and scars observable to a parent or emergency room physician. Surely no one still believes the old adage, "sticks and stones will break my bones, but names will never hurt me." Names do hurt!

When delivering punishment one must be sure that what one actually is delivering is, in fact, punishment! Whether or not something is punishing is not decided by the punisher, but by the person being punished. A teacher's scolding, designed to be punishing, may be taken as a successful bid for attention—in other words, a reward. An application of the "board of education" to one's hindquarters could be seen by a misbehaving child as a right of passage into manhood, something earning him admiration (reward) from his peers.

Accurately determining ahead of time just how an individual child will perceive an intended punishment is about as hard (and unsuccessful) as other efforts to read the future. The true test of whether or not an intended punishment was perceived as punishment is determined by its impact on the child. If the punished behavior lessens in intensity, duration, and/or frequency in the future, it was perceived as punishment. If the punished behavior does not decrease in the future, it was not perceived as punishment.

CHALLENGES TO PUNISHMENT

So far, the overall point of this chapter is that there may be a place for punishment in classrooms. Now it must be said that the preponderance of evidence, as well as informed opinion, supports the other side of the argument. Such evidence can be found in even the most superficial review of the literature.

Alvin Toffler (1990), for instance, describes three forms of power—force (violence), wealth, and knowledge. Force, even when it "works," produces resistance. Victims either try to escape or fight back. He describes force—the use of punishment—as "low-quality power" (p. 15). Further, the effects of punishment are not the opposite of reward. Punishment does not "subtract" responses where reinforcement "adds" them (Milhollan & Forisha, 1972). Typically, the arguments against the use of punishment, particularly physical punishment, center around several points.

Experimental research on punishment reveals, for instance, that "many of the characteristics of effective corporal punishment are not achievable or acceptable in the classroom setting" (Orentlicher, 1992, p. 3207). These include, among others, that it is most effective when delivered (1) with complete surprise (eliminates due process), (2) immediately after the occurrence of the misbehavior (impossible with a classroom full of students), (3) following *every* occurrence, and (4) with an intensity severe enough to cause pain.

A second regularly cited argument against the use of punishment is that educators could use more effective alternatives to accomplish the same end.

For instance, Skinner's views (the basis for behavior modification) ignore the punishment of undesired behaviors, instead concentrating upon the reinforcement of desired behaviors. Teachers could do likewise. Kessler (1985) argues that kids for whom corporal punishment will work can be controlled in other ways, whereas the students who are the "real problems" won't be deterred by it.

Other arguments against retaining corporal punishment as an educator option include: (1) that what is often claimed as a last-resort, when-all-else-fails, tool is used too soon and too often, therefore undermining the search for appropriate alternatives; and (2) that punishment turns kids off to learning and inadvertently teaches them that "might makes right." It teaches them, by example, that force is the solution of choice in any conflict—home, school, community. The bottom line is "punitive methods . . . don't work in the long run" (Skinner, 1980, p. 79).

Given the negative connotation that the term *punishment* carries, should we call it something else? Perhaps. But, according to Kohn (1991), punishment is such a disagreeable style of interaction that it cannot be disguised by referring to it by some other name. Perhaps people continue to use punishment because to do so reinforces the punisher. I recall one of my graduate professors saying, "Although punishing a child may not have any long-lasting impact on the child's behavior, if it makes you feel better, go ahead and do it." When a behavior occurs that is aversive to us, we punish it. By our response of punishing, the annoying behavior is removed, constituting reinforcement of our punishing behavior.

"Anyone can beat a child with a rod as the primary way of conditioning his behavior. That takes no sensitivity, no judgment, no understanding, and no talent. To depend on corporal punishment as the principal method of discipline is to make that critical error in assuming that discipline equals punishment" (Campbell, 1977, p. 84). Given that so little is known about the long-term consequences of punishment, especially physical punishment, reason dictates caution. It makes sense to explore alternatives, including reasoning, discussion, use of logical consequences, time-out, isolation, and setting boundaries, rules, and limits (Greven, 1991).

The statement, "Spare the rod and spoil the child," has special meaning to me in that I have spent a year in northern England (sheep country), six months in Australia (also, sheep country), and some time in New Zealand where there are more sheep than people. To the best of my recollection I never saw a shepherd using a rod to hit a sheep. The rod, even in biblical times, was used by the shepherd to *guide* the sheep and to *protect* them from the menace of wolves. Somehow over the years the meaning behind "Spare the rod and spoil the child" has changed whereby the rod is no longer viewed as an instrument for guiding and protecting, but seen as an instrument for hitting and inflicting pain upon one's charges. Personally I prefer the guidance and protection connotation.

ORGANIZATIONS FAVORING THE ABOLISHMENT OF CORPORAL PUNISHMENT

The following list of organizations, although certainly not exhaustive, shows the wide support that exists for the abolition of corporal punishment.

- American Academy of Pediatrics
- American Association for Counseling and Development
- American Association of Colleges for Teacher Education
- American Association of School Administrators
- American Bar Association
- American Humanist Association
- American Medical Association
- American Nurses Association
- American Personnel and Guidance Association
- American Psychiatric Association
- American Psychological Association
- American Public Health Association
- Association of Junior Leagues
- Association of State Departments of Education
- Council for Exceptional Children
- National Association for the Advancement of Colored People (NAACP)
- National Association of Elementary School Principals
- National Association of Secondary School Principals
- National Association of School Psychologists
- National Association of Social Workers
- National Association of State Boards of Education
- National Committee to Prevent Child Abuse
- National Council of Teachers
- National Education Association (two million members)

- National Foster Parents Association
- National Mental Health Association
- National Parent Teachers Association

THE DEMOGRAPHICS OF PUNISHMENT

Of note in the study of corporal punishment is the fact that physical punishment is not the educator's tool of choice for *all* students in *all* schools in *all* communities, states, or countries. Demographic factors clearly exist. The child of choice is the frail male. "Students who are more capable of striking back are treated more humanely" (Boonin, 1979, p. 395). It is not the school bully who is the object of corporal punishment, but students in elementary schools and pupils of small stature in junior high schools (Ball, 1989).

Nationwide, is it sheer coincidence that the ten worst states by percentage of students struck by educators just happen to be in the South— Arkansas, Mississippi, Alabama, Tennessee, Georgia, Texas, Louisiana, Oklahoma, South Carolina, and Missouri (U.S. Department of Education, 1997)? Could it be that all of the "bad kids" in our nation just happened to be born in, or have moved to, these states? Of course not. Within my home state of Pennsylvania, school districts in the west have a higher incidence of allowing and using corporal punishment than do schools in the east (*Erie Morning News*, 1993, p. 4A). Could it be that more "bad kids" gravitate to the western part of the state? Probably not.

According to Orentlicher (1992), corporal punishment occurs more often in rural schools and in smaller schools. Male students are disciplined more frequently (and more severely) than female students, with black males receiving more disciplinary actions than white males (Radin, 1988, Gregory, 1995). African American students and those with special learning disabilities are more likely to receive corporal punishment. Socioeconomically, poor white males are paddled more often than middle-class whites (Baker, 1987). Less-educated families and those with a greater number of children living in the household are particularly supportive of corporal punishment (Ellison & Sherkat, 1993). Schools with more inexperienced teachers are more likely to use corporal punishment.

Worldwide, most every industrialized country in the world *except* the United States, Canada, and one state in Australia, prohibits corporal punishment in schools. The trend toward outlawing corporal punishment in schools is not new. Its elimination dates back to the 1800s including, among many other countries, the Netherlands (1820), Italy (1860), France (1881), Finland (1890), Russia (1917), Norway (1936), China (1949), Sweden

(1958), Denmark (1967), Germany (1970), Ireland (1982), United Kingdom (1986), New Zealand (1990), and South Africa (1996). In 1998 England extended the ban to all private schools. Imagine, even England, a country that for centuries imprisoned, flogged, keel-hauled, branded, beheaded, and burned its enemies, has been able to outlaw corporal punishment. Many of these countries also have outlawed the use of corporal punishment by parents (i.e., England, Sweden, Norway, Finland, Denmark). With its newly elected liberal government, Germany, too, is moving toward banning parents and teachers from striking children.

In one of my more spirited class lectures on discipline, I approached a student who I knew recently had served in the military and, as part of a classroom demonstration, "slapped" him across the face. The "slap," exaggerated for the benefit of the audience, barely touched him. Still, a slap is a slap, and he noticeably recoiled with surprise. I asked him whether or not his superior officers in the military had a right to slap him. He answered "No! Of course not." I then asked him (and the rest of the class) if they found it at all strange that the military (an organization designed to prepare well-trained, physically fit, macho young men and women who "can take it") does not permit soldiers to be slapped, and yet school children, many of whom are young and frail, can be hit by their "superiors"—their teachers. An extended silence followed my question. With only twenty-seven states in the United States having banned corporal punishment in schools, let alone in homes, we have a long, long way to go. What are we waiting for?

James Dobson, when asked, "Do you think corporal punishment will eventually be outlawed?" responded, "It is very likely." When asked "Why?" he responded, "There are those in the Western world who will not rest until the government interferes with parent-child relationships . . . it has already happened in Sweden, and the media seems determined to bring that legislation to the United States. It will be a sad day for families" (Dobson, 1992, pp. 63–64).

CENTER FOR THE STUDY OF CORPORAL PUNISHMENT IN SCHOOLS

No discussion about punishment, in particular corporal punishment, would be complete without a reference to the work of Irwin A. Hyman, director of the National Center for the Study of Corporal Punishment and Alternatives in the Schools (NCSPAS), 255 Ritter Hall South, Temple University, Philadelphia, PA 19122 (215–204–6091). Hyman, a professor of psychology and director of NCSPAS since the late 1970s, is internationally known for his research, his advocacy, and for dissemination of materials concerning corporal punishment and its alternatives.

As an expert on corporal punishment, Hyman has written and delivered scholarly papers, published journal articles, written books, designed workshops, and delivered testimony before the United States Congress. A sampling of his work includes publications in *Phi Delta Kappan* (1984*), Today's Education* (1978), *Children Today* (1982), *Journal of Interpersonal Violence* (1988), *Education Digest* (1989), and *Holistic Education* (1990).

One of his books, *Reading, Writing and the Hickory Stick: The Appalling Story of Physical and Psychological Abuse in American Schools* (1990), sheds a disturbing light on what is happening in some American classrooms. Another, *Corporal Punishment in American Education: Readings in History, Alternatives* (Hyman & Wise, 1979), is self-described as the definitive text on corporal punishment. His book, *The Case against Spanking* (1997), describes how to discipline a child without hitting, while his book, *School Discipline and School Violence: The Teacher Variance* (1996), discusses how discipline and school violence may interact. You can obtain a complete listing of his works, as well as other NCSPAS publications and papers, by contacting the center.

Another organization worth contacting is End Physical Punishment of Children-USA (EPOCH-USA). They are located at 155 West Main Street, Suite 100–B, Columbus, Ohio 43215, and can be reached by calling (614) 221–8829. EPOCH-USA is an American affiliate of EPOCH-WORLD-WIDE, a multinational federation committed to ending corporal punishment through education and legal reforms.

WHAT PARENTS CAN DO IF THEIR SCHOOL DISTRICT USES CORPORAL PUNISHMENT

Does your school district use corporal punishment? Listed below are some of the things that you can do, including writing a letter (see Figure 3.1, Sample Letter to a Child's Teacher) to your child's teacher, as suggested by the Center for Effective Discipline, Columbus, Ohio (1998).

- Check with your school district's administration to see if corporal punishment is allowed.
- If it is, get a copy of the district's discipline policy regarding how and when corporal punishment can be administered.
- You may be able to write a letter stating that you do not want your child to receive corporal punishment. A sample letter follows. Even if the district says that it does not have to honor your wishes, write the letter anyway. If possible, have your family physician or pediatrician sign it.
- Tell your child that you do not want him/her paddled and tell him/her to tell

you if it happens.

- If a teacher paddles your child, request a written copy of your rights to a due process hearing procedure.
- If your child is injured take the child to a physician or to an emergency room. Take colored pictures of the injury. Ask the physician to report the injury to the police and the child protection agency.
- Talk with your child. He or she may be fearful that you will blame him/her. While your child may have deserved punishment for misbehavior, assure him/her that he/she should not have been paddled leading to an injury.

Figure 3.1
Sample Letter to a Child's Teacher

A sample letter to your child's teacher regarding your position on corporal punishment might read as follows:

Date:

Dear _____,

Our family does not believe that school children should be disciplined by paddling. We believe that it sends children the message that hitting people is a way to solve problems.

We know that our child will make mistakes. When that happens, we hope that you will help our child learn what is appropriate behavior and how to act more appropriately in the future. If you are having problems with our child, please contact us, and we will make every effort to come to school to help you. Do not paddle our child.

Sincerely,

_____

Name:
Address:
Telephone Number:

cc: superintendent:
         principal:

SELECTED RESEARCH ON DOBSON'S "A PLACE FOR PUNISHMENT" MODEL

Are you interested in Dobson's model? Are you ready to try some of his techniques? If you are, be sure first to consult some of his original sources, several of which are cited below. In addition, you should read more on the short-term and long-term effects of supplying punishment—perhaps you could contact the National Center for the Study of Corporal Punishment and Alternatives in the Schools. What has been presented in this chapter, or any other single chapter, is not enough for you to run out, start using the abbreviated knowledge and skills, and expect to get results. There is no substitute for the original. Learn more about teaching respect and responsibility to children, about barriers to learning, discipline in morality, the strong-willed adolescent, and shaping a child's will. Buy his books, borrow his books, read his books!

Although I have included Dobson's views on discipline among the six discipline models presented in this text, technically, Dobson does not really have a model. At least it is not a model in the same sense that the other five discipline authors presented in this book have a model. All of the other authors outline specific hierarchical teacher/parent responses to children's misbehavior.

For instance, the Canters have their names-on-the board type responses (do this, then do this, then do that), Jones has his "layer cake" set of responses, Dreikurs has his progressively more severe goals of misbehavior-triggered responses, Glasser has his steps in Reality Therapy, and Gordon has his effectiveness training schematic that identifies what skill to use in what situation. My wife, a high school English teacher, and I had a similar response, recently, when listening to a one and one-half hour cassette tape by Dobson. When the tapes were over, we turned to each other and, like that television commercial several years ago showing the two older ladies examining their hamburgers, asked each other "Where's the beef?" There was no doubt that both of us felt better after having listened to the tapes, but we could not recall one specific thing that we had learned that we could apply Monday morning when we went back to school.

Why, then, have Dobson's ideas been included? His is the only discipline position that sees a real place for supplying punishment. And, because so many Americans still seem to rely on punishment, what Dobson has to say should be of interest. Although Dobson's model has been placed on the behaviorist or Skinnerian side of the Skinner-Rogers' dichotomy, B. F. Skinner himself has said, "I believe that there is no longer any use for corporal punishment in school and much is to be gained by suppressing it." But the fact is that punishment, whether being supplied at home or in school, is here to stay for the foreseeable future. Only by studying the subject can parents and teachers make more educated decisions on whether the use of punishment will increase or decrease.

Dobson's "A Place for Punishment" model has been the focus of very little scientific research. When students of mine in an independent learning course titled *Psychology of Discipline* are studying the chapter on Dobson, they regularly write or e-mail expressing the difficulty they are having in locating anything in the scientific literature regarding Dobson's model. I write or e-mail back that the frustration they have experienced was, in fact, part of the lesson. I then ask them to consider how such an independently untested model such as Dobson's can be so popular among the masses.

Most of the sources on Dobson's views that do exist have been written by Dobson himself. Some of these sources are listed below. His model, although popular among some laypeople and selected religious groups, has not been a major focus of master's theses, doctoral dissertations, or other empirical studies. Hence, a review of Dobson's model in the academic literature on classroom management comes up almost empty-handed.

Discussions of Dobson's model are either included with a string of behaviorist-oriented programs (such as the Canters') or offered as a contrast to other discipline models (such as Glasser's). This is surprising given the popularity of his model. Although Dobson's model itself is not widely referenced in the academic literature, numerous citations on the subject of supplying punishment are available.

Bobgan, M., & Bobgan, D. (1990). *Profits of psychoHeresy II: Critiquing Dr. James C. Dobson*. Santa Barbara, CA: EastGate.

A must read for anyone desiring a fuller understanding of Dobson's teachings.

Dobson, J. (1992). *The new dare to discipline*. Wheaton, IL: Tyndale House.

The latest edition of Dobson's original book, *Dare to discipline* (1970), where, often through a series of questions and answers, Dobson provides his common sense approach to child rearing.

Dobson, J. (1978). *The strong-willed child*. Wheaton, IL: Tyndale House.

A book dedicated to helping a parent's or teacher's will prevail over that of the child or student. Chapter 7 of the book argues strenuously against Thomas Gordon's Parent Effectiveness Training Model.

Dobson, J. (1978). *Preparing for adolescence*. Wheaton, IL: Tyndale House.

Working with adolescents is not for the timid. Parents (and teachers) must expect the occasional war of wills which they must win.

Focus on the family. Newsletter of focus on the family: With Dr. James Dobson. Colorado Springs, CO: Focus on the Family.

A monthly newsletter addressing timely parental concerns regarding child rearing.

Hyman, I. A. (1997). *The case against spanking: How to discipline your child without hitting*. San Francisco: Jossey-Bass.

The author explains in a passionate and compelling style why spanking or hitting children is abusive, destructive, and counterproductive. Alternative, more constructive, methods of discipline are offered.

Hyman, I. A. (1990). *Reading, writing, and the hickory stick: The appalling story of physical and psychological abuse in American schools*. Lexington, MA: Lexington Books.

Dr. Hyman takes a long, hard, well-referenced look at discipline practices that have been tolerated for too long in homes and schools.

Hyman, I. A. (1988). Should children ever be hit?: A contemporary answer to an historical question. *Journal of Interpersonal Violence*, 3(2):227–230.

A brief article that maintains, using evidence from the Sumerian Age to modern times, that hitting a child is never warranted.

Hyman, I. A. (1982). Discipline in the 1980's: Some alternatives to corporal punishment. *Children Today*, 11(1):10–13.

Describes workshops and research activities of the National Center for the Study of Corporal Punishment and Alternatives in the Schools. Implications of various theoretical points of view for responding to discipline problems are described.

Hyman, I. A. (1978). Is the hickory stick out of tune? *Today's Education*, 67(2):30–32.

Addresses some of the classroom management problems faced by teachers. The article includes interesting cases to illustrate practical applications of theory.

Hyman, I. A., & Dahbany, A. (1997). *School discipline and school violence: The teacher variance approach*. Boston: Allyn & Bacon.

This 382-page book focuses upon providing preservice and in-service teachers with an overview of the various models of discipline and helps readers apply the theory in a systematic manner.

Teachers in focus. Colorado Springs, CO: Focus on the Family.

Like the *Focus on the family* newsletter for parents, *Teachers in focus* is a newsletter that addresses, from Dobson's point of view, the many and varied needs of teachers, including discipline.

LEARNING MORE ABOUT DOBSON'S "A PLACE FOR PUNISHMENT" MODEL

- To learn more about James Dobson and his ideas on classroom (as well as home) management, contact:

  Focus on the Family
  P.O. Box 35500
  Colorado Springs, CO 80935
  Phone: (719) 531–3400 or (800)A-FAMILY
  FAX: (719) 548–4670
  E-mail: mail@fotf.org

- If you would like to view more of Dobson's ideas, check into his web site: www.fotf.org
- Search one or more of the many Internet web sites using such terms as "James Dobson," "Focus on the Family," "discipline," "strong-willed child" as keywords.
- Subscribe to Dobson's *Focus on the Family* and *Teachers in Focus* magazines.
- To learn more about the National Center for the Study of Corporal Punishment and Alternatives in the Schools (NCSCPA), to access a "discipline hotline," or to contact Dr. Irwin Hyman (NCSCPA director), phone 215-204-6091.

TEST YOURSELF

This is a sampling of the kinds of factual and open-ended questions that you should be able to answer after having read this chapter.

1. What are three reasons to explain the continued popularity of punishment?
2. How would you classify Dobson's views according to the four theoretical

frameworks presented in chapter 2?

3. Name two of Dobson's more popular books outlining his views on how to discipline children.

4. What is the title of Dobson's Colorado-based organization?

5. What are three guidelines for administering punishment?

6. Contrast the terms natural, logical, and contrived consequences.

7. Cite five organizations that favor the abolition of corporal punishment.

8. Offer two examples to support the claim that punishment is related to the demographics of our population.

9. Where is the National Center for the Study of Corporal Punishment and Alternatives in the Schools located?

10. What are three things that parents can do if schools use corporal punishment with their children against their will?

11. According to Dobson, should punishment be a "last resort"? Why?

12. Defend or challenge the statement, "Spare the rod and spoil the child."

13. Defend or challenge Dobson's belief that you cannot learn how to rear (teach) children by turning to the scientific inquiry.

14. How do Skinner's and Dobson's views on the use of punishment differ?

15. How difficult would it be to find articles by or about Dobson's views in the professional literature read by educators?

ASK YOURSELF: IS THIS MODEL FOR YOU?

Although you would want to defer making any final decision until you read still more, at this point what are your feelings toward Dobson's approach to discipline? What strengths and weaknesses do you see in his approach? Does his approach to discipline reflect your fundamental views on how you believe people should be treated? Could you defend the use of this approach to your students and their parents, to your colleagues, and to your administrators? Could you remain committed to his approach—even when the going got tough? If you were to adopt his approach, could you go to sleep at night and not feel that there simply has to be a better way to discipline? At this point, is Dobson's approach for you?

CHAPTER 4

Lee and Marlene Canter: Assertive Discipline: A "Take-Charge" Approach to Classroom Management

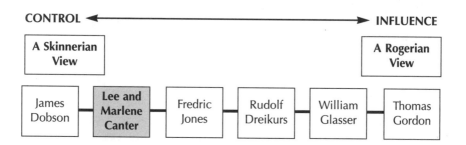

CONTROL ←————————————————————→ INFLUENCE

A Skinnerian View					A Rogerian View

James Dobson	**Lee and Marlene Canter**	Fredric Jones	Rudolf Dreikurs	William Glasser	Thomas Gordon

Lee J. Canter (1947–), prior to founding Lee Canter and Associates in 1976, worked with child guidance agencies throughout California. Marlene Canter (1948–) began her career teaching students with special needs. Known for their work in the fields of education and parenting, together they have written more than forty books and produced more than ten video programs—as well as producing a myriad of support materials geared to helping educators teach and parents raise responsible children. Most recently they have worked with several universities to develop course materials for delivery in a distance-learning master's program for educators. Through professional development workshops, seminars, and graduate courses, the Canters have taught the Assertive Discipline model, a model that holds to the underlying principle that teachers have *a right to teach* and that students have *a right to learn*. Their model has been taught to more than one million people, both in the United States and abroad.

OBJECTIVES

This chapter will help you, among other things, to:

- Classify, using the theoretical frameworks presented in chapter 2, Lee and Marlene Canter's Assertive Discipline model.
- Explain the popularity of Lee and Marlene Canter's views regarding the use of assertive discipline.
- Identify and explain Canters' three response styles.
- Explain the importance of teacher-prepared rules.
- Explain the importance of positive recognition.
- Identify the parts of a Canter-type I-Message.
- Explain Alfie Kohn's challenge to the use of rewards.
- Explore whether Canters' Assertive Discipline model is for you.

WHERE DOES THE CANTERS' MODEL FALL WITHIN THE FOUR THEORETICAL FRAMEWORKS DISCUSSED IN CHAPTER 2?

The Canters' Assertive Discipline model clearly finds a place in French and Raven's Social Bases of Power framework under "coercive" and "reward" powers. It finds a home in Wolfgang and Glickman's Schools of Thought framework as an interventionist strategy. The Canters' position falls on the Skinnerian side of the Skinner-Rogers' dichotomy. In Lewis' Keeping It Simple framework, Assertive Discipline is equated with "control."

"C" FOR CONTROVERSY; "C" FOR CANTER

Of all the models of classroom management, none is more controversial than the Canters' "take-charge" Assertive Discipline model. Advocates swear by it; nonadvocates swear at it. It seems that no one occupies a middle ground. Although the controversy continues, it came to a head in the late 1980s. This is when *Educational Leadership*, the journal for the Association for Curriculum and Supervision Development, published a series of good-guy/bad-guy articles on Assertive Discipline.

Curwin and Mendler (1988b) started it off in an article titled "Packaged Discipline Programs: Let the Buyer Beware." They argued that prepackaged training programs may save time, but that obedience models (their belief about Assertive Discipline) often yielded quick results at the expense of developing responsible students who understand the important principles underlying school rules. In the same issue of *Educational Leadership* (1988b), in "Let the Educator Beware: A Response to Curwin and Mendler," Lee Canter defended his approach as an effective and practical behavior management strategy that leads to improved student and teacher self-concepts.

Later that same academic year, Render, Padilla, and Krank (1989) argued in "What Research Really Shows about Assertive Discipline" that the claims for Assertive Discipline made by the Canters were not supported by the limited research that has been conducted. McCormack's (1989) rebuttal, "Response to Render, Padilla, and Krank: But Practitioners Say It Works," immediately followed. Curwin and Mendler (1989) stepped forward once again and in "We Repeat, Let the Buyer Beware: A Response to Canter" defended their challenge to Assertive Discipline.

The debate did not end here. In the professional journal *Phi Delta Kappan*, Lee Canter published "Assertive Discipline: More Than Names on the Board and Marbles in a Jar" (1989). In this article, Canter argued that many people who speak against Assertive Discipline misinterpret or misunderstand the model. They have "selective hearing," paying attention only to one or two parts of a total program—names on the board and marbles dropped in a jar.

An overlooked key element in Assertive Discipline is its reliance on catching students being good and letting them know that they have been caught. This theme, actually present since the conception of Assertive Discipline, is heavily stressed in the Canters' revised *Assertive Discipline* (1992), whose telling subtitle is *Positive Behavior Management for Today's Classroom*. Appropriate use of praise is an integral component of the Canters' discipline program. In fact, the Canters "suggest that teachers should find something for which to praise every child at least once a day" (Ferguson & Houghton, 1992, p. 84). Although the Canters recant nothing in the original book, the 1992 edition hopes to take the reader "beyond 'taking charge' in the classroom" (Canter & Canter, 1992, p. xviii).

A "TAKE-CHARGE" ATTITUDE: BECOMING THE *ALPHA* MALE

One of the best ways that I have heard to describe the posture and position that an assertive discipline-trained teacher should assume is to try to become the classroom equivalent of an *alpha* male wolf. Just as the *alpha* male wolf controls the pack, the *alpha* male teacher (male or female) controls a classroom of students. Although some readers might react negatively to this wolf pack/classroom analogy, it should be stressed that in both situations the welfare of those under the *alpha* male may be heightened.

Every nature program that I have ever watched that described the hierarchy of power within a wolf pack has pointed out the benefits to the entire pack of having a clearly established *alpha* male—the one at the top, the one that directs, the one that settles arguments, the one that insures the well-being of the community. For many parents and teachers, what works for the family of wolves can work for the family at home or in the school classroom. Everyone would be better off if someone was clearly in charge, if someone had the authority. Who better than the parent or the teacher? What might be overlooked in this wolf pack/classroom analogy is that where there is an *alpha* male (the wolf with all the power), there also is an *omega* male (the wolf at the bottom of the back with absolutely no power). At least as shown in the nature programs, the life of the *omega* male can be very difficult.

Critical to the effectiveness of the Canters' Assertive Discipline is that teachers assume a "take-charge" attitude in the classroom. The idea of assertion is one of the most important features of the Canters' model (Davidman & Davidman, 1984). Teachers must develop an assertive attitude. The importance of feeling assertive—and acting assertive—is so important to the Canters that this single point dominates the first three chapters of the revised *Assertive Discipline* (1992).

Taking charge, in a Canter sense, does not mean trampling over others, although critics of Assertive Discipline claim otherwise. Taking charge is simply a less palatable way of saying that teachers should be "empowered"— a concept that has gained and continues to gain widespread acceptance within the educational community. If "take charge" is too harsh a way of saying what the Canters want to say, perhaps it should be restated as "assertive teachers are empowered teachers."

RESPONSE STYLES

Teachers, according to the Canters, fall into one of three categories regarding their response styles—the major factor affecting the tone in a classroom. The three response-style categories are assertive, hostile, or nonassertive.

An assertive teacher protects the rights of both the teacher and the students. With this style, teachers make their expectations known to students and in a calm and businesslike manner continually insist that students comply with those expectations. (Note: The term expectation as used here can be equated with the term demand. Elsewhere in this book, the term expectations will be discussed under the topic of the self-fulfilling prophecy whereby its meaning will be closer to one of "I have confidence in your ability to succeed at a given task.") Assertive teachers back up their words with actions—with positive and negative consequences.

A hostile teacher resorts to aversive techniques such as sarcasm and threats. These teachers view the classroom world as one of us (teachers) versus them (students). They feel they must rule with an iron fist or else chaos will reign. Hostile teachers, and the behaviors they use, hurt students' feelings, provoke disrespect (odd given that hostile teachers actually are desperately trying to gain respect) and a desire to retaliate, and undermine students' needs for security, safety, and belonging. It is hard to imagine any positive and lasting learning taking place in such a hostile environment.

A nonassertive teacher is passive, often inconsistent, and reluctant to impose demands on student behavior. It becomes clear to students that such teachers lack direction and focus. Nonassertive teachers do not know where they are going, and, because of this, it is hard for them to do what any leader must do—secure the willingness of others to follow. No clear standards are evident, and, still further, no evidence exists that actions would be taken by the teacher to back up such standards even if they did exist.

- Assertive teachers get their needs met first, and then go on to act in the best interests of their students.
- Hostile teachers get their needs met first, but do not go on to act in the best interests of their students.
- Nonassertive teachers do not get their needs met and do not go on to act in the best interests of their students.

Some teachers are uncomfortable with the idea of "getting their needs met first." They believe that teaching is a service profession of sorts and, therefore, that they are there to serve the needs of the customer. The customer's (student's) needs come first. The best way to explain the Canters' feelings on this point is to call the reader's attention to the standard speech delivered by airline flight attendants just before takeoff. They say something to the effect of, "Should we lose cabin pressure and oxygen be required, oxygen masks will drop from the ceiling. If you are traveling with small children or elderly companions, first place the mask on yourself, and then attend to the needs of those around you."

The message here is clear. If you help yourself first, you will be in a better position to render assistance to those around you. But if you attend to their needs first (such as helping an infant or child), it is unlikely that they will be able to assist you. By taking care of your immediate needs first, you are not being selfish or greedy; you are actually acting in the best interests of everyone. As in other human service professions, if professionals meet only the needs of their clients to the exclusion of meeting their own needs, they will soon burn out and be of little help to either their clients or themselves.

As a teacher, what are the minimum needs that you must have met in the classroom before you can get on with the task of helping students? Do you have a need for students to be in their seats ready to start class when the bell rings? Do you have a need for students to raise their hands and be acknowl-edged before speaking? Normally, the list is not too long. As a teacher you are entitled to have your legitimate needs met first. Nonassertive teachers do not realize this fact. You then have a responsibility to do your best to help meet the needs of your students. Hostile teachers ignore this responsibility. Clearly, the Canters believe that an assertive response style best serves both teachers and students.

Personally, as a teacher I have a need to:

- start class on time;
- have students stay awake and do only work related to the class while in my class;
- have assignments submitted on time;
- be treated, and have them treat each other, civilly; and
- be formally addressed as "Dr. Tauber" and not by my first name.

That's it! These are the needs that I feel I must have met before I can help my students meet their own needs. These and other similar needs are rea-sonable—they are legitimate. I have a right to expect that these needs be met. Some teachers are comfortable with students strolling in after the class has started; I am not. Some teachers overlook students' lack of civility; I do not. Some teachers do not mind (some even prefer) being called by their first name; I do mind.

Not only are these my legitimate needs, but most serve as sort of on-the-job training for teacher education majors who, in a very short time, will become classroom teachers themselves. My behaviors, my demands that cer-tain legitimate needs be met, act as modeling for them. Chances are they, too, will enumerate these same needs to their students.

RESPONSE STYLES IN ACTION

You are teaching, and two students toward the back of the classroom are chattering to each other and not paying attention to the lesson.

Nonassertive Response: "Please (almost pleading) try to stop talking while I am teach-ing. How many times do I have to warn you?"

Comment: Even while enforcing legitimate rules in the classroom, nonassertive teachers have a tendency to plead. Doing so is demeaning. It also undermines the teacher's effectiveness as a disciplinarian. Asking students to "try" to stop talking is not really what you want. What you want is the students to actually stop talking. Asking, "How many times do I have to warn you?" opens the door to unwanted sarcastic student responses such as, "How about five hundred times?"

Hostile Response: "Hey, you two. Where are your manners? You are the most inconsiderate kids I have ever had the misfortune of teaching. Now turn around and shut up if you know what is good for you."

Comment: Hostile teachers see the situation as "me versus them." They take everything personally. All tactics—sarcasm, put-downs, challenges to one's heritage—are deemed appropriate to use if they get results. Any means to the end of the teacher's "winning," complete with angry body language and tone of voice, is acceptable. If students comply, it is usually out of fear.

Assertive Response: While continuing to lecture, the teacher moves over to the chattering students and says, "Bill and John, the rule in this class is that while one person is talking the rest of the class will remain quiet and listen. I want you to stop talking, turn around and face front, and pay attention to the lecture."

Comment: Assertive teachers act in a calm, confident, and businesslike manner. They let their discipline plan do all of the work. The response they desire is clearly communicated. It is also clear that they are prepared to enforce their discipline plan.

RULES AND A DISCIPLINE PLAN

To be assertive, one must assert something. For the Canters, that something is rules. Rules form the basis for a teacher's discipline plan, what the Canters call "limit setting." The Canters are realistic; they accept the fact that discipline problems in the classroom will occur. Given that the best defense is a good offense, they plan for the inevitable student misbehaviors by designing a well-thought-out discipline plan—one organized in a hierarchy of severity of teacher-supplied consequences to match degrees of student behavior—both unacceptable and acceptable. The plan should be approved by the administration, shared with (taught to) students on the first day of class, sent home to parents (asked to sign and return), and enforced fairly with all students.

The rules, as with all effective rule making and rule enforcing, are few. They might include, among others:

- No one may interfere with my teaching for any reason.
- No one may interfere with any students' efforts to learn for any reason.
- No one may cause physical or psychological harm to himself or herself or to other students.

• Good behavior will be rewarded.

Still other rules might be more specific such as:

• Raise your hand and be acknowledged before speaking.
• Only one person may speak at a time.
• Walk quietly to and from lunch and all specials.
• Come to class prepared with paper and pencil.
• All homework is due when assigned.

Students understand that negative consequences will follow when they break the rules, and they know that positive consequences will follow when they observe the rules. The rules are few in number, simple, direct, and unambiguous. A clear if-then, cause-and-effect relationship exists between the rules and desired outcomes. If you follow such and such rule, then such and such will follow. These rules protect both the teacher's and the students' rights. They constitute a classroom's version of a Magna Carta or Bill of Rights.

Fairness in enforcing a discipline plan requires some sort of record keeping. The Canters' record-keeping methods of using "names on the board" (so often attacked by critics as being too public an admonition [Gartrell, 1987]) and "marbles in a jar" are nothing more than instruments to keep these records. Placing a student's name on the board (or on a clipboard) for breaking a rule and then adding a check mark next to it each time that rule again is broken is simply a way of recording data (see Table 4.1, Names on the Board).

Table 4.1
Names on the Board

MISBEHAVES	CONSEQUENCE
First time	Name on board (warning)
Second time	One check (15 minutes after school)
Third time	Two checks (30 minutes after school)
Fourth time	Three checks (30 minutes after school, and call parents)
Fifth time	Four checks (remove from room—principal or vice principal)

Figure 4.1
Marbles in a Jar

Dropping a marble in a glass Mason jar (as shown in Figure 4.1, Marbles in a Jar) when students do something that the teacher approves of, such as following a rule, is simply an audible signal to all that the class has earned a reward—for example, two extra minutes of recess.

If you find "names on the board" and "marbles in a jar" objectionable, the Canters argue that you should select other, more acceptable methods. Use your creativity.

In specific instances when names are placed on the board, complete with possible check marks next to them for repeated violations of the rules, the Canters instruct teachers to enforce the discipline plan's consequences and then wipe the slate clean. Once the sentence has been served, the student has a clean slate. Tomorrow is a new day. No grudges are held.

The fact is, to implement any discipline plan fairly, you must collect data—lots of data—and then use some method to record such data. In the Canters' model, it is the analysis of the data, not the possible capricious behavior of a teacher, that triggers the supplying of positive or negative consequences in the discipline plan.

POSITIVE RECOGNITION: A CANTER EMPHASIS

Positive recognition of students following rules is more important in the Canters' model than most people realize. In fact, one of Canters' posters says that the teachers should "Praise Every Child Every Day!" Although critics, the Canters claim, have overlooked this fact, rewarding a student or an entire class for engaging in desirable behavior has always been a cornerstone of their model. This stress upon the positive is made abundantly clear in the revised edition of *Assertive Discipline* (1992). Of the seventeen chapters in the book, the three longest are chapter 6, "Creating Your Classroom Discipline Plan, Part 2: Positive Recognition"; chapter 10, "Teaching Responsible Behavior, Part 2:

Using Positive Recognition to Motivate Students to Behave"; and chapter 15, "Using Positive Support to Build Positive Relationships."

As with all behavior modification systems, the teacher must identify what it is that *each student* values as a reward. This can be hard to do, whether for an elementary teacher having a classroom of thirty students or for a secondary teacher meeting with 180 students throughout the day. Once having determined what each student values as a reward, the teacher must decide what schedule of reinforcement (fixed interval, fixed ratio, variable interval, variable ratio) to use *with each* student in distributing the rewards. All the while the teacher must guard against handing out too many rewards too often or the student may become immune to their effect. Once again, this can be hard, time-consuming work. While all of this is going on, the teacher must proceed with the business of teaching reading, writing, and arithmetic and all else that must be taught in today's busy classrooms.

Canter-produced supplemental materials, such as collections of ready-to-fill-in awards, seasonal motivators, monthly citizen slips, and bulletin boards for reinforcing positive behavior, can help with the supplying of rewards. Many of these resources can be duplicated, filled in, and handed out with minimal teacher time and effort being expended.

The Canters' emphasis shows up in other ways, too—even surrounding the dispensing of negative consequences. For instance, by making the classroom rules clear and taking the time to teach students these rules, teachers put students in a knowledgeable position. They now have information that they can use to gain control over their own destinies. They can choose to follow or break the rules. They also know what the consequences (positive or negative) will be. Being in a position to make an informed choice is, the Canters would argue, positive.

Holding all students—minorities and nonminorities, boys and girls, socioeconomically privileged and socioeconomically deprived—accountable for obeying the rules is also positive. Not making excuses for students ("What can you expect, he comes from a single-parent family") and not letting them make excuses for themselves ("But he called me a bad name first") sends a message that, no matter what their circumstances, you think enough of them to expect that they will obey the rules just like any other student. To expect less would be condescending.

SEVERAL OTHER ASSERTIVE DISCIPLINE TACTICS

Other strategies recommended by the Canters help capture the flavor and tone of their model. Two of these strategies are the "broken-record technique" and the "consistency of consequences."

The broken-record technique involves a teacher's insistent, but matter-of-fact (not mean) repetition of his or her original message. This is especially effective with students who try to divert the teacher's attention. Each teacher request, no matter what the student's argument, merely repeats the request as originally stated—like a broken record. Teachers should use the exact words, same tone, same volume, and so on, each time the request is delivered. For example:

Teacher: Becky, stop talking and turn around.

Becky: But Heather was asking me a question.

Teacher: Becky, I want you to stop talking and turn around.

Becky: But Heather wants my help with the assignment.

Teacher: Becky, the rule in this classroom is that no one may talk during the review period.

Becky: But, but, I just wanted to help Heather.

Teacher: That may be the case, but right now I want you to stop talking and turn around.

Becky: Oh, all right! (she sulkingly turns around in her seat).

Teacher: Thank you (polite and sincere).

The Canters warn, though, that three times repeating a request is plenty. After that, the student has, in effect, "chosen" to have a predetermined consequence supplied. Because assertive teachers know what they will do if and when a student does not comply, there is less chance that they will get upset. After all, their discipline plan has been designed to handle just such contingencies. At the same time, when a student does quickly comply, be sure to inform him or her of how pleased you are that he or she "chose" to cooperate.

The consistency of consequences equates with the saying, "It is as sure as death and taxes." The consequences "chosen" by the students through their behavior will be administered. Students who misbehave during the early morning periods and get their name on the board will receive their consequence (for example, loss of recess time). No matter how good they are all afternoon or no matter how many fellow students' lives they save using the Heimlich maneuver during lunch, the consequence of losing recess time will occur. Earned negative consequences, as well as positive consequences, are consistently applied. Positive and negative consequences, the key to any conditioning-oriented models, "are clearly linked to Skinnerian conceptions of human behavior and behavior modification" (Davidman & Davidman, 1984, p. 171).

DELIVERING YOUR ASSERTIVE MESSAGE ASSERTIVELY

Delivering an assertive message does not mean having to be mean, loud, abusive, or threatening. Instead, assertive messages should be delivered in a firm, calm, confident, businesslike manner that leaves no doubt in a student's mind that the teacher will accept nothing less than total compliance with the reasonable rules and limits of the classroom. Although all limit-setting messages include a nonverbal (i.e., body language) component, how one delivers the verbal portion of an assertive limit-setting message is more open to adjustment by a teacher.

Teachers can (and should) work on several components of their verbal messages including:

- Tone of voice in the delivery should be firmly neutral and businesslike. It should not be harsh, sarcastic, or intimidating. At the same time, it should not be weak, squeaky, wispy, or crackly, implying a lack of commitment.

- Eye contact is important for messages to have their greatest impact. Teachers should look students straight in the eyes. However, teachers should not insist that students look them back in the eyes. First of all, there is no easy way to enforce this and, second of all, there may be students who come from homes where it is disrespectful of children to do so with adults. Although some teachers may find looking students directly in the eyes difficult to do, the Canters argue that because the assertive teacher has a well-prepared, comprehensive discipline plan, he or she is operating from a position of strength—and knows it.

- Gestures can add much to verbal messages. A palm of the hand held upright ("stop"), a deliberate pendulum-type swing of a palm-up hand ("no more of that"), an index finger held to one's lips ("quiet now"), or two hands, palms open, pushing down together ("tone it down") all can strengthen a verbal message. Notice that in each of these examples an openness (i.e., palms open) or a slow deliberateness (i.e., pendulum swing of the palm-up hand) is exhibited. Openness and deliberateness convey a message of strength and confidence. Clenched fists and rapid movements convey a message of weakness, frustration, and nervousness. Teachers are cautioned not to wave their fingers or fists in students' faces.

- Use of a student's name grabs the attention of the offender, even over long distances, and makes the assertive message that follows more powerful, personal, and penetrating. Note: Even at a noisy party it is possible to tune into messages from across the room when one's name is heard.

I-MESSAGES: THE CANTER WAY

One particular verbal message advocated by the Canters is the I-message. I-messages tell students how their behavior is affecting the teacher and how the teacher wants that behavior to change. I-messages contain three parts. They include:

- "I feel (name the feeling) . . . "
- "When you (state the problem) . . . "
- "I would like (say what you want to happen to make things better) . . . "

Consider Miss Karns, a teacher who has a student, David, who is talking while she is trying to explain to the class a concept in British history. Miss Karns' I-message might go something like this. "David, I feel annoyed when you are talking to students while I am trying to lecture, and I want you to stop talking and give me your full attention." The I-message contains the feeling (annoyed), the problem (you are talking while I am lecturing), and the preferred behavior (I want you to stop talking and give me your full attention). There is little doubt as to what the teacher wants to have happen in order to "make things better"—presumably for both the teacher and the students.

The point of a Canter-type I-message is clarity, leaving no room for misinterpretation by students as to how they are supposed to mend their ways. Underlying an I-message is the fact that consequences will follow—cooperation will be rewarded and lack of cooperation will be punished. This position is consistent with a Skinnerian-type view of human nature. Students will likely alter their behavior in order to enhance the chance that reward consequences will follow and that punishment consequences will be avoided.

To point out the drastic differences between a Skinnerian-type view and a Rogerian-type view of human nature, one needs only to look at the specific design of I-messages as advocated by the Canters and those proposed by Thomas Gordon (a discipline model you will study later in this book). Their respective I-messages, although both contain three parts, are as different as night and day. Where the Canters' ends by telling the students exactly how they are to change their behavior in order "to make things better," Gordon's leaves the decision of how and whether to change their behavior up to the students. Of note is the fact that Gordon has included I-messages as a successful confrontational skill since the conception of his Teacher Effectiveness Training model more than two decades ago. The Canters' version of an I-message is a much more recent addition to their assertive discipline model of discipline.

DOES ASSERTIVE DISCIPLINE WORK?

It depends upon what you mean by "Does it work?" Does it help new, as well as experienced, teachers gain (regain) control over the classroom? Yes. According to Hill (1990, p. 73), "Teachers and administrators who use Assertive Discipline do tend to gush about its benefits." Hill (1990) describes a Connecticut middle school principal as having nothing but praise for the program. Yet, still another Connecticut school, believing that they "were manipulating and controlling behavior instead of instilling values" (Wade, 1997, p. 34), dropped their emphasis upon Assertive Discipline. They substituted schoolwide celebrations for rewards and problem solving for teacher-supplied consequences.

In a more formal investigation, McCormack (1986) reports that in her elementary school study, Assertive Discipline works to reduce off-task behavior of students of varying reading levels, socioeconomic status, ethnicity, sex, and parental influence. Further, Assertive Discipline works for teachers who have varying qualifications, experience, and knowledge of the subject. Ferre (1991) reports that rural teachers who used Assertive Discipline over a nine-week period reduced the off-task and disruptive behavior of kindergarten students.

Student teachers trained in Assertive Discipline reported feeling "adequately prepared to employ appropriate techniques of classroom discipline" (Barrett & Curtis, 1986, p. 56). University supervisors and supervising teachers also rated these Assertive Discipline-trained student teachers higher than those not so trained.

If "Does it work?" means that it creates a classroom where shared ownership exists, then the answer may be "No." After all, the classroom is the students' classroom too, isn't it? While the Canters clearly want the teacher to be the "boss" in the classroom, other educators would prefer the teacher to be the "leader"—a position more fitted to a democratic environment (Crockenberg, 1982). To be fair, a recent article by Lee Canter (*Learning*, 1996) suggests that teachers first establish a rapport with learners, then deal with rules. Such an emphasis upon rapport first, rules second, should help in the development of a classroom sense of community.

If you are uncomfortable using a model that is "only a common-sense combination of behavioral psychology and traditional authoritarianism" (McDaniel, 1986, p. 65), then again the answer may be "No." If you believe that Assertive Discipline, like other behavior modification-based programs, treats the symptoms, not the causes, offers only short-term benefits, has limited transfer value to out-of-school environments, and devalues self-discipline (Palardy, 1996), then the answer is "No."

If you believe that praise and rewards, fundamental to Assertive Discipline, can be interpreted by the learner as a sign of *low* teacher expectations as do Miller and Hom (1997), then the answer may be "No." If you are uncomfortable using a "single-mandated" model, one that dictates rather than reflects, you may even view the Canters' Assertive Discipline as detrimental (Ashton & Urquhart, 1988).

If you are swayed by people "voting with their feet," then the answer to whether or not Assertive Discipline works is an emphatic "Yes." Walk into any store that sells teaching-related materials, and you will find Assertive Discipline displays. No discipline model has more books, workbooks, plan books, record-keeping books, videocassettes, audiocassettes, and other supplementary materials (for teachers, bus drivers, paraprofessionals, and parents) available than does Assertive Discipline. Assertive Discipline workshops continue to be widely available and eagerly attended—throughout the world.

Whether or not Assertive Discipline works is one question. Another question is even if it does work, should it be used in today's classrooms? The answers to these two questions can partially be found by reading the works cited at the end of this chapter. Given the controversy surrounding Assertive Discipline, more citations than usual are included here. The final answer to whether the system works—and if it does work, whether it should be used— lies with individual educators.

PUNISHED BY REWARDS

Any behavior modification-based system, and Canters' Assertive Discipline is no exception, heavily depends upon teachers dispensing rewards when students exhibit desirable behaviors and withholding rewards when students exhibit undesirable behaviors. Nothing could be more fundamental to Skinner's operant learning principles than the wielding of rewards by the person in power.

Yet, Alfie Kohn, in his book with the rather startling title, *Punished by Rewards: The Trouble with Gold Stars, Incentive Plans, A's, Praise, and Other Bribes* (1993), argues that for children, adolescents, and adults alike, the best way to *lower* performance and to *lower* creativity at school or at work is for the person(s) in power to use a system based upon rewards! Kohn argues, in this book as well as in others (listed at end of the chapter), that rewards:

- punish,
- rupture relationships,

- ignore reasons,
- discourage risk taking, and
- discourage self-discipline.

One example of a nationwide program dependent upon the use of rewards is the popular pizza chain's Book-It program, whereby students or classes are given pizzas as a reward for reading books. Although at first glance this seems like as good idea, Kohn and others would argue that rewarding people for doing something such as reading substitutes external motivation for internal motivation. Sought-after rewards begin to take the place of students reading and, among other things, experiencing suspense and excitement, gaining knowledge and information, and learning about exciting worlds near and far. Kohn (1996) argues that if you really want to get kids hooked on reading, give them real literature, not workbooks; give them more choices about what to read and who to work with.

When students are rewarded for reading, the underlying message to them is, "We know that reading is an awful thing to do, and we know that you would never want to do it on your own, so we are going to reward (bribe) you into engaging in this dastardly undertaking." Yet, most of us know that reading is, in and of itself, not only fun, but fundamental. Perhaps teachers should spend more time thinking about how to make reading activities and selections fun and less time designing reward systems.

Over the years, I have surveyed many of my college students who themselves participated in one form or another of a Book-It program. One student reports, "I remember how excited I would be to read my books to get my free pizza—excited enough to lie. I sometimes did not read the book at all or else chose easy books." Another student reports, "I don't think that this program teaches anything to students except how to cheat and lie. Every student in class wanted to win the pizza party at the end of the year, so they were going to do whatever they had to do to win. I would go to the library and pick the shortest and easiest book possible. Most of the time I didn't even read the book. I would just tell the teacher the summary that was written on the back cover of the book."

A third student confessed that she loved to read then as she does now, but in fourth grade she thought, "Well, this is a stupid exercise so who cares if I lie? Well, I knew, and I felt like a real heel, but I still did it." Another student says that she remembers her third grade classroom where a chart hung in a prominent place showing the stars next to the students' names for every book that they read. Although lying was less likely because of the report that had to accompany every completed book, "picking the easy ones to avoid more work than was necessary was definitely true." A final student reports watching a child get beat up out on the playground at recess because he had not read a sufficient number of books and so the entire class was going to miss out on its promised pizza party.

It has been asserted that such programs connecting academics (i.e., reading) to food will simply result in a bunch of fat kids who hate reading. It might be argued that the Book-It program, as well as similar reward-based programs, would enjoy more long-term success if instead of giving a pizza for every book read (claimed to be read), they would give a book to every student who purchased a pizza! What do you think?

While conducting a workshop on discipline, a physics teacher in the audience came up to me at break and shared something that she had just received in the mail. She knew that I would be interested because it dealt with our shared love of physics (my college major). She showed me an advertisement for a reward-based system called the "Jimmy Joule Physics Incentive Program." (Note: Joules are units of work in physics). The kit, for only $159.95, consisted of two hundred Jimmy Joule tokens (similar to poker chips), thirty stickers, twenty heat sensitive pens, twenty pencils, ten balsa gliders, ten rulers, twelve bumper stickers, twelve window decals, and more. The earned Jimmy Joule tokens could be used to purchase one or more of the incentives. Having taught physics, I am convinced that the subject matter, itself, when exploited by a creative teacher, possesses the potential for student motivation. Jimmy Joules are not needed.

SELECTED RESEARCH ON THE CANTERS' ASSERTIVE DISCIPLINE MODEL

Are you interested in the Canters' model? Are you ready to try some of their techniques? If you are, be sure first to consult several of their original sources, many of which are cited at the end of this chapter. What has been presented in this chapter, or any other single chapter, is not enough for you to run out, start using the abbreviated knowledge and skills, and expect to get results. There is no substitute for the original. Learn more about empowering the teacher, roadblocks to being assertive, response styles, positive recognition, defusing confrontations, and redirecting off-task behavior. Buy their books, borrow their books, read their books!

The Canters' Assertive Discipline model has been the focus of much research. A search of any academic library will reveal many such sources, some written by the Canters, others written about their model. Selected articles by Kohn also are cited. A number of these sources are listed below. Note the wide variety of citations and the variety of responses—some pro and some con.

Clearly, no one is neutral regarding the Canters' Assertive Discipline!

Canter, L. (1996). *The high performing teacher.* Santa Monica, CA: Lee
     Canter & Associates.

Shows teachers how to empower themselves to face the challenges of teaching, avoid burnout, lower job-related stress, and maintain their enthusiasm for the profession.

Canter, L. (1996). Discipline alternatives. First, the rapport—Then, the
     rules. *Learning, 24*(5):12,14.

The article details the basic principles of the Assertive Discipline program.

Canter, L. (1994). *Scared or prepared.* Santa Monica, CA: Lee Canter &
     Associates.

Introduces preventative strategies that teachers can use to protect themselves and their students, and to create a safe, violence-free learning environment.

Canter, L. (1989). Assertive discipline—More than names on the board and
     marbles in a jar. *Phi Delta Kappan, 71*(1):57–61.

Explains the proper interpretations of the Assertive Discipline program, stressing that teachers must communicate clear classroom rules, teach kids how to follow them, use positive reinforcement, and use firm, negative consequences.

Canter, L. (1988). Let the educator beware: A response to Curwin and
     Mendler. *Educational Leadership, 46*(2):71–73.

Defends the Assertive Discipline model critiqued by Curwin and Mendler in the same *Educational Leadership* issue.

Canter, L., & Canter, M. (1997). *Assertive discipline: Positive behavior man-*
     agement for today's classrooms. Santa Monica, CA: Lee Canter &
     Associates.

Teaches teachers how to prevent behavior problems by learning proactive techniques that teach students how to make responsible behavior choices.

Canter, L., & Canter, M. (1993). *Succeeding with difficult students.* Santa
     Monica, CA: Lee Canter & Associates.

Introduces new strategies for reaching the most challenging students with whom nothing seems to work.

Chance, P. (1993). Sticking up for rewards. *Phi Delta Kappan*, 74(10):787–790.

Defends the use of rewards suggesting that it is ironic that a straight forward contingency between work and rewards should be called manipulative.

Curwin, R. L., & Mendler, A. N. (1989). We repeat. Let the buyer beware: A response to Canter. *Educational Leadership*, 46(6):83.

Challenges Assertive Discipline on the basis that instead of emphasizing respect and responsibility in addressing behavior problems, it tells students, "Behave or else."

Curwin, R. L., & Mendler, A. N. (1988b). Packaged discipline programs: Let the buyer beware. *Educational Leadership*, 46(2):68–71.

Claims that obedience models such as Assertive Discipline often yield quick results, but at the expense of not developing responsible students.

Hill, D. (1990). Order in the classroom. *Teacher Magazine*, 1(7):70–77.

Presents both a challenge to, and a defense of, Assertive Discipline. Critics claim it is dehumanizing, humiliating, and decreases intrinsic motivation. Proponents claim that teachers who effectively use the system mold it to their individual teaching styles.

Kohn, A. (1996). *Beyond discipline: From compliance to community*. ASCD: Alexandria, VA.

Kohn argues against the use of rewards that teachers use to force compliance and for the establishment of a more equal-rights community.

Kohn, A. (1996). By all available means: Cameron and Pierce's defense of extrinsic motivators. *Review of Educational Research*, 66(1):1–4.

Debates the findings of Cameron and Pierce's (1994) claim that extrinsic rewards may not undermine intrinsic motivation.

Kohn, A. (1996). Should we pay kids to learn? *Learning*, 24(5):6–7.

Presents a point-counterpoint debate on whether we should pay students to read.

Kohn, A. (1994). Bribes for behaving: Why behaviorism doesn't help children become good people. *NAMTA Journal*, 19(2):71–94.

Argues against using punishment and rewards to motivate children, maintaining that, although penalties and prizes may change behavior in the short term, they do not help children become responsible decision makers in the long term.

Kohn, A. (1993). Rewards versus learning: A response to Paul Chance. *Phi Delta Kappan*, 74(10):783–787.

Kohn argues that an engaging curriculum, not the manipulation of children through rewards, offers the real hope for the problem of diminished motivation in schools.

McCormack, S. (1989). Response to Render, Padilla, and Krank: But practitioners say it works. *Educational Leadership*, 46(6):77–79.

In response to the Render et al. citation questioning the effectiveness of Assertive Discipline, the author maintains that, from a practitioner's standpoint, it works.

Palardy, J. (1996). Taking another look at behavior modification and Assertive Discipline. *NASSP Bulletin*, 80(581):66–70.

Argues that behavior modification has significant limitations, as it treats symptoms, not causes. It yields only short-term benefits, has limited transfer value to other environments, and values managed conduct over self-discipline.

Render, G. F., Padilla, J.N.M., & Krank, H. M. (1989). What research really shows about assertive discipline. *Educational Leadership*, 46(6):72–75.

Argues that Assertive Discipline claims of effectiveness are not supported by the limited research conducted to date.

Render, G. F., Padilla, J.N.M., & Krank, H. M. (1989b). Assertive discipline: A critical review and analysis. *Teachers College Record*, 90(4):607–630.

After an overview of Assertive Discipline, the authors criticize the method as primarily meeting teachers' needs, being too authoritarian, and lacking evidence to back up claims.

LEARNING MORE ABOUT THE CANTERS' ASSERTIVE DISCIPLINE MODEL

- To learn more about Lee and Marlene Canter and their ideas on classroom management, contact:

  Canter & Associates
  P.O. Box 2113
  Santa Monica, CA 90407
  Phone: (800) 262–4347
  FAX: (310) 394–6017
  E-mail: www.canterweb.com

- Search one or more of the many Internet web sites using "Lee Canter," "assertive discipline," "rewards," "Alfie Kohn," and "Canter & Associates" among other terms as keywords.

TEST YOURSELF

This is a sampling of the kinds of factual and open-ended questions that you should be able to answer after having read this chapter.

1. What are three reasons to explain the continued popularity of Canters' Assertive Discipline?

2. How would you classify the Canters' views according to the four theoretical frameworks presented in chapter 2?

3. Defend or challenge the *alpha* male analogy used in the chapter to explain the position a teacher is to assume in Assertive Discipline.

4. Contrast the Canters' three response styles (assertive, nonassertive, hostile).

5. Create an "original" statement for each of these three response styles that a teacher might deliver to a misbehaving student.

6. Explain how the airline host/hostess preflight announcement to passengers can be used by advocates of Assertive Discipline to justify teachers getting their needs met first.

7. Identify four needs you believe that you must have met before you can get on with meeting the needs of your students.

8. What do the Canters mean by their recommendation that teachers use a "broken-record" technique?

9. Defend how Assertive Discipline emphasizes positive recognition over punishment.

10. Explain what the term "marbles in a jar" means and how you might use the

concept in a school environment.

11. What are two components of teachers' verbal messages that can help them deliver their assertive messages assertively?

12. What are the three components of the Canters' I-messages and how do they differ from Gordon's I-messages?

13. Who is the author of the book *Punished by Rewards* and what is your reaction to his claims that rewards and incentives do more damage than good?

14. Explain how a major pizza chain's Book-It program could be doing more harm than good.

15. Do you see yourself using Assertive Discipline in your classroom? Why?

ASK YOURSELF: IS THIS MODEL FOR YOU?

Although you would want to defer making any final decision until you read still more, at this point what are your feelings toward the Canters' approach to discipline? What strengths and weaknesses do you see in their model? Does their approach to discipline reflect your fundamental views on how you believe people should be treated? Could you defend the use of this model to your students and their parents, to your colleagues, and to your administrators? Could you remain committed to their model—even when the going got tough? If you were to adopt their model, could you go to sleep at night and not feel that there simply has to be a better way to discipline? At this point, is the Canters' approach for you?

CHAPTER 5

Fredric H. Jones:
Positive Discipline

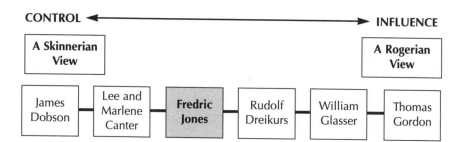

CONTROL ◄─────────────────────────────► INFLUENCE

| A Skinnerian View | | | | | A Rogerian View |

| James Dobson | Lee and Marlene Canter | **Fredric Jones** | Rudolf Dreikurs | William Glasser | Thomas Gordon |

Trained as a clinical psychologist, Fredric H. Jones (1940–) began his professional career on the faculty of the Neuropsychiatric Institute at the University of California at Los Angeles (UCLA), designing and implementing programs for retarded, autistic, and schizophrenic children. He has served on the faculty of the University of Rochester, working in the areas of nonadversarial classroom management and teacher training. Since 1978, Dr. Jones has been an independent consultant working directly with individual school districts. His work is best revealed in his books *Positive Classroom Discipline* (1987) and *Positive Classroom Instruction* (1987).

OBJECTIVES

This chapter will help you, among other things, to:

* Classify, using the theoretical frameworks presented in chapter 2, Fredric Jones' Positive Discipline model.
* Describe the value of using body language rather than words to discipline.

- Explain the use of classroom structure as a discipline strategy.
- Explain the use of limit setting as a discipline strategy.
- Explain the use of responsibility training as a strategy of discipline.
- Explain the use of backup systems as a discipline strategy.
- Defend the importance of positive classroom instruction to the disciplinary process.
- Explore whether Jones' Positive Discipline model is for you.

WHERE DOES JONES' MODEL FIT WITHIN THE FOUR THEORETICAL FRAMEWORKS DISCUSSED IN CHAPTER 2?

Jones' Positive Discipline model clearly finds a place in French and Raven's Social Bases of Power framework under "coercive," "reward," and, most appropriately, "legitimate." It finds a home in Wolfgang and Glickman's School of Thought framework as an interventionist strategy. Jones' position leans towards the Skinnerian side of the Skinner-Rogers' dichotomy. In Lewis' Keeping It Simple framework, Positive Discipline is equated with some "control" and some "manage."

FROM THEORY TO PRACTICE

Dr. Jones' work with classroom management began when he found two teachers who could cause a room full of emotionally and behaviorally handicapped junior high school students to function as a productive, respectful group of young people. From the outset two things were clear: (a) these teachers were not working as hard as their colleagues who were rapidly becoming candidates for a burnout workshop, and (b) their classroom atmospheres were warm, relaxed, and nurturing. When asked how they got such wonderful results, these teachers could not describe specific skills. Rather, they attributed their results to amorphous variables such as "meaning business." Thus began a decade-long process of exploring the skills of the "natural teachers" in conjunction with research on classroom management.

LAYER CAKE APPROACH

Like a chocolate layer cake, Jones arranges the skills of discipline management into four layers as shown in Figure 5.1: A Layer Cake Approach.

1. Classroom Structure: the prevention of discipline problems by arranging the

Figure 5.1
A Layer Cake Approach

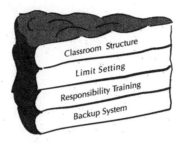

classroom environment so that problems will be relatively unlikely to occur. Classroom Structure includes topics as diverse as room arrangement, working the crowd, procedures for the first day and week of school, classroom rules, classroom chores, and communication with parents.

2. Limit Setting: the subtle process of meaning business in the classroom by which rule enforcement becomes both relaxed and nearly invisible. Limit setting focuses upon the body language by which the natural teacher signals to the students both a commitment to high standards and a calm resolve to follow through.

3. Responsibility Training: the implementation of group incentives whereby students learn to internalize responsibility for their own actions. These advanced incentive systems allow patterns of cooperation to be taught to the entire class rapidly and economically.

4. Backup Systems: the use of nonadversarial negative sanctions to resolve severe or repetitive behavior problems while avoiding the more public, stressful, and self-perpetuating measures that comprise the discipline codes of most schools.

CLASSROOM STRUCTURE

Working the Crowd

One of the more prominent characteristics of the natural teacher was that they spent a great deal of their time working the crowd. They spent a minimum of time in front of the class presenting and a maximum of time circulating among the students who were busy doing work. When asked why they spent so much of their time in this fashion, the teachers responded, "Well, students are not learning unless they are doing something, and I want to see what they are doing." Yet, the teachers were also quite aware that their movement among the students had a strong impact on the willingness of students to begin fooling around. Either you work the crowd, or the crowd works you. Jones observed that the single most powerful factor that governed the likelihood of a student's fooling around was the physical distance between the teacher and the student.

Room Arrangement

Working the crowd quickly led to an analysis of the arrangement of the furniture in the classroom since broad walkways seemed a precondition to easy cruising by the teacher. To make working the crowd easy, the teacher must be able to get from any student to any other student with a minimum number of steps and without tripping over furniture.

What's important is not where to place the furniture, but where not to place it. Remove the furniture barriers between you and the students! More effective room arrangements were characterized by an interior loop that allowed teachers to easily see every student's work with an easy stroll among the students. Typically, the teacher's desk was removed from the middle front of the classroom so that the students' desks could be brought up near the chalkboard. Moving the class forward so that the front row was approximately eight feet from the wall allowed the teacher to write on the board and then turn to address the group at the proximity of normal conversation.

Another structural component of the classroom of the natural teacher was assigned seating. These teachers could not even imagine a classroom in which the students simply sat where they wished. They said, "Well, without assigned seating, the ones who want to talk will sit in the back of the classroom next to their buddies. Those are the kids you want to place right under your nose." Being proactive by nature, these teachers understood that anything that they did not arrange to their advantage would ultimately be arranged to their disadvantage.

Specific Procedures and Routines

Contained in Jones' section on classroom structure is a collection of specific procedures that he has observed good teachers using to their great advantage. These include procedures for the first day of school, procedures for getting the class period started, the organization of classroom chores, and specific routines for "how to do this and how to do that."

A part of this section particularly worthy of note is Jones' discussion of classroom routines. As he rightly points out, rules are ultimately embodied in specific procedures and routines. Primary teachers, of course, work on them all year long. By contrast, high school teachers typically make a few announcements about procedures on the first day of school and then launch into the curriculum.

Such a shortchanging of the time required to teach routines is a false economy. The notion that students should know how to behave by now is both true and irrelevant. Students will naturally test to see what they can get away with, and they will adjust their behavior from one teacher to the next depending on what the market will bear.

Each procedure has to be taught like any other lesson in the curriculum complete with setting the stage, explanation, modeling, and practice, practice, practice until they get it right. Such an investment in training teaches not only what is expected but also how seriously you as a teacher take these procedures. Once again, the natural teachers seem to instinctively understand the role that investing in classroom procedures plays in setting the tone of the class for the entire semester.

LIMIT SETTING

While classroom structure deals with the prevention of discipline problems, limit setting deals with their remediation once they occur. It is with limit setting that the skills of the natural teacher become most difficult to decode because they are subtle and nearly invisible. A simple look can get a hard-to-manage student back on task. How do these teachers get such control at so little effort?

Jones describes meaning business as being 99 percent nonverbal communication—it is all body language. He reminds us that students can read you like a book. They know when you are tired or impatient or frazzled; they know exactly how long your fuse is; and they certainly know at any time during the day how far they can push you, how committed you are to dealing with a situation, and whether you will follow through. So, what are the nonverbal cues that the students are reading? And, how do teachers train their students what "No means?"

Jones stresses that the whole human race speaks the same body language (cultural differences being trivial compared to the similarities) so that, when you study body language, you are really studying biology—an area known as behavioral biology. Jones' analysis of the body language of meaning business is a contribution to that field. He has isolated three major factors: (1) the teacher's priority; (2) the teacher's emotional response; and (3) the teacher's physical response.

The Teacher's Priority

The priority is very simple: discipline comes before instruction. Yet, while most teachers would agree with this statement as a general principle, few teachers embody it in the moment-by-moment interactions of the classroom. Imagine, for example, that you are helping a student at his or her desk who is "stuck." You have spent two minutes with the student, and shortly you will be able to get closure and move on. You look up to see two students on the far side of the classroom disrupting.

Jones then asks his trainees, "Now, how many of you would like to finish helping the student you are working with before dealing with the talking across the room?" His trainees candidly respond that they would like to finish because they have invested time and effort and are close to closure. Indeed, that is exactly what teachers typically do. Unfortunately, they have just taught a crucial lesson to the class.

"Class, did you see what I just did? I talk a good game about standards and time on task, but talk is cheap. In fact, I find discipline management to be inconvenient, and I don't like to do it. So, when discipline and instruction are happening at the same time, which they typically do, I will deal with the instruction and ignore discipline. Instruction is on the front burner in my class, and discipline is on the back burner."

Dr. Jones reiterates that, if discipline management is not worth your time, it will certainly never be worth a student's time. So, terminate instruction and deal with the disruption now! Discipline comes before instruction *anytime* and *anywhere* because, ultimately, you do not have a choice. Either "No means no," or all of your classroom rules are just hot air. Children determine boundaries by testing, and unstable boundaries obligate the students to test you all year long.

The Teacher's Emotional Response

Our first response to a disruption in the classroom is a "fight-flight reflex"—that primitive response of all vertebrates to any event that they did not expect or do not like. We tense up, we dump adrenaline into the blood stream, and our brain begins to "downshift" from the cortex to the brain stem. This response can range from becoming mildly upset to going "ballistic."

But, because it takes adrenaline time to clear the bloodstream, and because a room full of students generates problem behaviors at a high rate, some teachers live on adrenaline or nervous energy all day long. The result for the teacher could be very destructive—hypertension and exhaustion. Yet, for the students it is not much better because the fight-flight reflex is by its very nature confrontational. When you add a verbal component to the fight-flight reflex you get *nag, nag, nag.*

An appreciation for the fight-flight reflex yields the first major principle of social power in the classroom: calm is strength and upset is weakness. If you are calm, who is in control of your mind and body? You are. If you are upset, who is in control of your mind and body? You are.

Discipline management is first emotional and second physical. Training teachers to mean business begins, therefore, with gaining voluntary control of the relaxation response as a means of aborting the fight-flight reflex before it dumps much adrenaline into the bloodstream. Jones repeatedly refers to "training" and "practice" in his book because he knows only too well that body language is performance, and performance is acquired only through coaching and practice.

His focus for the teacher, however, is always upon doing as little work as possible. The natural teachers, after all, are not working themselves to death, so why should you? For that reason, he examined the beginning of the teacher's response to the disruptive student in order to understand why a student might respond positively to a simple look. If, for example, students will get back to work simply because you look at them, then you will not have to walk all the way over to them in order to prompt them back to work. So, how do you begin to respond to a disruption?

The Teacher's Physical Response

Meaning business or failing to mean business happens very rapidly in the classroom. If we are going to fly off the handle, we will do so in a second or two. If the teacher can get off on the right foot in the first second or two by remaining calm, he or she will probably be in fairly good shape to deal with the situation.

By the time the teacher has turned toward the student, several seconds have passed. Consequently, Jones focuses on "the turn." By the time the teacher has turned, the emotional part of the response has been determined, and the teacher's body language has signaled to the students in a dozen different ways that the teacher either does or does not mean business.

While an experienced teacher can mean business at any time as he or she moves around the room, "the turn" as a practice exercise breaks down the initial response of the teacher into key behavioral components so that they can be studied and practiced. Key elements of "the turn" are as follows:

Excuse Yourself. Imagine that you are helping a student on one side of the classroom when you look up to see a disruption on the other side. Common courtesy would dictate that you excuse yourself from the student you are helping before dealing with the disruption. In addition, take a relaxing breath and give yourself a moment to clear your mind. When you stand and turn toward the disrupter, you may be met with an immediate escalation of the disruption such as back talk, and you will need to be calm *before* this occurs.

Stand Slowly and Turn Slowly. When you are calm you move slowly, and when you are upset you move rapidly. As you stand and turn, the students can literally "take your temperature." Jones has his trainees complete the turn "in a regal fashion" as though their body were exuding Queen Victoria's famous quote, "We are not amused." This is not as easy as it sounds. When you turn, turn from the top down in four parts—head, shoulders, waist, and feet.

If the teacher is animated at the moment the disruption occurs—for example, talking to the class—the change in speed is even more dramatic, and everyone in the class will know that the teacher has just gone from "instruction mode" to "discipline mode." By relaxing and slowing down, your body signals that something has just occurred in the classroom that must be dealt with before we proceed with instruction.

Point Your Toes. When you turn slowly toward the disruptive student, turn completely so that your toes are pointed toward the disruption. A partial turn indicates a partial commitment. With a full turn away from instruction and toward the disruption, the teacher sends a clear message—discipline comes before instruction.

A partial turn is a mixed message. It says to the students, "I know I ought to deal with this situation, but I don't really want to stop now and spend the time and effort." The teacher literally has one foot in and one foot out of discipline management. This half-baked response tells the students that they can give you pseudocompliance—some "smiley face" accompanied by a momentary return to work—and you will leave them alone. When the teacher returns to instruction, the disrupters return to fooling around.

In contrast, the more effective teacher conveys, what Jones calls, signal clarity. If all of the teacher's body messages say, "When this occurs, I will stop everything and deal with the problem," then the students will learn to respond to those signals. If, on the other hand, the teacher sends mixed messages indicating a general unwillingness to follow through unless forced, the students will continue their normal testing to see where the real limits lie.

The sudden change in the teacher's speed of movement from animated to slow tells the students that this same shift in the teacher's priorities is taking place. That change, however, is first of all in the teacher's mind. Body language, therefore, simply signals to the students what the teacher is thinking.

Whatever you are thinking will be signaled. For this reason, the setting of priorities, the relaxation and the body language are simply facets of the same response.

Get a Focal Point. Good eye contact creates an expectancy on the part of the teacher that grows the longer the teacher waits. That expectancy is easy for the students to decode—"I expect you to get back to work." When teachers glance around the room while waiting for the students to get back to work, they undermine the growing sense of expectation.

Good eye contact is another signal that tells the students you are focused on this event rather than being preoccupied with other events in the classroom—like instruction. Yet, it is important for teachers to realize that this is not a stare down. The teacher's body, as well as facial expression, is relaxed, and he or she is simply waiting. The teacher's recommended look at this point should be one of boredom—"I've seen it all before"; "I am not amused"; "Are you finished yet?" Teachers need to hone their bored look—even to the extent of practicing it before a mirror at home. They also should be careful not to end their "look" with even the hint of a smile. This can convey to the disrupting student that, in spite of everything, "I really did find what you did to be amusing." Ultimately, the student is in control of the situation. The student can either terminate the interaction with the teacher by getting back to work, or he or she can continue the interaction.

Hands Down. If you relax your biceps, your hands will be down at your sides rather than on your hips or folded across your chest. Waist-high gestures are animated, and shoulder-high gestures are ballistic. So relax your arms and find a comfortable position for your hands. At the beginning, teachers may find that placing their hands behind them is a forgiving posture because any nervous gestures in the hands cannot be seen.

Jaw Down. Relax your jaw. Clenching your teeth is one of the more predictable parts of a fight-flight reflex, and students can see it from anywhere in the room. Relaxing your jaw not only wipes any perturbed expression off of your face, but it also helps you relax the rest of your body and lower your blood pressure.

Move the Body, Not the Mouth. If the student does not give the teacher the body language of returning to work, the teacher must walk over to the student to prompt them from close range. Avoid "silly talk" such as, "Am I going to have to come over there?" or "This is the second time I've had to talk to you." Such nagging on the part of the teacher simply indicates a reticence to deal with the situation.

If you have to walk over to the student, stay until you get a stable commitment to work on their part. A common error on the part of teachers is to leave as soon as they prompt the students back to work. Do not be surprised if the students return to their disruption very quickly. Rather, put your palms flat on the table and simply watch (with your now perfected look of boredom) the students' work until they have done enough of the assignment to represent a meaningful commitment.

Walking over to the students to get them back to work, therefore, cannot be cheap. And, the price can certainly not be reduced by leaving quickly after you get there. This reality puts all the more premium on doing the first part of the limit setting correctly (i.e., the turn) so that you can save yourself the time-consuming trip.

Relax with Back Talk. Back talk on the part of the student, even innocuous back talk, has a very high likelihood of triggering a fight-flight reflex in the teacher. After all, the student has just escalated the situation by "calling the teacher out" in front of their peer group. Obviously, the student has just raised the stakes.

It is helpful for the teachers to realize, however, that they do not have to prove anything in front of the class. Rather, the student is taking all of the chances and doing all of the work. Simply let the student continue to do all the work, and sooner or later he or she will run out of gas. Clear your mind, relax your body, and let the words go in one ear and out the other.

By relaxing and keeping your mouth shut you have left all of your management options open. You can still respond when you see fit and how you judge to be appropriate.

Without training, teachers typically have a fight-flight reflex and open their mouths. No matter what teachers say, they lose. Everything the teacher says simply provides the structure for the student's rejoinder. Consequently, during training, Jones teaches that, "It takes one fool to back talk, but it takes two fools to make a conversation out of it." Most office referrals result from the teacher back talking with the student until the two of them have dug a hole so deep that there is no other way out. By being the "second fool," the teacher engages in "mud wrestling" with the student.

Camouflage. While the teacher may occasionally have to stop what he or she is doing and walk over to the student, doing so risks making limit setting that invites both the participation of peers and the embarrassment of the target student obvious to the peer group. One of Jones' rules is "Never go public if you can help it."

The natural camouflage for walking over to a student while limit setting is working the crowd. When teachers are working the crowd, they are continually walking toward every student, in turn, as they cruise around the room to check work. Strolling toward a student, therefore, would not cause any classmate to look up, particularly if the teacher pauses occasionally to look down at other students' work as he or she normally would. The disrupter, of course, sees the teacher moving his or her way. As the teacher draws near, most students typically decide that returning to work is a sensible thing to do.

That is to say, most of the real limit setting in the classroom is invisible because it is preventative. It is a by-product of working the crowd. One might think of working the crowd and limit setting as simply the preventative and the remedial versions of the same body language.

RESPONSIBILITY TRAINING (INCLUDING PATs)

Training students to be responsible is perhaps the central issue in discipline management because in learning to be responsible, the students learn to manage themselves. The more the students manage themselves, the less the teacher has to manage them.

What makes the management of responsibility tricky is that responsible behavior requires cooperation, and cooperation is voluntary. You cannot force someone to cooperate. If you try, you get the opposite—resistance.

Yet, before teachers can get cooperation from all of their students, they will have to answer one simple question thousands of times a day. That question is, "Why should I?" Why should a student be on time if the alternative is to socialize with his or her friends in the hall? Why should a student remember to bring three pencils to class if it robs them of the opportunity to stretch their legs and go sharpen a pencil whenever they want to? In classroom management, virtue is not its own reward. Quite to the contrary, goofing off is always the easy and pleasurable alternative to work.

Add to this the fact that moderate improvement in the area of cooperation does not really improve the quality of the teacher's life that much. For example, what is the practical difference between four students not having a pencil as opposed to two students not having a pencil? The teacher still has to manage pencils every class period. To set the teacher free, he or she needs cooperation from everyone. Getting cooperation from everyone in the class is the objective of Responsibility Training.

Responsibility Training is an incentive management program for the classroom. It is group management that seeks to gain cooperation from all of the students with enough fail-safe mechanisms built in to prevent the few chronic disrupters from ruining it for everyone else.

To help trainees relate to the novel features of Responsibility Training, Jones uses a parent's attempt to train a teenager to be responsible with money as an analogy. Jones asks, "What is the one thing a teenager must have in order to learn to be responsible with money?" Trainees respond in unison, "Money!" Indeed, you cannot learn money management without having money to manage.

So, what is the precious resource that students waste all day at school? Once again, the trainees answer in unison, "Time!" In order for students to learn time management, they must first have time to manage. So, Responsibility Training begins with a gift of time from the teacher—like an allowance for the teenager learning to manage money.

The teacher's gift of time to the class is called PAT—Preferred Activity Time. It is a time set aside for activities, typically creative learning activities, that the students would eagerly anticipate. PAT would occur more often with younger students—perhaps three times a day with first graders, and once a day with fifth graders. For secondary students in departmentalized settings, once per week per class period is common. The amount of time given is enough to allow a meaningful enrichment activity or learning game—typically fifteen to thirty minutes.

From the perspective of training students to be responsible, however, PAT is merely a "pump primer." The mechanism that really drives behavior is bonus PAT. It is through bonus PAT that students gain control over their own destiny by being able to *lengthen* the duration of PAT.

The types of bonus PATs include:

Hurry-up Bonuses

Hurry-up bonuses reinforce hustle and reduce time wasting. A classic example of a hurry-up bonus in family life would be the bed time routine. The parent might say, "Kids, time to get upstairs, wash your face, brush your teeth, get your pajamas on, and get into bed. It's 8:30 now, and as soon as you're in bed, we will have story time. But, remember, lights out at 9:00." The PAT is story time, of course, but the children control the length of it. The faster they move, the longer they get to snuggle in bed and listen to stories—something that they prefer. The more they dawdle, the shorter PAT becomes.

One of the prime opportunities to utilize PAT in the classroom is in lesson transitions. Typically, lesson transitions take from five to seven minutes because students dawdle. Students get out of their seats to hand in papers, sharpen pencils, get drinks of water, return to their desks, get out materials, and so on, at an unhurried pace, to say the least. Note, students don't mind wasting the teacher's time. The students know that as soon as the transition time is over, they will have to go back to work.

This lesson transition, however, can often be done in thirty to forty seconds if the students have a reason to hustle. The time saved is found time for learning. But the teacher must share this found time with the students. The teacher might say, "Before you get out of your seats, let me tell you what I want during this transition. First, I want you to hand in your papers. Then you may sharpen your pencils and get a drink of water. I want the cleanup committee to erase the board and straighten up the book shelves. I will give you two minutes to get all of this done, but you know you can get it done in less than a minute if you try. So, let's see how fast you can get it done, and all the time you save will be added to your PAT. Let's look at the clock and . . . begin."

Time gained is real time on the clock as opposed to being an arbitrary amount that the teacher awards. As soon as the lesson transition begins, the teacher begins to work the crowd. He or she prompts students to hurry as needed and breaks up side conversations between small groups of students that amount to incentives for dawdling.

The cleanup committee has, of course, been trained to do its job properly and has no doubt that, if it is done sloppily, it will have to be done again. And the class has been trained to move furniture safely and arrange it properly as one of many classroom routines. In addition, teachers may set additional limits as needed as they work the crowd.

A common error of untrained teachers is to use PAT in isolation as a management gimmick. Incentives, no matter how good, cannot bear the entire weight of classroom management. To the contrary, the greatest investment in management is always made at the level of classroom structure through working the crowd and well-established routines. Thus, hurry-up bonuses give trainees their first look at how Positive Classroom Discipline functions as a system.

Automatic Bonuses

Automatic bonuses increase the flexibility of Responsibility Training by permitting the teacher to include behaviors that cannot be timed. The most common behaviors are being at the right place at the right time with the right stuff.

Imagine, for example, that, as part of the routine for beginning class, the teacher awards one minute each if the students (1) are in their seats when the bell rings, (2) have a pencil, and (3) have their books. Imagine, further, that a student realizes with a half minute to go that he or she does not have a pencil. If the student simply says, "Hey, you guys, I need a pencil!" chances are someone will produce a pencil. When the whole class shares a vested interest in something happening, it will probably happen.

The beauty of this program from the teacher's point of view is that the student has not borrowed the teacher's pencil, and the teacher does not care if the student who lent it gets it back. Pencils are not the teacher's problem anymore—one less hassle that the teacher has to worry about.

Individual Bonuses

Once a teacher has a simple form of group accountability operating in the classroom, he or she can make a hero out of anyone by giving that student an opportunity to earn bonus minutes for the group. Such individual bonuses tend to be far more powerful than traditional behavior modification programs for students because they tap into the greatest source of social power in the class—the peer group.

A special case of an individual bonus is a program for highly oppositional students called Omission Training. Omission Training is so powerful that it can all but eliminate office referrals and is so important that Jones deals with it as a special topic. Omission Training is the general name given to an incentive system that trains someone *not* to do something. Since you cannot reinforce the nonoccurrence of a discrete event (I like the way you didn't just hit him), the only thing you can do is reinforce the student for not getting into trouble for a preset amount of time (you get a bonus minute for getting through the group discussion without interrupting).

A highly oppositional student could be made a hero by earning a bonus minute of PAT for the group by getting through half a class period without getting into trouble. The boundaries for PAT are simple—the student must want it, and the teacher must be able to live with it. Often, angry students are so busy being oppositional that they fail to perceive that PAT is for their enjoyment, too.

While the protocol for Omission Training is fairly complex as incentive systems go, it does give the teacher an alternative to the backup system that is both cheaper and more forgiving for the student. It is not only a win-win program, but it also provides a direct route for the teacher's helping a highly unpopular student to be accepted by the peer group.

Omission Training also provides a fail-safe mechanism for automatic bonuses. What if, for example, your students can earn a bonus minute for being in their seats when the bell rings? However, your most oppositional student decides not to be in his or her seat just to prove that he or she does not *have to*. The oppositional student, trying to prove his or her power, has just put the entire class in jeopardy of not earning PAT. This dilemma points out how tricky group management can be unless you are trained in the fine points.

One simple way of protecting both the group and the automatic bonus should this problem occur repeatedly is to simply omit the problem student from the bonus—called "cutting them out of the herd." If the rest of the students are in their seats when the bell rings, for example, they get the bonus minute. But if the problem student is not in his or her seat, the teacher deals with that student separately.

THE BACKUP SYSTEM

The backup system largely overlaps with the school discipline code—a hierarchy of negative sanctions ranging from a verbal warning to expulsion—that has as its purpose suppressing obnoxious behavior. Its problems are twofold. First, it tends not to work for the students who need it most because the same 5 percent of the student body are repeatedly sent to the office. Second, it is expensive for teachers who end up with extra conferences, phone calls, and incident reports and for administrators who must deal with all of the referrals.

Yet, some teachers almost never need to send a student to the office. Why? Three things seem to be crucial. First, they are good at classroom management and are perceived as meaning business. Consequently, most problems are either prevented or nipped in the bud. And, when the teacher has to give a warning, it is taken seriously because the teacher is taken seriously. Second, the teacher never embarrasses a student. Once again, working the crowd serves as camouflage so that a warning looks like any other private teacher/student interaction. During training, Jones focuses on the warning messages and small sanctions that the teacher can use while working the crowd to signal that "enough is enough." These small backup response options are private and invisible to the other students. And, third, these teachers never engage in back talk with a student.

Thus, the power of the backup system comes not from the size of the negative sanction, but from the person delivering it. No policy down in the office can compensate for a lack of skill in the classroom.

POSITIVE CLASSROOM INSTRUCTION

While Positive Classroom Discipline is a crucial part of Dr. Jones' training program for teachers, it is only half of the picture. The other half is Positive Classroom Instruction which deals with lesson presentation, corrective feedback, and motivation.

To provide a quick picture of the issues that link the two programs, imagine a teacher's timeless words as they transition to the guided practice portion of a lesson: " . . . and I'll be coming around to see how you are doing.

If you have any questions, look at my example on the board. But, if you still need help, raise your hand, and I'll be around to help you as soon as I can."

These words hardly leave the teacher's lips before a half dozen hands begin waving helplessly in the air. The teacher goes to the first student and asks, "Where do you need help?" The student responds, "I don't understand how to do this." The teacher asks, "What part don't you understand?" The student says, "All of it." The teacher begins to tutor the stuck student, which takes several minutes. Positive Classroom Discipline seems to work well until the teacher is confronted with the helpless hand raisers. Then, typically, the teacher relinquishes working the crowd for the life of a tutor, and classroom management bites the dust. At this point, guided practice should be used.

So, how do you conduct guided practice, and more specifically, how do you give corrective feedback to students so that you make them independent learners instead of helpless hand raisers? You can use what Jones calls, "Praise, Prompt, and Leave Subskills." He recommends that after praising what you can about the student's work, you should deliver a clear, quick, and simple prompt—a statement beginning "The next thing you need to do is . . ." Finally, you should leave and turn your attention to another student.

The prompt step deserves some elaboration. The prompt is designed to get the child started. Providing too much detail and direction is counterproductive. It is overwhelming. How many of you, while driving, have stopped and asked for directions, only to feel swamped and confused by too much information? Provide just enough information to get the student moving in the correct direction—even a step or two. You can always cruise by later to check on the student's progress and offer another clear, quick prompt.

Are you interested in Jones' model? Are you ready to try some of his techniques? If you are, be sure first to consult the original source, his book *Positive Classroom Discipline* (1987). What has been presented in this chapter, or any other single chapter, is not enough for you to run out, start using the abbreviated knowledge and skills, and expect to get results. There is no substitute for the original. Learn more about establishing rules and routines, recognizing the variations and limitations of limit setting, using Omission Training, initiating Preferred Activity Time, and using backup systems within and beyond the classroom. Buy his book, borrow his book, read his book!

SELECTED RESEARCH ON JONES' POSITIVE DISCIPLINE MODEL

Jones' Positive Discipline model has been the focus of research, but not as much as some other models. One reason for this lack of supportive or challenging research regarding his model is that Jones left academia and its world of publish or perish in 1978 to become a private consultant. Since then he has concentrated on developing his Positive Discipline model and writing books and guides describing that model. A thorough search of an academic library will reveal some earlier sources written or coauthored by Jones. A number of these sources are listed below.

Burka, A. A., & Jones, F. H. (1979). Procedures for increasing appropriate verbal participation in special elementary classrooms. *Behavior Modification*, 3(1):27–48.

A study that evaluated a comprehensive methodology to train teachers in group management skills to eliminate disruption and increase self-expression.

Cowen, R. J., Jones, F. H., & Bellack, A. S. (1979). Grandma's rule with group contingencies: A cost-efficient means of classroom management. *Behavior Modification*, 3(3):397–418.

Describes two different incentive techniques teachers can use to reduce the disruptive behavior of students including out-of-seat, talking-to-neighbor, and off-task behaviors.

Jones, F. H. (1997). Discipline alternatives. Did not! Did too! *Learning*, 24(6):24, 26.

Describes how the positive classroom management program trains teachers to remain calm, think before speaking, use effective body language, and mean business without being dragged into fruitless power struggles and student back talk.

Jones, F. H. (1979). The gentle art of classroom discipline. *National Elementary Principal*, 58(4):26–32.

A summary of a comprehensive approach to organizing and managing a teacher's day that integrates powerful, but cost-efficient, procedures for dealing with disruption, motivation, instruction, and communication.

Jones, F. H., Fremouw, W., & Carples, S. (1977). Pyramid training of elementary school teachers to use a classroom management "Skill Package." *Journal of Applied Behavior Analysis*, 10(2):239–253.

The study demonstrated that regular elementary teachers trained in the use of the "Skill Package" could effectively train colleagues in the use of a complex set of classroom management social skills.

Rardin, R. (1978). Classroom management made easy. *Virginia Journal of Education,* September: 14–17.

Describes Jones' Classroom Management Training, a set of concrete social interaction skills designed to address discipline, motivation, and instruction.

LEARNING MORE ABOUT JONES' POSITIVE DISCIPLINE MODEL

- To learn more about Fredric Jones and his ideas on classroom management, contact:

Fredric H. Jones & Associates, Inc.
103 Quarry Lane
Santa Cruz, CA 95060
Phone: (831) 425–8222

TEST YOURSELF

This is a sampling of the kinds of factual and open-ended questions that you should be able to answer after having read this chapter.

1. How would you classify Jones' views according to the four theoretical frameworks presented in chapter 2?
2. What is the title of Jones' popular book that outlines his views on how to discipline children?
3. Identify two of Jones' four teacher-controllable skill areas.
4. Contrast traditional classroom seating patterns with those suggested by Jones as it relates to more effective discipline.
5. What does Jones mean by "proximity control" and how might you make use of it in your classroom?
6. Complete the phrase, "Calmness is _____" and explain why this is true.
7. Complete the sentence, "Discipline always comes before _____" and explain why this is true.
8. Jones suggests that teachers do much of their disciplining, not with words, but with "body _____." Complete this sentence and explain why this is so.
9. Explain why Jones believes that a teacher should appear bored (i.e., thinking about their dirty laundry that needs to be washed) when looking at a misbehaving student.
10. Why might even a slight smile on a teacher's face at the end of his or her cor-

recting of a disruptive student be counterproductive?

11. What are PATs and how might you use them in your classroom?

12. How does Jones suggest that teachers use Omission Training to address highly oppositional students so that they do not ruin PAT for the rest of a class?

13. Identify two examples of what Jones means by having "backup systems."

14. In Jones' "Praise-Prompt-Leave" skill that is used as a teacher cruises the classroom while students are doing seatwork, what does he mean by "prompt?"

15. Do you see yourself using Jones' Positive Discipline in your classroom? Why?

ASK YOURSELF: IS THIS MODEL FOR YOU?

Although you would want to defer making any final decision until you read still more, at this point what are your feelings toward Jones' approach to discipline? What strengths and weaknesses do you see in his model? Does his approach to discipline reflect your fundamental views on how you believe people should be treated? Could you defend the use of this model to your students and their parents, to your colleagues, and to your administrators? Could you remain committed to his model—even when the going got tough? If you were to adopt his model, could you go to sleep at night and not feel that there simply has to be a better way to discipline? At this point, is Jones' approach for you?

CHAPTER 6

Rudolf Dreikurs:
Social Discipline

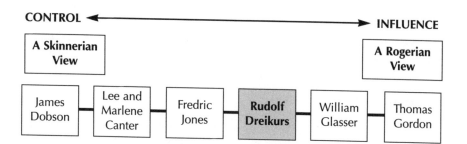

CONTROL ◄————————————————————————► INFLUENCE

A Skinnerian View				A Rogerian View

James Dobson	Lee and Marlene Canter	Fredric Jones	**Rudolf Dreikurs**	William Glasser	Thomas Gordon

Rudolf Dreikurs (1897–1972), a native of Vienna, Austria, was an associate of psychologist Alfred Adler. Dreikurs immigrated to the United States in 1937 and in 1952 founded the Alfred Adler Institute of Chicago, which reflects the optimistic approach that people are capable of changing and that human problems are inter-personal and socially embedded. Dreikurs espouses the values underlying Adler's Individual Psychology—an emphasis on equality, respect, cooperation, and self-discipline. Dreikurs' work has been continued and/or repackaged by such educators as Don Dinkmeyer, Sr., Don Dinkmeyer, Jr., Linda Albert, and Jane Nelsen.

OBJECTIVES

This chapter will help you, among other things, to:

- Classify, using the theoretical frameworks presented in chapter 2, Dreikurs' Social Discipline model.
- Identify the clues children give as a basis for their goals of misbehavior.

- Identify alternative teacher responses to children's misbehavior.
- Compare and contrast natural, logical, and contrived consequences.
- Compare and contrast praise and encouragement.
- Describe how to deliver effective encouragement statements.
- Explore whether Dreikurs' Social Discipline model is for you.

WHERE DOES DREIKURS' MODEL FALL WITHIN THE FOUR THEORETICAL FRAMEWORKS DISCUSSED IN CHAPTER 2?

Dreikurs' Social Discipline model clearly finds a place in French and Raven's Social Bases of Power framework under "legitimate" and "referent" powers. It finds a home in Wolfgang and Glickman's Schools of Thought framework as an interactionalist strategy. Dreikurs' position falls midway between the Skinner-Rogers' dichotomy. In Lewis' Keeping It Simple framework, Social Discipline is equated with "manage."

KIDS ARE PEOPLE, TOO

According to Dreikurs, children are social beings. Like all humans, they have a need to know that they belong. "Nature has not fitted him (man) to survive singlehanded" (Dreikurs, 1950, p. l). Children want evidence that they are significant. They want to be recognized. Is this too much to ask? I think not. A problem occurs, though, when children are unable to achieve these goals through socially accepted means; they may then resort to antisocial methods.

When students operate under the mistaken belief that misbehaving will gain them recognition and status, teachers must take action. But what action? As a practical matter, teachers should not—in fact, cannot—decide what action to take until they first identify which goal misbehaving students are seeking.

Dreikurs identifies four goals that describe the purpose of children's misbehavior. They include, from least to most serious:

1. Bids for attention
2. Power struggles
3. Revenge seeking
4. Displays of inadequacy

Children, in the mistaken belief that they do not belong, are discouraged and turn to disturbing behaviors to achieve their goals. By doing so, "they can be something special, be admired by peers, feel important, and gain status, merely by defeating the adults and violating their commands" (Dinkmeyer & Dreikurs, 1963, p. 42). In other words, if you can't be the best at being the best, be the best at being the worst. At least you will be noticed!

Misbehaving children will engage in purposeful behavior—behavior designed to achieve one or more of these goals. The key point is that the behavior is purposeful. "It is impossible to understand a person correctly unless one recognizes the purpose of his behavior" (Dreikurs, 1977, p. 176). Whether consciously or unconsciously, a child's choice of behavior is goal directed. Table 6.1, Behaviors with Undesirable Goals, outlines student

Table 6.1
Behaviors with Undesirable Goals

TYPES OF CLASSROOM BEHAVIOR		
Student's Goal	**Attacking Behavior**	**Defending Behavior**
Attention Seeking	The clown	Lazy
	The nuisance	Anxious
	The smart aleck	Speech problems
	The show-off	Bashful or shy
	Obtrusive	Untidy
	Walking question mark	Excessively pleasant
Power Seeking	Argues	Uncooperative
	Rebels	Dawdles
	Defiant	Stubborn
	Temper tantrums	Forgetful
	Disobedient (carries out forbidden acts)	Disobedient (won't do what he or she is told)
Revenge Seeking	Stealing	Sullen
	Vicious	Moody
	Destructive/Violent	Morose
	Revenge	Cruel
	Delinquent behavior	Refuses to participate
	Violent	
Escape by Withdrawal		Incapable
		Idle
		Hopeless
		Juvenile ways
		Won't mix
		Solitary activities

behaviors that typify each of the four goals (Balson, 1982, p. 50). Note that a student's behavior may manifest itself as either an "attacking" or "defending" behavior—actively or passively pursuing the same goal.

A hierarchy of sorts exists within these student behaviors. If bids for attention are unsuccessful in reassuring the child that he or she belongs, that child may well resort to more serious tactics such as revenge seeking or displays of inadequacy. Teachers would be well warned to deal with misbehaving children while they are seeking one of the less serious goals—for example, bids for attention or power struggles.

CLUES TO A CHILD'S GOAL FOR MISBEHAVING

How can teachers tell which goal of misbehavior a student is seeking? Dreikurs describes several distinct clues teachers can use to help them identify a child's goal:

- How do you feel when the child displays the misbehavior?
- How have you typically responded to the child's misbehavior?
- How has the child responded to your attempts at correction?

Two of these three clues deal with teachers examining themselves—their feelings and their previous efforts at correcting the child's misbehavior.

Teachers' Feelings

Teachers typically feel annoyed when a student is making a constant bid for their attention. The child is like a gnat that is always in their face; they wish the child would go away and stop bothering them. When a child is engaged in a power struggle, teachers feel their authority has been threatened. They feel angry. They feel a need to pull the child down off his or her high horse and show him or her who's boss. A feeling of hurt accompanies situations in which a student is seeking revenge. Teachers feel, "How could this child have done this to me?" Finally, teachers feel a sense of despair when a child is displaying helplessness or inadequacy. The point is to take a moment before acting and ask, "How am I feeling right now while the child is misbehaving?" An honest answer can go a long way toward identifying the child's goal of misbehavior.

A Teacher's Typical Response to Child's Misbehavior

When a child is making a bid for attention, it is common for teachers to remind and coax. They might remind a child twenty times a week to raise his or her hand before calling out an answer. For a child involved in a power struggle with teachers, too often teachers resort to fighting back or giving in: "No student of mine is going to get away with such and such" or "Why bother? What's the use? I may as well look the other way and give in." Where a child appears to be seeking revenge, teachers may retaliate in an effort to get even. Finally, teachers are often overheard to say, "I've tried everything with this student, I give up," when a child is displaying inadequacy.

These typical teacher responses to a student's misbehavior in most cases simply make matters worse. Reminding and coaxing lead only to more reminding and coaxing. Fighting back or giving in results in an unproductive and unhealthy win-lose or lose-win situation. Retaliating only confirms to the child that his or her initial efforts at revenge were justified—"See everyone is out to get me; look at what the teacher just did." Giving up on a student who has given up only helps confirm his or her inadequacy.

Child's Response to a Teacher's Corrective Efforts

When a child is making a bid for attention, reminding and coaxing seem to work—but only temporarily. The child stops the unwanted behavior only to resume it or another unwanted behavior soon afterward. The reason is that reminding and coaxing in no way help to make the child more responsible or more independent. In fact, these typical teacher responses do just the opposite; they make the child less responsible and more dependent. Remember also that the student's bid for attention is his or her mistaken way of trying to belong and be recognized. Belonging is a basic deficiency need as described by Maslow. It is episodic; just like eating and breathing, it is a need that must continually be replenished.

For those children who find themselves in a power struggle with the teacher, fighting back results only in an escalation or intensification of the struggle. If the student complies at all, he or she does so defiantly. Misbehaving children are discouraged; their inappropriate behavior is a last-resort effort to belong and gain status. Pulling children down off their high horses or cutting them down to size and showing them who's boss by fighting back only increases this discouragement. On the other hand, if a teacher responds by giving in, then students are sent clear but unintended messages—their needs come first, they can be boss, and no one can make them do anything they don't want to do.

If a teacher responds with an eye-for-an-eye, revenge-for-revenge strategy, one can expect children to do likewise. Like a snowball rolling downhill, getting bigger and bigger, where will it ever end? It is common for students seeking revenge not only to become violent or hostile but to feel justified in doing so. Before the teacher actually retaliated, the students only thought others were out to hurt them. When a teacher falls into the trap of actually retaliating, the students now have concrete evidence that others are out to get them!

Passive response or failure to respond at all can be expected of children who have teachers who throw their hands up in despair and give up. It is all too easy for a teacher, in frustration, to "take the picture of him as a student worth teaching out of her picture album" (Glasser, 1986, p. 53). Having teachers give up confirms those children's beliefs that they are incapable of doing anything—just what they mistakenly thought in the beginning. Now they have their teachers agreeing with them. They think, "Both of us can't be wrong. I must, in fact, be inadequate." Remaining passive and doing nothing enables students to guard what little self-esteem they have left by removing it from social tests (Charles, 1985, p. 76).

Recognition Reflex: A Final Clue

After examining your feelings while the child is misbehaving (noting how you have typically responded in the past and looking at how the misbehaving child has reacted to your responses), you are in a good position to judge which of Dreikurs' four goals of misbehavior the child is seeking. One final litmus test is to confront the child with a statement that represents that goal of misbehavior and look for a recognition reflex. The four confrontation statements are:

- "Could it be that you would like to keep me busy with you?"
- "Could it be that you would like to be boss and show everyone that no one can make you do anything?"
- "Could it be that you would like to hurt others as you think they have hurt you?"
- "Could it be that you would like to convince others that you are not capable?"

How long will it take, and what, exactly, is a recognition reflex? According to Dreikurs, Grunwald, and Pepper (1971, p. 41):

The recognition reflex may not come immediately because the child may have to think it over first. Therefore, one has to wait for his reaction. It is most dramatic to watch the child, how he first considers it, and then the corners of his mouth begin to expand in a knowing smile and a gleam appears in his eyes. He begins to recognize what he was up to.

With the child's goal now out in the open for both the child and the teacher to see, real progress can be made. Teachers can now respond in ways more likely not to reinforce the mistaken goals of misbehavior. Keep in mind that in the world of operant learning, "not reinforcing," is the only way to extinguish an unwanted behavior.

ALTERNATIVE BEHAVIORS FOR TEACHERS

Once a teacher has determined a child's goal of misbehavior, the teacher can make corrective responses. Alternative teacher responses to each goal of misbehavior are described in Table 6.2, Alternative Teacher Responses.

Bids for Attention

Teachers should ignore a student's bid for attention, where possible, and give attention to positive behavior when the student is not making a bid for

Table 6.2
Alternative Teacher Responses

BEHAVIOR	GOAL OF BEHAVIOR	TEACHER RESPONSE
Clowning Showing off Being late	Attention	1. Refuse to give special attention on request. 2. Allow consequences to take place.
Stubborn Apathetic Disobedient Untruthful	Power	1. Refuse to fight. 2. Admit your inability to make students do anything. 3. Allow consequences to take place.
Stealing Delinquent Moody Personally abusive	Revenge	1. Refuse to be hurt. 2. Avoid retaliation. 3. Maintain order. 4. Allow consequences to take place.
Truant Unable to learn Gives up easily Indolent	Withdrawal	1. Avoid criticism. 2. Look for slight improvement. 3. Acknowledge effort. 4. Never give up.

it. Student misbehavior that threatens to cause harm either to the student, fellow students, or the environment, of course, cannot be ignored. But much of the type of misbehavior that teachers find annoying (Dreikurs' signal for students making a bid for attention) can be ignored.

However, ignoring, alone, is ineffective because it results only in the student either escalating the misbehavior or moving to more serious misbehavior—for example, power struggles. Keep in mind that the student's bid for attention is a goal-directed behavior. Ignoring that behavior interferes with the child's achieving that goal. On the other hand, supplying attention when the child is not making a bid for it reinforces the cause-and-effect relationship between engaging in acceptable behavior and receiving attention. The student soon realizes that if the work is done—that is, he or she obeys the norms (rules)—then acceptance, belonging, and recognition will be achieved.

Something else occurs when a student sets to work believing that in doing so he or she will receive attention. The more learning that takes place and the more confidence that is gained the better the grades achieved on tests and the more that student feels to be the master of his or her own fate. Internal motivation starts to replace external motivation. Locus of control shifts from without to within. As a result, the student needs less and less of the teacher's overt attention, for now he or she is better able to get the same feelings of worth and recognition through his or her own achievements.

Power Struggles

As stated earlier, fighting back or giving in simply does not work. Both are win-lose situations. Teachers should disengage from a power struggle. Just as it takes "two to tango," it takes "two to tangle." The steam quickly goes out of a power struggle when students find themselves trying to sustain it when there is no one with whom to struggle.

Part of disengaging from a power struggle is helping the child understand the goal of the misbehavior (such as the need to be boss). According to Dreikurs, Grunwald, and Pepper (1971, p. 199), this "removes from him the conviction that he is just a bad child, and opens avenues for alternatives."

Just as it is ineffective simply to ignore a student's bid for attention, it is equally ineffective simply to withdraw from a power struggle. A teacher must do more. Remember that the child's behaviors are goal directed. "A child driven by the desire for power is always ambitious. But his ambition is directed exclusively at the defeat of the power of those who try to suppress him" (Dreikurs, 1968, p. 50). Withdrawing from the power struggle leaves that goal unattained. Teachers must redirect the student's need for power into constructive endeavors. But how?

Admit to a child that you don't know what to do about his misbehavior and then ask him or her, "What do you think we can do to solve the problem?" This gives the misbehaving student a prosocial opportunity (and responsibility) to "be the boss." Who knows, as a teacher you may be surprised by the quality of solutions generated. As is the case in Glasser's Reality Therapy, corrective plans generated by a student should be accepted only if they meet the teacher's need. Further, does it really matter who comes up with a solution to the problem behavior as long as it stops?

Admitting to students that you cannot make them complete a particular assignment or force them to turn in a paper if they do not want to acknowledges the fact that they and only they have the final power over their behavior. Students know this to be true, and by your saying so, students know you know it to be true. Once it is out in the open, students have less of a need to continue trying to prove it to be so. The fact is, the incomplete assignment or nonsubmitted paper is a smoke screen to hide the student's feeling of powerlessness. Often students act "big" to conceal just how "small" or discouraged they really feel.

Few people in this world want to take on the responsibilities of being the boss or the leader; why not capitalize upon those students who do? Assign them posts of responsibility. Let them be lunch monitor, take messages to the office, help younger children, oversee the distribution of materials, be a crossing guard, and so on. Most people, including children, take assignments of responsibility quite seriously. By doing so they are getting their needs for power, status, and recognition met. At the same time, they are going about it in a socially acceptable way.

Revenge Seeking

The first piece of advice is "don't retaliate" and "don't take it personally." Although the student's behavior is goal directed, it is not normally directed at you in particular. The child is striking out, you just happen to be there. As difficult as it may be, teachers must show that they care for the student and for his or her well-being.

I am reminded of the situation where a teenager says to a parent, "I hate you! I wish you weren't my parent!" These are razor-sharp, hurting words. The urge to retaliate is great. Think what it does, though, when the parent responds by saying, "Well, I still love you."

If the child's goal of misbehavior is acknowledged ("Could it be that you want to hurt others as much as you believe they have hurt you?") and then followed by sincere caring statements and caring actions, there will be less of a need for the student to continue seeking revenge. Once students begin to believe that they belong, there is little motivation to continue acts of revenge against the teacher or their peers. To do so would undo their sense of belonging, their sense of recognition.

Displays of Inadequacy

When a child exhibits displays of inadequacy, find something the child can do and at which he or she can succeed. Focus on the child's assets. Statements such as "I know you have it in you" and "I really believe you can do it" can motivate the child to try. Once the child is making an attempt, any attempt, the opportunity then exists for the teacher to offer encouragement.

Eventually you will want to wean the child from all of this external encouragement and praise. But for now, load it on. If you don't begin to convince the student that he or she is a capable person, who is going to? According to Balson (1982, pp. 72–73), these children "need positive reassurance by teachers of their worth and ability so they can begin to function usefully, constructively and cooperatively."

NATURAL, LOGICAL, AND CONTRIVED CONSEQUENCES

The effective alternative teacher responses identified in Table 6.2, Alternative Teacher Responses, consist of supplying consequences—but not just any consequences. There is no doubt that people's future behavior is influenced by the consequences of their present as well as past behavior. Teachers have control over supplying many of these consequences. But what consequences are we talking about? If we were to list examples of specific consequences that could be provided to learners, the list would be virtually endless and thus of little use to educators. If instead we were to group these specific consequences by categories, we would find that there are only three: natural, logical, and contrived.

Natural Consequences

Natural consequences are those that "naturally" flow from someone's behaviors. They are not imposed by anyone else—teacher, parent, spouse, boss. If anyone is responsible for supplying natural consequences, it is nature itself. If a child has body odor, nature has designed it so that others will sense (smell) the odor and naturally avoid the child's company. No adult has to tell the other children to engage in avoidance behavior. Of course, when adults, as responsible caregivers, "decide to let the child bear the consequences of his behavior, they must be a little bit cunning about it and sometimes look the other way and give him plenty of scope" (Dreikurs, 1950, p. 80).

If a student does not study for a test, then, naturally the odds are that the results will not be as good as if the student had studied. In this case, the fact that nature has designed a relationship between studying and performance supplies the unpleasant consequence—doing less well on the test. Adults who drive too fast for icy weather conditions are more likely to skid off the road. The relationship between tire adhesion and weather conditions may supply the unpleasant consequence of an accident.

There are, of course, times when teachers cannot let natural consequences unfold. A child using a Bunsen burner in an unsafe manner in chemistry lab or using a metal grinder in shop without safety glasses is likely to experience a "natural" accident. Should the child survive the accident, he or she would certainly be more cautious in the future. However, as teachers we must anticipate where such serious natural dangers exist and take preventive measures to avoid them. Letting nature take its course in these kinds of situations would be unconscionable.

Logical Consequences

Logical consequences are those supplied by someone else, not by nature. To a reasoning person, supplying logical consequences makes sense. There is a recognizable connection between a student's behavior and the consequence supplied by a teacher. The consequences must be "experienced by the child as logical in nature, or the corrective effect may be lost" (Dreikurs & Grey, 1968, p. 66).

If a child has body odor, it would be logical (reasonable) for a principal to require that the child attend to personal hygiene before being permitted to return to class. If a student does not study for a test and does poorly, it would be logical for a teacher to require that the student continue studying the material and take a makeup test before being permitted to go on. For the adult who drove too fast and had an automobile accident, it would be logical for the insurance company to raise his or her premiums or for the police to issue a ticket. In each case, the consequence is seen as related to the inappropriate behavior.

The three R's for logical consequences include related, respectful, and reasonable (Nelsen, 1987). If any one of the three R's is missing, it is not truly a Dreikurs-type logical consequence. Having a child clean up his or her spilled food in the cafeteria is a related consequence. If the teacher is not respectful and adds humiliation to his or her request that the spilled food be picked up—for example, saying aloud for all to hear, "Joe, when will you ever learn to stop being so messy when you eat? Don't be such a pig. Now clean up that mess"—it is no longer a proper logical consequence.

Further, if the teacher instructs Joe to pick up the spilled food from the entire cafeteria, not just the food he has spilled, this request is not reasonable—it doesn't follow logically. Suffering, either from being shown a lack of respect or from consequences that are not reasonable, has no place among Dreikurs' logical consequences.

Contrived Consequences

Contrived consequences (Shrigley, 1985) are invented or fabricated by someone else. A reasoning person would have difficulty understanding the connection between the misbehavior and the contrived consequence. With contrived consequences—unlike logical consequences—it is not at all clear why they follow from one's behavior. No logical connection exists. If a child has body odor, a contrived consequence would be to have the student write five hundred times, "I will always come to school clean." This type of writing-related punishment probably will have an effect, but not the desired one. Instead, the student will learn to hate writing! (Hogan, 1985). If a student does poorly on a test, a contrived consequence would be one hundred laps around the gym. For the adult who had the automobile accident, a contrived consequence would be seventy-five hours of public service work in the park. It is almost as if the consequence came out of thin air.

What might be a synonym for contrived consequences—those that do not logically or naturally flow from a student's misbehavior? If you guessed punishment, then you are correct. Contrived consequences are usually just another way of making a child suffer. Contrived consequences, or punishment, evoke the three R's of punishment: resentment, revenge, and retreat in the form of rebellion and/or reduced self-esteem (Nelsen, 1987).

Where possible, structure the environment so that natural consequences will likely occur. They are the best teachers. They accompany each of us out in the real world. Body odor will cause us to lose friends; chances are, we will take corrective measures. Not studying for tests will cause lower performance; chances are, next time we will adjust our studying habits. Driving too fast will cause accidents; chances are, we will be more careful in the future.

When natural consequences are not likely to occur, try your very best to supply logical consequences. They work because students can see that the consequences you supply are somehow connected or related to their behavior. The consequences are predictable; they make sense. They may even be judged as fair.

Table 6.3
Logical Consequences versus Punishment

LOGICAL CONSEQUENCES	PUNISHMENTS
1. Expresses the reality of the social person.	1. Expresses the power of a personal order, not the authority.
2. Is intrinsically related to the misbehavior.	2. Connection between misbehavior and consequences is arbitrary, not logical.
3. Involves no element of moral judgment.	3. Inevitably involves some moral judgment.
4. Is concerned only with what will happen now.	4. Deals with the past.

This is not to say that students graciously accept logical consequences; they don't always. But logical consequences depend less upon the whim or capriciousness of the consequence-supplier. They are more impersonal. A student's behavior, something over which he or she has control, triggers a logical consequence. It is entirely in the hands of the misbehaving student. This sets the stage for students to take responsibility for their own behaviors.

Educators normally have a difficult time justifying contrived consequences since no logical connection exists between them and the misbehavior. Contrived consequences are taken "personally." This undermines their effectiveness. Avoid contrived consequences at all costs. Use the more effective alternatives—natural and logical consequences.

Handling students' misbehavior with Dreikurs' natural and logical consequences demonstrates that "mistakes are wonderful opportunities to learn" (Nelsen, 1987, p. 67). Dreikurs (1964, p. 64) agrees when he says, "If we allow a child to experience the consequences of his acts, we provide an honest and real learning situation."

Of the three available consequences—natural, logical, and contrived—teachers have most control over delivering the last two. Table 6.3, Logical Consequences versus Punishment, contrasts these two consequences (Dreikurs & Grey, 1968, p. 82).

ENCOURAGEMENT *OR* PRAISE

According to Dreikurs (1964, p. 36), "Encouragement is more important than any other aspect of child-raising. It is so important that the lack of it can be considered the basic cause for misbehavior. A misbehaving child is a discouraged child." Balson (1985) states that "The most important obstacle to learning in school is discouragement" (p. 3). Nelsen (1987) supports this position when she declares, "It is obvious that the best way to help a misbehaving child is through encouragement. When discouragement is removed, the motivation for misbehavior will be gone also" (p. 87).

All human beings *require* encouragement; *some* human beings *desire* praise. Problems arise when praise is mistakenly delivered as intended encouragement. Praise and encouragement are not synonyms. Praise focuses on the person or product; encouragement focuses on the process or effort.

Not all persons or products are praiseworthy. That is a fact of life. Further, praise loses its associated honor if too many people receive it. The Super Bowl is designed to honor the best football team—not the one that tried the hardest, practiced the longest, or was the most dedicated. There will be one, and only one, winner—one team worth public acclaim, one team glorified. Although this may be acceptable in the world of professional sports, its applicability to education is questionable.

On the other hand, all students can be encouraged in the process of creating, or for their effort related to completing, a product. Every child can be encouraged—should be encouraged—must be encouraged. Dinkmeyer, McKay, and Dinkmeyer (1980, p. 51) have delineated the basic differences between praise and encouragement, which are described in Table 6.4, Praise versus Encouragement. Other authors, such as Nelsen (1987), offer similar distinctions.

In his paper "Some Words of Encouragement," Reimer (1967, pp. 71–73) offers teachers some language for encouragement. Examples include:

- "You do a good job of . . .

  This stresses the activity itself, not its finished product. Even a comment about something small and insignificant to us may have a great impact on a child.

- "You have improved in . . .

  Growth and improvement are the nuts and the bolts that build student self-worth and confidence. Students may not be where we would like them to be, but if they are making progress, note that progress. It does wonders.

- "You can help me (us, the school, and so on) by . . .

  To feel useful and helpful is important to everyone—including children; we have only to give them the chance.

- "You are really working at . . .

  Recognition of one's diligence and persistence from teachers helps sustain learners on their way to turning an activity attempted into an activity completed. Further, these two work habits themselves will transfer to other endeavors.

Table 6.4
Praise versus Encouragement

PRAISE	ENCOURAGEMENT
1. Praise is a reward given for a completed achievement.	1. Encouragement is an acknowledgment of effort.
2. Praise tells students they've satisfied the demands of others.	2. Encouragement helps students evaluate their own performance.
3. Praise connects students' work with their personal worth.	3. Encouragement focuses on the strength of the work, helping students see and feel confident about their own ability.
4. Praise places a cold judgment on the student as a person.	4. Encouragement shows acceptance and respect.
5. Praise can be cheapened by over-use withheld as punishment.	5. Encouragement can be freely given because everyone deserves to receive it.
6. Praise is patronizing. It's talking down praiser enjoys a superior position.	6. Encouragement is a message between equals.

"In summary, encouragement recognizes effort and improvement, shows appreciation for contribution, accepts students as they are now, minimizes mistakes and deficiencies, focuses on assets and strengths, and separates the deed from the doer" (Balson, 1982, p. 112). Teachers who continue to use praise, rather than encouragement, perpetuate the erroneous link between the student's self-worth and his or her achievement.

PRAISE VERSUS ENCOURAGEMENT RESEARCH— AN EYE-OPENER!

Dreikurs believes, like most Rogerians, that encouragement, not praise, holds the potential for motivating students and building their self-esteem, self-confidence, and self-discipline. Most things written by or about Dreikurs, such as Hitz and Driscoll's (1988) article, "Praise *or* Encouragement," stresses the importance of choosing either encouragement or praise—not both. Dreikurs recommends that we choose encouragement. Hanko (1994, p. 166) comes right out and says "There is a danger in perceiving praise and encouragement as synonymous."

While I had read many articles contrasting the two terms, encouragement and praise, I remained unconvinced that there really was any great difference between them. That all changed several years ago when I asked a student assistant to do some library research on these two terms. I asked her to go to the library and examine psychology and educational psychology books with the aim of answering four questions. In each case she was to note the author, title, and pages where the answers to these questions could be found. These questions included:

- Which authors/books offer a *definition* of praise and of encouragement?
- Which authors/books offer *concrete examples* of praise and of encouragement?
- Which authors/books offer *positive effects* of using praise and of using encouragement?
- Which authors/books offer *negative effects* of using praise and of using encouragement?

The student reported back to me after she answered each question. In the first three instances, the pattern was the same. She came to my office with a confident air about her, suggesting that she was successful in completing the task I had assigned. In each of these instances she presented me with a two-column ("praise" and "encouragement") list of authors/books where the answers to the questions could be found. For the first three questions, each of the two columns that she presented contained about the same number of responses. In other words, she had found a similar number of sources that provided *definitions, concrete examples,* and *positive effects* of using praise and encouragement.

When she appeared at my office door after setting about to answer the fourth question, her shoulders were slouched, her voice was meek, and she seemed anything but the poised, self-confident young lady I knew. I asked what the problem was. She said "Dr. Tauber, I don't think that I did what you wanted me to do." She was almost in tears. Reproduced below in Table 6.5, Researching Praise and Encouragement, are her actual two-column responses to the question, "Which authors/books offer *negative effects* of using praise and of using encouragement?"

No matter how hard she had looked, and knowing her I have every reason to believe that she was diligent in her search, she could not find anyone, anywhere, who had something negative to say about the use of encouragement. Whereas my research assistant thought she had let me down by not generating an equally long, two-column list of responses, in reality she had opened my eyes to the difference between praise and encouragement and how one may be fraught with danger, while the other seems to have no detrimental side effects. According to Albert (1996a), "Encouragement is the most powerful tool we possess" (p. 15).

Table 6.5
Researching Praise and Encouragement

Negative effects of using:	
Praise	**Encouragement**
Hitz & Driscoll, p. 7	
Hitz & Driscoll, p. 8	
Hitz & Driscoll, p. 9	
Hitz & Driscoll, p. 10	
Hitz & Driscoll, p. 11	
Madden, p. 142	
Madden, p. 143	
Madden, p. 144	
Pety & Kelly, p. 93	
Schirrmacher, p. 93	
Pitsounis & Dixon, p. 508	
Pitsounis & Dixon, p. 509	
Pitsounis & Dixon, p. 510	
Brophy, p. 7	
Brophy, p. 8	
Brophy, p. 10	
Brophy, p. 11	
Brophy, p. 13	
Brophy, p. 15	
Brophy, p. 17	
Brophy, p. 20	
Brophy, p. 21	
Brophy, p. 22	
Brophy, p. 23	
Green & Lepper, p. 50	
Green & Lepper, p. 54	
Meyer, p. 259	

DELIVERING ENCOURAGEMENT MESSAGES

Pretend that you have a student who turns in his or her completed project that you know he or she has been working diligently on for several weeks. This student expects some kind of response from you. You, depending upon the discipline model that you embrace, must decide what sort of response to deliver. First I will present "praise" messages and then I will present Dreikurs' recommended "encouragement" messages. See if the differences are evident. In both cases I will "deliver" them in an enthusiastic manner—the positive person's most obvious characteristic (Dinkmeyer & Losoncy, 1996).

Praise Messages

"That's wonderful!"

"It is one of the best projects I have seen in years."

"I am very proud of you."

"I knew that you were going to do a great job."

"Now this is the kind of work all students should be doing."

"I am going to display it right here on the wall (equivalent to the refrigerator door at home) for everyone to see."

Encouragement Messages

"What was the most difficult part of project?"

"Can you suggest any way that I could better present the skills to next year's students so that they can complete this project more easily?"

"If you were to do this project again, how might you proceed differently?"

"How does it feel to work on a task for so long and finally have it completed?"

"You must feel really proud of yourself!"

"May I send some of the other students who are still struggling with their projects to you for help?"

"Would it be okay if I put your project on display for others to view?"

Let me repeat, the student who submitted his or her project wanted some reaction from the teacher. He or she didn't necessarily want praise. Did you spot some major differences in the two forms of teacher feedback? For instance, in the praise messages, the teacher said that he or she was proud of the child. In the encouragement messages the teacher acknowledged that the child must really feel proud of himself or herself. In the praise messages the teacher took it upon himself or herself to display the child's work. In the encouragement messages the teacher asked the child's permission (i.e., sign of respect) to display his or her project.

In the praise messages, evaluation after evaluation flows from the teacher's mouth. Granted, these are positive evaluations, but they are still evaluations none the less. In the encouragement messages the teacher asks the student to evaluate his or her own work. This is a major difference. In the encouragement messages we see the teacher actually asking the student's opinion (i.e., "how could I better present these skills to next year's students?"), a sign of respect, and asking for the student's help (i.e., "May I send some of the other students who are still struggling?"), a sign, that at least in this instance, both the teacher and the student are colleagues or equals in the learning process.

At least one other major difference exists between the two types of messages. When a teacher praises a student, that is the end of it. There is little or nothing else to be said by either party—especially by the student. Reread the above praise messages. These messages provide little if any opportunity for the student to respond except, perhaps, to blush and say "thank you." When a teacher encourages a student, a continued dialogue is expected. The stage is set for the student to, among other things, evaluate his or her own work, analyze his or her own efforts, examine his or her own feelings, provide sought-after input for improvement, grant his or her permission, and so forth. The learner becomes an active participant in the learning process.

Are you interested in Dreikurs' model? Are you ready to try some of his techniques? If you are, be sure first to consult several of his original sources, including *A New Approach to Discipline: Logical Consequences* (Dreikurs & Grey, 1968), *Discipline without Tears* (Dreikurs & Cassel, 1972), and *Maintaining Sanity in the Classroom: Classroom Management Techniques* (Dreikurs, Grunwald, & Pepper, 1982). You should also read *Systematic Training for Effective Teaching* (Dinkmeyer, McKay, & Dinkmeyer, Jr., 1980). What has been presented in this chapter, or any other single chapter, is not enough for you to run out, start using the abbreviated knowledge and skills, and expect to get results. There is no substitute for the original. Learn more about encouragement as a prime motivator, deterrents to encouragement, discipline as an educational process, classroom meetings, and logical consequences versus punishment. Buy his books, borrow his books, read his books!

SELECTED RESEARCH ON DREIKURS' SOCIAL DISCIPLINE MODEL

Dreikurs' Social Discipline model, an extension of the ideas first proposed by Alfred Adler, the founder of Individual Psychology, has been the focus of much research—master's theses, doctoral dissertations, books, and journal articles. A search of any academic library will reveal such sources. A number of these sources are listed below. Note the wide variety of citations.

Dinkmeyer, D., & Eckstein, D. (1996). *Leadership by encouragement.* Boca Raton, FL: St. Lucie Press.
Presents a unique and powerful psychology that helps build an encouragement atmosphere in organizations.

Dinkmeyer, D., & Losoncy, L. (1996). *The skills of encouragement: Bringing out the best in yourself and others*. Boca Raton, FL: St. Lucie Press.

Presents skills to improve one's self-esteem, take ownership of one's life, and achieve a positive approach to living.

Dreikurs, R. (1968). *Psychology in the classroom*. New York: Harper & Row.

Presents the basic principles behind Adlerian psychology and then offers, in some detail, the practical application of the theory to classroom situations.

Dreikurs, R. (1950). *Fundamentals of Adlerian psychology*. Chicago: Alfred Adler Institute.

Building upon the premise that nature has not fitted us to survive single-handedly, Dreikurs explains Adler's Social Interest theory, whereby all of our actions (both good and bad behavior) are purposeful—dictated by our need to belong and to have a sense of community.

Dreikurs, R., & Dinkmeyer, D. (1963). *Encouraging children to learn: The encouragement process*. Englewood Cliffs, NJ: Prentice-Hall.

Directly links encouragement of children to learn with a recognition that their social striving (need to belong) is a primary, not a secondary, need. Offers principles of encouragement, supported with specific case studies of such principles.

Dreikurs, R., Grunwald, B. B., & Pepper, F. C. (1982). *Maintaining sanity in the classroom: Classroom management techniques*. New York: HarperCollins.

Offers specific Adlerian psychology-based steps for handling behavior difficulties and understanding the group dynamics of various classroom situations.

Evans, T. D. (1996). Encouragement: The key to reforming classrooms. *Educational Leadership, 54*(1):81–85.

Describes how encouragement training changes the way teachers run classrooms and relate to students. This source heavily cites Dreikurs, Adler, and Dinkmeyer & Dinkmeyer (i.e., STEP/STET [Systematic Training for Effective Parenting/Systematic Training for Effective Teaching]).

Goldberg, J., & Wilgosh, L. (1990). Comparing and evaluating classroom discipline models. *Education Canada, 30*(2):3–42.

Describes the development of a teacher checklist for comparing discipline models on dimensions relevant to classroom practice and research. Dreikurs' model is one of four models upon which the checklist is applied.

Kizer, B. (1988). *Adlerian therapy with aggressive children.* Educational Resources Information Center (ERIC) report. Accession No. ED 302790.

Argues that Adlerian therapy, clarified and refined by Rudolf Dreikurs, has retained its place in psychology because of its common-sense approach and concern for the individual.

Painter, G., & Corsini, R. J. (1990). *Effective discipline in the home and school.* Muncie, IN: Accelerated Development.

This book, based originally on the work of Alfred Adler, which was then further developed by Rudolf Dreikurs, offers solutions to specific child discipline problems. Part I focuses on the home; part II focuses on schools.

Sussman, S. (1976). *A critical examination of disciplinary theories and practices.* Toronto: York Board of Education.

Focuses on what is known about the development and control of human behavior that is relevant to schoolteachers. Examines and summarizes several approaches to classroom management including the Adlerian approach espoused by Dreikurs.

Trumble, L. D., & Thurston. P. (1976). Improving classroom management: A systematic application of Dreikurs' theory of misbehavior in the elementary school. *Planning and Changing, 7*(2):29–34.

Presents Dreikurs' theoretical framework in a tabular form that can easily be used in suggesting appropriate action for a particular misbehavior.

LEARNING MORE ABOUT DREIKURS' SOCIAL DISCIPLINE MODEL

- To learn more about Rudolf Dreikurs and his ideas on classroom management, contact:

  The Adler School of Professional Psychology
  65 East Wacker Place, Suite 2100
  Chicago, IL 60601–7203
  Phone: (312) 201–5900

Dreikurs' ideas—for example, goals of misbehavior and natural/logical consequences—serve as the basis for the popular STEP (Systematic Training for
Effective Parenting) and STET (Systematic Training for Effective Teaching)
books, guides, and workshops. Further, the work of contemporary authors such
as Jane Nelsen of *Positive Discipline* fame (not the same as Jones' *Positive
Discipline* model) and Linda Albert of *Cooperative Discipline* fame, repackage
Dreikurs' ideas in their books and workshops. A brief summary of the works of
these two Dreikurs-oriented authors appears in chapter 9. Thus, although
Dreikurs has died, his ideas are alive and well and still widely read. To learn more
about the STEP and STET programs, as well as *Cooperative Discipline*, contact:

American Guidance Service
P. O. Box 99
Circle Pines, MN 55014–1796
Phone: (800) 328–2560

- Search one or more of the many Internet web sites using "Dreikurs," "power
  struggles," "goals of misbehavior," and "logical and natural consequences,"
  among other terms, as keywords.

TEST YOURSELF

This is a sampling of the kinds of factual and open-ended questions that
you should be able to answer after having read this chapter.

1. How would you classify Dreikurs' views according to the four theoretical
   frameworks presented in chapter 2?
2. Name two of Dreikurs' books that outline his views on how to discipline
   children whether at home or in school?
3. What famous psychologist influenced Dreikurs' views on discipline?
4. Identify, in order from least to most serious, the four goals of misbehavior
   identified by Dreikurs.
5. Children's desire to pursue these goals of misbehavior is fueled by their need
   to meet what basic human need?
6. Which of the goals of misbehavior is associated with a teacher feeling
   "angry," feeling his or her "authority has been threatened," and feeling that
   it is time to "pull the child down off his or her high horse?"
7. Identify the typical, yet ineffective, ways that teachers usually respond to students seeking these four goals, and then identify the Dreikurs-recommend-
   ed alternative teacher responses.
8. What feelings do adults experience with each of these four goals of misbe-

havior?

9. Of the three types of consequences identified by Dreikurs, which one is most preferred? Which is least preferred? Why?

10. What is another name for a "contrived consequence?"

11. Which of the two teacher-supplied consequences, praise or encouragement, is recommended by Dreikurs and his followers? Why?

12. What was the eye-opening result of the author's research student's library research regarding praise and encouragement?

13. Create three "original" praise responses and three "original" encouragement responses that you might deliver to a student and explain how the statements differ.

14. Although Dreikurs is dead, what set of workshops and associated publications are offered today by the American Guidance Services that continue to promote and deliver Dreikurs' ideas to parents and teachers?

15. Do you see yourself using Dreikurs' Social Discipline model in your classroom? Why?

ASK YOURSELF: IS THIS MODEL FOR YOU?

Although you would want to defer making any final decision until you read still more, at this point what are your feelings toward Dreikurs' approach to discipline? What strengths and weaknesses do you see in his model? Does his approach to discipline reflect your fundamental views on how you believe people should be treated? Could you defend the use of this model to your students and their parents, to your colleagues, and to your administrators? Could you remain committed to his model—even when the going got tough? If you were to adopt his model, could you go to sleep at night and not feel that there simply has to be a better way to discipline? At this point, is Dreikurs' approach for you?

CHAPTER 7

William Glasser: Reality Therapy, Choice Theory, and Quality Schools

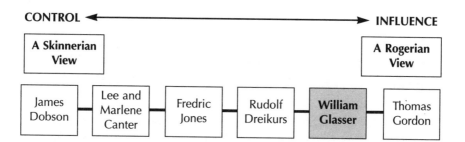

CONTROL ← → INFLUENCE

A Skinnerian View					A Rogerian View

James Dobson	Lee and Marlene Canter	Fredric Jones	Rudolf Dreikurs	**William Glasser**	Thomas Gordon

William Glasser (1925–) is a board-certified psychiatrist and founder/president of the Institute for Reality Therapy which in 1996 was renamed The William Glasser Institute. He is best known for *Reality Therapy: A New Approach to Psychiatry* (1965), a book that describes a method of psychotherapy recognized worldwide. Reality Therapy operates on the premise that it is more important for the client to confront his or her inappropriate behavior by dealing with the present rather than dwelling upon the past. Glasser translated his Reality Therapy counseling techniques into school-based procedures in his book *Schools without Failure* (1969). His recent interests have been in the application of *Choice Theory* (1998) and W. Edwards Deming's definition of "quality" to schools and school curricula. Glasser continues to write and lecture on these ideas. His books have been translated into seven major languages.

OBJECTIVES

This chapter will help you, among other things, to:

- Classify, using the theoretical frameworks presented in chapter 2, William Glasser's Reality Therapy, Choice Theory, and Quality Schools model.
- Identify the steps in reality therapy.
- Identify the elements necessary for the school to be seen as a good place.
- Explain how classroom rules should be formed.
- Explain the concept of choice theory.
- Name the basic human needs as identified by Glasser.
- Explain how these basic human needs can be used as a basis for motivating students.
- Defend how learning is the key to meeting all human needs.
- Explain the concept of quality schools.
- Explore whether Glasser's Reality Therapy, Choice Theory, and Quality Schools model is for you.

WHERE DOES GLASSER'S MODEL FALL WITHIN THE FOUR THEORETICAL FRAMEWORKS DISCUSSED IN CHAPTER 2?

Glasser's model clearly finds a place in French and Raven's Social Bases of Power framework under "legitimate" power. It finds a home in Wolfgang and Glickman's Schools of Thought framework as an "interactionalist" strategy. His position falls on the Rogerian side of the Skinner-Rogers' dichotomy. In Lewis' Keeping It Simple framework, Glasser's model is equated with "manage" and "influence."

INTRODUCTION

Recently, I met with a principal, and the subject of "Glasser" came up. He mentioned that a few weeks earlier he had traveled to Johnson City, New York, where he observed a school in which all the teachers had been trained in Glasser's model. To put it mildly, he was impressed. This reinforced two ideas of mine. First, no book on classroom management would be complete without Glasser. Second, there is little that is new in the world of discipline. Glasser's theories are as applicable now as they were twenty-five years ago when he introduced Reality Therapy to educators in *Schools without Failure*.

Of all the models presented in this book, none is recognized more often than is Glasser's. Educators around the world recognize Glasser's name and believe that they understand his model. Many state that they use his model, or at least use portions of it. Herein lies a major problem. Most educators do not fully understand Glasser's ideas. Further, when they state that they use his model, or at least parts of it, they are not, in fact, using it at all. Like all of the major classroom management models, Glasser's is meant to be used in its entirety, not piecemeal.

Glasser's Reality Therapy, Choice Theory, and Quality Schools model clearly finds a place in French and Raven's Social Bases of Power framework under "legitimate" and "referent." It finds a home in Wolfgang and Glickman's Schools of Thought framework as an interactionalist strategy. Glasser's position falls to the far right in the Skinner-Rogers' dichotomy. In Lewis' Keeping It Simple framework, his views are equated with "manage."

The best way to present Glasser's views is to highlight his work as it appears in several of his most influential books—*Schools without Failure* (1969), *Control Theory in the Classroom* (1986), *Choice Theory* (1998), and *The Quality School: Managing Students without Coercion* (1990). The first book applies Glasser's Reality Therapy, as then practiced in the world of psychiatry, to school classrooms. It provides teachers with a specific set of skills to use in sharing the responsibility for problem resolution—a strategy new to the American educational scene. The latter three books concentrate more upon what the school, as a total entity, must do to help students better meet their needs.

SCHOOLS WITHOUT FAILURE

In *Schools without Failure*, Glasser introduced educators to his concept of Reality Therapy. Why is it called Reality Therapy? Most educators don't know. Yet, to understand Reality Therapy, one first must understand the origin of the name itself. Keep in mind that Glasser is a trained psychiatrist who, through the publication of his earlier book *Reality Therapy: A New Approach to Psychiatry* (1965), challenged the traditional psychoanalytic approach to helping clients. He reasoned that clients could do little if anything to change past events. Hence, there was no reason to concentrate upon solving previously unresolved conflicts—for example, relationships with a parent. Clients could, however, do something about their lives right now— that is the reality of the human condition. People can control their behavior; they can, if helped, make good (prosocial) choices.

ELEMENTS OF REALITY THERAPY

Glasser stresses in *Schools without Failure* that before introducing Reality Therapy, the school must first be a good and fair place (rule formation). After that prerequisite has been established, Reality Therapy may be put into motion. The steps include securing student involvement, identifying problem behavior, evaluating inappropriate behavior, planning new behavior, gaining commitment, accepting no excuses, and avoiding punishment. The core of Reality Therapy is that, regardless of what has happened to us in our lives, we can choose present and future behaviors that are likely to help us meet our needs more effectively.

SCHOOL MUST BE A GOOD PLACE

Before any classroom management strategy can be expected to succeed, students must first perceive school as a good place to be. The strategy of supplying time-out (for example, in-school suspension or removing students from the classroom and placing them in the hall) or removing a child from a rewarding situation works only if that child perceives his or her school/classroom experience to be rewarding.

Similarly, in Glasser's model there is a shared responsibility between the teacher and the student. This acceptance of responsibility by students is far more likely to occur if they perceive school as a good place. Increased student choice is an outcome of increased student responsibility. A school that is a good place to be is, in fact, a school where students would normally choose, given alternatives, to be. They are getting their needs met. According to Gough (1987, p. 658), "Discipline problems do not occur in classrooms in which students' needs are satisfied."

Once students have chosen to be there, they have a stake in making their school an even better place to be. Students have less motivation to misbehave; there is less need for teachers to use strategies of classroom management.

What makes school a good place? "A good school could be defined as a place where almost all students believe that if they do some work, they will be able to satisfy their needs enough so that it makes sense to keep working" (Glasser, 1986, p. 15). It is one where students believe that they are important and that they have power. Both beliefs lead to increased self-esteem (Brandt, 1988, p. 39). More specifically, Glasser (1977, p. 61) describes a good school as a place where:

- People are courteous, especially the adults.
- One frequently hears laughter that springs from genuine joy brought about by involvement with caring people engaged in relevant work.
- Communication is practiced and not just preached. People talk with, not at, one another.
- Reasonable rules, recognized to be beneficial to both the individual and the group, exist.

- Administrators actively support and participate in an approach to discipline that teaches self-responsibility.

FORMING RULES

Of the criteria listed above for making school a good place, the one referring to reasonable rules deserves further elaboration. It does so because it is the one criterion that educators are best able to use tangibly to share the responsibility for solving problem behaviors. Reasonable rules do not just happen; they come about as a result of reasonable people using reason. This process is as important as the sensible rules that emerge. The process, as Glasser views it, is one involving both students and teachers.

Specifically, what does Glasser say about rules? First, "Reasonable rules, firmly enforced through separation from the program (not punishment) . . . are a necessary part of helping students become responsible enough to take advantage of what is made available to them" (Glasser, 1969, p. 194). He believes that students should know the rules. Although ignorance of the law (rules) is no excuse for breaking the law, there is little to be lost and much to be gained by clearly displaying the school rules. And because sharing the school rules is so easy to do, it would be a shame if problem behaviors occurred simply because the student did not know his or her action was against the rules. Copies of the rules can be passed out, included in student handbooks, sent home to be shared with parents, displayed in individual classrooms, and so on. Within reason, students should agree with the rules. The more reasonable the rule, the more likely the student will agree with it. What determines whether or not a rule is reasonable? Reasonable rules are those in which cause-and-effect relationships are clear. Walking in the halls (cause) is more likely to have students arrive safely to their next class (effect). On the other hand, running in the halls (cause) is more likely to result in accidents (effect). Such cause-and-effect relationships can easily be identified regarding activities such as throwing things, hitting other people, and taking turns to talk in class.

In fact, if you cannot show the existence of a cause-and-effect relationship for a rule, I would question the need for the rule in the first place. Without the logic of a cause-and-effect relationship, rules appear capricious, dictatorial, and unreasonable. Woe to the teacher or administrator who tries to make students obey unreasonable rules! You are doomed before you start. Further, in Glasser's model, unreasonable anything, including rules, would interfere with students believing schools are good places to be.

There will be those cases where, in spite of explaining the cause-and-effect reason for a rule, some students still will not agree with it. So be it. You can do little more. Chances are that reasonable rules will prevail. Peer pressure, exerted by the masses of students convinced by the explained logic of the rules, will help convince some holdouts.

Students should also play a role in both forming the rules and, when necessary, changing the rules. Although it may be more expedient for teachers simply to form the rules themselves, type them, and distribute them, Glasser suggests teachers do otherwise. There is no doubt that students who have part "ownership" in a rule have more incentive to follow it. Ownership is obtained by helping to form the rules in the first place.

As an assignment, education majors of mine who are placed in sophomore-level field experiences in local schools ask their elementary students to participate in forming five or six rules that would help the classroom run more smoothly. Sure enough, these students come up with almost exactly the same rules that the teacher would have formed if he or she had created them. "Walk, don't run," "One person talks at a time," "Keep one's hands to oneself," and "Be quiet when the teacher talks to another adult" are common favorites.

Of course, these elementary students are the products of prior years in school, complete with dictated rules, and as such would be expected to veer little in their rule formation. Still, when students help form the classroom rules, they do experience some degree of ownership. The rules are now partially their rules. Who wants to break something of their own? Not me. Not you. Not students.

STEPS IN REALITY THERAPY

Glasser's Reality Therapy carries more information than meets the eye. Reality Therapy is not a psychoanalytic-based approach to problem behaviors. Glasser is less interested in the experiences found in a child's past that might explain his or her problem behaviors than in having the child deal with the here and now—reality. The reality of a child's life, in or out of school, is that only in the present, not the past, can choices be made. He or she cannot do anything about the past; it is gone forever.

On the other hand, something can be done about the future, a point in one's life influenced by present choices. As a rational being, one can make tomorrow what one wants it to be. It depends upon the behaviors chosen now. Through a clearly defined set of steps, teachers can use Glasser's Reality Therapy to help create the facilitative and supportive environment necessary for children to embark upon a path of assuming increased responsibility for their own lives.

Glasser believes students are rational beings. They choose their behaviors.

They can choose to be good, or they can choose to be bad. Teachers need to structure the environment to help students make better choices. Reality Therapy helps to provide this structure.

The steps in Reality Therapy read somewhat like a recipe in a cookbook. As with any recipe, the finished product—in this case, improved student behavior—will not turn out as you expect unless you follow all the steps.

Step One: Secure Student Involvement—Be Personal

When school is seen as a good place, in which teachers display warmth and caring behaviors toward students, such involvement is relatively easy to achieve.

Step Two: Identify the Problem Behavior

The mutual trust and personal involvement begun in step one continue when the teacher asks a student to identify his or her own misbehavior. Although it would be more expedient for the teacher to simply tell the student what he or she has done wrong, this would rob the student of the chance to take responsibility for the behaviors.

Deal only with the present, not with the past. Simply ask, in as caring a manner as possible, "John, what are you doing?" If he tries to distract you by telling what someone else did, say, "John, at this point I do not want to know what so-and-so did. I want to know what you are doing." Keep at this question, even to the point of sounding like a broken record. Avoid bringing up John's history of past sins—his "rap sheet." Don't encourage John to give excuses for his misbehavior by asking him why he misbehaved.

Asking "why" implies that the reasons for the student's misbehavior will help bring about change. In fact, the opposite is likely to occur. Concentrating upon why a child has misbehaved gives him or her a way to avoid change. "Gaining insight into the unconscious thinking that accompanies aberrant behavior is not an objective; excuses for deviant behavior are not accepted, and one's history is not made more important than one's present life" (Glasser, 1965, p. 32). Ginott (1969) describes another major drawback to asking "Why?" Often when a teacher asks "why," as in "Why don't you every finish your work on time?" the teacher actually is conveying his or her disapproval or assigning blame to the student. In this situation, the teacher does not actually expect the child to answer the question. So, why ask the question in the first place?

We should be more interested in the responsible person we know the child can be and less concerned with the irresponsible person he or she was.

"What are you doing?" not "Why are you doing it?" is the question to be asked. If it sounds incredible to expect a student to admit what he or she has done wrong, keep in mind two points. First, you have already set the stage for cooperation in step one by securing student involvement. Second, the main reason students avoid owning up to their misbehavior is fear that they will be punished. Step seven in Reality Therapy, "Don't punish," removes this roadblock to honesty.

Step Three: Call for Value Judgments

It would, of course, also be more expedient for the teacher to judge the misbehavior and tell the student exactly why this behavior is bad for him or her. But to do so would be counterproductive to students assuming greater responsibility for their actions.

The judgment sought in this step is a cause-and-effect, not a moral one. A student who is caught copying homework (cause) will not learn the material (effect). A child who constantly bothers other children in the classroom (cause) will interfere with their ability to study (effect). A student who throws stones on the playground (cause) may cause a serious injury (effect). One chooses to display or not to display misbehavior.

Moral judgments, on the other hand, connect a child's misbehavior to something about his or her character as a human being—something most of us find difficult to change. A student who is caught copying homework is labeled a cheat; a child who constantly bothers others is labeled as lacking self-control; a child who throws stones on the playground is labeled a bully or troublemaker.

When students understand the cause-and-effect relationship between what they have done and what happens as a result, they are better able to come up with a concrete plan (Glasser's step four) for changing their behavior. Most important, the more practice students have in evaluating their own behavior, the more likely they are to internalize the value of changing their behavior. It is this act of internalizing that equips students with the commitment to make the change in behavior more lasting (Raffini, 1980, p. 103).

Step Four: Plan a New Behavior

By now, the strategy is clear—let students assume the primary responsibility for their misbehavior and for developing a plan to change that behavior. The teacher might ask, "Susan, what is your plan to make sure that this misbehavior does not occur in the future?" For those students new to the responsibility of planning new behaviors, a teacher might suggest a couple of plans and then leave it to them either to choose one or to make an original plan of their own. The key is that students choose; they start to take responsibility.

As students gain experience in planning new behaviors, the teacher will have to make fewer suggestions. With experience comes confidence; with experience and confidence comes an increased feeling of responsibility over one's life. Students make more good choices of behavior and fewer bad choices of behavior.

Occasionally, a student will come along who you believe is simply unwilling to take the responsibility for planning new behaviors. He might respond to your request to do so by saying, "I can't think of a plan." The temptation might be to give him one of yours and get the problem behavior settled. Don't give in to temptation. Instead, put the student in a time-out situation (such as a safe, comfortable, but rather sterile corner of the room) and tell him that he will remain there until he does formulate a plan. When he comes up with a plan acceptable to both of you, he can rejoin the class. This works, of course, only if you have relatively interesting lessons and exciting activities going on in the classroom, so that the misbehaving student would rather join in than remain in the time-out area.

As with much of what human beings tackle, the first time is the hardest. If we can get the misbehaving child to formulate one plan, even a simple plan as long as it works, we have set the stage for future occurrences.

Step Five: Get a Commitment

Don't overlook this simple, yet important step. Whether orally or in writing (the better choice), get a commitment. The sense of mutual trust that Reality Therapy is built upon increases the chance that plans for new behaviors will be carried out. After all, you "shook hands on it."

Step Six: Accept No Excuses

Asking for excuses, encouraging excuses, listening to excuses, and accepting excuses are all counterproductive. Excuses deal with the past. For Glasser, the goal is to deal with the future. If a plan for new behavior is not working, then either it must be reexamined to see how it can be made to work, or a new plan must be constructed. Our sights are ever forward—coming up with and successfully implementing a plan that does work. That is our collective goal. There is no place in Reality Therapy for accepting excuses.

Step Seven: Don't Punish

Punishment lifts responsibility from the student's shoulders. If a plan for new behavior is broken, it cannot be fixed by punishing the student. Punishment, or even the threat of punishment, destroys the warmth, trust, and feeling that school is a good place—all so necessary for Reality Therapy to work. Remember how important it is in step two, Identify the Problem Behavior, to have the student feel free of punishment in order to have him or her admit wrongdoing? Further, punishment is a contrived consequence that bears little relationship to the misbehavior.

Glasser is not saying that students should suffer no consequences for their misbehavior. He sees, as part of planning a new behavior, a place for supplying logical consequences—those that are a logical result of the misbehavior.

Step Eight: Never Give Up—Be Persistent

How long is never? You decide. Glasser (1977, p. 61) offers a good basic rule of thumb: "Hang in there longer than the student thinks you will."

The steps in Reality Therapy might be summarized as follows:

Involvement. Get into the student's world. Create a positive, caring atmosphere.

Behavior. What is the student doing? What does the student want? Focus on the present. Do not bring up past sins.

Evaluate. Is what the student's doing against the rules? Is it helping the student get what he or she wants?

Make a plan. Make a plan that is simple, small, specific, independent, positive, immediate, repeatable, and revisable (if needed).

Commitment. Document the plan. Have concerned parties sign it or shake hands on it.

Never accept excuses. Did the plan work? If not, what is the student's new plan?

Never, never punish. Punishment addresses the past, something that can't be changed. Reality Therapy addresses today and tomorrow. Allow natural and logical consequences to occur.

Never, never give up. Make it clear that Reality Therapy is the only game in town.

CHOICE THEORY IN THE CLASSROOM

Glasser originally labeled Choice Theory as Control Theory. His reasoning was that the only person we can control in our life is ourself. The sooner one learns this message the better. Unfortunately, Control Theory, at first glance, appeared to be more behaviorist than humanist in nature. Nothing could have been further from the truth. Hence, Glasser's recent renaming of Control Theory as Choice Theory.

For Glasser (1998), Choice Theory is founded on two important premises:

- All of our behavior is our best attempt to satisfy one or more of five basic human needs.
- All we can do is behave. In contrast to Stimulus/Response theory that claims that all of our behavior is externally motivated, Control Theory explains that all of our behavior is internally motivated.

Premise #1: Basic Human Needs Determine Our Choices

Glasser argues that the recommendations made by the Commission on Excellence in Education in *A Nation at Risk* (1983) that American schools should increase coursework requirements and raise academic standards misses the point. "The problem is that at least half of all students are making little or no effort to learn because they don't believe that school satisfies their needs" (Gough, 1987, p. 656). Hence, the emphasis of the first element in Glasser's Choice Theory is needs.

Normally, in any discussion of needs, educators immediately think of Abraham Maslow's Hierarchy of Needs: physiological, safety and security, belonging, esteem, and self-actualization. Glasser, however, has his own hierarchy, one parallel to yet different from Maslow's. See Figure 7.1, Glasser's Hierarchy of Needs.

Glasser asserts that our behavior, even our misbehavior, is our best attempt to alter the external world to fit our perception of our internal need-

Figure 7.1
Glasser's Hierarchy of Needs

Need to play and have fun

Need for power and influence

Need to be free and make choices

Need to belong

Need to survive

satisfying world. Although we all possess the same five human needs, each of us fulfills them differently. We develop an inner picture album of our own quality world and move forward trying to make reality better fit that quality world. My personal picture album, my definition of a quality world, includes the Florida Keys—Key West, in particular. Ever since Key West entered my mind as a significant part of my quality world, I have spent much of my waking time trying to get my reality (working full time in the cold, snowy North) closer to my picture album of a quality world—Key West. I take vacations in Key West, I eat key lime pie, I have purchased property in Keys, I read everything that I can find on the Keys. I search the Internet for Key West web sites. I have searched out job opportunities in the Keys. I review my finances to see if (when) I can move there. I talk about the Keys with anyone who will listen. And the list goes on and on.

Beyond the physiological need of survival and the psychological need of belonging, Glasser's and Maslow's hierarchies differ. Consistent with his belief that individuals are capable of making choices, Glasser cites such a need—the need to be free and make choices. He also cites as a basic human need, even for children, the need for power and influence. This need may be hard for some adults to acknowledge—harder still to accommodate. The last need, the need to play and have fun, is one that must exist side by side with school and community goals of academic scholarship.

Do today's schools provide sufficient avenues for students to meet their "choices," "power," and "fun" needs? Glasser would answer, "No, but they should—they must." If schools don't provide students socially acceptable ways of meeting these needs, come "h——" or high water, students will find ways of meeting them even if they have to resort to socially unacceptable ways of doing so. Hence, the emergence of discipline problems.

Students' innate need for "choices," "power," and "fun," once recognized and acknowledged by teachers, can be harnessed for use as a strong motivational tool. With appropriate and sufficient teacher direction (for example, structuring assignments), students can meet these three fundamental needs and learn, too. School, then, is perceived by students as helping, rather than thwarting, the meeting of these important needs.

Of these three needs, the one dealing with power raises the most eyebrows among educators steeped in the stimulus/response, behavior modification tradition. Yet power itself is neither good nor bad. "As a genetic need, it has no morality" (Glasser, 1986, p. 27). Like all needs, this need pushes us toward its fulfillment. In doing so, some students find themselves in conflict with the system. In those schools where appropriate avenues have not been provided for students to meet their needs, especially the need for power, inappropriate avenues will be found. Hence, discipline problems arise.

Glasser believes that "frustration of the need for power, even more than the need for belonging, is at the core of today's difficulties, not only in school, but every place else in our society where there are problems" (Brandt, 1988, p. 40). Students in a situation where they are unable to say "I'm at least a little bit important" will not work very hard to preserve or improve that situation (Brandt, 1988). Would you?

One often overlooked avenue for fulfilling this need for power, as well as fulfilling the other needs, is addressed in Glasser's *Reality Therapy* (1986). This avenue is through the use of groups or teams—the focus of his Learning-Team model. One need not look any further for an example of the importance of teams than the satisfaction most students experience in athletics, music (band, chorus), school government (model United Nations), drama, newspaper, and other team-related school efforts.

As social beings, we can gain a sense of belonging through the use of teams. The need for fun is also more satisfactorily met for most of us by doing things, even school-related tasks and assignments, together. School-related learning teams increase the opportunity for more people to exercise more choices—a Glasser need in and of itself—and thus experience more power and influence than is possible when working as individuals.

Most young people alone can exercise little power—either on the athletic or the academic field. A student's power springs from the collective strength, talent, knowledge, and dedication of all team members. "Only individuals who are very exceptional can obtain a sense of power by themselves. The rest of us have to obtain a sense of power through membership in some sort of team" (Gough, 1987, p. 660). Teachers must begin to create more experiences centered around learning teams.

Together, Glasser's needs can, and should, serve as the basis for real internal motivation on the part of learners. In the Performance Learning Systems' course, *Teaching through Learning Channels*, these basic human needs are identified as "'compelling whys' for students—meaningful, personal reasons for wanting to learn" (Pruess, 1997, p. 3).

Premise #2: What Choices We Make Are Internally Motivated

Nothing will change for the better until educators understand that the premise of Stimulus/Response theory—that human behavior is caused by external events—is wrong (Gough, 1987). Instead, Choice Theory holds that all human behavior is generated by what goes on *inside* the person. The outside world only supplies us with information. "We then choose to act on that information in the way we believe is best for us" (Gough, 1987, p. 656).

As living creatures we never *react*; all we can do is *act* (Glasser, 1986). Our choices are guided by our perception of our unmet, important needs. Hence, the emphasis of the second element in Glasser's Control Theory is *individual choice*.

Many people still mistakenly believe that they are not in control of their own lives. Ask depressed-looking students why they are depressed and chances are high that their responses will suggest that somebody or something has done something that *made* them *depressed*. They have no choice but to be depressed. "My boyfriend dumped me," "I did poorly on a math test," "My mom and dad are fighting again." Glasser would argue that people choose to be depressed. Perhaps it gives them an excuse for inaction; perhaps other people will feel sorry for them. Who knows for sure why they blame their predicament on other people or other things.

Glasser states that all behavior has four components: *actions, thoughts, physiological reactions*, and *feelings*. Although one can do little, directly, to control one's *feelings* and *physiological reactions*, one can control the other two components—*actions* and *thoughts*. Pretend you are an automobile where your rear tires, respectively, are labeled *feelings* and *physiological reactions*. Now, pretend your front tires, the ones that steer the car, are labeled, respectively, *actions* and *thoughts*. The fact is that the tires that steer the automobile—the parts over which you have complete control—determine the overall direction the car takes.

In a real-life example, take the college student who did poorly on a math test and, as a result, returns to her room all alone, pulls down the shade to make it dark, and puts on some depressing music. When a friend comes to the door and asks if she would like to go out for pizza, the response is, "I'm too depressed to go out." Chances are that these responses (*actions* and *thoughts*) will contribute to still further depression. On the other hand, the college student could have chosen the *actions* of going out for pizza, getting out into the warmth of the sunshine, and mingling with friends. The student also could have begun to think more positive *thoughts* such as, "Well, it was only the first of several math tests," "I could make plans to see the math tutor for help," "I could put more effort and time into doing the homework problems." Chances are that choosing these *actions* and these *thoughts*, just like the car's front tires, would begin to steer the college student's negative *feelings* and *physiological reactions* in a more positive direction!

LEARNING: THE KEY FOR MEETING ALL BASIC HUMAN NEEDS

What single activity in life best enables one to meet all of his or her basic human needs? The answer, and lucky for educators it is the answer, is learning and the acquired *knowledge* that results! Learning can, and most often does, lead to gaining knowledge and skills that, in addition to being personally rewarding, are salable on the job market. The diploma, the degree, the "sheepskin" awarded to successful learners can open many career-oriented doors that otherwise would remain closed. As a result, successful learners meet their need for *safety and security*. While learning, as argued earlier, the use of team-related activities helps one meet his or her need for *belonging*. This *belonging* need is further met throughout successful learners' lives as they join organizations, companies, divisions, departments, project teams, and so forth. As a case in point, I have just received my chair as recognition of twenty-five years' service to Pennsylvania State University. In a large way, I feel a sense of *belonging* to Penn State.

Learning also often results in the acquisition of *power*, the kind of *power and influence*, unlike simple physical power, that can last a lifetime. Everyone has heard the statement, "Knowledge is power." No truer statement was ever uttered! The need to be *free and make choices* is definitely enhanced through learning. Successful learners have more freedom and more choices than unsuccessful learners. Where one lives, what job one secures, how rapidly one advances in the job, how successful one is in child-rearing, how good a school one's child attends, how healthy one is (and stays), and more are all choices that are enhanced through learning. Finally, as the popular banner "reading is fun(damental)" proclaims, learning is (or at least it should be) *fun*. When one is learning something interesting, exciting, challenging, and useful, the time seems to fly by, little effort is needed, and one generally is self-motivated.

Think back over your own experiences. When have you ever had more *fun* than when you were actively learning something? Think of when you first learned to read, when you first learned about dinosaurs or King Arthur's Knights of the Roundtable, when you first learned to ride a bike or to snorkel, when you first learned to use a computer or calculator, when you first learned to make something in shop or home economics, when you first watched a seed germinate or a baby chick be born in biology class, when you first learned about the sinking of the *Titanic* or about the struggle of minorities while listening to Martin Luther King's inspirational "I Have a Dream" speech.

Truly, knowledge is a universal vehicle for meeting one's needs! This message, starting with literally placing a banner stating this point above all classroom doorways, needs to be driven home to learners. Teachers should spend more time designing interesting and challenging lessons and less time trying to figure out how to use "carrot and stick" approaches to make students learn. Once students actually begin to believe that learning is the key to their meeting their needs, students will be self-motivated. Discipline problems will cease to exist, since people, including students, who find themselves in an environment where their basic human needs are being met have little time, energy, or inclination to misbehave. Why should they misbehave; why should they disturb an environment that is conducive to their meeting their needs? Learning, something much more productive, is a lot more enjoyable!

A brief postscript regarding one of Glasser's identified needs is in order. Glasser argues that most animals seem to have a basic need to have fun. He cites nature programs showing the endless romping of lion cub siblings. Although the lion cubs appear simply to be having fun, they are, in fact, learning—watching their parents and practicing on each other how to bring down and kill prey. Glasser goes on, though, to say that there is one animal that appears to have no basic need to have fun. That animal is the sea turtle. Before the reader begins to think that Dr. Glasser has become senile, consider the following. The mother sea turtle climbs up the beach, digs out a hole in the sand, deposits her eggs, and then disappears into the ocean. When the sea turtles hatch, there is no parent around to teach them anything; they are on their own. Baby sea turtles come into this world knowing all that they need to know. Therefore, they have no need to learn; hence, they have no need to have fun! Personally, I am glad that human beings must learn, otherwise life as we know it would be very, very boring.

THE QUALITY SCHOOL: MANAGING STUDENTS WITHOUT COERCION

Glasser's most recent book builds upon the work of W. Edwards Deming, the man who has taught countless managers. It was Deming who, with the aid of the MacArthur government after World War II, taught the Japanese to achieve high quality at low cost (Aquayo, 1990). Deming proceeded to teach the Japanese the same effective methods that American managers rejected—primarily to establish a trusting relationship between managers and workers.

The Japanese learned well. They threaten the American auto industry, have captured the motorcycle market (except for Harley-Davidson and BMW), and dominate the electronics field. In education, the West looks with envy at, if not the Japanese system of education itself, the products of that system. What about here in America? Only recently have we fought back. For example, Ford Motor Company's focus on quality as "Job 1." Glasser believes that schools must also fight back. They must become Quality Schools.

To fight back, American schools must have leaders who are dedicated to quality. Remarkable parallels exist between the American manufacturers who ignored Deming when he suggested that they make quality their number one priority after World War II and today's school managers who seem unconcerned that only a few students in any school do what we—or even they—would call high-quality work (Glasser, 1991). Doing enough simply to "get through" never was enough for students, teachers, or administrators.

Glasser (1990, p. 3) explains that "Dr. Deming's ideas can be brought undistorted into our schools so that the present elitist system, in which just a few students are involved in high-quality work, will be replaced by a system in which almost all students have this experience." Creating a Quality School consists, in large part, of school leaders (from state superintendents to teachers) moving from coercive "boss-managing" to noncoercive "lead-managing." To do so successfully, schools must create (teach) a quality curriculum (Glasser, 1992).

Reduced to its essentials, boss-managing contains four elements:

- The boss sets the task and the standards for what the workers (students) are to do, usually without consulting the workers. Bosses do not compromise.
- The boss usually tells, rather than shows, the workers how the work is to be done. Rarely is worker input solicited.
- The boss, or some designee, inspects (grades) the work. Workers tend to do just enough to make an acceptable "grade."
- When workers resist, the boss uses punishment (coercion) almost exclusively to try to make them do as they are told. An us-against-them, adversarial relationship develops (Glasser, 1990).

Lead-managing, the needed reform suggested by Glasser, contrasts point by point with boss-managing. Lead-managing contains four basic components:

- The leader engages the workers in discussion about the quality of work and makes an effort to fit the job to the needs of the workers.
- The leader models the job to be done and solicits suggestions for improvement.
- The leader asks the workers to inspect and evaluate their own work.
- The leader is a facilitator, providing workers with the tools and a supportive (noncoercive), nonadversarial atmosphere to get the job done (Glasser, 1990).

The crucial difference between these two managerial styles lies in an understanding of how people, workers or students, are motivated. Boss-managers continue to believe that motivation is something one does to another person: workers must be made to work—often through the use of coercion. Lead-managers hold a different view. They believe that people have innate needs that can be met if a facilitating environment exists. In doing so, these people will engage in productive, as well as prosocial, behavior. Discipline problems, as we know them, would be minimized.

Glasser's preferred lead-manager style addresses how we treat others. What we teach them, too, is important. "Workers will not work hard unless they believe there is quality in what they are asked to do" (Glasser, 1990, p. 89). Hence, a Quality School requires a quality curriculum. Among the many Glasser ingredients for a Quality School is an emphasis upon useful skills, not on information simply committed to memory. Students are asked to demonstrate how what they have learned will be used in their lives, now or later. There is a greater emphasis upon writing than upon reading. The former guarantees the latter—the reverse is not true.

A Quality School (teachers) will not accept low-quality work from any student. Students set their own ever increasing standards for quality in the same fashion that an athlete continues to try to better his or her standing record. Effective teaching, perhaps in the mold of Jaime Escalante in the film *Stand and Deliver*, would exist. According to Glasser (1991), a Quality School would probably look much like the public schools in Johnson City, New York. We simply need more of them.

SELECTED RESEARCH ON GLASSER'S REALITY THERAPY, CHOICE THEORY, AND QUALITY SCHOOLS MODEL

Are you interested in Glasser's model? Are you ready to try some of his techniques? If you are, be sure first to consult several of his original sources, many of which are cited below. What has been presented in this chapter, or any other single chapter, is not enough for you to run out, start using the abbreviated knowledge and skills, and expect to get results. There is no substitute for the original. Learn more about the differences between Reality Therapy and conventional therapy, the needs that drive us all, how all motivation comes from within, learning teams, and lead management. Buy his books, borrow his books, read his books.

Glasser's writings have been the focus of much research—master's theses, doctoral dissertations, journal articles, and books. A search of any academic library will reveal many such sources, some by Glasser, others written about his model. A number of these sources are listed below. Note the wide variety of citations.

Brandt, R. (1988). On students' needs and team learning: A conversation with William Glasser. *Educational Leadership, 45*(6):38–45.

Ron Brandt, Executive of the Association for Supervision and Curriculum Development (ASCD), interviews Glasser on the subject of Control Theory, in general, and on the use of learning teams, in particular.

Cockrum, J. R. (1989). Reality therapy: Interviews with Dr. William Glasser. *Psychology: A Journal of Human Behavior, 26*(1):13–16.

Discusses incorporation of Control Theory and Reality Therapy, the growth of Reality Therapy, and the development of an Educator Training Center.

Glasser, W. (1998). *Choice theory: A new psychology of personal freedom.* New York: HarperCollins.

Describes a noncontrolling psychology that gives people the freedom to meet their basic human needs and to enhance personal relationships whether in a home or work environment.

Glasser, W. (1997). A new look at school failure and school success. *Phi Delta Kappan, 78*(8):597–602.

Describes the success of Choice Theory as it was used at the Schwab Middle School in Cincinnati, Ohio, and at the Huntington Woods Elementary School in Wyoming, Michigan.

Glasser, W. (1996). The theory of choice. *Learning, 25*(3):20–22.

Contrasts Choice Theory and S-R theory. Goes on to describe the use of Choice Theory at Schwab Elementary School in creating a quality school.

Glasser, W. (1994). *The control theory manager.* New York: HarperCollins.

Combines the Control Theory of Glasser with W. Edwards Deming's ideas to explain what quality is and how lead-managers can achieve it in the workplace.

Glasser, W. (1992). The quality school curriculum. *Phi Delta Kappan, 73*(9):690–694.

Describing schools as places where even good students believe much of the curriculum is not worth learning, Glasser maintains that the answer is to increase the quality of what they are asked to learn.

Glasser, W. (1991). The quality school. *Principal Matters, 3*(3):17–27.

In this Australian journal, Glasser discusses the connection between Control Theory and student motivation, contrasts boss-management and lead-management, and stresses the need for high-quality school work from both students and teachers.

Glasser, W. (1990) *The quality school: Managing students without coercion.* New York: HarperCollins.

Applies W. Edwards Deming's ideas about quality workplaces to developing quality schools.

Glasser, W. (1989). Quality: The key to discipline. *Phi Kappa Phi Journal,* 69(1):36–38.

Until students have a much clearer idea of what a good education is and how it can be gained from what they are asked to do in school, they will not produce quality work or behavior.

Glasser, W. (1986). *Control theory in the classroom.* New York: HarperCollins.

True to its title, the book applies Glasser's Control Theory (now Choice Theory) ideas to the school classroom.

Schmoker, M., & Wilson, B. W. (1993). Transforming school through total quality education. *Phi Delta Kappan,* 74(5):389–395.

Presents W. Edwards Deming's views on Total Quality Management and then offers examples of how the technique can be applied in schools (such as the Glasser-trained Johnson City Schools' staff).

Wade, R. K. (1997). Lifting a school's spirit. *Educational Leadership,* 54(8):34–36.

Describes one school's experience substituting Glasser-type activities for the Canters' Assertive Discipline.

Wubbolding, R. E. (1986). *Using reality therapy.* New York: HarperCollins.

Explains Reality Therapy and describes how we all carry around a picture album of our quality world. Applies the material to counseling, relationship, and work environments.

LEARNING MORE ABOUT GLASSER'S REALITY THERAPY, CHOICE THEORY, AND QUALITY SCHOOLS MODEL

- To learn more about William Glasser and his ideas on classroom management, contact:

The William Glasser Institute
22024 Lassen Street
Suite 118
Chatsworth, CA 91311
Phone: (800) 899–0688
Phone: (818) 700–8000
FAX: (818) 700–0555
E-mail: wginst@earthlink.net

- Search one or more of the many Internet web sites using "William Glasser," "reality therapy," "control theory," "choice theory," and "quality schools," among other terms, as keywords.

- Subscribe to the *Journal of Reality Therapy* that is sponsored by Northeastern University and The William Glasser Institute and published bi-annually in fall and spring. This journal would be a fine addition to an institution's professional or an educator's personal library. The address for the editorial office is:

Journal of Reality Therapy
203 Lake Hall
Northwestern University
Boston, MA 02115
Phone: (617) 373–2485

- To whet your appetite, I have included the titles of several articles published in the *Journal of Reality Therapy*.

A reality therapy staff development model. *11*(2):20–21, 1992.

Control theory: The missing correlate in the effective school movement. *7*(1):10–11, 1987.

Class meetings: Fulfilling students' pathway to power. *9*(1):43–48, 1989.

The theories of B. B. Skinner and William Glasser: Relevance to reality therapy. *8*(2):69–73, 1989.

Reality therapy in the elementary/junior high school. *5*(1):16–18, 1985.

Efficacy of reality therapy in the schools: A review of the research from 1980–1995. *16*(2):12–20, 1997.

Resolving conflicts in life. *10*(1):71–72, 1990.

Survival, belonging, power, fun and freedom on the high seas. *15*(2):102–103, 1996.

From boss manager to lead manager: A personal journey. *16*(2):31–44, 1997.

- To learn more about the Johnson City Schools, a recognized model for Glasser's vision of a Quality School, contact:

Johnson City Schools
666 Reynolds Avenue

Johnson City, NY 13790
Phone: (607) 763–1230

Until the early nineties, the Johnson City Schools hosted once a week, all-day tours for educators from across the nation. Unfortunately, the district has been a victim of its own success—too much disruption, too often, from too many visitors. The Johnson City Schools remain committed to Glasser's ideas regarding Reality Therapy, Choice Theory, and Quality Schools and, on a more limited basis, still can be contacted by interested educators.

TEST YOURSELF

This is a sampling of the kinds of factual and open-ended questions that you should be able to answer after having read this chapter.

1. How would you classify Glasser's views according to the four theoretical frameworks presented in chapter 2?

2. Give the title of three of Glasser's books that outline his views on how to discipline children.

3. What are three elements necessary for school to be seen as a "good place"?

4. How would Glasser's method of forming classroom rules differ from Dobson's or the Canters' method of forming classroom rules?

5. What is so unique about "Step Two: Identify the Problem Behavior" as it exists within Glasser's Reality Therapy?

6. What is so unique about "Step Four: Plan a New Behavior" as it exists within Glasser's Reality Therapy?

7. What step in Glasser's Reality Therapy is most difficult for more traditional teachers to accept? Why?

8. What is Glasser's current nomenclature (i.e., name) for Control Theory? Why the change?

9. Which of Glasser's basic human needs raises the most eyebrows among educators steeped in the stimulus/response, behavior modification, tradition? Why?

10. Glasser's Choice Theory holds that all human behavior is generated by what goes on _____ the person. Supply the missing word and explain how his view is diametrically opposed to the views held by behaviorists.

11. Explain how "learning" can be the vehicle for students meeting all of their basic human needs.

12. Contrast boss-managing with lead-managing as it applies to the organization and supervision of a classroom.

13. Glasser cites what person from industry as his model for developing the Quality School?

14. Do you see yourself using Glasser's Reality Therapy in your classroom? Why?

15. Explain how you would translate Glasser's Choice Theory into the design and operation of your classroom.

ASK YOURSELF: IS THIS MODEL FOR YOU?

Although you would want to defer making any final decision until you read still more, at this point what are your feelings toward Glasser's approach to discipline? What strengths and weaknesses do you see in his model? Does his approach to discipline reflect your fundamental views on how you believe people should be treated? Could you defend the use of this model to your students and their parents, to your colleagues, and to your administrators? Could you remain committed to his model—even when the going got tough? If you were to adopt his model, could you go to sleep at night and not feel that there simply has to be a better way to discipline? At this point, is Glasser's approach for you?

CHAPTER 8

Thomas Gordon: Teacher Effectiveness Training

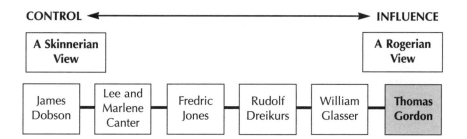

CONTROL ◄─────────────────────────────► INFLUENCE

A Skinnerian View					A Rogerian View
James Dobson	Lee and Marlene Canter	Fredric Jones	Rudolf Dreikurs	William Glasser	**Thomas Gordon**

A licensed clinical psychologist, Thomas Gordon (1918–) has served on the faculty of the University of Chicago and is the founder and president of Effectiveness Training, an education corporation that operates a network of professionals in thirty-one countries offering training programs for parents, teachers, administrators, and leaders in business, industry, and organizations of every type. Thomas Gordon's master's thesis advisor at Ohio State University was Carl Rogers—hence the Rogerian influence shown in his work. Gordon's book *P.E.T.: Parent Effectiveness Training* (1970) has sold close to two million copies. His other books, including *T.E.T.: Teacher Effectiveness Training* (1974), apply his Effectiveness Training model to targeted audiences. As an active writer, with a new Effectiveness Training book published in 1993, *Sales Effectiveness Training* (Zaiss & Gordon), he almost single-handedly continues to represent a Rogerian view of management—classroom, home, and industry.

OBJECTIVES

This chapter will help you, among other things, to:

- Classify, using the theoretical frameworks presented in chapter 2, Thomas Gordon's Effectiveness Training model.
- Identify the parts of a T.E.T. Rectangle.
- Identify how the T.E.T. Rectangle is used as the basis for selecting appropriate teacher responses.
- Explain the concept of problem ownership.
- Identify the twelve roadblocks to communication.
- Identify alternatives to roadblocks.
- Define the concept of active listening.
- Identify the three parts of a properly stated I-message.
- Explain the differences between a Canter-type and Gordon-type I-message.
- Identify the steps in Gordon's Conflict Resolution or Win/Win skill.
- Explore whether Gordon's Effectiveness Training model is for you.

WHERE DOES GORDON'S MODEL FALL WITHIN THE FOUR THEORETICAL FRAMEWORKS DISCUSSED IN CHAPTER 2?

Gordon's Teacher/Parent Effectiveness Training model clearly finds a place in French and Raven's Social Bases of Power framework under "referent" power. It finds a home in Wolfgang and Glickman's Schools of Thought Framework as a noninterventionist strategy. Gordon's position most clearly reflects the Rogerian view within the Skinner-Rogers' dichotomy. In Lewis's Keeping It Simple framework, his views are equated with "influence."

TWO COMMON PROBLEMS

Two interpersonal communication problems regularly occur in the classroom: how to respond when a student "owns" a problem, and how to respond when the teacher "owns" a problem. In the first case, the student's behavior is acceptable to the teacher; it does not interfere with the teacher's meeting his or her needs. In the second case, the student's behavior is not acceptable to the teacher; it interferes with the teacher's meeting his or her needs. Different, yet precise, responding skills are required in each case. Gordon's Teacher Effectiveness Training (T.E.T.) gives teachers a model to which they can refer to help them decide which skill to use and when.

T.E.T.: SOME BACKGROUND

"Effectiveness Training" is a communication model that translates a humanistic ideology into a complete and consistent set of practical skills. It clearly finds a place in French and Raven's Social Bases of Power framework under "referent." It finds a home in Wolfgang and Glickman's Schools of Thought framework as the most extreme noninterventionist strategy. Gordon's position falls on Rogers' side of the Skinner-Rogers' dichotomy. In Lewis' Keeping It Simple framework, Effectiveness Training is equated with "influence."

Gordon first described the model in his book, *P.E.T.: Parent Effectiveness Training* (1970), followed by *T.E.T.: Teacher Effectiveness Training* (1974) and *L.E.T.: Leader Effectiveness Training* (1977). The general applicability of the model exists because of the similarities in all interpersonal relationships and the corresponding need for communication skills, whether the relationship is one between parent and child, teacher and student, or manager and employee. The Effectiveness Training model describes the process of communication between two people.

THE T.E.T. RECTANGLE

The Teacher Effectiveness Training model is best represented by a rectangle or window through which one views the behaviors of all other people (see Figure 8.1, The T.E.T. Rectangle). The top part of the window depicts behaviors of the other person (student or teacher) that you find "acceptable"; the bottom part of the rectangle depicts behaviors that you find "unacceptable." The user of the model must first decide whether the other person's behaviors are acceptable or unacceptable.

According to Gordon, "acceptable" means that the other person's behavior does not interfere with your meeting your needs. It does not mean that you give your blessing to the behavior or that you necessarily wish it would continue. "Unacceptable" means that the other person's behavior does interfere with your meeting your needs. It does not mean that you find the behavior to be repugnant or immoral; you would just like it stopped.

We normally have little difficulty identifying examples of both categories of behaviors. The dividing line separating the acceptable from unacceptable is fluid; it moves up and down. Self, Others, and Environment all affect the line's movement. There are days when you (Self) feel especially good, when all is going well; you judge many behaviors of the other person to be acceptable. On those days when, for whatever reason, you don't feel so good, the line moves up; you judge far fewer behaviors to be acceptable and many more to be unacceptable.

Others themselves influence the line. Teachers are simply more or less accepting of some students than of others. It is not being unprofessional; it

Figure 8.1
The T.E.T. Rectangle

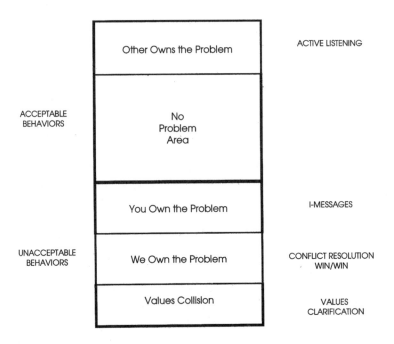

is simply being human. It could be how Others dress, act, respond in class, or attend to personal hygiene that causes teachers to be more or less accepting of their behaviors. Reasons aside, the fact is that it happens. We cannot be equally accepting all the time of all of our students (or bosses, friends, peers). It would be a superhuman task to do so.

Finally, the Environment in which the Other's behavior occurs influences whether or not we will find it acceptable. An acceptable student behavior that occurs when the principal is not present may suddenly be judged unacceptable when the principal walks into the classroom.

It is crucial to use the T.E.T. rectangle to decide first whether the other person's behavior is acceptable or unacceptable. Gordon identifies one responding skill for the former and several for the latter. Proficiently applied, the best of responding skills are of little value if the circumstances surrounding the situation do not warrant that particular response. The responding skill must be congruent with the initial acceptable-unacceptable decision.

An acceptable behavior may or may not warrant a responding skill. When the other person's behavior is deemed acceptable and he or she shows no sign of experiencing a problem, then no responding skill is necessary. It is in this part of the model that maximum student learning can take place. The goal of the T.E.T. model is to enlarge this "No Problem" area.

On the other hand, when the other person's behavior is deemed acceptable but it is obvious that he or she is experiencing a problem, a responding skill is necessary. Although people may not come right out and say they are experiencing a problem, they often give verbal or nonverbal signals that such is the case. People experiencing a problem act atypically. They may cry, sulk, scream, give curt responses, express feelings of sadness, bitterness, disappointment, frustration—and more. All of these, if they represent unusual behaviors for him or her, are cues that the person is experiencing a problem. Here we have a situation in which you can accept the other person's behavior (he does have the right to cry, to be disappointed, doesn't he?), but you want to facilitate his solving his problem. Remember, he owns the problem; it belongs to him.

PRACTICE WITH "OTHER OWNS THE PROBLEM" SITUATIONS

In the following situations, assume that you accept the other person's behavior, that what he or she is saying or doing does not tangibly interfere with your meeting your needs. At the same time, it is obvious the other person is experiencing a problem. You want to help. What would you say in response to the following personal problems? (Some suggested responses appear later.)

1. You are eating lunch in the faculty room. Mr. Knouse, a fellow teacher, comes up to you and says, "Nothing I do with my students seems to work. I'm not sure I'm cut out to be a teacher. What do you think?"

2. You have a primary student named Eileen who usually works extra hard to overcome her lack of natural ability in mathematics. When you ask her why she is not working on her math assignment, she responds by saying, "This work is too hard. I can't do it. I am just too stupid!"

If you are like most people, despite good intentions, you would probably respond with what Gordon calls "roadblocks to communication." Their net effect is to close off the very communication you want to enhance, that which could help the other person come to grips with, and possibly solve, his or her problem. Roadblocks not only cause the other person to want to escape your presence, they also make it less likely he or she will seek you out as a listener the next time a problem occurs.

ROADBLOCKS TO COMMUNICATION

There are twelve roadblocks to communication:

1. Ordering, directing
   ("You must . . . " "You have to . . . " "If you know what is good for you . . . ")
2. Admonishing, threatening
   ("You had better . . . " "If you don't, then . . . ")
3. Moralizing, preaching
   ("You should . . . " "You ought . . . " "A good student would . . . ")
4. Advising, giving solutions
   ("What I would do is . . . " "Let me suggest . . . " "Why don't you . . . ")
5. Lecturing, giving logical arguments
   ("The facts are . . . " "Yes, but . . . " "Don't you realize . . . ")
6. Judging, criticizing
   ("Have you lost your marbles . . . " "You are acting foolishly . . . ")
7. Praising, agreeing, me-tooing
   ("You are absolutely right . . . " "The same thing happened to me . . . ")
8. Ridiculing, shaming
   ("That is a dumb attitude . . . " "You are just talking silly . . . ")
9. Analyzing, diagnosing
   ("I know why you are upset, you are just . . . " "Your problem is . . . ")
10. Sympathizing, consoling
    ("Don't worry, I know how you feel . . . " "You'll feel better tomorrow . . . ")
11. Probing, questioning, interrogating
    ("Who . . . " "What . . . " "When . . . " "Why . . . ")
12. Withdrawing, humoring
    ("Let's talk about it later . . . " "Say, have you heard the one about . . . ")

Several response categories sound as if they would be obvious roadblocks (for instance, "threatening," "criticizing," and "ridiculing"), while other response categories (such as "praising," "giving solutions," and "consoling") seem, at least at first glance, to be quite appropriate ways of responding. Let's examine further some of these seemingly appropriate response categories.

Take, for example, "giving solutions." When another person owns a problem, avoid giving solutions. How committed to your solution of his or her problem do you expect the other person will be? Not very. If your solution does not work, who takes the blame? You do. After all, it was your solution. If the solution actually does work, how does the person who had the problem feel? Initially, relieved: but later, perhaps a little humiliated. Why? If the other person had been given the chance to talk out the problem, he or she may also have come up with a solution—maybe even a better one than yours.

Do we so readily offer solutions because it makes us, as the solution-giver, feel good? Do we feel that, unless we offer solutions, we haven't been of any help? Do we offer solutions because we do not have enough faith in the other person's ability to come up with his or her own? If we keep handing people solutions, when, if ever, will they develop the confidence to solve their own problems?

Underlying our temptation to give solutions is a feeling that good teachers or good parents are supposed to lift problems off their charges' shoulders. But when we do for others what they (if given the chance) can do for themselves, we hurt them, not help them. When someone asks for your opinion or solution, do not be so ready to give it. The person with the problem who says, "What do you think I should do?" or "What would you do in my place?" may not really want you to answer. Often, such statements are just an awkward way to end, for the moment, what he or she has to say and turn the dialogue over to you, the listener. Don't respond by telling the person what you would do in his or her situation. You are not in that situation!

Further, responding with a solution to the person's problem assumes that the words he or she has used adequately reveal the real, often underlying problem being faced. The real problem may not surface until much later in the dialogue. For instance, if a person says, "I am so mad at him, I could kill him," do we really believe his words? Do we actually think he is contemplating murder? Or do we take his words as simply a signal of some other problem that he has not revealed?

Another roadblock is "probing," "questioning," or "interrogating." Although probing and interrogating seem inherently inappropriate, what could be wrong with questioning? The moment you ask a question, the person who owns the problem must typically answer your question. This is especially true in schools where students have been conditioned to answer when teachers ask. By asking questions, you take control of the conversation. Chances are, once started you will ask questions until you have enough information to offer your solution. Note the number of references to "you(r)" in the preceding sentence. Can parents and teachers know just the right question to ask out of the thousands that could be asked? How are they able to select that question based on just a sentence or two from the person who owns the problem? Even trained clinical psychologists would not act on such little information.

Finally, "analyzing" or "diagnosing" is another roadblock to communication when a teacher responds to a student who owns a problem. This is a Catch-22 situation. If the teacher's analysis or diagnosis is incorrect, the student feels as if the teacher has not really listened at all; if the analysis or diagnosis is correct, the student may feel exposed. He may not be ready to handle the fact that someone else has him figured out even before he himself has.

ALTERNATIVES TO ROADBLOCKS

At this point some readers may feel a little guilty, for it is all too easy to remember times when we have responded with roadblocks to communication. But if not roadblocks, what then? Gordon suggests "silence," "noncommittal responses," "door openers," and, finally, "active listening."

To keep communication lines open, attentive silence often works. Body posture and eye contact show the person with the problem that you are tuned in, yet silence leaves him or her with the responsibility to continue. Both the pressure and the respect that silence displays convey a faith in the other person's own problem-solving ability.

Noncommittal responses are simply grunts of one sort or another that, properly delivered, convey that the listener is not only tuned in to the sender's problem, but tuned in to the intensity of the problem. "Oh," "My gosh," "You don't say," "I see," and "No fooling" are all powerful ways to interact with a sender while simultaneously avoiding any roadblocks to communication. Selecting the proper noncommittal response demonstrates that you are in tune with the intensity of the sender's feelings. A response such as "No fooling" may be appropriate for a child who tells you he got drenched on the way to school, but inappropriate for the high school student sobbing that she just bombed on her College Board exams.

Door-openers are fairly straightforward. "Do you want to talk about it?" and "Let's hear more of what you have to say" convey the message that you are ready and willing to listen to whatever the sender wants to say about his problem. If he chooses not to talk, so be it. It is his problem; he has the right to talk about it or not talk about it. If he doesn't take you up on your offer, have you failed him? No. What you have done with the door-opener is let him know that you are ready now, and probably are the kind of person who will be ready in the future, to listen to him. A door-opener that is not immediately taken advantage of when given still has the benefit of setting a positive foundation for the future.

Active listening is even more effective than silence, noncommittal responses, or door-openers. It is, in theory, the same as Carl Rogers' Reflective Listening—listening to the client (student) and mirroring the message and feelings behind the message for his or her immediate confirmation. If this form of response seems unusual, remember that it is not at all uncommon for people seeking professional help with their personal problems to pay hard-earned money to a counselor who does little else but listen! Listening, especially active listening, is therapeutic.

Figure 8.2, Decoding the Feelings-Oriented Message behind the Student's Words, diagrams the active listening process. In the diagram the student is experiencing strong feelings that are debilitating to his or her moving on with the everyday demands of life. The teacher's job, acting in the role of a Rogerian-type facilitator, is to help the child understand the underlying feelings he or she is experiencing. Strange as it may seem, teachers should not necessarily believe the student's actual words. Words are a code, often a poor code, used to convey an underlying message—one usually rooted in strong feelings.

Consider the following statement. "The problem with the problem is not the problem, the problem with the problem is the strong debilitating feelings that surround the problem, that is the problem!" Is this just some sort of tongue-twister? Nope! For instance, two students, both juniors in high school, could have basically earned the same relatively low Preliminary Scholastic Aptitude Test (PSAT) scores. The first person could feel devastated, discouraged, and reluctant to ever take them again—all but ruling out going to college. The second person could feel that although he or she wishes the score had been higher, there is not much that can be done about it now except to buckle down and prepare better for the SATs that will be offered during his or her senior year. Hence, very different feelings can surround the exact same problem. It is these feelings that must be addressed. In effect, the feelings surrounding a problem are often more important to address than the actual problem itself (i.e., feeling overwhelmed by the demands of schoolwork, feeling scared because your parents have been fighting, feeling embarrassed because you did not make the basketball team and you had been bragging that you would).

Figure 8.2
Decoding the Feelings-Oriented Message behind the Student's Words

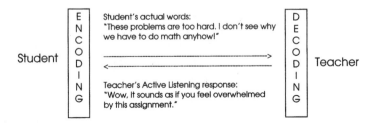

Active listening operates like the sounding board of a guitar. The hollow box of the guitar makes no sound of its own. Its sole job is to amplify the faint sounds of the plucked strings so that they can be heard. Active listening, too, amplifies. It helps amplify the feelings—sometimes quite faint—of the person who owns the problem so that he or she can "hear" them better.

An active listener should respond by using emphatic leads. Gazda, et al. (1995), categorize such leads as visual ("Looks as if you . . . ", "From your point of view . . . "), auditory ("As I hear it, you . . . ", "What you seem to be saying is . . . "), olfactory ("You smelled trouble when . . . ", "You experienced the sweet smell of success when . . . "), gustatory ("It soured you when . . . ", "You wanted to savor the moment . . . "), and generic ("You sense that . . . ", "You seem to believe . . . "). In each case, the sender (the person with the problem) has the chance to affirm or disaffirm the listener's attempt to decode his message. The sender might say, "Yes, that's exactly how I feel," or "No, it's not that; it's more like . . . "

What might be appropriate responses to the two situations identified earlier (Mr. Knouse and Eileen), in which it is clear that they own a problem and that you want to help?

1. "Mr. Knouse, you really seem to be upset today. Do you want to talk about it?" Just think how tempting it would be to send one or more of the roadblocks to communication. For example: "I know just how you feel" (consoling); "You are just feeling upset because you had an argument with the principal" (diagnosing); "I think you are one of the best teachers in the school" (praising); "Why don't we forget about it and have a cup of coffee?" (withdrawing).

2. "If I hear you correctly, Eileen, you feel pretty frustrated with today's mathematics assignment. Is that right?" (Note that you do not tell her she is frustrated. You ask her if that is how she thinks she feels. She will affirm or disaffirm your active listening response.)

Each of these alternative responses is designed to keep the lines of communication open. Each conveys faith that the individual with the problem is the best person to solve, or at least handle, the feelings associated with the problem.

The phrase, *handle the feelings*, points out the reality of our world because many student (as well as adult) problems cannot be solved. At best, only the debilitating feelings associated with the problem can be handled. A fellow teacher's spouse becomes ill, a child's parent is suddenly unemployed, a student is not selected to his first-choice university—all are problems without immediate solutions. Yet the feelings about the problem are still there. This is where active listening shines.

Do these two active-listening responses seem too artificial or too clinical? They will not seem that way to the person who is knee-deep in a problem. For a moment, put yourself in Mr. Knouse's or Eileen's place. Haven't each of the active-listening statements above left the door open for you to talk more about your problem if you want to? When used in a real situation, in which the owner of the problem is looking for a listener, wouldn't each of these statements convey a degree of trust and confidence in your ability to solve your problem?

Finally, teachers also can actively listen to students who have positive problems (i.e., William just found out that he won a financially significant academic college scholarship; Susan just passed a dreaded calculus exam. Both have to tell someone the great news). Once again, until the feelings, positive or negative, are handled, little learning will take place.

I-MESSAGES: WHEN YOU OWN A PROBLEM

What skill does Gordon recommend using when you, the teacher, own the problem? My professional training, first as a classroom teacher and then as a guidance counselor, stressed what I should do to serve the needs of those of my students who owned problems. After several years of teaching and counseling, I wondered what I was supposed to do when I owned a problem. How could I get my needs met? I found the answer in Gordon's Effectiveness Training model. It has a set of responding skills not only to help me to help others who own problems but also to help me when I own a problem.

When I own the problem, I look through Gordon's T.E.T. rectangle, classify the other person's behavior as unacceptable (by interfering with my meeting my needs), and recognize the need to confront the other person to get him to stop his behavior. How you confront another person can be the key to getting your needs met.

For those who have power over others who cause them a problem, too often their answer is to make others alter their behavior. When others interfere with our needs, it is tempting to send power-based messages. Gordon calls these "you-messages." "You stop that talking while I am teaching or else!" "If you know what is good for you, you will stop acting like a crybaby and start cleaning up the garage." One can picture the teacher (or parent) shaking his or her finger at the other person while uttering these messages. Perhaps it is obvious, but it bears saying: you-messages incorporate one or more of Gordon's twelve roadblocks to communication. They send solutions (yours), moralize, lecture, ridicule, threaten—sometimes all at one time. In short, they close off communication.

But don't teachers (and others in power) have the right to bark these kinds of commands? Perhaps they do; but should they? You-messages may force the other person to alter his or her behavior, but at what cost? They often result in defiant compliance, cause the other person to lose face, and weaken the relationship between the two of you. After all, you have won, and he or she has lost. Why take this chance when an alternative to you-messages, "I-messages," exists?

A properly constructed I-message consists of three parts:

- A nonblameful description of the other person's behavior that is interfering with your meeting your needs
- A tangible effect now or in the future that the behavior is having on you
- A feeling that tangible effect is causing you

Below are two situations in which, as a teacher, you might judge student behaviors to be unacceptable. Immediately following each situation is an I-message designed to confront the student, get him to change his behavior willingly, allow you both to save face, and to do as little damage as possible to the relationship.

Situation One: John, an eager third-grade student of yours, continually blurts out answers before being formally called upon. The effect of his behavior is that no one else has an opportunity to answer, and you are not sure the other students are following your lesson.

I-Message: "John, when you call out the answers before I have had a chance to call on other students, I am not sure the whole class knows the material. As a result, I may not be doing as good a job as your parents pay me to do."

Situation Two: Before leaving school, you rearrange the students' desks into a semicircle in preparation for a theater exercise you plan to do first thing the next morning. You write a note asking that the pattern of the desks be left untouched. The next day you come in only to find that the custodian has put the desks back into a straight-row pattern.

I-Message: "When you ignore my note asking that you leave the student desks in their semicircle pattern and place them back into straight rows, I must take time at the beginning of class to rearrange them. As a result, I feel really pressured by not having enough time adequately to present my theater exercise."

From the teacher's point of view it would be tempting to send a you-message such as, in the first example: "John, stop trying to show everyone how smart you are" (diagnosing); "John, a good little boy would raise his hand and wait to be called" (moralizing); or "If you blurt out the answer one more time without raising your hand, you are in real trouble" (threatening).

Each of the alternative I-messages contains the necessary three parts. In reference to John, who blurts out answers, the first sentence of the I-message points out the behavior that is interfering with the teacher's meeting his or her own needs and then describes the tangible effect the behavior is having on the teacher. The second sentence describes the teacher's feelings.

An I-message does not tell the student how to change his or her behavior. That is left up to the student. Further, an I-message does not say anything about the other person; it concentrates only upon the speaker. I-messages tell how "I" am being tangibly affected and how "I" feel. Unlike you-messages, in which the other person is likely to dig in his or her heels and resist or fight back, I-messages are received differently. It is hard for the other person to get defensive when the focus of the I-message is not on him or her. An I-message conveys, as does active listening, a trust in the other person. It says that our relationship is strong enough that if I tell you that what you are doing interferes with my meeting my needs, you will probably volunteer to alter your behavior.

Gordon's three-component confrontation model consistently shows positive results (Watson & Remer, 1984) when compared to messages consisting of just one (behavior, tangible effect, or feeling) or two (behavior and tangible effect, behavior and feeling, or tangible effect and feeling) components. The evidence is convincing for using the complete, three-component I-message to resolve interpersonal conflicts.

On the outside chance that the other person will get defensive when you send an I-message, you have a skill to help handle the problem the student feels he or she has: active listening. After using active listening to defuse the student's defensive feelings, you would once again present your I-message.

No doubt some teachers are skeptical about exposing their feelings so openly to a student. I-messages require a teacher to be honest with students and acknowledge that they have the power through their behaviors to interfere with teachers meeting their own needs. This is the "tangible effect" portion of the message. When one adds admitting true human feelings such as fear, discouragement, frustration, or vulnerability—the "feelings" portion of the message—sending an I-message may take more courage and trust than teachers possess. To these doubters I respond by saying that there is one other very strong reason why I-messages work so well. If, as a teacher, parent, boss, spouse, or good friend, you have helped others by active listening when they had problems, they will be looking for opportunities to reciprocate—to pay you back. They will want to help you as they feel you have helped them. Your I-message gives others the opportunity to respond by altering their behavior so that you may get your needs met.

I-messages work on the assumption that you and the other person have an ongoing relationship. It is one that has basically been beneficial to both of you. Teachers need students, and students need teachers. Further, it is assumed that as a teacher you probably have had opportunities to use active listening with one or more of the students to whom you are sending your I-message. Thus, they have a reason to reciprocate your earlier helping behaviors. Remember that the alternative to an I-message is a finger-shaking you-message. Often the other person will say, "Gee, I'm sorry. I didn't realize that it was affecting you. How about if I . . . "

Most people use I-messages with others who possess equal power, realizing that they are not in a position to enforce the demands of a you-message. Almost by default and, perhaps somewhat reluctantly, I-messages are used when you-messages are perceived to be ineffective. Gordon suggests that we not wait until we have no choice but to use I-messages. I agree.

DIFFERENCES BETWEEN A CANTER AND A GORDON I-MESSAGE

At this point you may wish to review chapter 3 on Assertive Discipline in order to determine how the Canters' version of an I-message differs from Gordon's. To help make this contrast clearer, the design of both I-messages are shown below. The first one is a Canter-type I-message; the second one is a Gordon-type I-message. Can you spot the fundamental differences in the two messages? Do you understand how these fundamental differences clearly reveal the contrasting philosophical positions held by the Canters and by Gordon?

A Canter I-Message

- I feel (name the feeling) . . .
- When you (state the problem) . . .
- I would like (say what you want to happen to make things better) . . .

A Gordon I-Message

- When you do (nonblameful description of other's behavior) such and such . . .
- The tangible effect on me (now or in the future) is . . .
- That makes me feel (name the feeling) . . .

A Canter-type I-message tells the other person exactly how he or she is supposed to change—supposed to mend his or her ways. It is, I suppose, assumed that the other person is too insensitive or too uncaring to voluntarily respond in a way that would make your life better. Thus, you must tell them how to change. A Gordon-type I-message never tells the other person how to change. Instead, the message leaves it up to the other person to decide voluntarily how to respond in order to make your life better.

A Canter I-message carries with it an air of enforcement—change in the way I tell you to change—"Here is exactly how I want you to change your behavior!" The threat, "Change your behavior or else," is implied. A Gordon I-message carries with it an air of trust and mutual respect—"I trust that if I share with you how your behavior is interfering with my meeting my needs, you will respect me enough to voluntarily change that behavior."

CONFLICT RESOLUTION

There are times, as shown in Gordon's T.E.T. rectangle, when your aim is not simply to facilitate others meeting their needs or your meeting your needs. Instead, a skill is required to resolve a conflict of needs. In a more power-based model, the conflict would be resolved in either a win-lose (method l) or lose-win (method 2) fashion. Resolutions in which either party "wins all" are not considered acceptable. Why? Philosophically, such a resolution is inconsistent with a noninterventionist's beliefs. Practically, such a resolution harms the ongoing relationship—it causes resentment. After all, who likes to be around someone who always wins at your expense?

Gordon offers an alternative, no-lose, win-win, "conflict resolution" skill referred to as "method 3"—a skill that does not endorse compromise. In compromise, both parties lose! Therefore, they play a game of sorts whereby they demand more than they know they will receive in the hopes that compromise will get them what they really wanted in the first place. A lack of trust exists between the two conflicting parties. It does not have to be that way.

Gordon's conflict resolution consists of six steps:

1. Define the problem. Using active listening to help determine the other person's needs and I-messages to convey your needs; define the problem in terms of those needs, not in terms of conflicting solutions.
2. Generate possible solutions. This is also known as brainstorming. When quantity is sought, quality will emerge. Now that the problem has been defined in terms of needs, not conflicting solutions, both parties are free to be creative in generating solutions. Write down these solutions. No evaluation is done in this step.
3. Evaluate solutions. Both parties evaluate the solutions with an eye to whether or not the solution(s) will meet their needs. Discard solutions that do not

meet one's needs. The odds are, if step two was done well, one or more solutions will survive that are deemed to meet both people's needs. Hence, no compromise!

4. Choose a solution. Examine surviving solutions for their workability. Choose one "best" solution. Avoid voting; seek consensus. Clarify for all concerned parties exactly what the agreed-upon solution is.

5. Implement the solution. Agree upon who is to do what, when, and how well. Remember that both parties now are motivated to make this solution work because they see it as a means of getting their needs met. Approach parties not living up to their part of the bargain with an I-message, not punishment. No nagging is permitted.

6. Evaluate the solution. Build in an agreed-upon "check-back" time to determine if the solution works. If it does, great. If the solution proves to be unsatisfactory, review previous steps to identify the breakdown. If all else fails, you still have other solutions that survived your step three.

Conflicts resolved using method 3 stay solved. Further, because the conflict is resolved in a manner that meets both person's needs, the ongoing relationship is strengthened, setting the basis for resolving future conflicts of needs more easily. It worked once, and both came out winners. Who would not want to use this mutually acceptable conflict resolution process with future conflicts?

DON'T KEEP T.E.T. A SECRET

Tell your students that you value your relationship with them and, as a result, have decided to use some skills that should enhance that relationship. Explain at an appropriate level for the audience (for instance, elementary or high school) the philosophy behind Gordon's model—trust and faith in the other person. Explain the fundamentals of active listening and I-messages. Acknowledge that you may sound a little phony when you first practice these skills, but because of the value you place on strengthening your relationship, you feel it is worth it. Gordon's Teacher Effectiveness Training model and the skills contained within it work best when both parties are informed. In this way, no one feels that something is being used on them.

A significant side benefit of using the T.E.T. skills with others is that, through modeling, they too may start to use it as their vehicle for problem solving. Just imagine the decrease in discipline problems in schools if students were to use active listening and I-messages on one another. It is a fact that students are going to confront one another, with or without the knowledge of Gordon's communication model—for that matter, so are teachers and administrators. The alternative of an I-message is a less desirable and less effective power-based you-message. Combine the benefits of active listening and I-messages to bring about a win-win solution using Gordon's conflict resolution steps. Conflicts solved this way stay solved!

Do active listening and I-messages work all the time? Does method 3 guarantee results every time? The answer is definitely "No!" Human interaction is not an exact science. We are playing the odds, looking for those skills that work with most people in most situations most of the time. Active listening works better than roadblocks to communication. I-messages work better than you-messages. Method 3 works better than a win-lose or lose-win method of resolving conflicts of needs. Gordon's skills help keep the lines of communication open between a teacher and a student or, for that matter, between any two people.

Having once taught physics and mathematics at the high school level, I thought my greatest achievement as a teacher would be to have graduated students knowledgeable of such material as Newton's laws and quadratic equations. In hindsight, although subject-specific information is certainly important, if I had to choose with what knowledge and skills students left school, I would choose communication skills. Such skills promote the most effective discipline—self-discipline—in school as well as in society. Until something better comes along, the communication model I would use would be Gordon's.

Are you interested in Gordon's model? Are you ready to try some of his techniques? If you are, be sure first to consult one of his original sources, in particular *T.E.T.: Teacher Effectiveness Training* (1974). What has been presented in this chapter, or any other single chapter, is not enough for you to run out, start using the abbreviated knowledge and skills, and expect to get results. There is no substitute for the original. Learn more about what teachers can do when students own problems, what teachers can do when they own problems, the many uses for active listening, modifying the environment, the no-lose method of resolving conflicts, and what to do when values collide. Buy his books, borrow his books, read his books!

SELECTED RESEARCH ON GORDON'S TEACHER EFFECTIVENESS TRAINING MODEL

Gordon's Teacher Effectiveness Training model has been the focus of much research—master's theses, doctoral dissertations, and journal articles. A search of any academic library will reveal such sources, some by Gordon, others written about his model. A number of these sources are listed below. Note the wide variety of citations.

Bear, G. C. (1983). Usefulness of Y.E.T. and Kohlberg's approach to guidance. *Elementary School Guidance and Counseling, 17*(3):221–225.

Examines the usefulness of these two models of effective, or values, education and concludes that gains in self-esteem are higher among the Effectiveness Training participants.

Chanow-Gruen, K. J., & Doyle, R. (1983). The counselor's consultative role with teachers, using the T.E.T. model. *Humanistic Education and Development, 22*(1):16–24.

Concludes that T.E.T., a program specifically designed to enhance communication, human relationships, and conflict resolution, has much to offer.

Cornell, A. W. (1993). Turning abstractions into teachable skills. *Perspective,* May/June:26–27.

An interview with Thomas Gordon that concentrates upon his graduate experiences with Carl Rogers, the continuing impact the experiences have had on his thinking, and the ongoing development of the Effectiveness Training model.

Dembo, M. H., Sweitzer, M., & Lauritzen, P. (1985). An evaluation of group parent education: Behavioral, P.E.T., and Adlerian programs. *Review of Educational Research, 55*(2):155–200.

Presents an extensive review of three group parent education programs, each of which has application to educational settings.

Gaskins, I. (1988). Teaching as parenting, or "more die of heartbreak." *Freshman English News, 16*(3):16–19.

Suggests that good teaching, like good parenting, allows students to take responsibility for their own problems—behavioral and academic.

Gordon, T. (1988). The case against disciplining children at home or in school. *Person-Centered Review, 3*(1):59–85.

Examines and evaluates the commonly held belief that kids must be controlled by parents and teachers. Documents that punishment and reward are hazardous to the mental and physical good health of children.

Gordon, T. (1981). Crippling our children with discipline. *Journal of Education, 163*(3):228–243.

Describes a democratic and egalitarian parenting model that is seen as an alternative to adult, power-based control of children.

Gordon, T. (1981). Problem solving: How to help others do their own. *Nursing Life*, *1*(1):57–64.

Presents active listening as a more effective way to eliminate roadblocks to communication. Incorporates examples from the health field. Content applicable to all audiences.

Gordon, T. (1981). Problem solving: When you need to confront other people. *Nursing Life*, *1*(2):57–63.

Argues that you can get people who cause you problems to solve them through a no-lose method of conflict resolution. Content applicable to all audiences.

LEARNING MORE ABOUT GORDON'S TEACHER EFFECTIVENESS TRAINING MODEL

- To learn more about Thomas Gordon and his ideas on classroom (as well as home) management, contact:

  Effectiveness Training Inc.
  531 Stevens Avenue
  Solana Beach, CA 92075–2093
  Phone: (619) 481–8121

  Note: Although the California office of Effectiveness Training no longer delivers T.E.T. workshops, this training can be obtained through an organization called Teacher Education Institute, Winter Park, FL (1–800–336–2208). Finally, of note is the fact that C. M. Charles, a noted author in the area of classroom management, has finally decided to include Gordon's Effectiveness Training model in the most recent edition of his discipline book. One can only wonder why it took so long for him to do so!!

- Search one or more of the many Internet web sites using "Thomas Gordon," "active listening," "I-messages," "conflict resolution," and "values clarification," among other terms, as keywords.

TEST YOURSELF

This is a sampling of the kinds of factual and open-ended questions that you should be able to answer after having read this chapter.

1. How would you classify Gordon's views according to the four theoretical frameworks presented in chapter 2?
2. Give the title of two of Gordon's books that outline his views on how to dis-

cipline children whether at home or in school.

3. What special relationship did Gordon have with Carl R. Rogers and how did it ultimately affect the design of his Effectiveness Training model?

4. Why is it important for a teacher to determine who owns the problem before he or she decides upon a course of action?

5. Define the terms "acceptable" and "unacceptable" as presented by Gordon and contrast them with their more traditional definitions.

6. Of all the areas in a Gordon Effectiveness Training rectangle, which one does Gordon want to increase in area? Why?

7. Identify four of Gordon's more surprising roadblocks to communication *and* then explain why they are roadblocks.

8. Identify three alternatives to roadblocks that are recommended by Gordon.

9. Define the Gordon-recommended skills of Active Listening and explain how they can help others who own a problem.

10. Identify the three parts of a properly stated I-message.

11. Create an "original" I-message and then defend how it should help get the desired results, help both parties save face, and do the least damage to the ongoing relationship.

12. Describe how the skills of Active Listening and I-messages are crucial to Gordon's Win/Win skill of Conflict Resolution.

13. Why is the term "compromise" an inappropriate description of what happens in Gordon's Conflict Resolution?

14. Do you see yourself using Gordon's Effectiveness Training model in your classroom? Why?

15. Do you see yourself using Gordon's Effectiveness Training model in your personal life? What results would you expect?

ASK YOURSELF: IS THIS MODEL FOR YOU?

Although you would want to defer making any final decision until you read still more, at this point what are your feelings toward Gordon's approach to discipline? What strengths and weaknesses do you see in his model? Does his approach to discipline reflect your fundamental views on how you believe people should be treated? Could you defend the use of this model to your students and their parents, to your colleagues, and to your administrators? Could you remain committed to his model—even when the going got tough? If you were to adopt his model, could you go to sleep at night and not feel that there simply has to be a better way to discipline? At this point, is Gordon's approach for you?

Figure 8.3
Choosing a Discipline Model that Is Right for You

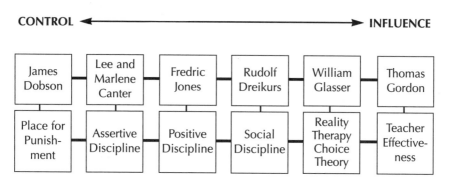

CONTROL ◄───► INFLUENCE

James Dobson	Lee and Marlene Canter	Fredric Jones	Rudolf Dreikurs	William Glasser	Thomas Gordon
Place for Punishment	Assertive Discipline	Positive Discipline	Social Discipline	Reality Therapy Choice Theory	Teacher Effectiveness

TIME TO CHOOSE ONE OF THE SIX "TRIED AND TRUE" DISCIPLINE MODELS

By this point in your reading and study you have been exposed to four theoretical frameworks (i.e., chapter 2) for use in evaluating the six tried and true discipline models presented in chapters 3 through 8. At the end of each of the six discipline model chapters—Dobson, Canters, Jones, Dreikurs, Glasser, and Gordon—you were asked whether the discipline model was one that you could enthusiastically adopt.

It probably would be a good idea to review the theoretical frameworks presented in chapter 2 before selecting a discipline model in which you will make a major investment of time, energy, and commitment (see Figure 8.3). Remember, some discipline models, those reflecting Skinner's beliefs, assume that the system is fine; it is the child that needs changing. Other discipline models, those reflecting Rogers' beliefs, assume that the curriculum and the child are okay; it is the system that needs changing. Unless you have the time and energy to learn more than one model well, which model do you think is best for you? Now is the time to choose!

PART III

THEORIES AND PRACTICES RELATING TO MORE EFFECTIVE CLASSROOM MANAGEMENT

The following chapters present articles on discipline-related topics that are often underrepresented, incorrectly presented, or overlooked completely in studies of classroom management. Chapter 9 summarizes the views of other recognized theorists who have something to say on the subject of discipline. Chapter 10 deals with what an educator can do to "prevent" problem behaviors. Chapter 11 presents some surprising, and perhaps controversial, ideas about discipline. Chapter 12 presents, in an "A through Z" format, brief teacher behaviors that address both prevention and correction of problem behaviors in the classroom. Chapter 13 discusses violence in schools' classrooms. The final chapter in this section, chapter 14, introduces Educational Resources Information Center (ERIC) as a vehicle for locating information on classroom management-related topics that address both prevention and correction of problem behaviors in the classroom.

Use these articles as a focus of discussion. Consider how the topics presented have been used on you in your present or past role as a student. Ponder how you can use these same topics in your current or future role as a teacher. Take nothing at face value. Investigate further the topics presented with an eye to collecting challenging or corroborating evidence.

CHAPTER 9
Other Noted Authors: What They Have to Say about Discipline

OBJECTIVES

This chapter will help you, among other things, to:

- Identify the works of discipline authors other than the "tried and true" authors presented in chapters 3 through 8.
- Pigeonhole the works of these authors into one or more of the "tried and true" discipline models presented in chapters 3 through 8.

The authors presented in chapters 3 through 8 represent major "tried and true" discipline models, in most cases complete with structure and strategies that have undergone the scrutiny of scholarly testing and can be traced back to one or more of the theoretical foundations presented in chapter 2. Each of these models has stood the test of time—two decades or more! But there are other noted authors who have written on the subject of discipline. A number of these authors and their views on classroom management are presented in this chapter.

As you read what these authors have to say, try to pigeonhole their approaches into one of the four theoretical frameworks presented in chapter 2. This should not be a difficult task. Also, try to determine which of the six "tried and true" models presented in chapters 3 through 8 would be best aligned with each author's approach. Once again, the task should not be difficult because most of these authors' approaches simply restate or repackage one of these "tried and true" discipline models. You especially will see the views of Dreikurs (i.e., as revealed in the work of Linda Albert and Jane Nelsen), Glasser, and Gordon seeping through in the approaches of these newer authors. Of note is the fact that not one of the authors in this chapter advocates the use of punishment as a classroom management tool.

If, after reading this chapter, your appetite has been whetted regarding one or more of these authors, you should read some of their original works (some are cited in this chapter) and, if you are still interested, consider attending a workshop on the author(s) of your choice.

Linda Albert: *Cooperative Discipline*

Stephen G. Barkley: *Project T.E.A.C.H.*

Richard Curwin and Allen Mendler: *Discipline with Dignity*

Forrest Gathercoal: *Judicious Discipline*

Haim G. Ginott: *Communication Discipline*

Herb Grossman: *Multicultural Discipline*

Madeline Hunter: *Enhancing Teaching (Preventative Discipline)*

Larry Koenig: *Smart Discipline*

Jacob S. Kounin: *Withitness* (and more) *Discipline*

Jane Nelsen: *Positive Discipline* (not the same as Jones' *Positive Discipline* model)

William A. Rogers (Australian author): *Decisive Discipline*

Michael Valentine: *A Family-Systems Approach Adapted to Schools*

Harry K. Wong: *The First Days of School*

LINDA ALBERT: *COOPERATIVE DISCIPLINE*

Linda Albert, Ph.D., has been a classroom teacher, college professor, educational consultant, syndicated columnist, and author of a number of books, a video series, and other publications on discipline in school and at home. As a former student of Rudolf Dreikurs, Albert draws heavily upon his work in the development of her Cooperative Discipline program. She has been providing courses on the Cooperative Discipline approach to discipline for more than two decades. Like Jane Nelsen (discussed later in this chapter), Albert has taken, as well as expanded, the ideas of Dreikurs and packaged them in a way that many educators and parents find both attractive and useful. Linda Albert may be contacted by e-mail at LindAlbert@aol.com.

Cooperative Discipline

Reflecting the fundamental beliefs of Dreikurs, Albert believes that students choose their own behaviors. She further believes that the long-term goal of student behavior is to overcome feelings of discouragement and to fulfill a basic human need to belong. She believes that students misbehave for a reason. They are trying to achieve one of four short-term goals—attention, power, revenge, and avoidance of failure. Unfortunately, when children seek these inappropriate short-term goals they can actually become *more* discouraged and *less* able to meet their need to belong. Hence, matters worsen. Cooperative Discipline instructs parents and teachers on how to recognize which short-term goal a child is seeking and then to influence the child's behavior in a positive manner.

As a comprehensive program, Cooperative Discipline deals with, among other topics, helping students satisfy their need to belong, addresses the importance of building a student's self-esteem, discusses three styles of classroom management, and stresses the importance of teachers forming Action Plans.

In order to experience a sense of belonging students must believe that they are *capable* of completing the tasks at hand, feel *connected* with teachers and peers, and know that they make some *contribution* to the group. Albert calls these the "Three Cs." Each of these "Cs" can be enhanced by teachers. They can, for instance, enhance a student's belief of being *capable* by "making mistakes okay," enhance a feeling of being *connected* by "offering acceptance" and "showing appreciation," and enhance a feeling of *making a contribution* by "working in teams" and designing opportunities for students to "interact with the class, school, and community." Once students feel that they belong, they are less likely to misbehave.

When it comes to building a student's self-esteem, the key word is encouragement! Of all the tools for building student self-esteem that we possess as teachers or parents, encouragement is the most powerful. Once again, the "Three Cs" come into play as pedagogical tools for teachers to use in encouraging students. Unlike the giving of rewards, where only a few are found deserving, encouragement is for everyone, all the time—students and teachers, alike.

Cooperative Discipline introduces three styles of classroom management—hands-off, hands-on, and hands-joined. Albert makes a strong case for the hands-joined style of management where students are respected, have a say in making decisions, and play a role in designing their own education. The end result, according to Albert, are students who behave more cooperatively.

As with all endeavors, the more effectively one plans the more one is likely to experience success. With Albert, this planning takes the form of a Written School Action Plan. The plan consists of a number of steps including pinpointing the student's behavior, identifying the student's goal of misbehavior (i.e., attention, power, revenge, avoidance of failure), choosing an appropriate teacher response for the moment, selecting encouragement techniques to help build student self-esteem for the future, involving students and parents, and monitoring the plan's progress.

To learn more about Linda Albert's ideas, read:

Albert, L. (1996a). *Cooperative discipline*. Circle Pines, MN: American Guidance Service.
Albert, L. (1996b). *A teacher's guide to cooperative discipline*. Circle Pines, MN: American Guidance Service.
Albert, L. (1989). *Cooperative discipline: How to manage your classroom and promote self-esteem*. Circle Pines, MN: American Guidance Service.

Note: American Guidance Service (AGS) is located at 4201 Woodland Road, Circle Pines, MN 55014–1796. Training in Cooperative Discipline is available by contacting the Cooperative Discipline Institute, 800–954–7704.

STEPHEN G. BARKLEY: *PROJECT T.E.A.C.H.*

Stephen G. Barkley is executive vice president of Performance Learning Systems. In addition to his administrative responsibilities at PLS, he has developed a series of videotapes around such themes as raising student expectations and live-event learning. Mr. Barkley can be contacted at Performance Learning Systems, Inc., 466 Old Hook Road, Suite 25–26, Emerson, NJ 07630. Phone: 800–526–4630.

Project T.E.A.C.H.

Classroom management involves knowing yourself and your students, your agenda and that of your students. Performance Learning Systems (PLS) program, Project T.E.A.C.H. examines the how and why of these ideas.

Knowing Your Students

Project T.E.A.C.H. training begins by presenting twelve verbal communication skills. The first set of skills—Open-ended Questions, Close-ended questions, Confirmatory and Leading Paraphrases—enhance a teacher's ability to engage students (parents and colleagues, too) in dialogues that aid in clarity and understanding. These skills help uncover the true agenda of those with whom you are working. Knowledge of a person's agenda helps you develop a better approach to problem solving that is acceptable to all. The verbal communications skills of Project T.E.A.C.H. aid in gaining student cooperation and producing long-term changes in behavior.

Letting Your Students Know That You Know Them (and have heard them)

Training in Positive Phrasing, Empathy, Support, and Approval Statements increases a teacher's ability to communicate concern and acceptance to students. Effective use of the skills, especially Empathy, Support, and Approval Statements, communicates the teacher's concern for student ideas, feelings, and actions. These skills are crucial in lowering resistance before considering problem solving options. These skills encourage students to act on their own best interests for change.

Knowing Yourself and Your Management Style

Teachers can be effective with a management style that ranges from highly autocratic to highly noninterventive. The key is to be consistent and congruent. Consistency builds trust and perceived fairness. Say what you will do—and then do it. Congruent body language and voice tone are crucial to any successful management style. Body language and voice tone must match skill use. A sarcastic remark made with a smile on your face is still a sarcastic remark and will be perceived as such by students.

After studying the Problem Solving Inquiry, Contingent Action Proposal, Disapproval and Authority Statements as problem-solving options, teachers in Project T.E.A.C.H. practice these skills in role plays with other course participants. Congruent body language and voice tone are essential to the effectiveness of these skills also.

Truly great teachers know themselves and their students so well that while maintaining a consistent and congruent management style for the most part, they are able to use a different style when necessary to help a student achieve some success. For example, they are able to shift from sharing the decision-making power to being directive as needed by individual students.

An Illustration. A teacher with a noninterventionist style is most comfortable encouraging students to define problems and explore possible options. However, when working with a student who is unable or unwilling to work in this way, the teacher might offer a Contingent Action Proposal with unequal options, such as "You could choose to refrain from disrupting the class or choose to report to the time-out room."

Communicating is key to developing effective classroom management, whatever the style. Listening is crucial—and verbal training improves listening. By being conscious of verbal options and choices, teachers are able to be reflective and to enhance the environment for themselves and their students.

To learn more about Project T.E.A.C.H., in particular, and Performance Learning Systems, in general, visit their web site at www.pls-ed.com, or read:

Hasenstab, J., & Wilson, C. (1989). *Training the teacher as a champion.* Nevada City, CA: Performance Learning Systems.
The Heart of Teaching (Newsletter). Nevada City, CA: Program Learning Systems.
Cake, F. S., & Vernetson, T. (1988). Project T.E.A.C.H. in Alachua Schools. *Florida ASCD Journal,* fall, 45–47.

RICHARD CURWIN AND ALLEN MENDLER: DISCIPLINE WITH DIGNITY

Dr. Allen N. Mendler is an educator, school psychologist, and nationally known seminar and workshop presenter on the subject of discipline and behavior management. Dr. Richard L. Curwin, too, is an educator, with teaching experience both in basic and higher education. Like Mendler, Curwin serves as a private consultant and seminar and workshop presenter. Together they have written a number of books, have authored individual as well as coauthored articles in professional journals, and have produced a series of staff development videotapes. They can be reached by mail at Discipline Associates, P.O. Box 20481, Rochester, NY 14602, and by phone at 800–772–5227. Their web site is www.disciplineassociates.com.

Discipline with Dignity

Although the ideas and strategies outlined in the book, *Discipline with Dignity* (1988), can work with all students, Curwin and Mendler's approach is especially useful for students who have lost all hope and who have given up on themselves. These students, usually only about 5 percent of the student body, end up consuming a significant amount of the teacher's classroom management time and energy. Note: Fredric Jones (i.e., *Positive Discipline*) identified approximately this same percentage of students whose chronic misbehavior makes life miserable for teachers.

Discipline with dignity helps educators develop a repertoire of preestablished consequences to apply when students ignore behaviors that they have agreed to in their social contracts. Punishment is not one of the consequences. Instead, measures designed to bolster student self-esteem and to hone social problem-solving skills and self-regulation are used. *Discipline with Dignity*, a responsibility and empowerment-based versus obedience-based discipline model, creates an atmosphere of democracy, encouragement, hope, and warmth where clearly defined limits (with student input) and skills in resolving conflicts are taught and applied.

Specifically, the model contains three hierarchical dimensions including *Prevention, Action,* and *Resolution*. Briefly, *Prevention* describes what teachers can do to prevent discipline problems from happening in the first place. The old adage, "An ounce of prevention is worth a pound of cure," was never more true. This dimension has seven stages including, among others, the all-important step of setting up a social contract with the class. A social contract is a mutually developed set of specific and clear rules and consequences that define acceptable and unacceptable behaviors in the classroom.

The *Action* dimension provides teachers with the knowledge and skills to stop misbehavior when it occurs. Sample skills include proximity control, tone of voice, and body language. Finally, the *Resolution* dimension equips teachers and students with the knowledge, skills, and confidence necessary to confront and negotiate with dignity resolutions to the behavior of continually misbehaving students.

Some guiding principles to applying discipline with dignity in the classroom include, among others, recognizing that:

- long-term behavior changes are more desirable than simply short-term fixes.
- teachers should stop doing ineffective things. Often this means stop using traditional carrot and stick, reward and punishment, techniques to which chronically misbehaving students have become immune.
- classroom rules must make sense to students in the here and now.
- teachers should model what they expect from students negating the usefulness and value of the oft-stated comment "Don't do as I do, do as I say (command)."
- at all times, even when in the act of disciplining, students should be treated with dignity! Without being treated with dignity, students may begin to think that it is preferable to misbehave than to be seen as stupid. No one, including students, wants to be embarrassed or seen as stupid and incapable, especially in public. Discipline *can*, and *should*, and *must*, be administered with dignity.

The consistent application of discipline with dignity can and does lead to increased mutual respect between student and teachers where power struggles can become a thing of the past.

To learn more about Curwin and Mendler's ideas, read:

Curwin, R., & Mendler, A. (1988). *Discipline with dignity*. Alexandria, VA: Association for Supervision and Curriculum Development.

Curwin, R., & Mendler, A. (1987). *Discipline with dignity: Resource handbook*. Bellevue, WA: Bureau of Education & Research.

Mendler, A., & Curwin, R. (1983). *Taking charge in the classroom*. Reston, VA: Reston Publishing.

FORREST GATHERCOAL: *JUDICIOUS DISCIPLINE*

Forrest Gathercoal is a professor in the School of Education at Oregon State University, Corvallis, Oregon. He has taught law courses for educators for more than twenty years. He also has taught educational psychology, conducted workshops on civil rights and student discipline, and served as a consultant to colleges and school districts across the country. Earlier in his career he taught elementary and secondary music and was a guidance counselor, high school coach, and vice principal. He can be contacted at 541–737–5982.

Judicious Discipline: Its Theory

An uncomplicated, yet workable, rule has evolved from the classrooms of successful teachers throughout our country. Simply stated: "You may do what you want in this classroom until it interferes with the rights of others." It is their way of acknowledging individual differences among their students while recognizing the need for an educational environment free from disruptive forces. Teachers taking this position and applying it in an evenhanded manner to student conduct are teaching and respecting their students' constitutional rights. At the same time, they are creating a classroom environment in which students are able to learn about their responsibilities to the other members of the class.

Judicious Discipline, fashioned upon this principle, creates an educational and ethical perspective for school management based on the Bill of Rights. Because students have Constitutional rights, our schools and classrooms today are microcosms of the United States. But having rights does not mean students have a license to do as they please. By teaching students their citizenship rights, providing them an opportunity to experience individual liberties, and helping them to understand the needs and demands of their social responsibilities, we are empowering students to govern and think for themselves. Educators have always believed teaching citizenship is an important aspect of their educational mission. *Judicious Discipline*, however, takes that belief one step further to acknowledge and respect students as citizens.

The Educational Aspect

One of our educational system's more glaring contradictions is the auto-cratic public school system we use as a model for teaching students to be responsible citizens in a democratic society. If classroom management in our schools parallels the autocratic environment of most American homes, it follows that parents and educators together may be preparing citizens who are unable to understand or function well in a participatory society. *Judicious Discipline*, on the other hand, uses our nation's justice model for an educational approach to student discipline and responsibility. As a result, students will not only be respected as citizens and learn to think for themselves within a democratic community, but they will have an opportunity to experience the joys and sorrows of being accountable for their own actions.

Often educators find themselves inventing an endless parade of rules hoping to create the illusion of being in control. But once a teacher's line is crossed, the illusion of being in control begins to unravel. Until students are allowed to experience a proprietary interest in rules and decisions, student control and a good learning environment will always be at risk.

Students who waver from democratically imposed boundaries need an educator nearby, not a parent substitute or a quasi-law-enforcement officer to pull them back into line. When a behavior problem does occur, it is an unswerving and dedicated educator who pauses to think—"What needs to be learned here?" Every student behavior problem then becomes an educational challenge. Educators must learn to approach discipline as professional educators by helping students learn and develop attitudes necessary to live productively and responsibly in a democratic setting.

Judicious Consequences

There are two aspects to judicious consequences. The first is that the consequences should be commensurate with the rule violation. The second is that they be compatible with the needs of the student and the school community. Commensurate denotes that the consequence is consistent with and flows logically from the student's misbehavior. The compatible aspect begins with identifying issues central to the educational and self-esteem needs of each student as well as the mission and ethical practices of professional educators.

If students know that consequences for their misconduct will be judicious in nature, as opposed to punishing, then consequences become akin to curricular issues. When students believe they are in the capable hands of professional educators, judicious consequences will be perceived by students as ways to make amends and get back on track. As this plateau of mutual trust and professional responsibility is achieved, good educational and ethical practices become the model for student discipline.

Classroom discipline is not a process isolated from other school activities, rather it is an integral part of the tenor and tone of each school. The current educational reforms, reflecting as they do a greater emphasis on democratic practices, provide logical support for discipline strategies based upon equity and fairness. Judicious discipline, described by William Glasser as "An excellent approach to discipline, one that fits with my concepts," offers educators a systematic framework that promotes and sustains democratic decision making while helping students learn the rights and responsibilities incumbent upon all citizens in our society.

To learn more about Forrest Gathercoal's ideas, read:

Gathercoal, F. (1997). *Judicious discipline.* 4th ed. San Francisco: Caddo Gap Press.
Gathercoal, F. (1996). *A judicious philosophy for school support personnel.* San Francisco: Caddo Gap Press.
McEwan, B. (1994). *Practicing judicious discipline.* San Francisco: Caddo Gap Press.

HAIM G. GINOTT: *COMMUNICATION DISCIPLINE*

Dr. Haim G. Ginott (deceased) was an educator whose ideas have permeated the American scene—both in the home and in the school. Ginott was a professor of psychology at Adelphi University and at New York University Graduate School.

Ginott and Other Rogerian-Oriented Authors

Ginott's ideas reflect, in fact may be the basis for, the work of today's contemporary Rogerian-oriented discipline authors. For instance, his advice not to ask "why?" mirrors the advice given by William Glasser. His suggestion that we use alternatives to praise reflects Rudolf Dreikurs' long-standing position on this topic. Ginott's emphasis upon listening, what he calls using a "healing dialogue," is similar to Thomas Gordon's facilitating skill of active listening.

His suggestion for how adults should handle anger, too, reflects Gordon's recommended confrontation skill of sending I-messages. Ginott's suggestions that teachers send sane messages (those that concentrate on the facts of situation), avoid using sarcasm, and avoid labeling students, as well as his concern that students and teachers, alike, save face in any and all confrontations, are characteristic of Rogerian-oriented discipline authors.

Ginott, as a humanist, endorses the use of congruent communication which, like Gordon's communication skills (Active Listening and I-messages), helps students to build a more positive self-esteem through recognizing the feelings they have about themselves, about others, and about the home, school, and community in which they exist. Ginott's communication between a teacher and child, particularly in a discipline situation, stresses the circumstances of the problem never the child's nature or personality.

The importance Ginott ascribes to the role of the teacher is highlighted dramatically in a sobering quote from his book, *Teacher and Child* (1971). It reads:

> I am the decisive element in the classroom. It is my personal approach that creates the climate. It is my daily mood that makes the weather. As a teacher, I possess tremendous power to make a child's life miserable or joyous. I can be a tool of torture or an instrument of inspiration. I can humiliate or humor, hurt or heal. In all of my situations it is my response that decides whether a crisis will be escalated or de-escalated, and a child humanized or dehumanized. (p. 13)

Ginott, like other Rogerian-oriented authors, not only champions the humanist's position but also challenges those who hold opposing views. For instance, where James Dobson says that if a child appears to be asking for punishment, give it to him, Ginott tells adults to help the child handle his/her guilt and anger, not comply with his request for punishment. Ginott's beliefs regarding how parents and teachers can effectively discipline children are timeless. His ideas, though appearing dated, seem to have no expiration date.

To learn more about Haim G. Ginott's ideas, read:

Ginott, H. G. (1965). *Between parent and child*. New York: Avon.
Ginott, H. G. (1969). *Between parent and teenager*. New York: Macmillan.
Ginott, H. G. (1971). *Teacher and child*. New York: Macmillan.

HERB GROSSMAN: *MULTICULTURAL DISCIPLINE*

Until his retirement, Dr. Grossman taught courses in classroom management in the education and special education departments at San Jose State University, San Jose, California. He also directed the bilingual/cross-cultural special education program at the same institution.

Introduction

The population of the United States is rapidly becoming less EuroAmerican. By the year 2000, non-EuroAmericans are expected to compose one-third of the U.S. population and well over one-third of the student population. Currently, non-EuroAmericans are in the majority in the twenty-five largest school districts in the United States. The three fastest growing groups are Hispanics, African Americans, and Southeast Asians. As a result, fewer students will fit the stereotype of EuroAmerican middle-class students and fewer students will respond positively to and profit from classroom management techniques that have been designed with EuroAmerican middle-class students in mind.

Culturally Inappropriate Classroom Management

Many classroom management techniques that work with EuroAmerican middle-class students are less effective and often ineffective with students who have been brought up by adults who have used different management techniques with them. To avoid the problems created by using culturally inappropriate management approaches, teachers require cultural sensitivity, cultural literacy and, in some cases, attitudinal/behavioral change. To be culturally sensitive is to be aware of the ways in which cultures differ and the effects of these differences. Among these effects are the general problems culturally diverse students experience in school because of their cultural differences, how cultural differences may cause students to behave in ways that are acceptable in their cultures but not in school, and how these differences may lead students to react in unanticipated ways to behavior management techniques.

To be culturally literate is to have a detailed knowledge of the cultural characteristics of specific ethnic and socioeconomic groups. Being sensitive to cultural differences in general is not sufficient. In order to adapt their management techniques to the specific cultural characteristics of their students, educators also need to have an in-depth knowledge of the specific cultures that are represented in their classes. This knowledge is not merely about holidays, food, dances, music, and so forth. It includes values, behavioral norms, acceptable and effective reinforcements, patterns of interpersonal relationships, and so on. The following are only a few of the many characteristics that educators need to consider when choosing which management techniques to use with students from different ethnic or socioeconomic backgrounds.

- Whether they work and learn better individually or in groups
- Whether they think their individual desires and goals are most important or that they should usually submit to the will and welfare of the group
- Whether they function better under cooperative or competitive situations
- Whether they are indifferent or responsive to praise and criticism from others
- Whether they respond better to impersonal rewards like toys, candy, time off, or personal rewards such as praise, smiles, and pats on the back
- Whether they are present- or future-time oriented
- Whether they prefer formal or informal relationships with adults

Cultural literacy can help educators avoid many types of classroom management problems. Uninformed teachers may misunderstand students' behavior and try to solve problems that do not exist. For example, they may think that students brought up to not be assertive or to volunteer their opinions unless encouraged to do so by adults are insecure or lacking in self-confidence and try to remediate their "problems." They may also fail to notice problems that do exist. Teachers who are not tuned in to the nonverbal ways students from different cultures communicate may miss a request for help or a signal of distress from students who communicate their needs in subtle and indirect ways. And they may use culturally ineffective techniques to deal with problems. This can occur if they use individual rewards to motivate a student who identifies with the group and is uncomfortable with individualistic approaches. It can also happen when the use of negative reinforcements such as public reprimands, writing student's names on the board, and so on, backfire because they cause students greater loss of face than they are able to tolerate.

Teachers who do not agree that they need to be culturally literate when working with a group of ethnically and socioeconomically diverse students will have to change their attitudes about how to deal with the diversity among their students. And those who agree that culturally appropriate management techniques are important, but are reluctant to use them because of the many community and administrative pressures not to do so, will have to find the courage and commitment to do what they know is best for a diverse student population.

Disempowering Classroom Management

Students who are empowered by their teachers are helped to believe they can achieve because students themselves have the power to shape their destinies and futures. Those who are disempowered come to believe they lack the ability or potential to accomplish their own goals or those that are shared by most members of their group. Deprecating students' backgrounds and treating them prejudicially has a harmful effect on their self-concepts and sense of power.

To empower students, teachers should demonstrate their conviction that students can and will succeed. Teachers should avoid emphasizing teacher-management techniques over self-management techniques that can lead students to believe that they are unable to manage themselves. The elimination of teacher prejudices, including those based upon a student's culture, is one of the most important steps educators can take to reduce disciplinary problems with minority students.

To learn more about Herbert Grossman's ideas, read:

Grossman, H. (1995). *Classroom behavior management in a diverse society.* Mountain View, CA: Mayfield.
Grossman, H. (1991). Trouble-free teaching: Solutions to behavior problems in the classroom. *Adolescence, 26*(102):495–496.
Grossman, H. (1990). *Trouble-free teaching: Solutions to behavior problems in the classroom.* Mountain View, CA: Mayfield.
Grossman, H. (1984). *Educating Hispanic students: Cultural implications for instruction, classroom management, counseling and assessment.* Springfield, IL: Thomas.

MADELINE HUNTER: *ENHANCING TEACHING (PREVENTATIVE DISCIPLINE)*

Dr. Madeline Hunter (deceased) was an educator whose ideas have permeated the American educational scene from pre-school to university classrooms. She was the principal of the elementary lab school at the University of California at Los Angeles and, most recently, professor in administration and teacher education at the UCLA graduate school of education. She was widely sought as consultant and keynote speaker.

A Hunter Lesson: Preventative Discipline

Madeline Hunter's ideas relate more to the elements of presenting an effective classroom lesson than they do to directly establishing and maintaining good classroom discipline. Yet, as most experienced teachers will tell you, presenting an effective lesson goes a long way toward thwarting potential discipline problems. An effectively presented lesson is one of many measures teachers can take to *prevent* problem behaviors.

In order to "do a Madeline Hunter lesson," teachers have to include a number of specific steps that enable them to make deliberate and appropriate decisions based upon the best psychological research available. Thus, a teacher is cast in the role of a *professional* decision maker—one who makes decisions by turning to a recognized body of pedagogical knowledge. Included in a Hunter lesson are, among other steps:

- establishing an anticipatory set
- defending why the objective(s) is important
- teaching the lesson's main concepts
- checking students' understanding
- providing guided and independent practice

For successful teachers, a Hunter-type lesson offers little that is new or unique. These teachers have been doing these steps intuitively. But, intuition, alone, is insufficient as a widespread basis for *professional* decision makers. Instead, Hunter helps teachers see the psychological basis, the pedagogical logic, and the educational justification behind each of her recommended steps. Thus, teachers become and, more important, feel confident in what they are doing and ready and able to explain why they are doing what they are doing. Further, the steps in a Hunter-type lesson provide the basis for successful *mentoring* or *coaching* of new and/or less experienced teachers by administrators, supervisors, and more experienced colleagues.

The very structure recommended by Hunter that so many teachers have come to depend upon, on occasion, has come under challenge. Some educators see a Hunter-type approach as too rigid, too mechanical, and, often, too mandated. Hunter responds by defending what she calls a "professional researched-based" approach to teaching rather than the more common "trial and error" approach practiced by too many teachers. Further, she claims that there really is no such thing a Hunter-type lesson, adding that even within the steps dictated, not by her, but by researched-based pedagogy, there is a good bit of teacher flexibility.

Although Hunter's recommendation that teachers apply sound psychological principles of learning when creating lessons helps, in itself, to prevent behavior problems, other Hunter ideas more directly address the subject of discipline. For instance, in an article titled "Do your words get them to think?" (1985), Hunter and coauthor Bailis identify a number of classroom situations where the way a teacher responds can contribute to student *think stoppers* or *think starters*.

Think stoppers are direct commands issued by the teacher. They place all of the responsibility upon the teacher's shoulders for eliciting a specific (i.e., the teacher's) response from the student. *Think stoppers* are a form of discipline where little or no potential for the development of student self-control exists. Usually it results in a teacher-student test of wills.

Think starters, on the other hand, "not only encourage a student to think but indicate that you *expect* him to think and make decisions" (Bailis & Hunter, p. 43). As an example, the authors offer the classroom situation where one student is making disruptive noises while another student is trying to speak. A *think stopper* teacher response might be "Be quiet!" A *think starter* teacher response might be "Peggy, find a place where you can do a good job of listening. Thanks."

To learn more about Madeline Hunter's ideas, read:

Bailis, P., & Hunter, M. (1985). Do your words get them to think? *Learning, 14*(1):43.

Brandt, R. (1985). On teaching and supervising: A conversation with Madeline Hunter. *Educational Leadership, 42*(5):61–66.

Hunter, M. (1994). *Mastery teaching.* Thousand Oaks, CA: Corwin Press.

Slavin, R., & Hunter, M. (1987). The Hunterization of America's schools. *Instructor, 96*(8):56–58, 60.

LARRY KOENIG: *SMART DISCIPLINE*

Dr. Larry Koenig founded the Up with Youth Company in 1985, an organization devoted to enhancing the self-esteem in young people. He is recognized as an effective public speaker and humorist, and regularly delivers workshops throughout the country. Dr. Koenig has authored several books including *Smart Discipline: A Workbook for Parents* and *Smart Discipline for the Classroom*. PBS aired a two-part series on Smart Discipline in the fall of 1995. Dr. Koenig can be contacted at 800–255–3008 or at his web site: www.smartdiscipline.com.

Smart Discipline for the Classroom

The purpose of the Smart Discipline system is to assist teachers in developing a personal plan of action to handle discipline problems in the classroom. Because of the excess of misbehaviors in today's classrooms, not having an effective discipline plan will thwart an instructor's goal of teaching. If you are a teacher, this needs no further explanation.

Back in the dark ages of the fifties and sixties, all a teacher needed to be effective was a good lesson plan. Things have changed. In the nineties (and beyond), that's not enough. Now, a plan for handling student behavior is just as necessary. And, it must, among other things, be one that:

- identifies disruptive behaviors and their causes,
- addresses drawbacks to using traditional approaches,
- provides prevention strategies,
- offers intervention strategies,
- permits customizing by individual teachers, and
- is quick and easy to use.

Smart Discipline encompasses these goals. Also, you will find Smart Discipline adaptable to the different needs and personalities of children. More importantly, the system provides for "Plan A" and "Plan B" strategies that are progressive and always provide a "next step."

Plan A strategies take seconds to implement. They are quick and easy methods to both strengthen a teacher-student relationship and gain immediate cooperation.

Plan B strategies take more time to implement but are designed to turn around the attitudes and behaviors of specific children. Most frequently, they will be used when Plan A methods have not produced satisfactory results.

All of the strategies in Smart Discipline are presented in a logical progression. However, that does not mean that they have to be used that way—quite the opposite. Smart Discipline is designed with flexibility in mind. It is meant for you to pick and choose methods according to what "fits for you" in a given situation with a particular child.

To learn more about Larry Koenig's ideas, read:

Koenig, L. (1994). *Smart discipline for the classroom.* Baton Rouge, LA: Koenig and Associates.

Koenig, L. (1988). *Smart discipline: A workbook for parents.* Baton Rouge, LA: Koenig and Associates.

JACOB S. KOUNIN: *WITHITNESS* (AND MORE) *DISCIPLINE*

Jacob S. Kounin, until his death in 1995, was professor emeritus at Wayne State University. While there, he served in the Department of Education: Theoretical and Behavioral Foundations/Instructional Programs. Dr. Kounin's observations of classrooms resulted in his creation of a series of labels (i.e., withitness) to describe effective and ineffective teacher actions that related to classroom control. His work has repeatedly been cited in discipline-related publications.

Withitness and Overlapping

Who doesn't want to be "with it"? What I am referring to here is not wearing trendy clothes or having fashionable hair styles, reading the latest bestsellers, or using up-to-date slang. Kounin (1977) defines withitness as the teacher's demonstrating that he or she knows what is going on in the classroom. Nothing (or little) seems to get by a with-it teacher. With-it teachers seem to have eyes in the back of their head. No one can pull the wool over their eyes—don't even bother trying. The student's perception is that a with-it teacher will catch you and will deal with you!

With respect to classroom management, teachers with withitness demonstrate proper target identification and timing when supplying desists, procedures designed to stop behavior. Target identification refers to catching the correct culprit, disciplining the right misbehaving child. If more than one child is misbehaving or if onlookers and imitators have appeared, the withitness teacher singles out the central figure, the instigator. Identifying the wrong student and, even worse, punishing the wrong student seriously undermine one's effectiveness and credibility as a disciplinarian. Teachers who are able to clearly identify appropriate offenders, while at the same time avoiding involving innocent bystanders, are preferred by students (Lewis & Lovegrove, 1984). Although mistaken identifications may be defended as one of those great lessons in life (the world is not perfect), few children appreciate this message. They see the situation, and you, as unaware and unfair.

With-it teachers also demonstrate proper timing. They execute their classroom management strategy before the deviant behavior spreads and increases in seriousness. A simple kitchen fire extinguisher can, if used early enough, stop a catastrophic fire. Yet, if one waits too long to intervene, that same simple fire extinguisher will be useless. It is no different in classroom management.

Although it may take a little time and energy to establish one's self as possessing withitness, that reputation can go a long way toward discouraging discipline problems from occurring. The payoff is more time and energy left to teach and for children to learn.

The ability to handle two or more situations at the same time constitutes what Kounin calls "overlapping." Any seasoned teacher knows that this skill needs to be developed, and developed early, or events can get out of hand leading to possible discipline problems. No teacher can afford the luxury of becoming immersed in just one issue, problem, or event at a time. Events don't occur just one at a time, therefore, they can't always be handled just one at a time.

Movement Management

Classrooms are filled with instructional and procedural activities that must be initiated, sustained, and terminated. These activities need to be managed. More effective teachers avoid movement mistakes including, what Kounin calls, "smoothness" and "momentum." Smoothness, or lack of jerkiness, refers to the teacher's ability to stay on track with a lesson and avoid tangents and digressions. Momentum refers to a teacher's ability to initiate and sustain the activity flow in a classroom so as to maximize work involvement and to minimize deviant behaviors.

More effective teachers control the momentum, or rate of flow of activities in the classroom. They avoid slowdowns such as overdwelling, in which a teacher continues to pay attention to a misbehavior even after it has ceased. Kounin calls this a teacher's "nag quotient." Another example of overdwelling is overelaborating on tasks and topics beyond that needed for student comprehension. Kounin calls this the teacher's "yack quotient." Another example of momentum is called fragmentation. Fragmentation occurs when a teacher asks individual students to complete tasks that more easily could be completed by the whole group.

Maintaining Group Focus

Maintaining a group's focus involves "group alerting" and "accountability." Group alerting refers to the degree to which a teacher can get nonreciting children's attention and get them engaged in recitation. For instance, teachers could create a bit of suspense before calling on a specific student, ranging from the nature of the question itself to pausing before a student is randomly called on in order to "keep all students on their toes."

Accountability refers to the teacher's monitoring students' task performance so as to communicate that he or she knows what students are doing and what they are accomplishing.

To learn more about Jacob Kounin's ideas, read:

Kounin, J. S. (1970). Observing and delineating technique of managing behavior in classrooms. *Journal of Research and Development in Education*, 4(1):62–72.

Kounin, J. S. (1977). *Discipline and group management in classrooms*. New
     York: Holt, Rinehart & Winston.
Kounin, J. S. (1983). *Classrooms: Individuals or behavior settings? Monographs
     in teaching and learning*. Bloomington: Indiana University.

JANE NELSEN: *POSITIVE DISCIPLINE* (NOT THE SAME AS JONES' *POSITIVE DISCIPLINE* MODEL)

Jane Nelsen is a licensed marriage, family, and child counselor with
a doctorate in educational psychology from the University of San
Francisco. She has authored and/or coauthored at least eleven books
and has produced audio soundtracks and videotapes describing the
ideas behind Positive Discipline. She regularly delivers workshops for
parents and teachers. Dr. Nelson can be contacted at 800–879–0812.
Her books and other materials can be obtained by contacting most
local bookstores or by calling Empowering People (P.O. Box 1926,
Orem, UT 84059) 800–456–7770.

Positive Discipline

For Nelsen it is important that parents and teachers understand why children do not behave the way they used to, and why both controlling and
overpermissive discipline styles are ineffective. Her ideas might best be summarized by reviewing some of the guidelines for discipline presented in her
book, *Positive Discipline*. First and foremost, she believes that misbehaving
children are "discouraged children" who have mistaken ideas on how to
achieve their primary goal—to belong. Their mistaken ideas lead them to
misbehave. We cannot be effective in helping students to stop their misbehavior unless we address their mistaken beliefs.

If, as the reader, you have read the early chapter devoted to Rudolf
Dreikurs and his Social Discipline model, you must recognize the fundamentals of Dreikurs' ideas underlying what Nelsen has to say. Note Nelsen's
emphasis upon the root of misbehavior—children feeling "discouraged."
These are words right from Dreikurs. Where does that discouragement come
from? Dreikurs says, and Nelson backs up, that discouragement comes from
a child's belief that he or she does not belong. Given that the need to belong
is a basic human need, children have little choice but to engage in actions,
even misbehaviors, that they believe will help them meet this unmet need.

One of Nelsen's earliest chapters in her book is titled "Four Mistaken
Goals of Behavior." Like Dreikurs, Nelsen helps the reader to identify each
mistaken goal, to resist reacting in a traditional (i.e., ineffective) manner, and
to respond in a more appropriate (i.e., more effective) way.

Nelsen believes that punishment may "work" if all you, as a teacher, are interested in is stopping the misbehavior momentarily. She asks whether punishers are aware that the long-range results from punishment often are Resentment, Rebellion, Revenge, or Retreat. She asks the reader to get rid of the crazy idea that in order to make children do better, first you have to make them feel worse. Note that Dreikurs, too, would avoid the use of punishment.

If punishment is not the consequence of choice, what does Nelsen recommend? Knowing that her work flows from the fundamental beliefs of Rudolf Dreikurs and Alfred Adler helps the reader to answer this question. Jane Nelsen would use logical consequences instead of punishment and would make sure that these consequences are Related, Respectful, and Reasonable. While we are using all of these R words, Nelsen suggests that we teach children that mistakes (i.e., misbehaviors) are wonderful opportunities to learn. How does she suggest we do this? She teaches the use of the Three R's of Recovery after one has made a mistake. These include, Recognize your mistake with good feelings; Reconcile the fact that "I didn't like the way I handled that"; and Resolve to focus upon solutions rather than blame or excuses.

Finally, the longest chapter in her book, *Positive Discipline*, is titled "Using Encouragement Effectively." As the reader knows from his or her earlier study of Dreikurs, encouraging children (as opposed to praising them) is the most important skill parents and teachers can learn in helping children. Nelsen quotes Dreikurs as saying that "Children need encouragement, just as plants need water. They cannot survive without it" (*Positive Discipline*, 1987, p. 88). Elements of encouragement include, among others, winning (not demanding) cooperation, mutual respect (another R word), improvement (not perfection), redirecting misbehavior, and avoiding criticism (even "constructive" criticism).

To learn more about Jane Nelsen's ideas, read:

Nelsen, J., Lott, L., & Glenn, H. S. (1997). *Positive discipline in the classroom*. Rocklin, CA: Prima.

Nelsen, J. (1996). *Positive discipline*. New York: Ballantine.

Nelscn, J., Dufy, R., Escobar, L., Ortolano, K., & Owen-Sohocki, R. (1996). *Positive discipline: A teacher's A-Z guide*. Orem, UT: Empowering People.

Nelsen, J., & Glenn, H. S. (1992). *Time out: Abuses and effective uses*. Orem, UT: Empowering People.

WILLIAM A. ROGERS (AUSTRALIAN AUTHOR): *DECISIVE DISCIPLINE*

William A. Rogers (BTh [Hons], Dip Min, Dip Teach, Bed and MEd [Melbourne]), an Australian educator, lectures widely in Australia and in other countries on topics involving discipline, classroom management, and peer-support programs for teachers. Rogers has worked in the United Kingdom as a consultant to the Elton Report, *Discipline in Schools: Report of the Committee of Enquiry* (1989) and made many additional visits to the United Kingdom since. He has written a number of articles and books and has produced a video package on classroom management. He can be contacted at P.O. Box 261, Yarraville, Victoria, 3013, Australia (Phone/Fax: 03–9314–0779).

Decisive Discipline

As the lesson begins, the teacher tells two boys to be quiet: "Stop (he emphasizes the verb) talking please!" One of the students has a last word. "We were only talking about the work—gees!" He folds his arms, pouts loudly, eyes rolling to the ceiling. With all eyes watching, the teacher leaves the blackboard and walks across the room to confront the student. "Look, I don't care what you were talking about!" The student answers back, "What about Melissa and Denise? They were talking; you didn't say nothing to them!" (louder pout, skewed eye contact). "I'm not talking to them, I'm talking to you!" The teacher is entering terminal-frustration mode. And so it goes; each transaction is a mini-battle for verbal and emotional supremacy.

Effective teachers utilize a "language of discipline" and do so under emotional pressure, day after day. Does it matter what we say in discipline transactions, how we say it, or when we say it? Ample research and student opinion say, "Yes."

Decisive teachers *expect* compliance; they don't *demand* it. Decisive teachers recognize that they cannot actually make students do anything. Instead, their verbal language and body language convey an expectation that their reasonable requests will be followed. Their language is brief (thus avoiding "over servicing" a student's bid for attention or power), clear and directed (redirected, if necessary), rule-focused, calm and businesslike, and assertive when the situation demands it.

Decisive Discipline Language

Decisive discipline language embraces several factors.
The Language Is Planned and Conscious. One's verbal repertoire is not left

to chance alone. While we can't plan for every discipline contingency, we can plan for the common ones—from talking out of turn and seat-wandering, to interpersonal put-downs, answering back, and arguing. Although a lot of these behaviors are "low-level," their very frequency increases teacher frustration. We can even plan what to say when we have to employ the most intrusive measures—that is, ejecting a student from the room.

The Emphasis of the Language Is Assertive. The teacher's language is not hostile, aggressive, or sarcastic, neither is it indecisive or debating. The teacher's response is brief and clear. It does not attack the person; it addresses the inappropriate behavior.

The Language Moves from Least-to-Most Intrusive. If teachers can keep the language transactions at the least intrusive level, they will keep the unnecessary "heat" down. Instead of snatching objects off a student's desk, give a directional "choice." For example, "Lisa, I want you to put the comic in your bag or on my desk—thanks." ("Thanks" is said expectantly, not pleadingly or sarcastically.) Choice gives the ownership back to the student.

The level of teacher intrusiveness should correlate with the level of student disruption—low-, medium-, or high-level. It is not the severity of the consequences, but the certainty of the consequences that makes them work. The key is to avoid boxing yourself or the student into a no-win situation. Rogers suggests four, ever increasing, levels of decisive teacher action. These include:

Step one. Tactical ignoring of disruptive behavior. It involves signaling that you are aware of the disruptive, often attention-seeking, behavior but refuse to acknowledge it.

Step two. Directional language addresses the behavior you want to see. "Dave, I want you to put the pen down, thanks, and face this way." Saying "thanks," or "ta," helps mitigate those times when a simple direction to a student may be taken as something much more—a challenge, an ultimatum. "When/then" or "yes/when" is better than, "No you can't because. . . . " "Hey, may I go to the toilet?" said at the start of a lesson may be quickly, even positively, countered with, "Yes, when I've finished this part of the lesson."

Step three. The calm, yet firm, repeating of step two can be enhanced by dignifying what Rogers calls "secondary behavior"—the behavior that often follows a teacher's directive statement. When Melissa is directed to stop talking to a classmate, turn around, and face front, she responds by saying, "I was just showing him how to solve the assignment. Why are you picking on me?" This is the student's effort, conscious or not, to divert the teacher's attention away from the primary behavior—talking while the teacher is presenting a lesson. Dignifying a secondary behavior simply acknowledges that it *may* be true; it does not necessarily condone it. "That may be the case, Melissa, but I want you to stop talking, turn around, and pay attention to the lesson." Dignifying her "reason" for talking helps defuse the situation and helps avoid an unwanted and unwarranted escalation of the problem. Who knows, she may well have been trying to help her classmate.

Step four. If redirection, rule restatement, and providing students with alternative choices do not work, the teacher imposes some form of time-out, ranging from in-class isolation to exiting the classroom. Time-out sends a clear message to the entire school community about nonnegotiable behavior. Unless ineffectively administered, time-out is not punishment. The time-out space, although not solitary confinement, should be nonreinforcing. Otherwise, it becomes positive reinforcement, not time-out. Like all of Rogers' steps, time-out should be administered with dignity and respect.

The Tone of the Language Is Important. Sixty percent of *what* we say is *how* we say it. Tone, then, also needs to be part of our conscious style. "Paula, what are you doing?" "Nothing." "Actually, you're out of your seat. What are you supposed to be doing?" "I wasn't the only one out of my seat." "Maybe you weren't, but I'm speaking to you—what are you supposed to be doing?" "My work." She sulks off back to her desk as the teacher leaves her in order to work with another group.

Read the above teacher language aloud in a sarcastic tone of voice; read it in a hostile, aggressive, and finger-pointing tone; try saying it in a pleading, be-nice-to-me-please tone. Our body language and voice-tone need to be congruent with what we say.

Joint Rules, Rights, and Responsibilities

Decisive discipline language works best when the three R's—Rules, Rights, and Responsibilities—are clear. The three R's, especially important in what Rogers calls the "establishment phase," provide teachers and students with mutually desirable goals whereby decisive discipline can be seen as a means of achieving them. Rules should be discussed, perhaps even negotiated. They should be clear, positively stated, few in number, logical, and "owned" by all over whom they apply. Perhaps the most overlooked aspect of rules is that they need to be taught and, if necessary, retaught. Rules, and their enforcement, should be perceived as fair! They are necessary to protect our rights—students' and teachers'.

Central to the success of the three R's is still another R word—Respect. Rules *can* be enforced and people *can* be held accountable without publicly imposing shame, ridicule, embarrassment, or unnecessary confrontation.

Rogers: His Use of Other Discipline Models

Rogers' approach borrows from other discipline gurus' models—especially Dreikurs and Glasser. He contrasts logical consequences and punishment just as Dreikurs does—favoring, of course, logical consequences. He offers attention seeking and a need to belong as motives for misbehavior just as Dreikurs does. He expands upon Glasser's *The Quality School* contrast of the characteristics between a boss and a leader—favoring the latter posture. He stresses the value of rules and avoids asking misbehaving students why they have misbehaved as does Glasser in *Schools without Failure*. He maximizes student choice as does Glasser in *Control Theory in the Classroom*.

Hey mate! To learn more about Bill Rogers' ideas, read:

Rogers, B. (1998). *You know the fair rule: And much more.* Hawthorn, Victoria: The Australian Council for Educational Research.

Rogers, B. (1997). *Cracking the hard class: Strategies for managing the harder than average class.* Gosford, New South Wales: Scholastic Australia.

Rogers, B. (1995). *Behaviour management: A whole-school approach.* Gosford, New South Wales: Scholastic Australia.

Rogers, B. (1993). *The language of discipline: A practical approach to effective classroom discipline.* Plymouth, England: Northcoate House Publishers.

Rogers, B. (1989). *Making a discipline plan.* Melbourne, Australia: Thomas Nelson.

MICHAEL VALENTINE: *A FAMILY-SYSTEMS APPROACH ADAPTED TO SCHOOLS*

Michael R. Valentine received his Ph.D. from the University of California at Los Angeles (UCLA) in education with a specialization in clinical psychology and psychopathology. He has served in a variety of positions as a teacher, counselor, administrator, and school psychologist at the basic-education and higher-education levels. He is a tested and experienced workshop leader and author. He can be contacted at 23565 Via Paloma, Coto de Caza, CA 92679. Phone: 717–858–7803.

Family-Systems Approach

"My approach," says Valentine, "relies on the strengths and capabilities of adults and children, rather than on their assumed weaknesses or disabilities.

It is a simple truth that adults who believe in children, and who get involved and set in motion the external factors necessary to insure that the child will be successful, usually are successful in achieving that goal.

"The three major underlying components of my model are (1) analyzing belief systems, (2) analyzing communication patterns, and (3) developing effective nonpunishing backup techniques to ensure success."

Component One: Analyzing Belief Systems

Analysis of erroneous teacher belief systems is an important first step in this approach because people usually act congruently with their beliefs about inappropriate behavior. In looking at popular belief systems of educators about why children do what they do, the question becomes, "Is the child seen as capable of doing what is wanted, or does the belief system imply that the child is incapable of controlling the specific behavior?" The ultimate way to determine if the child is capable is by observable evidence. Has the child ever done what is wanted? If so, then the child is capable, and all the previously entertained excuses need to be set aside for change to occur. Once this is clearly seen by teachers, the real issue is changed from "Can the child do or control the behavior?" to "What needs to be done to get the child to do the desired behavior?"

The logic of the system is simple. If you believe that the student is incapable of doing what you want him to do, then you will not directly and clearly tell him to do what you want him to do. However, if the belief system is challenged by objectively collecting evidence and thereby proving that the student is in control of his or her behavior, then it becomes reasonable and congruent with that new way of seeing things to tell the student in very specific and concrete terms to do what you want.

Component Two: Analyzing Communication Patterns

The intent of this second component is to illustrate to teachers that adults who do not believe that a child is capable of performing the desired behavior usually use vague, indirect, and unclear communications and behavioral interventions that, unfortunately, say to the child, "Keep on doing the inappropriate behavior." Again, it is the contention of this approach that if actual teacher-student communications were videotaped or recorded verbatim, it would be evident that in most incidents when children act inappropriately, adults do not give them clear, direct, specific, and concrete messages to stop the inappropriate behavior and start doing what they wish them to do.

Vague and Indirect Communication Patterns. Vague and indirect communication patterns are quite common. They include, among others:

- Ignoring inappropriate behavior. Teachers just hope and pray that the inappropriate behavior will go away.
- Actually encouraging inappropriate behavior. "That was real cute. Why don't you show the other students how obnoxious you can be?" Don't be surprised if the student does what he or she was told!
- Using behavioral contracts or threats. "If you don't do these 10 problems now, you are choosing to stay after school." The potential message for the child is: "It's your choice, do X or Y, either one is okay with me." Do you really mean this?
- Asking questions. "How many times do I have to tell you to stop that?" Do you really want an answer to this question?
- Asking for an effort to change. "Please *try* to get to class on time." Is *trying* really good enough?
- Asking the child to think about the behavior. "Think twice before you do that again."
- Issuing warnings. "Don't you ever let me catch you doing that again." Is the message "Don't get caught?"
- Giving abstract meaningless directions. "Grow up."

Even though at times vague communication patterns work with some children, they rarely work with hard-to-handle children. Vague, indirect communication patterns must be analyzed to determine whether a clear message to perform is present.

Direct Messages. Clear, direct messages convey to the child in very specific terms what is to be done. For example, the statement, "John, sit in your seat now, and stay there until I tell you to get up. While you are there, do these ten problems neatly and correctly. Have them finished in fifteen minutes to a C-level or better. Start immediately, do absolutely nothing else but these problems, and do not stop until you are finished," is a clearer, more direct message than the typical vague teacher message of "Get to work."

Direct messages reflect an underlying adult belief system that: (1) It is reasonable, from the adult's personal value system, to tell the child and expect the child to do the particular behavior; (2) the adult sees the child as capable of doing what is asked; and (3) the child has to do what is requested—the child has no choice. This is not a hostile, authoritarian, or dogmatic position. Instead, this is a clear, objective statement of what is expected, couched in a context of love, caring, and positive expectations. It is amazing how teachers (and parents) can almost always get children to stop inappropriate behavior when they make up their minds, use clear messages, and mean it.

Component Three: Backup Techniques

Backup techniques by teachers should set the stage for the child to complete the required behavior with success. These techniques in essence say to the child, "When you don't do the desired behavior on your own, you can count on teachers to give you guidance and structure to make sure you are successful." The choice is "Would you like to be successful on your own?" or "Would you like us to help you be successful until you get the message that you can be successful on your own?" It is not, like most of the psychological and educational approaches of the day which in some form state, "Would you like to be successful (for instance, go to school) or fail (for instance, drop out of school)?"

Some children, especially those with long histories and habit patterns of being out of control, will test adults to see if they mean what is said. Even if teachers change their minds about the student's capabilities and, consequently, now give clear messages to do a specific behavior, the student may not be convinced. When this occurs, the goal for adults is to back up what is wanted in a nonhostile, nonpunishing way and convince the child to do what is wanted. Although the number of backup techniques is limited only by the adults' imagination, the structure is always the same—an emphasis on success versus success, never on success versus failure.

When parents, teachers, and school personnel see students as being capable, expect students to behave and perform appropriately, and give clear, specific, concrete communication, they will usually get most students to do what they want. The problem is getting teachers to "believe" in the children and in themselves and then not back off until the student is successful. In essence, there are no magical cures, no new techniques—just a systematic way of "believing" in people, education, and hard work.

To learn more about Valentine's ideas, read:

Valentine, M. (1988). *Difficult discipline problems: A family systems approach.* Dubuque, IA: Kendall/Hunt.
Valentine, M. (1987). *How to deal with difficult discipline problems in schools: A practical guide for educators.* Dubuque, IA: Kendall/Hunt.

HARRY K. WONG: *THE FIRST DAYS OF SCHOOL*

Harry K. Wong, Ed.D., is a practicing classroom teacher with almost four decades of experience. He is well published with books and journal articles, as well as video and audio tape series. He can be contacted at Harry K. Wong, 1030 West Maude Avenue #507, Sunnydale, CA 94086. Phone: 408-732-1388.

The First Days of School: How to Be an Effective Teacher

Dr. Wong and Rosemary Tripi Wong coauthored the successfully selling book, *The First Days of School: How to Be an Effective Teacher* (1998), which has been described as a user-friendly resource for teachers who realize just how important it is to get the year started right. Building upon the ideas generated in an earlier publication by Brooks (1985, p. 77) titled "The first day of school," Wong believes that students, especially adolescents, come to school with certain first-day questions. These include:

- Are they in the right room?
- Where are they supposed to sit?
- What are the rules of this teacher?
- What will they be doing in this course?
- How will they be evaluated?
- Is the teacher going to be interested in them as individuals?

Dr. Wong devotes several chapters in his book to, among other topics, communicating positive expectations and stressing the importance of teachers' establishing effective classroom management procedures, not just rules! This contrast between procedures and rules is important to the Wongs because rules, often seen as a challenge by students, need to be enforced, often through the use of punishments—something the authors wish to avoid. Procedures, on the other hand, produce less student resistance, especially, as recommended by the Wongs, if the teacher teaches (and if necessary reteaches) the procedures at the very start of the year.

The importance of arranging and assigning student seating, when and how to take roll, regularly posting assignments, and maintaining an effective grade record book also are discussed. Much of what has been so well received in the Wongs' book is presented and expanded in their eight-part video series called *The Effective Teacher*.

Finally, because the school year goes well beyond just the concerns of the first day, they include in their book a chapter on lesson mastery where one finds Bloom's Taxonomy used as a basis for writing lesson by lesson objectives.

To learn more about Harry K. Wong's ideas, read:

Wong, H. K. & Wong, R. T. (1998). *The first days of school: How to be an effective teacher.* Sunnydale, CA: Harry K. Wong Publications.

TEST YOURSELF

This is a sampling of the kinds of factual and open-ended questions that you should be able to answer after having read this chapter.

1. Which contemporary author(s) presented in this chapter best reflects the views of Rudolf Dreikurs?

2. Linda Albert, in her Cooperative Discipline, identifies three C's that must be present in order for students to feel that they "belong." These include, feeling capable, connected, and _____.

3. How could you design a classroom so as to foster Albert's three C's?

4. Steve Barkley, in his description of Project T.E.A.C.H., claims that "_____ is the key to developing effective classroom management whatever the style" used by teachers. Do you agree?

5. Define the term "judicious discipline" as described by Forrest Gathercoal.

6. How does the definition of "judicious discipline" as used by Gathercoal differ from how behaviorists might define the term discipline?

7. How could you design a classroom so as to foster Gathercoal's definition of "judicious discipline"?

8. Describe how Madeline Hunter's ideas regarding the enhancement of teaching qualifies as a form of preventative discipline.

9. What is your reaction to Mendler and Curwin's position that discipline must be delivered with dignity?

10. Create an original example of how you might deliver Mendler and Curwin's ideas regarding discipline with dignity in your classroom.

11. Under what conditions does Nelsen, in her presentation of Positive Discipline, say that punishment may "work"?

12. William Rogers, in his presentation of Decisive Discipline, identifies four steps to using language that proceeds from least-to-most intrusive. What are these steps?

13. What is the definition of "secondary behavior" as used by William Rogers?

14. According to Michael Valentine, what would be an example of vague and indirect communication pattern? What would be an example of a less vague and more direct communication pattern?

15. Which of the authors' works presented in this chapter interested you the most? Why?

CHAPTER 10

Ideas for Preventing
Problem Behaviors

OBJECTIVES

This chapter will help you, among other things, to:

- List the steps in the self-fulfilling prophecy process.
- Defend the importance of the self-fulfilling prophecy as a pedagogical tool.
- List specific categories of punishment.
- Defend whether or not educators are as much in favor of punishment as they may, at first, appear.
- Identify seven performance skills used by actors that could be used by teachers.
- Defend the claim that teachers should make more use of performance skills in their classrooms.

There is no doubt that preventing discipline problems before they occur is preferable to correcting them after they take place. The articles that follow address such preventative measures. Perhaps these very readable articles will whet your appetite for further study! The articles include:

- "Teachers as Pygmalions: good or bad, what we expect we generally get"

  The self-fulfilling prophecy is presented as a pedagogical tool to benefit all, not just a select few, students.
- "Changing teachers' attitudes toward punishment"

  An exercise to challenge whether or not teachers really see a place for punishment in today's schools.
- "Acting lessons for teachers: Using performance skills in the classroom"

Award-winning teachers attest to their use of performance skills in the classroom. Shouldn't more teachers use these skills?

TEACHERS AS PYGMALIONS: GOOD OR BAD, WHAT WE EXPECT WE GENERALLY GET!

Introduction

Most teachers know a little bit about the Pygmalion Effect, or the idea that one person's expectations can affect the behavior and achievement of another person. Everyone who has seen George Bernard Shaw's play *Pygmalion* or viewed the movie *My Fair Lady* can remember the remarkable transformation in Eliza Doolittle that takes place as a result of Professor Higgins' beliefs (i.e., expectations) about her. Yet few educators understand exactly how to use the Pygmalion Effect or self-fulfilling prophecy (SFP) as a purposeful pedagogical tool to convey positive expectations and, at the same time, avoid conveying negative expectations.

How many of you think that you are reasonably good judges of character? With years of teaching experience under your belt, are you more often than not able to size up students correctly? Sure, occasionally you are wrong, but most often you are correct. Right? Many teachers believe that they can tell ahead of time—sometimes at just a glance the first day of school—how certain students are likely, over time, to achieve and to behave.

Try the following exercise. Pretend that you are not reading an article designed to make you more sensitive to the power of teacher expectations. Instead, jot down the first descriptive thoughts that come to your mind when you think about the following kinds of people. Be honest, now. Only you will see what you write.

Generally, what descriptors might you use to characterize:

- a teenager from a family that has strong and vocal Democratic Party (or Republican) ties.
- a significantly overweight teenage girl.
- a primary school student from an affluent family who is an *only* child.
- a middle school student whose two older siblings you had in class several years ago—each were often troublemakers.
- an Asian student who is the son of a respected university mathematics professor.
- a teenage boy who is thin, almost frail, and very short for his age.

• a primary child, with at least six known siblings, who lives with his divorced (and currently pregnant) mother who receives food stamps.

In spite of your best efforts to resist forming predictions regarding these students and their academic and/or behavioral future, did you catch yourself forming expectations—even fleetingly? If your answer is "yes," then the self-fulfilling prophecy probably is set in motion. Keep in mind the adage, "First impressions (i.e., expectations) are _____ impressions." Everyone knows that the missing word is "lasting." As an additional exercise, try asking your colleagues what they might expect from the students described above. Don't be surprised at their expectations-oriented answers.

The basis of the SFP is that once a student has been pegged ahead of time as, say, "troublemaker," "nonscholar," or "likely to be self-centered," the chances are increased that our treatment of this student will, in effect, help our negative prophecies or expectations come true. Here the SFP would work to the detriment of the student. On the other hand, we could peg a student as "cooperative," "a scholar," or "likely to be a self-starter," thus increasing the chances that our treatment of him or her will convey these expectations and, in turn, contribute to his or her living up to our original positive prophecy. In this case, the SFP would work to the benefit of the student. The fact is, teachers, more often than not, get from students what they expect from them!

History of the Self-fulfilling Prophecy

The term "self-fulfilling prophecy" was first coined by sociologist Robert K. Merton in a 1948 *Antioch Review* article titled "The Self-Fulfilling Prophecy." As part of his explanation of the SFP, Merton drew upon a fellow sociologist's theorem: "If men define situations as real, they are real in their consequences" (Thomas, 1928, p. 257).

Robert Rosenthal did much to call attention to the SFP among educators in his classic book, *Pygmalion in the Classroom* (1968). In this book, he and his coauthor Lenore Jacobson describe an experiment in which elementary teachers' expectations of students were manipulated. The two researchers, presumably using the results from a test with the impressive sounding title *Harvard Test of Inflected Acquisition*, which had been administered schoolwide, led the teachers in eighteen classrooms to believe that approximately 20 percent of their students were expected to "bloom" academically and intellectually during the school year. In reality, the test was a relatively new intelligence test titled the *Flanagan Test of General Ability*.

The test results, of course, were never actually the basis for identifying which students were designated to bloom. Instead, the designated student "bloomers" were randomly assigned so that the only differences between the bloomers and the rest of the student body were in the minds of the teachers. When retested later using the same test, the designated bloomers did, in fact, show intellectual gains.

At the end of the school year, when asked to describe the classroom behavior of their students, the children from whom intellectual growth was expected (i.e., designated "bloomers") were described positively by their teachers as having a greater chance of being successful in life and of being happier, more curious, more interesting, more appealing, and better adjusted. On the other hand, when the nonbloomer-designated students bloomed, and some did, these same teachers described these students negatively—less likable, less likely to succeed in life, less happy.

It was almost as if the teachers were thinking, "How dare a student achieve if I did not expect him or her to!" The fact of the matter is that most people, including teachers, do not like to be wrong. When nonblooming-designated students actually achieved, teachers were forced to admit that they may have misjudged (i.e., formed the wrong expectations of) these students' ability and behavior.

As a case in point, if you were a teacher and you had a student perform significantly better on a test than you would have predicted, would you look first at alternative reasons why this happened before admitting that you may have misjudged the child's capabilities? Would you be tempted to go back and rescore his or her exam believing that you must have made an error? Would you try to recall who was sitting next to this student when the test was administered and check this person's exam for any all too obvious similarities in answers—i.e., the nonbloomer must have cheated?

If, as Wagar claims, "The ultimate function of a prophecy is not to tell the future, but to make it" (1963, p. 66), then each time teachers "size up" a student, they are, in effect, influencing this student's future behavior and achievement. This is an awesome burden for educators to carry. The burden can be lessened if educators better understand the SFP and then remain diligent in trying to control it.

Mechanisms of the Self-fulfilling Prophecy

First and foremost, the SFP is a process—a process that consists of a series of definite steps. Each of these steps can be impacted positively by informed educators. Whether educators are informed or not, the SFP will continue to operate. Surely it is better to have the SFP operate under our (the educator's) control. The following five-step model (Good and Brophy, 1978) explains how the SFP works.

- Step 1. Teacher forms expectations.
- Step 2. Based upon these expectations, the teacher acts in a differential manner.
- Step 3. The teacher's treatment tells each student (loud and clear) what behavior and what achievement the teacher expects.
- Step 4. If this treatment is consistent over time, and if the student does not actively resist, it will tend to shape the student's behavior and achievement.
- Step 5. With time, the student's behavior and achievement will conform more and more closely to that expected.

In four out of five steps, the teacher plays a pivotal role—that is, "the teacher forms expectations"; "the teacher acts in a differential manner." Because Steps 3, 4, and 5 are a continuation of Steps 1 and 2, only Step 1 and Step 2 will be elaborated.

Step 1. Teacher Forms Expectations. Whether because, like other human beings, teachers do not like to face the future with any more unknowns in their life than they have to, or because they feel that their experience working with students enables them to "size up" each new year's group of kids, teachers do form expectations—often during the very first day of school. If first impressions are lasting impressions, then some students are at a definite advantage while still others are at a significant disadvantage. How is this fair? How is this equitable?

The most surprising point about Step 1 in the SFP is not that teachers form expectations, but that teachers (and others) form expectations on various and sundry factors that ought to have little or nothing to do with a student's future achievement and behavior. There is a significant body of SFP research that shows that teachers form expectations of students on such characteristics as body build, gender, race, ethnicity, given name and/or surname, attractiveness, dialect and/or primary language, and socioeconomic level.

Let's examine, further, some of these highlighted student characteristics that can trigger a teacher's expectations. The research is clear that when it comes to a person's body build, mesomorphs (those with squared, rugged shoulders, small buttocks, and muscular bodies) are expected to be "better" than ectomorphs (thin, frail-looking bodies) and endomorphs (chubby, stout, fat bodies with a central concentration of mass). Among other expectations, mesomorphs are predicted to be better fathers, more likely to assume leadership positions, be more competent doctors, and most likely to put the needs of others before their own.

With respect to attractiveness, the adage "beauty is good" prevails whether in storybook heroes and heroines or in real life. All other things being equal, beautiful people are expected to be better employees—most likely to be hired, given a higher salary, and to advance more rapidly in an organization than their ugly-duckling counterparts. Beautiful people are perceived (expected) to make better parents, be better public servants, and to be more deserving of benefits bestowed upon them.

With respect to dialect and/or primary language, one only has to imagine a New York Wall Street stockbroker's first impressions when a rural West Virginia job applicant first opens his or her mouth. Competent or not, a negative "hillbilly" impression often is formed of the candidate. This scenario may be little different from the expectations some BBC News-speaking London folks might have when they first hear an Edinburgh or Northern England Jordee high school graduate first speak. A candidate's competence can be overshadowed by his or her dialect.

Finally, one's name, often the first thing that we "know" about someone, can trigger expectations. For instance, my brother's name is Randy. Does that generate any particular expectations in the reader's mind? It certainly does in the United Kingdom.

In the United States, primarily white, middle-class females continue to teach more and more diverse student bodies, that less and less resemble the teachers themselves—i.e., color, race, ethnicity. When minority students, who by far possess the most unusual names (at least in the eyes of teachers), come to class, teachers cannot help but be influenced. The repercussions of a child's being saddled with a "strange" name can last a lifetime. It has been said that parents take more time selecting a name for the family pet than they do for choosing names for their children.

Step 2. Teachers' Differential Treatment of Students. Different expectations can lead to different treatments. How does one person convey his or her expectations to another person? Robert Rosenthal's (1973) Four-Factor Theory identifies *climate, feedback, input,* and *output* as the factors teachers use to convey expectations.

> *Climate* refers to the socioemotional mood or spirit, often communicated non-verbally (e.g., smiling and nodding more often, providing greater eye contact, leaning closer to the student), created by the person holding the expectation. Do you catch yourself creating a warmer, more supportive climate for students for whom you hold higher expectations? I do!
>
> *Feedback* refers to providing both affective information (e.g., more praise and less criticism of high expectations students) and cognitive information (e.g., more, and more detailed, as well as higher quality feedback as to the correctness of higher expectation students' responses). Do you provide more feedback on the papers of those students whom you believe will actually read and digest what

you write—that is, the students for whom you hold higher expectations?

Input translates into the fact that teachers tend to teach more to students of whom they expect more—often in one-to-one situations. With students of whom you expect more, do you catch yourself suggesting and/or providing additional resources for them, believing that they will actually use these resources? At times, I do.

Output is where teachers encourage through their verbal and nonverbal behaviors, greater responsiveness from those students of whom they expect more— providing them with greater opportunities to seek clarification and/or to ask for further explanation.

These factors, each critical to conveying a teacher's expectations, can be controlled if only teachers are more aware that these factors are operating in the first place. Even if a teacher does not feel in his or her heart that a particular student is capable of greater achievement or significantly improved behavior, that teacher can at least *act* as if he or she holds such heightened positive expectations. This *act* can be made more convincing by the teacher controlling the four factors of *climate, feedback, input,* and *output.* After a period of time, the teacher may well be surprised to find that the student, believing the teacher's positive expectation messages, improves his/her achievement and behavior.

Communicating Expectations

Weinstein (1991) looks beyond patterns of differential teacher-student interactions to include the structure and organization of the classroom. She suggests that making changes in the instructional environment is another way of communicating positive expectations to students. Among Weinstein's suggested structural changes are (pp. 337, 345):

- Curriculum—*all* students should receive higher-order and more meaningful tasks
- Grouping practices—should be heterogeneous and interest based
- Evaluation system—should reflect the view of multiple intelligences and learning styles
- Motivation—should use cooperative rather than competitive teaching strategies
- Teacher-student relations—should foster pastoral care

Summary

The three most important words in real estate are *location, location, loca-*

tion. In education, the three most important words may well be *expectations, expectations, expectations.* Children have a natural desire to learn; all that is required is for those around them (parents, teachers, peers) to send them positive expectations messages. Teachers have a responsibility to understand and to better control the self-fulfilling prophecy as it operates in today's classrooms. Like "Little Toot" in the children's story *The Little Engine That Could,* who tries to make it up the steep mountain, a teacher's repeated positive expectations messages to students can help children progress from "I think I can; I think I can," to "I know I can!" As a result, students can become their own Pygmalions.

Much more information on the self-fulfilling prophecy can be found in the well-referenced 1997 book by Robert T. Tauber, *Self-Fulfilling Prophecy: A Practical Guide to Its Use in Education* (ISBN: 0–275–95503–6). It is available from Greenwood Publishing (203–226–3571).

Self-fulfilling Prophecy "Selected Citations"

In order to show how the SFP is influenced by most basic human characteristics, I have listed selected citations that, from their titles alone, reinforce the power of expectations. You may wish to obtain these sources and read then in their entirety.

Age: Simmons, G. (1987, February 1). Myths about aging are self-fulfilling prophecies. *Times-News* (Erie, PA), 7–C.

Attractiveness: Hunsberger, B., & Cavanagh, B. (1988). Physical attractiveness and children's expectations of potential teachers. *Psychology in the Schools, 25*(1):70–74.

Birth Order: Baskett, L. M. (1985). Sibling status effects: Adult expectations. *Developmental Psychology, 21*(1):441–445.

Body Build: Staffier, J. R. (1972). Body build and behavioral expectations in young females. *Developmental Psychology, 6*:125–127.

Ethnicity: Bonetati, D. (1994, April). *The effect of teachers' expectations on Mexican-American students.* Paper presented at the annual meeting of the American Educational Research Association, New Orleans, LA.

Gender: Sprouse, J. L., & Webb, J. E. (1994). *The Pygmalion Effect and its influence on the grading and gender assignment on spelling and essay assessments.* ERIC Document, ED 374096.

Given Name/Surname: Demetrulias, D. M. (1991). Teacher expectations and ethnic surnames. *Teacher Education Quarterly, 18*(2):37–43.

Quality of Dress: Davis, B. (1992). Dress for respect: The effect of teacher dress on student expectations of deference behavior. *Alberta Journal of Educational Research, 38*(1):27–31.

Race: Murray, C. B., & Clark, R. M. (1990). Targets of racism. *The American School Board Journal, 177*(6):22–24.

Single Parent vs. Two Parents: Grymes. J. M. (1993, November). *Pre-service teachers' expectations for children from different family structures.* Paper presented at the Annual Meeting of the Mid-South Educational Research Association, New Orleans, LA.

Socio-Economic Status: Rist, R. C. (1970). Student social class and teacher expectations: The self-fulfilling prophecy in ghetto education. *Harvard Educational Review, 40*:411–451.

Special Needs Students: Schleper, D. R.(1995). Well, what do you expect? *Perspectives in Education and Deafness, 13*(3):2–3.

An Inspirational SFP Story: How Miss Thompson Influenced Teddy!

If you don't think your expectations of others—be they children or spouses or fellow employees—have a profound effect, you are wrong. Your positive behavior and attitude towards others are major factors in obtaining the behavior from them that you desire. Consider the story about unattractive and unmotivated Teddy Stallard.

Teddy certainly qualified as one of the children least interested in school. Musty, wrinkled clothes; hair never combed. One of those kids in class with a deadpan face, expressionless—sort of a glassy, unfocused stare. When Miss Thompson spoke to Teddy, he always answered in monosyllables. Unattractive, unmotivated, and distant. He was just plain hard to like. Even though his teacher said she loved all in her class the same, down inside she wasn't completely truthful.

Whenever she marked Teddy's papers, she got a certain perverse pleasure out of putting X's next to the wrong answers and when she put F's at the top of his papers, she did it with flair. She should have known better. She had Teddy's records, and she knew more about him than she wanted to admit. The records read:

1st Grade: Teddy shows promise with his work and attitude, but poor home situations.

2nd Grade: Teddy could do better. Mother is seriously ill. He receives little help at home.

3rd Grade: He is a slow learner. His mother died this year.

4th Grade: Teddy is very slow, but well behaved. His father shows no interest.

Christmas came and the boys and girls in Miss Thompson's class brought her Christmas presents. They piled their presents on her desk and crowded around to watch her open them. Among the presents there was one from Teddy Stallard. She was surprised that he had brought her a gift. Teddy's gift was wrapped in brown paper and held together with Scotch tape. On the paper were written the simple words, "For Miss Thompson from Teddy." When she opened Teddy's present, out fell a gaudy rhinestone bracelet, with half the stones missing, and a bottle of cheap perfume.

The other boys and girls began to giggle and smirk over Teddy's gifts, but Miss Thompson at least had enough sense to silence them by immediately putting on the bracelet and putting some of the perfume on her wrist. Holding her wrist up for the other children to smell, she said, "Doesn't it smell lovely?" The children taking their cue from the teacher, readily agreed with "oohs" and "ahs."

At the end of the day, when school was over and the other children had left, Teddy lingered behind. He slowly came over to her desk and said softly, "Miss Thompson you smell just like my mother . . . and her bracelet looks really pretty on you, too. I'm glad you liked my presents." After Teddy left, Miss Thompson got down on her knees and asked God to forgive her.

The next day when the children came to school, they were welcomed by a new teacher. Miss Thompson had become a different person. She was now a person committed to loving her children and doing things for them that would live on after her. She helped all children, especially the slow ones, and especially Teddy Stallard. By the end of that school year, Teddy showed dramatic improvement. He had caught up with most of the students and was even ahead of some. She didn't hear from Teddy for a long time. Then one day, she received a note that read:

"Dear Miss Thompson: I wanted you to be the first to know. I will be graduating second in my class. Love, Teddy Stallard."

Four years later, another note came:

"Dear Miss Thompson: They just told me, I will be graduating first in my class. I wanted you to be the first to know. The university has not been easy, but I liked it. Love, Teddy Stallard."

And four years later:

"Dear Miss Thompson: As of today, I am Theodore Stallard, M.D. How about that? I just wanted you to be the first to know. I am getting married next month. The 27th, to be exact. I want you to come and sit where my mother would sit if she were alive. You are the only family I have now. Dad died last year. Love, Teddy Stallard."

Miss Thompson went to the wedding and sat in the place where Teddy's mother would have been. Miss Thompson deserved to sit there—she had done something for Teddy he could never forget.

The above story was taken from a speech given by Winston Churchill, "A Colossal Military Disaster," dated June 4, 1940, before the House of Commons. Just imagine how many more times this story could have been repeated in classrooms over the past sixty years if teachers were more aware of the power of the SFP!

CHANGING TEACHERS' ATTITUDES TOWARD PUNISHMENT

Introduction

Of the various options available to teachers in altering student behavior, none has been written about—and practiced—more than punishment. With all of this information available, teachers who advocate using punishment should be expected to make a strong defense for its use. But as one who does not believe in the use of punishment, I have devised a nonthreatening, yet revealing, activity designed to challenge the position of teachers who say they support the use of punishment. It could be presented, perhaps by an administrator, at a staff meeting or as an in-service exercise.

Step One

Ask the teachers, "How many of you see a place for punishment in today's schools?" Follow this up with a restatement of the question as follows, "Although it may not be your first choice of a discipline measure, how many of you at least see a place for it in today's schools?" After an initial reluctance to raise their hands, it is not uncommon to see more than half of the educators present raise their hands in agreement. Count the number of raised hands and write the number on the chalkboard or easel pad.

Step Two

Ask the teachers, "How many of you believe that the actions of teachers when dealing with student behavior should be purposeful, planned, and conscious?" Because most teachers understand that they must be accountable for their actions, most hands will be raised. If a significant number of hands are not raised, however, you might ask the teachers to think of the consequences of having the only adult in a classroom acting in an unpurposeful, unplanned, and unconscious manner.

Step Three

This step, which has several parts, is designed to determine the attitudes of the teachers toward six of the most frequently used categories of punishment: frustration, humiliation and embarrassment, fear and anxiety, boredom, physical discomfort, and pain (Mager 1968). Do not reveal these six categories beforehand. Instead, ask the participants to take a stand on their willingness to administer each type of punishment as it is introduced. You can expect some interesting responses.

Frustration. Ask the teachers, "How many of you would purposefully plan to frustrate your students, by, say, presenting information at a faster pace than students can handle, by teaching one set of skills and testing for another, or by using materials with too high a reading level?" Ask for a show of hands for each question and write down the totals. Chances are that only a fraction of the number who initially indicated that punishment is acceptable will admit that, as professionals, they would purposefully plan to frustrate their students. Yet, frustrating students—whether on purpose or inadvertently—is a common form of punishment.

Humiliation and Embarrassment. Ask the teachers, "How many of you would purposefully plan to humiliate and embarrass a student by, say, calling attention to a child's soiled clothing, unusual surname, or physical appearance, inability to solve a simple math problem, or to perform a simple physical education exercise? Are there times when humiliation and embarrassment of students are justified?" Once again, count the raised hands. Although there may be more in support for punishment by humiliation and embarrassment than for frustration, the number will still be far fewer than that of those who originally approved of punishment in a generic sense.

Fear and Anxiety. Ask the teachers, "How many of you would consciously plan to instill fear and anxiety in your students?" Describe some examples of instilling fear: a 200–pound adult screaming and shouting at children; a teacher threatening to expose the "ignorance" of a student by forcing him or her to solve problems at the chalkboard in front of the class. Explain how anxiety can be caused by announcing to students that you don't award very many A's or B's, by telling students ahead of time that they probably will not understand a lesson, or by arbitrarily changing course requirements or grading standards. For those who challenge the implied severity of the examples offered for fear and anxiety, point out that when teachers set out to purposefully instill fear and anxiety in their students, they *must* cause "distress or uneasiness of the mind; apprehension of danger, misfortune, or pain; tension, foreboding, worry" (Mager 1968). Otherwise it is not really punishment! When you check the hand count of those who would purposefully instill fear and anxiety in students, few hands will be raised.

Boredom. Now ask, "How many of you come to school planning to bore your students?" After the laughs and snickers stop, point out that there is little punishment more dreaded than being bored to death by ineffective and unimaginative teaching. Expect few, if any, hands to be raised in favor of this type of punishment.

Physical Discomfort. When you ask the teachers about their willingness to punish students by supplying physical discomfort, most will assume that this means hitting or paddling the child. But, physical discomfort is not the same as corporal punishment. Physical discomfort includes such things as purposefully making a classroom too hot or too cold, having students sit still for extended periods of time, denying students the opportunity to get a drink of water or go to the lavatory, or speaking too softly or too loudly. I once had a seventh-grade English teacher who would punish students by having them hold books in their outstretched arms for extended periods of time. I don't remember whether or not his attempts to supply physical discomfort altered my behavior. I do know that I hated English that year. Once teachers understand the nature of punishment by physical discomfort, you won't find many hands raised in its favor.

Pain. Finally, ask the teachers, "How many of you would feel comfortable administering corporal punishment?" Perhaps it is the fear of being sued. Perhaps your state is one of a few that forbids corporal punishment. Perhaps your staff is aware of the research showing that only short-term benefits accrue from corporal punishment. Perhaps the image of a large adult striking a small child makes teachers feel guilty. Whatever the reason, expect no more than 10 percent of the teachers to approve of this form of punishment. For those who still voice the belief, "Spare the rod and spoil the child," you may wish to point out that the "rod" in the biblical verse referred to "a shepherd's tool for guiding and protecting the flock, not for beating them" (Barnard and Thornburg, 1989).

Step Four

Announce that you have completed your presentation of the specific categories of punishment. Point out to the audience the disparity between their initial show of raised hands (often approaching 70 to 75 percent) in general support of punishment and the lack of support shown for each specific category of punishment. You will find a number of teachers who, after indicating their initial support for punishment, did not raise their hands for a single category. This very disparity is the message of this activity. Logically, one cannot support something, in general, and not be in support of at least one or more of its specific instances. Perhaps, when push comes to shove, teachers really are not so much in favor of punishment as they may have thought. I strongly believe the latter.

ACTING LESSONS FOR TEACHERS: USING PERFORMANCE SKILLS IN THE CLASSROOM
(Coauthored by Cathy Sargent Mester)

Introduction

It is a Wednesday morning and the clock shows 9:00 A.M. Faculty and staff have gathered for an in-service program. Some teachers have a cup of coffee; others have coffee and doughnuts. The stage is set for a morning of "in-servicing!" The workshop leader welcomes the educators and begins by asking them to read a series of prepared quotations handwritten on poster board in large print that he tapes, one at a time, to the walls of the classroom. Participants then are asked to determine the message that is common in each of the displayed quotations. The task is not difficult. Among the quotations hung on the wall are:

- *Enthusiasm* is the key to being a successful teacher (Soenksen, 1992).
- Effective teachers motivate their students with an *enthusiastic* style of teaching (Brophy & Good, 1986).
- One of the five delivery characteristics associated with effective teaching is the projection of *enthusiasm* for the subject matter (Goulden, 1991).
- A teacher who is not able to convey *enthusiasm* for his or her subject (even though he may feel it inwardly) labors under a great handicap. Students are unwilling to accept a teacher who cannot transmit to them something of the excitement of his field (Jordan, 1982).

A great teacher is not just someone who is approachable as a person, although this is not an uncommon characteristic of a great teacher. A great teacher also isn't simply a scholar—one who knows a lot—although knowing a lot about one's field certainly can contribute to greatness. What one knows must be communicated. Jordan (1982) reminds us that "the Teacher as Scholar is important, that the Teacher as Person is crucial, and that the Teacher as Communicator is indispensable" (p. 124). Teacher enthusiasm, the common factor in the displayed quotations, is fundamental to effective communication.

Effective actors, too, must communicate what they know. But, unlike teachers, actors long have recognized the need to develop specific skills, especially means and methods of expression, to enhance their communication. The bulk of this book is devoted to helping teachers develop acting skills that can help them communicate better.

The workshop leader continues by stating that teacher enthusiasm is a pedagogical necessity. Cautious, but slightly nervous, the participants agree. One participant, though, volunteers that classrooms do not just contain teachers, they contain students, too. Therefore, one might argue—in fact, one should argue—that enthusiastic teaching is of little value unless effective student learning takes place. Measures of effective learning consist of, among other factors, heightened student interest, positive student attitude, more on-task student behavior, and greater student achievement.

Instructor Enthusiasm: Its Relationship to Student Achievement

At this point, the workshop leader asks those gathered to read the remaining quotations, prepared as handwritten signs that are taped, one at a time, on the remaining two walls of the classroom. Among the quotations displayed are:

- Children taught at a high level of *enthusiasm* were more attentive, interested, and responsive (Burts et al., 1985).

- Research has shown correlational and causal links between teacher *enthusiasm* and student achievement (Gillett, 1980).

- Teachers trained in how to enhance their *enthusiasm* had students whose on-task time was significantly greater than for nontrained teachers (Bettencourt, Gillett, & Hull, 1983).

- Students repeatedly indicate that they learn more from those who evince *enthusiasm* and concern for the quality of teaching, even though they may frequently complain about their own required extra effort (Browne & Keeley, 1985).

The connection between teacher enthusiasm and desired student learning outcomes is clear. Researchers document it; practitioners testify to it. Teacher enthusiasm is one "means" to the "end" of greater student achievement.

Another point that emerges from these quotations is that teacher enthusiasm is a quality associated with effective teaching across all disciplines and at all grade levels. Teacher enthusiasm is as important in English as it is in physics, as important in social studies as it is in mathematics, and as important in elementary school and high school as it is in college.

Teacher enthusiasm plays a central role in holding students' attention, generating students' interest, and developing students' positive attitudes toward learning. Highly enthusiastic teachers are highly expressive in vocal delivery, gestures, body movement, and overall energy level. All of these are crucial ingredients that, in turn, contribute to greater student achievement.

Eison (1990) believes that in the classroom, a teacher's enthusiasm is often contagious; so too is his or her lack of enthusiasm. He believes that "enthusiasm and energy can carry the day" (p. 24). Who has not personally experienced the infectious enthusiasm generated by singers in a outdoor concert (e.g., Beach Boys), by players of a well-performed Nutcracker Suite, or by a stirring symphony and its conductor? That same infectious enthusiasm can exist in classrooms.

McKeachie, a recognized name in the field of pedagogy, claims that probably no characteristics are more important in education than a teacher's enthusiasm and energy (1986). Lowman (1984) argues that a factor found prominent in most research on teaching effectiveness is the instructor's ability to stimulate enthusiasm for the subject—a skill often related to the teacher's perceived enthusiasm. Sincere enthusiasm helps create, as well as maintain, a good learning environment (Campbell, 1981). Teacher enthusiasm has a positive impact—greater student achievement—on kindergarten youngsters, college students, and all those in between. The evidence is overwhelming in favor of teacher enthusiasm!

A teacher's zest for teaching, like an actor's zeal for acting, is revealed in his or her displayed enthusiasm. It is obvious in their expressiveness. Weimer (1993) in her book, *Improving Your Classroom Teaching*, devotes an entire chapter to the importance of enthusiasm. Early in the chapter she boldly declares, "Enthusiasm: Do It!" She states that one should not try to be enthusiastic, one should, instead, focus upon things that will convey your enthusiasm to the class. We agree.

Exactly how teachers or professors are supposed to "convey this enthusiasm" is the emphasis of the 1994 book by Tauber and Mester, *Acting Lessons for Teachers: Using Performance Skills in the Classroom*, available from Greenwood Publishing.

Boosting Teacher Enthusiasm Through Performing

Effective teachers are perceived as more enthusiastic teachers. Teacher enthusiasm, in turn, often leads to greater student achievement. The question, now, is how can teachers become more enthusiastic? As the quotation at the beginning of this chapter says, "It is not *who* you are but *what* you do that conveys enthusiasm."

Years ago, one of the authors supervised student teachers. Prior to entering the classroom for the first time, many of these student teachers had bouts of severe anxiety—the teacher's version of "stage fright." In an effort to calm their nerves, the author reassuringly offered this profound statement. "Don't worry. Just go in there and be yourself." In hindsight, this was terrible advice to give because many of these student teachers were, in fact, less than exciting human beings. If they went into the classroom and "remained themselves," they would have been boring teachers.

We can't imagine a director telling stage frightened actors to just go on stage and "be themselves." According to Hanning (1984), "You [teachers] don't have a 'self' to be when you start out as a teacher; that is you don't have a teacher-self. You have to develop one, and you do that by acting a part, by performing a role . . . as you would (in) a theatre" (p. 33).

At first glance performing a role—acting a part—may appear out of place to some educators. It shouldn't. In many ways, teaching in the classroom is not unlike acting on the stage or in the cinema. In both the theatre and the classroom, the character "onstage" must hold the attention of the listeners by using a variety of captivating devices. Teachers have the additional burden of having to hold the attention of their audience 180 or more days a year!

According to Lowman (1984, p. 11), "classrooms are fundamentally arenas in which the teacher is the focal point, just as the actor or orator is on a stage—teaching is undeniably a performing art." He further argues that, like other performers, teachers must convey a strong stage presence, often using overt enthusiasm, animation, and humor to accomplish this goal. Rubin (1985), too, argues that "teaching was (is) a performing art" (p. 100) and supports this belief by including chapters titled "The Classroom as Theatre," "Teacher as Actor," and "Lesson Staging."

According to Rubin (1985), school, like drama, is meant to be experienced directly. When a student who has missed a class asks, "What did we do in class yesterday?" his or her teacher often is at a loss to offer an appropriate response. Although the teacher might like to say, "Gee, you really lucked out. We didn't do a thing in that class"; more often they respond by saying something to the effect that "You had to be there in order to understand what happened in yesterday's class." A missed session might be described, but the real spirit of the event is missed.

Teachers act the role of teachers—a role that can, and does, vary from school to school and classroom to classroom. The classroom teacher is onstage. "The acting or performing dimension of the teaching act is highly relevant to a large portion of the teacher's role. Verve, color, humor, creativity, surprise, and even 'hamming' have characterized most great teachers" (Baughman, 1979, p. 27).

Despite the parallel between the two professions, very little has been written about how teachers might employ techniques used by actors to develop Hanning's concept of teacher-self. Nor has much been written about theatrical or acting devices for holding the audience's attention that might be suited to that same goal in the classroom. This book attempts to address this void.

There are a number of specific things teachers can do—most with a foundation in drama—in order to appear more enthusiastic. If educators "act" enthusiastic as teachers, over a period of time they may, in fact, "become" more enthusiastic as people. One needs only to look at the world of drama in order to see where people regularly "act" as something they most often are not in real life. Actors constantly are developing their "acting-self" in a manner similar to Hanning's recommendation that teachers develop their "teacher-self." Actors use acting skills. More successful actors more successfully use these performance skills. Teachers, too, can, and should, use these same skills. These performance skills have the potential for boosting a teacher's perceived enthusiasm.

A Craftsperson's Toolbox

We envision a teacher's performance skills, his or her teaching strategies, as analogous to the tools carried by any craftsperson, including actors. This analogy is supported by Rubin (1985) when he explains that the artistry part of teaching consists of "master craftsmanship" (p. 15). In the craftsperson's toolbox there are two categories of tools. Some tools are used more frequently and thus kept ever handy in the top tray. Other tools are used less frequently and, therefore, stored in the bottom of the toolbox.

Such a variety of tools enables the knowledgeable craftsperson to have the right tool handy to accomplish the desired task. Without the right tools, ever kept sharp, and the knowledge of how to use them, a craftsperson would be limited in his or her effectiveness. The same holds true for teachers.

The Craftsperson Himself or Herself

Although having the right tool for the job helps, a prerequisite to this is possessing the knowledge to use that tool in the first place. Tools do not operate themselves. But, even prior to knowing *how* to use a tool, one needs to know *what* tool, from those available, should be used in a given situation. It reminds us of students trying to solve problems in a physics course. The mathematics used in physics itself normally is not the stumbling block. The real difficulty for students is deciding (knowing) what formula, of the many available, best applies to the circumstances of the present problem.

The common ingredient in the above scenarios is "knowledge." Actors must know their lines before they can expect to deliver them effectively. Teachers must know their subject matter before they can expect to teach it effectively to others. Subject Matter Mastery is the first acting/teaching skill that we will address. In our craftsperson analogy, Subject Matter Mastery is not something viewed as a tool to be carried in the toolbox. Subject Matter Mastery is carried in the craftsperson's head—always ready, constantly used.

Without the proper mastery of content knowledge, the delivery, no matter how exciting, becomes as Shakespeare wrote, "full of sound and fury, signifying nothing" (*Macbeth*, Act V, Scene 5). On a more recent note, Spencer Tracy is reported to have offered this advice to an aspiring actor, "know your lines and don't bump into the furniture." Teachers must know their material.

In an often-cited experiment, an actor, introduced to a conference audience as Dr. Fox ("The Dr. Fox Effect"), presented an enthusiastic lecture that not only contained little content but used double-talk, irrelevant examples, and contradictory examples (Perry, 1985). The audience rated the lecture highly, citing that, among other things, it stimulated their thinking. Is it possible, then, to secure and hold the attention of an audience but, in the end, deliver little in the way of content? Teachers who lack subject expertise *may* be able to use acting skills, in the famous words of Abraham Lincoln, to fool some of the people all the time and all the people some of the time; but those who lack subject matter knowledge will not be able to fool all the people all of the time.

The evidence is clear—enthusiastic teachers, those who are expressive in their manner and method, do more regularly earn higher student evaluations. Further research supports that these same expressive teachers generally have students who exhibit higher achievement (Abrami, Leventhal, & Perry, 1982). Where you find enthusiastic teachers, you find greater student achievement. These teachers are delivering the goods—the requisite content!

The Actor's/Teacher's Top-Tray Tools

Through both research and interviews with award-winning faculty, we have identified three acting/teaching skills that should be used regularly by teachers. They are:

- Animation: Voice
- Animation: Body
- Effective Use of Classroom Space

The justification for including these three skills as top-tray tools (skills) is presented in separate chapters that follow. Suffice it to say, it would be unheard of for actors to ignore the importance of vocal animation (e.g., pitch, volume, voice quality, rate) in their attempts to hold an audience's attention and get their message across. Should teachers be any less concerned about their effective use of voice? Actors take lessons and practice, practice, practice these skills. Should teachers, too, work at improving the impact of such a resource?

In a like manner, no successful actor could, nor would, overlook the importance of physical animation and effective use of space. The power of body language, perhaps even more convincing than verbal language, is not lost on the successful actor. Nor is the value of one's physical placement within the stage setting. Teachers, too, should be sensitive to their physical animation and use of space.

The Actor's/Teacher's Other Tools

Also, through research and interviews with award-winning faculty, we have identified four acting/teaching skills that are most effective when used occasionally—whether in the theatre or in the classroom. These skills include the use of:

- Humor
- Role-Playing
- Props
- Suspense and Surprise

Once again, successful actors work long and hard at perfecting each of these skills. With respect to role-playing, no doubt, some actors feel more comfortable in some roles than in others. Yet, through a combination of sweat and talent, most are able to carry out many roles in a convincing manner. We believe that teachers, too, can convincingly take on various roles.

Like actors, teachers can hone their skills in the use of props, can make better use of subject matter-related humor (e.g., pun, short story, joke, riddle) and can create attention-getting suspense and surprise. Not only *can* teachers use all of these acting-related tools, we argue that they *must* use these tools. These tools, in conjunction with the educator's top-tray tools, can help teachers deliver their message more effectively. All of these "tools," these performance skills, are explained in detail in our book, *Acting Lessons for Teachers: Using Performance Skills in the Classroom* (Tauber & Mester, 1994). According to Nazzal's (1996) review of the book, "It should be required reading for all individuals aspiring to be great teachers."

Summary

Clearly, teachers' perceived enthusiasm can be enhanced through the judicious use of the performance skills outlined above, which until now may have been seen only as relating to the acting world. These skills, whether used by teachers or actors, are simply a means to an end. They are the tools of one's craft. The more of these acting tools teachers have at their disposal, and the better they are able to use them, the more effective these teachers will be in the classroom. Award-winning faculty attest to their regular and conscious use of performance skills in the classroom. If it works for them, it can work for you, too!

TEST YOURSELF

This is a sampling of the kinds of factual and open-ended questions that you should be able to answer after having read this chapter.

1. In any relationship (teacher-student, boss-employee), who is the Pygmalion?

2. In the article, "Teachers as Pygmalions: Good or Bad, What We Expect We Generally Get!," why was it argued that the self-fulfilling prophecy is a "process" and what effect does that have for the practitioner in the classroom?

3. Do you believe, in actual practice, that the title of the article, "Teachers as Pygmalions: Good or Bad, What We Expect We Generally Get!," is true?

4. In the article, "Teachers as Pygmalions: Good or Bad, What We Expect We Generally Get!," what are the four factors identified by Rosenthal for conveying expectations and how can that knowledge help you as a classroom teacher?

5. Identify the six categories of punishment described in the article, "Changing Teachers' Attitudes Toward Punishment."

6. Identify two original classroom examples of each of the six categories of punishment described in the article, "Changing Teachers' Attitudes Toward Punishment."

7. In the article, "Changing Teachers' Attitudes Toward Punishment," what logical discrepancy existed between many teachers' attitude toward punishment in general and their attitude toward specific categories of punishment?

8. In the article, "Changing Teachers' Attitudes Toward Punishment," how should teachers attempt to resolve this logical discrepancy?

9. By making reference to the article, "Acting Lessons for Teachers: Using Performance Skills in the Classroom," describe how a teacher's performance skills can act as preventative discipline.

10. By making reference to the article, "Acting Lessons for Teachers: Using Performance Skills in the Classroom," provide evidence to back up the importance of teacher enthusiasm to both successful teaching and to student achievement.

11. List the seven performance skills presented in the article, "Acting Lessons for Teachers: Using Performance Skills in the Classroom."

12. Which of the seven performance skills presented in the article, "Acting Lessons for Teachers: Using Performance Skills in the Classroom," have you personally observed to be most effective in holding your interest while learning?

13. By making reference to the article, "Acting Lessons for Teachers: Using Performance Skills in the Classroom," explain the point of the toolbox analogy.

14. By making reference to the article, "Acting Lessons for Teachers: Using Performance Skills in the Classroom," explain how you might incorporate two or three of the performance skills in teaching a lesson.

15. By making reference to the article, "Acting Lessons for Teachers: Using Performance Skills in the Classroom," which performance skill(s) do you predict will be most difficult to incorporate in your teaching? Why?

CHAPTER 11

Some Surprising Ideas about Discipline

OBJECTIVES

This chapter will help you, among other things, to:

- Identify three situations where one may wish to be cautious in delivering praise.
- Identify alternative teacher behaviors that may be delivered in place of praise.
- Explain how negative reinforcement can have a positive side.
- Define, and suggest uses for, the four teacher-supplied consequences presented in a consequence grid.
- Explain how power may be viewed by students as a goal of misbehavior.
- Identify three alternative teacher behaviors that may be delivered in place of fighting back or giving in.

The ideas that follow may take the reader by surprise. How can there be a negative side to praise? How can there be a positive side to negative reinforcement? You mean it is possible to defuse power struggles? Tell me quick. Hopefully these very readable and, perhaps controversial, articles will whet your appetite for further study!

The articles include:

- "The Negative Side of Praise"

  Praise may not be the teacher's tool of choice once one examines the negative side effects that can occur. Perhaps encouragement should be used instead of praise.

- "The Positive Side of Negative Reinforcement"

  Most educators do not understand the concept of negative reinforcement and thus use it at the wrong time for the wrong purpose and then complain that it didn't work.

- "Defusing Power Struggles: Alternatives to 'Fighting Back' or 'Giving In' "

  It is not how many power struggles you have but how you resolve them that is important. The alternative teacher behaviors presented result in a win-win situation for both parties.

THE NEGATIVE SIDE OF PRAISE

Introduction

Effective classroom management involves getting students not only to stop some behaviors, but to start other behaviors. From educational psychology and teaching methods courses to induction-year and in-service programs, the virtues of teacher-supplied praise are acclaimed as a tool for getting students to start or increase desired behaviors. Who could possibly challenge the value of praise for modifying student behavior?

According to Kohn (1991), though, "Many well-meaning teachers continue to assume that what works for training the family pet must be appropriate for shaping children's actions" (p. 500). What follows may be highly disconcerting to educators enamored with offering positive reinforcement, especially praise.

Praise Defined

Brophy (1981) defines praise as "teachers' positive responses to students' good work or good conduct that go beyond mere affirmation or positive feedback" (p. 270). Acknowledging a student's correct answer, without verbally and/or nonverbally embellishing the acknowledgment, would not qualify as praise.

The more students engage in acceptable behaviors (the goal of supplying praise), the less they are likely to engage in unacceptable behaviors—those for which they might then have to be disciplined. At first glance, using praise appears to be classroom management at its best—teachers motivating students to do what is correct, not motivating them simply to stop doing what is judged to be incorrect.

Praise: Its Origin

Praise finds its origin in operant learning theory where students' future behaviors are thought to be governed by the consequences of their present behaviors. Concepts such as behavior modification, shaping, and contingency management prevail. Proponents believe that if pleasant consequences follow students' behaviors, those behaviors are more likely to occur in the future. If unpleasant consequences follow the behaviors, those behaviors are less likely to occur in the future.

In order to modify student behavior, educators can *supply* a reward (something perceived as psychologically or physically pleasant) or *remove* a reward; they can supply an aversive stimulus (something perceived as psychologically or physically painful) or remove an aversive stimulus. Supplying a reward is called positive reinforcement; removing a reward is called time-out. Supplying an aversive stimulus is called punishment, and removing an aversive stimulus is called negative reinforcement. There are no other choices of consequences.

Where does praise fit? Educators commonly state that praise is an example of positive reinforcement. They are sometimes correct, but they may also be incorrect. The effect of educator-administered praise is influenced by a student's perception of that "praise." There are at least three situations where delivering praise is inappropriate. Administering praise at the wrong times and in the wrong situations may precipitate inappropriate student behavior—that which later may need to be disciplined.

Situation One: When Praise Is Perceived As a Personal Evaluation

Praise may be inappropriate when the student perceives it as a personal evaluation. First and foremost, praise *is* an evaluation, and most people do not like to be evaluated. Although praise suggests the person being evaluated has met the mark this time, will the person be worthy of praise in the future? What about all the times in the past when students did not receive praise? Does that suggest they were unpraiseworthy?

"Undoubtedly, the most threatening aspect of praise is the obligation it puts upon us to be praiseworthy people" (Farson, 1963, p. 63). Praise often establishes standards that we, then, are expected to live up to constantly. "Such messages give rise to intellectual evaluative threat, and impose a pressure for repeat performance" (Thompson, 1997, p. 57). Feedback in the form of "You're an 'A' student" suggests that being praiseworthy is a enduring human quality that will forever persist. But is it? Consider the student who earns all "A's" on a report card and then is singled out for praise by his or her teachers and parents. Woe be the student whose grades then fall. This responsibility to remain forever praiseworthy is the source of great anxiety as students become frightened about the prospect of not being able to live up to expectations (Dreikurs, 1965).

Although educators are cautioned to keep a professional distance between themselves and their students, too much distance can be harmful. Offering praise often increases that distance. According to Farson (1963), praise is normally delivered by someone of greater status to someone of lesser status. The master praises the apprentice; the apprentice does not praise the master. The person with the greater status remains in control of the relationship; the person with the lesser status continues to be controlled—and sooner or later realizes it.

For those who receive praise and perceive it as an attempt at manipulation, praise is something that has to be handled—even denied! It is just as difficult for many people to cope with positive criticism (praise) as it is to cope with negative criticism (punishment). Both are clearly evaluations; both demand a response. Often that response, especially when delivered in a public forum to adolescents, is defensive.

Listen to people's responses when they receive praise. It makes no difference whether the praise is directed toward an outfit they are wearing, a term paper they have completed, a curriculum they have revised or, in my case, a deck I recently built. The defensive responses to praise are the same. Some examples of defensive statement include: "I really can't take full credit for it," "You're just saying that, but thank you," and "It's not all that great, look at these mistakes."

We also exhibit defensive physiological responses when receiving praise. Watch students who are being praised and who view that praise as a personal evaluation. They blush, their hands turn clammy, they avoid eye contact, their pulse rate increases. All of these are signs that their bodies are attempting to cope with praise.

Is it any wonder that when students are asked which of two forms of praise about themselves they would most believe—praise given to their face or praise accidentally overheard—the majority answer the latter (Tauber, 1991)? Overheard praise is judged as less manipulative and, thus, more sincere.

Why do people become so defensive when receiving praise? As children, when we accepted praise at face value, we repeatedly got burned. We soon learned that praise very often signaled that a criticism was about to follow as in, "Your paper was fine, *but* you . . . Keep up the great work." This often-delivered praise-criticism-praise message is called the sandwich effect.

Finally, we have learned that some of the praise we receive is simply offered to make others' lives, not ours, more pleasant. Praising students for being quiet during study hall makes the teacher's life easier. It may also gain a teacher recognition for being an effective disciplinarian. When educators have an ulterior motive for supplying praise, children will surely pick up on it. Students quickly become suspicious of the motivation behind those who deliver praise, and thus the value of praise, even when it is unselfishly delivered, is also suspect.

In a school environment where some educators see it as their "obligation to modify student behavior" (Axelrod, 1977, p. 158), praise can become a too-often-used tool that sends a message that students are only acceptable when they receive praise.

Situation Two: When the Student Does Not Feel Praiseworthy

It is ironic that when one feels the least deserving of praise, those around him or her who care use that very occasion to deliver statements of praise. We all know the saying, "The road to hell is paved with good intentions." Good intentions or not, praising someone who does not feel praiseworthy is generally an ineffective interpersonal communication behavior. Among those who hold negative opinions of themselves, receiving a compliment that they think is undeserved can lead to a distrust of the sender of the praise (Clarizio, 1980).

Take the child who is in tears about the fact that she did not get selected for the varsity diving squad. Well-intentioned teachers (and parents) are likely to deliver praise. They might say, "Well, I think you are one of the very best divers the school has!" At this point the child faces a dilemma. Someone is lying to her. Either the school's selection committee is lying to her, or you, her trusted teacher, are lying to her. One is saying she is not among the best, while the other is saying she is among the very best. Whom should she believe?

People who receive praise in scenarios similar to the one above soon realize that the praise is being sent just to help make them "feel better." But what is the student to think when she recalls the lavish praise you offered regarding the short story she had written last week? Did you really think the story was praiseworthy or were you once again simply trying to make her feel better? How is the student to know when praise-givers are or are not telling the truth?

Messages of praise do not help students resolve their problems and, more important, do not help them handle the debilitating feelings surrounding their problems. Without a resolution of these problems and/or feelings, students cannot get on with their school lives (e.g., listening to a lecture, completing an assignment, participating in a group exercise). Unsolved problems and lingering uncontrolled feelings increase the likelihood that students will not be doing what they are supposed to be doing—hence, possible behavior problems.

Situation Three: When the Student Does Feel Praiseworthy

In this situation, the person receiving praise already feels deserving of praise. He or she feels especially good about something—doing particularly well on a school exam, completing a demanding and time-consuming school project, breaking a long-standing school record in sports. The specific examples, and age levels to which they apply, are endless.

One might ask, "Why not offer praise?" No harm is likely to occur by offering praise, given that praise would be consistent with how the child already feels about himself or herself, but a real opportunity is missed for helping the student attribute his or her success to his or her own doing.

Schools should capitalize upon every opportunity to help students see that their successes (and failures) primarily are attributable to causes under their control. Attribution theory (Weiner, 1980; Hunter & Barker, 1987) defines four explanations students offer for their successes and failures—task difficulty, luck, effort and ability. Task difficulty and luck are external attributions that, if believed, allow students to avoid responsibility for what happens to them. Although both effort and ability represent internal attribution, only effort is controllable by the student—hence its desirability as an attribution factor.

Students need help in seeing that it is *their* effort, an internal source of motivation, that most influences their successes and failures. They can choose to increase or decrease this attribution factor and, thus, exert a significant influence upon what happens in their academic, as well as personal, lives. They control their behavior, both good and bad. Glasser (1986) argues, "Our behavior always arises from within ourselves, never from an outside stimulus, that all we can do is *act*; as living creatures we never *react*" (p. 18).

Statements of praise do not reinforce the internal attribution of effort. Saying "I'm so proud of you," reinforced by demonstrable nonverbal behaviors, may ignore the cause and effect relationship between a student's effort (behavior) and success.

Alternative to Praise: Situation One

When there is danger that praise will be seen as a personal evaluation of worth, one needs to differentiate between praise and feedback. Providing students with corrective feedback or knowledge of results is a well-established learning principle (Page, E. B., 1958; Ausubel, D. P., 1968). It should be used and used often. Students need to know if their behaviors, whether serving a volleyball or solving a division problem, are correct or are at least moving them toward achieving mastery. Teachers are in a prime position to offer this feedback.

It is possible to tell a student that she is incorporating all of the proper steps in executing her volleyball serve, and that he has correctly solved the problem and apparently grasps the basic concept behind division, without offering praise.

Educators who rely upon praise soon realize that not everyone can be praiseworthy. The fact is, praise loses its associated honor if too many people receive it. Consider offering encouragement instead of praise. Balson (1982) summarizes his views on encouragement by noting that it "recognizes effort and improvement, shows appreciation for contribution, . . . focuses on assets as strengths, and separates the deed from the doer" (p. 112). This advice is as important in classroom management as it is in learning.

What are you to do if you are just so proud of a child's accomplishments that you are going to burst unless you praise him or her? Consider sending an appreciative I-message. According to Gordon (1976), "One of the most meaningful 'gifts' we can give others is to share with them how they specifically bring us delight, pleasure, joy, warmth" (p. 32). An appreciative I-message conveys our positive feelings without the evaluation implied by praise.

I-messages have three parts: (a) what the child has done, (b) what tangible effect it has on you, and (c) your feelings regarding that tangible effect. One might say to students, "When I am late arriving to class because of a phone call from a parent and all of you are at your assigned tasks, this makes it easier for me to move on with the lesson, and I just want to say thanks."

Appreciative I-messages take more time both to compose and to deliver than do statements of praise. One of the reasons for this is that appreciative I-messages, unlike most statements of praise, are supported by observable evidence. This makes the message more believable and, thus, more influential.

Teachers may also send I-messages (nonappreciative) when a student's behaviors are interfering with the teacher's meeting his or her needs. An example of such a three-part I-message would be, "David, when you call out the answers to all of the questions I ask, I don't know whether the rest of the students know the material. That makes me feel unsure."

Instead of using a message such as, "David, do not answer until I call upon you!" an I-message is more apt to get David to (a) voluntarily change his behavior, (b) allow both of you to save face, and (c) do the least damage to your ongoing relationship.

Alternative to Praise: Situation Two

Praise is delivered so often in this situation because we don't possess the requisite skill to listen, really listen, to people who are experiencing strong feelings surrounding either academic or personal problems. After all, teachers are supposed to teach, and too often that means talk, not listen.

Educators must learn how to listen—actively listen. Teachers can act as facilitators; they can use a Rogerian form of reflective counseling. They can, with training and practice, learn to listen for the feelings the student is sending and then feed them back to the student for affirmation or denial. This is exactly the kind of help professional counselors deliver. They listen. They leave the responsibility for change up to the client (student). The client comes away from such interactions better able to handle tomorrow's problems. This is not so with praise. Praise ends a dialogue. What is left to say after someone has lavished praise upon you?

Educators should read Gordon's (1974) *T.E.T.: Teacher Effectiveness Training* and begin to use his suggested skills of passive listening, noncommittal acknowledgments, door-openers and, of course, active listening. Saying to our student, "It sounds as if you are really disappointed about not getting chosen for the diving team," lets the student know that you are there, you are listening, you *hear* her hurt.

You can't make her disappointment go away even though you may want to. You can, through active listening, keep the lines of communication open so that she has a better chance of coming to grips with this "tragedy" in her life. She knows that she can talk out her problems without fear that you will give her undeserved praise, will offer a solution (yours), will moralize (into every life a little rain must fall), or will offer any other of the twelve roadblocks to communication (Gordon, 1974).

Educators should begin their facilitating responses with phrases such as, "It sounds as if you feel . . . " or "What I hear you saying is . . . " In each case your verbal and nonverbal responses to students who are hurting must clearly convey that they may freely affirm or deny your efforts at decoding their message.

Alternative to Praise: Situation Three

When someone is feeling especially praiseworthy, an educator should do one, or both, of two things. One, reply with a message that highlights the cause-and-effect relationship between the student's attribution of effort discussed earlier. Two, actively listen just as you should do with people feeling undeserving of praise.

Think of a time when something happened that you just had to share with someone before you could get on with your life. Recently, a colleague came to show me a desk copy of a book he had been sent by a publisher. He was so proud that his name was cited four times in the index. I responded, "It sounds as if you feel pretty proud about having your work cited by other authors." He replied, "Not so much proud, but satisfied." One minute later he was on his way getting on with his life. He just had to tell someone.

A student is beaming from ear to ear after having raised her grade from a "C" to an "A" in your biology class. You might say, "It looks as if you feel that study group you formed has paid off. Earning an 'A' feels pretty good, huh?" Here, you not only attributed her success to her effort, you also actively listened to her by reflecting her feelings. Haim Ginott (1965), too, distinguishes between *unhelpful* praise and *helpful* praise. Most of his examples of *helpful* praise center around the child attributing his successes to his or her own actions.

Summary

The temptation to use praise should be resisted when that praise is either perceived by the student to be an evaluation, felt to be undeserved, or felt to be deserved. Rather than spontaneously punctuating each student's actions with praise, teachers should become more informed, and thus more selective, in their use of praise (Wolfgang & Brundenell, 1982) and use the more effective alternatives to praise outlined above.

THE POSITIVE SIDE OF NEGATIVE REINFORCEMENT

Introduction

Educators need more effective strategies of classroom management. One strategy that teachers and administrators overlook is the positive use of negative reinforcement. This sounds like a contradiction in terms, but it is not.

Two Major Problems

Educators face two major problems in taking any corrective action designed to improve classroom discipline. First, they must select a specific theory of classroom management. Second, they must understand the theory well enough to apply it effectively. Teachers can make decisions about the first problem fairly easily because relatively few tried and true theories of classroom management exist.

Of these limited theories of classroom management, researchers have written most about those with behavior modification-type components. As a result, it is behavior modification that educators throughout the nation believe they understand well enough to apply as a corrective strategy. The theory seems as simple as "supply a carrot" for desired behavior and "apply a stick" for undesired behavior. Unfortunately, this theory, as well as many other behaviorist theories of classroom management, is deceptive in its apparent simplicity. The one portion of behavior modification educators least understand—and, as a result, effectively use least—is negative reinforcement. They overlook it as a *positive* strategy of classroom management.

Negative Reinforcement Quiz

To set the stage for a defense of this rather bold assertion about negative reinforcement, you should take the following quiz before reading further.

1. If you were doing a crossword puzzle on the subject of behavior modification and you were asked for a word that means the same thing as negative reinforcement, what word would you select?
2. Negative reinforcement usually results in students:
   a. Stopping (decreasing) a behavior the teacher wants stopped.
   b. Starting (increasing) a behavior the teacher wants started.
3. Do you believe students look forward to negative reinforcement?
   a. Yes b. No
   Why?
4. Do you consciously use (or plan to use) positive reinforcement with students?
   a. Yes b. No
   Why?
5. Do you consciously use (or plan to use) negative reinforcement with students?
   a. Yes b. No
   Why?

The Goals of Behavior Modification

To understand negative reinforcement and appreciate its usefulness as a positive classroom management strategy, one must first understand behavior modification. Behavior modification is essentially a consideration of the consequences a teacher supplies in order to modify a student's behavior.

Specifically, what changes in student behavior might a teacher desire? A teacher wants either to maintain, start (increase), or stop (decrease) student behavior. There are no other choices.

Available Consequences

Although there are numerous specific examples of the consequences of what a teacher does to modify behavior, all can be grouped into four categories. These categories are defined according to whether the teacher's response involves supplying or removing a reward, or supplying or removing an aversive. These four choices of consequences are known, respectively, as positive reinforcement, time-out, punishment, and negative reinforcement.

Teacher Use of Consequences

Of the four responses available, most teachers are familiar with and seem to accept the use of positive reinforcement. Punishment, although used often, is many times done so without a thorough understanding of its side effects. Time-out, although frequently used, is incorrectly perceived as just another form of punishment. Negative reinforcement is the least understood and least accepted as a strategy, let alone a positive strategy, of classroom management.

How do students respond to these four consequences? Put yourself in the place of the student in the following examples and imagine the effect upon your behavior that the teacher-supplied consequences would have.

Would you be motivated to start or increase a given behavior if, as a consequence of your behavior, you received a reward? If you had turned in a term paper with an extensive bibliography and earned an "A," would you not be more likely to continue including extensive bibliographies in future term papers? Sure you would! Supplying a reward (something desired by the student) as a consequence of the student's demonstrating a desired behavior is called positive reinforcement. We all use it, it is used on us, and it works.

Suppose, instead, that you were engaged in a behavior where, as a result of that behavior, a reward was taken away. What effect would that have on you? Most people would either stop, or at least decrease, behaviors whose consequence is the loss of a reward. Take the student who clowns in class, and no one, including his or her peers, pays any attention. Following a predicted brief increase in his or her clowning intensity that still leads to no notice by his or her peers, the clowning stops. After all, why engage in a behavior that results only in the loss of a reward—that is, attention? Removing a reward as a consequence of undesired behavior is called time-out.

Now imagine the effect upon you when, as a result of engaging in a given behavior, the teacher supplies an aversive. Mager (1968) identifies pain, fear and anxiety, frustration, humiliation and embarrassment, boredom, and physical discomfort as typical aversives available to teachers. Supplying an aversive, in sufficient quantity, usually has the effect of stopping, or at least reducing, the behavior—at least in the presence of the person supplying the aversive.

Score: 2–1

Thus far, we have discussed two responses, time-out and punishment, that have the effect of stopping or reducing a student's behavior. It is presumed that only one response, positive reinforcement, has the effect of starting or increasing a student's behavior. This seems a little lopsided. Teachers would be more successful in modifying student behavior if they had a second response available to start desired student behaviors. And they do! This second response is negative reinforcement—the elimination or removal of an aversive or noxious stimulus (McConnell, 1990). Negative reinforcement accomplishes the same outcome as positive reinforcement: it motivates a student to start or increase a behavior.

Figure 11.1, A Consequence Grid, summarizes the four categories of responses available to teachers in behavior modification.

Unjustified Concerns

Even if negative reinforcement works, some educators may question whether the end justifies the means. Does not negative reinforcement somehow do some damage? After all, how can something described as negative be positive? I suspect we have the same inherent mistrust of negative reinforcement as we have of negative numbers (or anything associated with the word "negative") in mathematics. The mistrust is unjustified. To address these concerns, let us answer the questions asked in the quiz earlier.

In question 1, most educators state that "punishment" is a synonym for negative reinforcement. Nothing could be more incorrect. The Consequence Grid clearly shows punishment to be the supplying of an aversive—fear, humiliation, and so on. Negative reinforcement is just the opposite. It is the removal of an aversive.

Figure 11.1
A Consequence Grid

	TEACHER SUPPLIES A CONSEQUENCE	TEACHER REMOVES A CONSEQUENCE
A REWARD STIMULUS (causes student mental or physical pleasure)	POSITIVE REINFORCEMENT (starts or increases desired student behavior)	TIME-OUT (stops or decreases unwanted student behavior)
AN AVERSIVE STIMULUS (causes student mental or physical anguish)	PUNISHMENT (stops or decreases unwanted student behavior)	NEGATIVE REINFORCEMENT (starts or increases desired student behavior)

As surprising as it may seem, the answer to question 2 should be "b," starting a behavior the teacher wants started. Note that this is exactly the outcome achieved with positive reinforcement.

Question 3 should be answered with a resounding "yes." Who would not look forward to having an aversive removed? Take the child who wishes to get a drink of water (thirst is the aversive), and the teacher says, "Yes, as soon as you can sit quietly for five minutes, you may get a drink." The teacher desires to have the child begin to sit quietly and uses as a consequence, the removal of a student-perceived aversive, thirst. This is negative reinforcement. When the child demonstrates the desired behavior (sits quietly for five minutes), the teacher permits the student to remove the aversive by getting a drink.

Far more educators answer "yes" to question 4 than to question 5. This is unfortunate, as positive and negative reinforcement accomplish similar results. Negative reinforcement is just one more option available to educators who choose behavior modification as the basis for classroom management. To use it, though, it must be understood.

Examples of Negative Reinforcement

To gain practice with negative reinforcement, examine the following statements and attempt to identify (1) the specific behavior the teacher wants modified, and (2) what aversive stimulus will be removed if the student demonstrates the desired behavior:

- If you are able to complete your work on time for three days in a row, you will no longer have to stay inside for recess.
- If you score 80 percent or higher on the exam, you will not have to turn in a final paper.
- If you get all of your assignments in on time throughout the ten weeks, you will be able to drop your lowest grade.
- If you stay at the assigned task for the entire study period, there will be no need to phone your parents.

In each of the above examples, the student is saddled with an aversive stimulus (or the threat of it). The student's way out is to change his or her behavior—do what is expected of him or her. If the student does, the aversive stimulus is lifted—for instance, the student no longer has to stay in for recess. There is no punishment, because no aversive stimulus is being supplied. There is no time-out, because no reward is being removed. And there is no positive reinforcement, because no reward is being supplied. What works here is negative reinforcement—removing an aversive stimulus following the demonstration of a desired behavior.

Quiz Results from Educators

I have administered this same quiz to more than a thousand elementary and secondary student teachers, teachers of all grade levels, administrators, and school guidance personnel. The results were disturbingly similar—few respondents understood the concept of negative reinforcement. Seventy percent thought punishment, or a word meaning the same thing as punishment, was a synonym for negative reinforcement. Sixty-six percent thought negative reinforcement stopped, not started, behavior. Ninety-nine percent would regularly consider using positive reinforcement in the future, yet only 38 percent said likewise for negative reinforcement.

Of those saying they would consider using negative reinforcement, the vast majority gave inappropriate reasons for why they would use it. They said something to the effect of "Everyone needs a good kick in the pants once in a while"—once again, confusing punishment with negative reinforcement.

Summary

Without making a value judgment in favor of behavior modification over any of the other theories of classroom management, I hope that whatever discipline model you use, you use it effectively. If behavior modification is your choice, then you have an obligation to learn it well, and that includes not overlooking the positive effects of negative reinforcement as a classroom management strategy.

DEFUSING POWER STRUGGLES: ALTERNATIVES TO "FIGHTING BACK" OR "GIVING IN"

Introduction

One of the most time-consuming and unrewarding duties of an educator is having to deal with discipline problems. Power struggles between teachers and students is an especially troublesome category of misbehavior. Teachers must learn how to effectively defuse power struggles.

Goals of Misbehavior

Dreikurs, Grunwald, and Pepper (1971) identify four goals of misbehavior: attention, power, revenge, and display of inadequacy. These goals form a hierarchy that reflects the degree of discouragement felt by the student. Attention, at the top of the hierarchy, represents mild discouragement. Display of inadequacy, at the bottom, represents intense discouragement. Students unsuccessful in gaining a sense of significance or a feeling of belonging at one end of the hierarchy—attention—may move down that hierarchy to the next and more serious goal of misbehavior—power.

When educators recognize that a student's misbehavior has a purpose and see the psychological motivation behind his or her actions, they can respond in a purposeful and helping manner. Teachers need to recognize the misbehavior for what it represents—the student's expression of discouragement, attempt to gain significance, or effort to belong.

Power As a Goal of Misbehavoir

Glasser (1986) identifies the need to gain power as a basic human need. Power, in spite of the cultural taint which it carries, is in itself neither good nor bad (Glasser, 1986, pp. 24–25). But efforts to fulfill an unmet need for power can cause conflict between teachers and students. Power struggles are a type of student misbehavior that not only interferes with classroom learning but often escalates to the point where the administrator becomes involved.

Students seeking power believe they can be somebody only if they do what they want to do and/or refuse to do what they are instructed to do. Remember this is a youngster's logic here, not an adult's. If a teacher tries to teach a student a lesson by "pulling the child down off his or her high horse," the teacher only increases the student's underlying sense of inferiority. The student in a power struggle acts "big" to conceal how "small" he or she really feels. The student's manifest behavior is a front to save face.

How do you know when you are having a power struggle with a student? Dinkmeyer and Dinkmeyer (1976) state that you need to examine your own feelings toward the student's behavior. In a power struggle, you most often feel angry. You feel provoked. You feel as if your authority has been threatened. You have a tendency to react by either fighting back or giving in. Let's examine these two common, although ineffective, ways an educator reacts to a power struggle.

Fighting Back

If an educator fights back and is successful in subduing the student, what really has been accomplished? The child may defiantly comply, but the relationship between the student and teacher has been hurt. The educator's actions impress upon the child the value of power, and as such the desire for more power is increased. When students lose to an educator in a power struggle, they learn that it is the powerful who win; if only they had more power, they reason, they too could win.

How do students typically deal with losing again and again? Consider rebellion, resentment, striking back (at the teacher or another student who is less powerful), blaming others, apple polishing, bossing others, fear of trying, and lying. In effect, the teacher's efforts to win in the power struggle may backfire (Tjosvold, 1976). Schmuck and Schmuck (1979) suggest that students who feel powerless view the classroom as a threatening and insecure place, thus further increasing their feelings of discouragement and thwarting their efforts to gain significance and to belong.

In reality, though, an adult simply cannot win in a power struggle with a student. Sound strange? Adults must be guided by a sense of responsibility and moral obligation. The student sees no such boundaries, parameters, or rules. The student will use any means to the end of winning in the power struggle. He or she can be amazingly creative and inventive.

Giving In

What happens if the educator gives in during the power struggle? The student learns, through operant conditioning, that power really does work. Because the student has been rewarded by winning, we would expect the student to engage even more frequently in this same behavior.

What happens to the child when he or she wins all the time in these power struggles? The child learns to see life as get-get-get; he or she learns that his or her needs are more important than anyone else's; he or she feels unloved (after all, how can adults show any real love to a child who constantly wins at their expense?); and he or she has difficulty developing peer relationships.

It appears, on the surface, that there are only two responses open to a teacher in a power struggle—fight back or give in. Both of these win-lose reactions have severe, undesirable side effects for the educator and the child. But is there any other alternative? There are, in fact, several.

Successful Alternative: Withdraw from the Conflict

One response is to withdraw from the conflict. Is this just another way of giving in? No! Often when a child finds himself or herself in a power struggle, he or she would like to get out of the predicament if only he or she knew how. Unfortunately, the student has already committed himself or herself. The student has challenged the teacher, perhaps refusing to do something that was asked of him or her. All the student's classmates have seen the challenge made. The student would like to get out of the predicament and at the same time save face.

This is a rather bold statement to make. What makes me believe a student often seeks a face-saving exit from the power struggle? Consider an example from your own life. Have you ever been zipping down the interstate and, for whatever reason, found yourself engaged in a power struggle with another driver? Without really thinking, the other driver cuts you off slightly, so in turn you tailgate the driver. The power struggle is on.

As you start to think about what you are doing, using all the adult logic you can muster, you ask yourself, "Why am I doing this? We could get killed. Why don't I just stop this silly power struggle?" But it is not so easy to stop the jousting once it has begun.

Think of how you feel when the other driver turns off at the next exit. The power struggle has ended. You feel relieved! His or her pulling off (withdrawing from the struggle) let the struggle end with both of you saving face. No winners, no losers.

Further, imagine if you had not taken up the challenge in the first place and had just let his or her cutting in go by unnoticed. Would you be perceived as weak? I think not. In fact, you may even consider yourself quite strong for having resisted the challenge. Thus, withdrawing from a conflict often takes more courage than fighting back. It should not be confused with simply giving in.

Returning to the classroom, assume that you have a student named Billy who has been absent for several days and is frustrated and discouraged at being behind the other students. He misbehaves. He says, with the whole class looking on, "I'm not going to make up all that work; you can't make me!" You feel your authority has been threatened. After all, what will all the other students think if you let Billy get away with this challenge? Note that after Billy has made the challenge, he too is thinking about what the rest of the class will think if he knuckles under and does the makeup work. The power struggle has begun.

Your first reaction might be, "I'll show you. Just watch me make you do the school work." Or you might think, "It just isn't worth the hassle, I'll give in and let him get out of doing the work." Neither of these are appropriate reactions.

Instead, try withdrawing from the conflict. Don't take up the challenge. Imagine how difficult it will be for the power struggle to go on, let alone escalate, if only one person is involved in the struggle. After all it "takes two to tango." Suggest a time and place when just you and the student can talk over this problem. Meeting at another, more convenient time has the added advantage of allowing the problem to be aired in private and not in front of the class as an audience—or "peanut gallery" as Buffalo Bob of the 1950's *Howdy Doody* show would say.

Successful Alternative: Plan Ahead for Power Struggles

A second response is to plan ahead in anticipation of power struggles. At the start of the year, explain to the students how you plan to handle power struggles when they come up. Explain that it is natural to have such struggles, but that it is important how they are resolved. Point out your logic for the need to save face (on the part of both parties), the need for tempers to calm down, and the need for the power struggles not to interfere with the scheduled learning activities.

Enlist students' support for this plan. If we add to this planning ahead the assumption that students generally perceive school as a safe and caring place and that they generally have a good rapport with teachers, withdrawing from a conflict can be a sign of coolheadedness and strength, an attempt to see school, like society, as a place where problems should be faced up to and handled in a calm, effective manner.

Another dimension of planning ahead is making sure that the students understand the bases for your power in the classroom. French and Raven

(1960) offer five bases of power for an educator, including legitimate power. Generally, students perceive that the teacher has the right to prescribe behavior; they respect the teacher's social position or office. Students understand that the teachers have a contract to teach, that by law they must fulfill these duties. In the heat of a power struggle, where personalities are often at odds, it is helpful to refer to the school's expectation that classes go on as planned and that interruptions be handled at other times. This becomes a reason for "talking about it later," a temporary out for both the educator and the student.

Successful Alternative: Acknowledge Student Power and Solicit Cooperation

A third response to a power struggle is to help youngsters see how to use their power constructively. This is often done by first acknowledging the actual power the child possesses, pausing to let the message sink in, and then enlisting his or her voluntary cooperation. This is an extremely powerful response. Like all attempts at discipline, it works best when students have a rapport with the teacher and generally see school as a good place.

For example, assume you are an English teacher responsible for the school newspaper. The paper is about to go to press but is missing several critical pictures that your one and only student photographer, Lynn, has not developed. In your attempt to persuade her to get on with this developing task, a power struggle emerges. The student says, "Well, you know I'm the only one who knows how to develop those pictures, and if I don't do them, there will not be any pictures for the newspaper." You feel angry. You feel provoked. You feel your authority has been threatened. You have all the feelings associated with a power struggle. You are tempted to tell her off, even though you know what she has said is absolutely true.

You instead admit the obvious to Lynn that she does, in fact, have the power to determine whether or not the paper will go to press complete with pictures. You then pause to let this acknowledgment of her power "sink in." Finally you go on to enlist her help or cooperation. You might say, "You are correct, Lynn. You are the only one who knows how to develop those pictures. Without your developing skills the newspaper will have to go to print without the pictures." Pause for a moment or two. Continue by asking "Will you help us by developing the pictures?"

If she agrees, then all you did to get her cooperation was to admit the obvious about her power. Your admitting that Lynn has that power defuses it, permits her to no longer need to flaunt it, and sets the stage for her to not only become a hero by developing the pictures, but to develop them and save face at the same time.

If you choose to give in to your natural tendency to fight back, you may or may not get the pictures developed. If they are developed, with defiant compliance on the student's part, chances are they will be of poor quality. When pictures are needed again, I would not count on Lynn. The teacher-student relationship has been damaged. Your admitting the obvious, that Lynn possessed power over the immediate situation, was not just a sign of significance for her. It was a sign that she has a legitimate place in the group she belongs.

Summary

Power struggles are inevitable. What is not inevitable are the ineffective ways educators typically respond to these struggles. Power struggles are also natural. Basic human needs must be fulfilled. The acquisition of power is, "especially for young people, the most difficult (need) to fulfill" (Glasser, 1986, p. 27). And yet for students, "There is no greater work incentive than to be able to see that your effort has a power payoff" (Glasser, 1986, p. 27).

Only motivated students engage in power struggles. This is a healthy sign. Channel that need for power. Use the alternatives outlined above as more effective ways to respond to power struggles.

TEST YOURSELF

This is a sampling of the kinds of factual and open-ended questions that you should be able to answer after having read this chapter.

1. What was your *initial* reaction to the title of the article, "The negative side of praise?" What was your reaction *after* having read the article?

2. Identify the three situations described in the article, "The negative side of praise," where educators should be cautious in sending praise.

3. What was your *initial* reaction to the title of the article, "The positive side of negative reinforcement?" What was your reaction *after* having read the article?

4. According to the article, "The positive side of negative reinforcement?" There are two ways to *start* a desired behavior and two ways to *stop* an unwanted behavior. What are they?

5. According to the article, "Defusing power struggles: Alternatives to fighting back or giving in," what three alternative teacher behaviors exist in a power struggle?

CHAPTER 12

"A" Through "Z" Suggestions for More Effective Classroom Management

OBJECTIVES

This chapter will help you, among other things, to:

- Identify specific classroom management strategies.
- Classify specific classroom management strategies.

A THROUGH Z SUGGESTIONS

Discipline problems do not just occur out of the blue; they are precipitated. Home and other out-of-school environments can exert a major influence upon children that, in turn, affects their readiness to learn when they come to school. As teachers, we can't do much about these out-of-school factors. We can, though, address those in-school factors that influence a child's willingness to learn. The suggestions presented in this chapter, when regularly and consciously applied, will improve classroom management.

Will you discover anything new? Shrigley (1985, p. 31) provides an answer when he states, "I concede that successful teachers have been using many of the coping skills casually; however, I challenge them to consciously sequence the coping skills into a systematic plan." Such plans are needed even more today given the mentoring role experienced teachers are asked to play.

Successful teachers may respond to many of the following suggestions by saying, "We already do it." While that may be true for them, most student teachers and new teachers can't respond with such confidence.

Those who regard themselves as teachers, not disciplinarians, consider that in the real world of the classroom one cannot choose to be one and avoid being the other. Discipline is a prerequisite to successful teaching. Effective classroom management is only a means to an end—effective teaching and effective learning. Discipline is a necessary but not sufficient condition for effective teaching.

All of the suggestions in this chapter are things you can do on your own. None involve any major change in school or departmental policy. Are these suggestions simply "tricks of the trade"? Not really. Each suggestion has a grounding in theory. Take advantage of these suggestions. Use these suggestions. Get started now!

Teachers looking for a single theoretical thread to connect each of the alphabetized suggestions may be disappointed. Although some are neutral enough that they can be accepted by most folks, your acceptance or rejection of others probably will be based upon your philosophical position (i.e., Skinner versus Rogers) as presented in chapter 2.

Although there may be no single, overall organizing scheme, many of the suggestions can logically be categorized. Some of these categories are outlined below. You are encouraged to create still other categories and to continue adding suggestions to your repertoire of classroom management strategies.

Respect for Students

"C" for Individual or Private Correction

"M" for Mr. or Miss

"N" for Learn Their Names

"N" for Personal Needs: Your and Theirs

"T" to Say "Thank You"

Preventing Discipline Problems

"C" for Catch Students Being Good

"O" for Organized

"O" for Overprepare

"S" for Surprise Them, or "How Did You Know That?"

Conveying a Professional Attitude

"C" for Calm and Businesslike

"G" for Don't Hold a Grudge

"P" for Don't Take It Personally

"U" for Be Up

"X" for Exemplify Desired Behavior; Don't Be a Hypocrite

Specific Classroom-Related Techniques

"A" for Act; Don't Just React

"A" for Assign Responsibility

"B" for Back Away

"E" for Enforce; Don't Negotiate

"E" for Eye Messages

"I" for Identify Specific Misbehaviors

"P" for Premack Principle (Grandma's Rule)

"P" for Punctuality

"R" for Return Assignments and Tests Quickly

"S" for Secure Their Attention—First!

"V" for Visibility (and At Times Invisibility)

"W" for Wait-Time

"W" for "We," Not "You"

Keeping a Teacher's Role in Perspective

"F" for Friendly versus Friends

"J" for Judge and Jury

"T" for Threats and Warnings

Just in Case

"D" for Make a Deal with a Fellow Teacher

"E" for Prepare an Emergency Plan

This ABC format may seem simplistic, but it was never intended to be anything more than a way to highlight a series of straightforward and practical classroom management strategies. These strategies are rearranged below in alphabetical order.

"A" for Act; Don't Just React

"A" for Assign Responsibility

"B" for Back Away

"C" for Calm and Businesslike

"C" for Catch Students Being Good

"C" for Individual or Private Correction

"D" for Make a Deal with a Fellow Teacher

"E" for Prepare an Emergency Plan

"E" for Enforce; Don't Negotiate

"E" for Eye Messages

"F" for Friendly versus Friends

"G" for Don't Hold a Grudge

"I" for Identify Specific Misbehaviors

"J" for Judge and Jury

"M" for Mr. or Miss

"N" for Learn Their Names

"N" for Personal Needs: Yours and Theirs

"O" for Organized

"O" for Overprepare

"P" for Don't Take It Personally

"P" for Premack Principle (Grandma's Rule)

"P" for Punctuality

"R" for Return Assignments and Tests Quickly

"S" for Secure Their Attention—First!

"S" for Surprise Them, or "How Did You Know That?"

"T" for Say "Thank You"

"T" for Threats and Warnings

"U" for Be Up

"V" for Visibility (and At Times Invisibility)

"W" for Wait-Time

"W" for "We," Not "You"

"X" for Exemplify Desired Behavior; Don't Be a Hypocrite

"A" for Act; Don't Just React

There is a big difference between acting and reacting. To act is to be in command; to react is to have the situation be in command. Teachers should do more acting, taking charge using the best knowledge base available, and less reacting, letting the circumstances dictate their behavior. Teachers who spend their time reacting are always followers—waiting until something happens before they take action. Teachers who spend their time acting are leaders—more often controlling what happens whether in classroom instruction or in classroom management.

Don't be a "fire-putter-outer." This is someone who looks at classroom management as a tool similar to a fire extinguisher. In this analogy, classroom management techniques are kept handy to douse the discipline fire should one occur. In reality, it is not a matter of *whether* discipline problems occur, but *when* discipline problems occur. Whereas most people hope they will never have to use the available fire extinguisher, hoping not to have to use classroom management strategies is an unrealistic expectation.

Teachers should spend time prior to the start of school planning their discipline strategies just as they spend time planning teaching strategies and ordering teaching materials. Discipline must be established, and discipline must be maintained throughout the school year. Skills are needed to make it happen.

The teaching profession is not too unlike the medical profession when we give lip service to preventative measures, yet still too often wait for symptoms to show before we take action. The "ounce of prevention is worth a pound of cure" adage applies as much to education as it does to medicine. Making things happen by acting is much preferred to letting things happen by simply reacting. Effective teachers act; they don't simply react!

"A" for Assign Responsibility

The more students are responsible for their own behaviors, the less they need teacher-supplied classroom management. Therefore, if for no reason than to reduce the time and energy devoted to classroom management, teachers should work to increase the pool of responsible students.

Too often teachers assign responsibility only to those students who have already shown they are responsible. What point is there to curing the already cured? How do students who are not responsible ever learn to become more responsible unless they practice being responsible? It reminds me of a childhood friend whose mother said he was allowed to go swimming with us only after he learned how to swim! He never did go swimming with us. To this day he cannot swim.

Learning to be more responsible is much like learning anything else. It involves a process of trial and error—one hopes more of the former than of the latter. Yet, teachers often treat the learning of responsibility as something completely different from other learning.

For instance, if a student was just starting to learn trigonometry, a teacher would require that the student practice solving trig problems (trial component). At the same time, the teacher would expect the student to make some mistakes, occasionally fail, and even periodically regress (error component). But "some mistakes" and "occasionally fail" would not be enough evidence to assume that the student is incapable of doing trigonometry. So too, when students occasionally fall short of being as responsible as we might have hoped, it would be equally unfair to assume they are incapable of being responsible.

Assigning responsibility can take many forms. A teacher could assign less responsible students the in-class tasks of distributing materials, helping to collect assignments, and so on. Later, the teacher could use out-of-class, yet well-defined and controlled activities such as having a student take attendance forms to the office. Another example might be a teacher's assigning an older student the responsibility of working with a younger student—perhaps teaching her a specific academic skill or showing him how to use a piece of playground equipment.

The general rule would be that the assigned tasks would start off small and build in importance and trust as the student showed he or she was capable of handling responsibility.

Just as it is true that "nothing breeds success like success," "nothing breeds responsibility like responsibility." Although increasing student responsibility is itself a desirable goal, remember its implication in the area of classroom and school discipline. More responsible students require less external (teacher-supplied) discipline.

"B" for Back Away

When you call upon a student to answer a question or when you acknowledge a student who has asked a question, the natural tendency is to move close to him. When you do this, what happens? The closer you move in his direction, the quieter his answer or question will be. After all, why should he speak loudly when you are, or soon will be, right next to him? What ends up happening is that the two of you carry on a dialogue and the rest of the class feels left out.

What else happens as you approach the student who is speaking? Your line of sight, your eye contact, with the rest of the class is lost. When your eye contact is lost, your nonverbal communication with the class is lost too.

If other students cannot hear what that one student is saying, if they lose eye contact with you, and if, as a result, they no longer feel involved in the discussion, their attention will turn elsewhere. Often this "elsewhere" results in the need for the teacher to take disciplinary measures. It doesn't have to happen.

Keep your students involved in what is happening in class discussions. When calling upon a student to answer, *back away* from him. This forces him to increase the volume of his voice so that you can hear him from across the room. If you can hear him, so can all of the other students!

Moving away from the student who is answering leaves you with a clear line of sight across the entire class. You can see the student who is answering. But you can see the faces of many of the other students—perhaps one or more of whom have approving or disapproving looks on their faces and can then be asked to comment. The student with the confused look can be straightened out. The students over in the corner just beginning a little neighborly conversation can be thwarted. The discussion continues; all are involved.

As effective as the concept of backing away is, occasionally do the exact opposite. Move very close to the person who is answering—eye to eye. Put the student on the spot. Invade his personal space—but not for too long— just long enough so that students do not know what to expect. In football it is like having a strong running game, but every once in a while going to the air with a pass. The other side never knows what play might come next. The quarterback who varies his game plan is usually more effective in the long run—so, too, with teachers.

Do move about the classroom. Look at your notes ahead of time and judge which portions of the lecture you can deliver while away from the desk or podium. Consider using an overhead projector that has a brief outline of your notes on it. This frees you to move about the room and more closely monitor student behavior. Let a student seated by the overhead uncover sections, so you don't have to run to the front of the room. A flip chart with the same brief outline works as well to free you from teaching solely in the front of the room.

Your movement about the classroom takes advantage of another well-known classroom management tool—proximity control. The closer you are to students the more likely they are to remain at task and, consequently, the less likely they are to misbehave.

"C" for Calm and Businesslike

When disciplining a student, do so calmly. I cannot stress this point strongly enough! Save your emotional energy for more appropriate times— animated lectures, spirited class discussions. Be businesslike, polite but firm, as you go about disciplining a student. Even a misbehaving child is entitled to respect. A police officer who pulls you over for speeding has every right to implement the state's discipline plan and write you a ticket. He or she has no right to belittle you, to rant and rave at you.

When a student misbehaves, get on with the act of implementing your discipline plan. Skip the screaming, finger shaking, penetrating looks, and sarcastic comments. Implementing your discipline plan in a calm manner keeps the misbehaving student's attention on the relationship between his or her behavior and the logical consequences that flow from that behavior. The ongoing relationship the two of you have is far less likely to be weakened. Remember that although the discipline episode will pass, you and the student must work together for the rest of the year.

I know of no author writing on the subject of discipline who would condone any other teacher posture then remaining calm and businesslike when disciplining a student. If you let students set you off or make you lose your temper, then you are no longer in control! Whether it is a 105–pound female or a 210–pound male, the thought of the only adult in the classroom being out of control is very scary. You are the teacher; you are supposed to be in control. To effectively control others, you must first control yourself!

One other important reason for remaining calm and businesslike when you discipline students is that your behavior will be a model for them. Discipline yourself in manners, voice, disposition, honesty, punctuality, consistency, and fairness (Stefanich & Bell, 1985, p. 20). Students will learn not only from the specific discipline you dispense, but also from *how* you dispense it. When you lose control, your unintended lesson of "flying off the handle" could well be remembered longer than the intended discipline lesson.

Be conscious of how you act when you discipline students. Others surely are—I guarantee it! Work at being able to discipline a student with as little disturbance to the normal classroom operation as possible. Teacher calmness has another thing going for it: students prefer it. Students judge as one characteristic of their "best" teachers the fact that such teachers remain calm when "telling off" miscreants (Lewis & Lovegrove, 1984). Everything is to be gained by disciplining in a calm and businesslike manner; nothing is to be gained by doing otherwise.

"C" for Catch Students Being Good

Try to catch students being good, not just being bad. Given that students' behavior in the future is, to a great degree, governed by the consequences of their present behavior, it makes just as much sense to reward good behavior as it does to punish bad behavior. In fact, it makes more sense.

Make sure students know they have been caught! Try sending an appreciative I-message to those students whom you catch being good. You might say, "Class, when all of you are sitting at your seat so quietly doing your work, it makes it possible for me to help other students who need assistance, and I really appreciate it." Or you could say, "Class, when you put your materials away after our art time, it saves me a lot of time and effort, and I really want to thank you." Finally, you could say, "When all of you continue doing your seat-work when I am called out in the hall to talk to the principal, it helps convey to the principal that I am doing a good job as a teacher. That makes me feel proud. Thanks!"

In each of these examples, I assume that you actually feel the way you say you feel. Why not simply acknowledge these feelings and supporting facts? Catch the students being good *and* let them know that you have caught them.

Sometimes catching students being good, as an effort to enhance students' acceptable behaviors, can also be used to lessen unacceptable behaviors. This is done by trying to catch students engaging in behavior that is *incompatible* with the behavior the teacher is trying to stop. For instance, the behavior of a student's sitting in his seat doing his work is incompatible with the behavior of that same student's being out of his seat wandering about the classroom. A student cannot do both at the same time—the two behaviors are incompatible. If the teacher's goal is to reduce the student's out-of-seat behavior, a traditional response might be to punish the student for being out of his seat. A more effective way to accomplish this same goal is for the teacher to catch the student in his seat and provide a desired consequence.

The more that students are "caught" being good, the more reason they have to continue being good. The more that students are "caught" being good, the less reason they have to misbehave.

"C" for Individual or Private Correction

Correction is an integral part of classroom discipline. How one corrects students can make the difference between achieving effective and ineffective results. More effective results are achieved when teachers individually correct and privately correct students.

According to Lasley (1981, p. 9), "Individualized corrections are directed only at those students who exhibit misbehavior. Direct, individual commands are difficult for students to ignore." Saying "David, put your library book away and start your math exercises on page ten," or issuing the command, "Becky, stop passing notes, and get your assignments ready to take home," makes it clear to whom the teacher is talking and what the teacher expects David and Becky to do. Generalized comments—for example, "Everyone get busy"—might enable David to keep reading his library book and Becky to continue passing notes while at the same time assuming that they are in fact "busy."

Private correction is generally unobtrusive to classroom processes and audible to almost no one other than the misbehaving student, or at least to only a small group of nearby pupils. Only the teacher and the misbehaving student are involved. Because no one else is involved, neither the teacher nor the student is under quite so much pressure to take a stand and save face by not backing down (Lasley, 1981). Private correction follows the adage, "Praise in public [except perhaps some secondary students], punish in private."

Shrigley (1985, pp. 26–27) presents four intervention skills, a form of "teacher telegraphy," designed to privately inform disruptive students that their behavior is unacceptable. These skills, in hierarchical order, are planned ignoring, the use of signals, proximity control, and touch control (actually touching a student—shoulder or upper arm). Teachers may choose to use planned ignoring, if only briefly, for slight infraction. Inaudible facial expressions and gestures such as putting your index finger up to your lips serve to put the misbehaving student on notice. Proximity control, or standing near the misbehaving student, is the next step. Finally, subtle and unobtrusive touch control (with appropriate age and gender consideration) leaves little doubt in the student's mind that you disapprove of his or her behavior.

If you are going to correct student misbehavior, do it effectively. Provide individual and private correction.

"D" for Make a Deal with a Fellow Teacher

To effectively use operant conditioning principles, one must be aware of the four available teacher-supplied consequences. These include positive reinforcement, negative reinforcement, time-out, and punishment. As time-out, consider striking a deal with a fellow teacher, preferably one who is teaching students of a different grade level than yours, so that he or she will take your "problem child" and you will take his or hers. In an elementary school, your sixth-grade problem, John, could be sent temporarily to Miss Homes' second-grade classroom. Miss Homes is primed to occasionally expect a sixth-grade "guest." She knows that he has been sent to her as part of a time-out arrangement. She knows that he has work to do and is to get on with it. No fuss, no bother.

This is a less drastic and less punitive, as well a more pedagogically sound, classroom management technique than putting John out in the hall or sending him to the office. The technique removes John from an environment in which, at least for the present, he is having trouble coping. Going to Miss Homes' room temporarily removes John from his friends, his peers, his audience. In turn, Miss Homes may occasionally send one of her second graders to your sixth-grade classroom.

Note that the purpose of striking a deal with a fellow teacher is not to embarrass or punish the child—that is a whole separate operant learning consequence called punishment. The purpose is simply to place the child in a different environment where he can once again get back at task. There should be no particular fanfare and no fuss made when the student is moved from one room to another. It should not be tongue lashing, or calling the sixth grader a "little second grader." Time-out as a classroom management technique is not punishment. Do not, by your inappropriate execution of a time-out arrangement, accidentally turn time-out into punishment!

How long is his temporary stay in Miss Homes' room? That depends. It could be your decision when you think he is ready to return and join his fellow sixth graders. It could be his decision, if you so agree, to return when he thinks he is capable of returning.

"E" for Prepare an Emergency Plan

Prepare a plan to handle those school or classroom emergencies (health, discipline) that may occur in a teacher's life. It should go without saying that the time to form an emergency plan is *not* during an actual emergency. The plan should be worked out ahead of time.

For instance, a teacher may need to take a child who has suddenly become ill to the nurse. What is the teacher to do with the rest of the class? Simply telling them to keep on with their work may not be the best answer. A teacher could work out ahead of time a code that when quickly delivered to a fellow teacher would tell that teacher to "please keep an eye on my unsupervised class while I attend to an emergency." No long explanation would be required—the code word would simply and quickly execute the emergency plan.

Have you ever been in a hospital when a "code blue" message came over the public address system? Everyone who needs to know knows where to go and what to do. Everyone else goes on about his or her regular business less disturbed, if not undisturbed, by the announcement. This emergency plan strategy for a hospital helps the staff to more efficiently, effectively, and smoothly do their job. It is no different for schools.

One could envision still other situations where assistance might be needed in the classroom to handle an overly rebellious student or to take an urgent phone call down in the office. Once again, in an emergency, time is of the essence. A quickly and clearly executed emergency plan worked out ahead of time can save the day.

"E" for Enforce; Don't Negotiate

I never have been certain whether stores displaying the sign YOU BREAK IT, YOU BOUGHT IT! would or could enforce what the sign says. The fact is I never want to put myself in a position to find out.

Just imagine how ineffective such a statement would be if, when something was broken by a careless customer, no action was taken by the store manager. The threat or, more accurately, the logical consequence of having to pay for something that you have broken would be a hollow warning at best. Once the word got around, future customers would feel less inclined to heed the sign's warning since the manager did not enforce store policy.

Anyone and everyone who writes on classroom management will tell you that teachers must enforce their discipline policy and must do so consistently. The more consistent the enforcement, the more the students will realize that is the policy that triggers a teacher's disciplinary response, not the teacher. Discipline is seen as less personal, less arbitrary. Students learn that it is useless to argue, useless to try to negotiate a reduced "sentence." Arguing and negotiating have a chance of working only on people, not on a discipline policy. And it is policy, assuming it is a fair policy, that is at stake here.

Don't give in to students who try to argue or negotiate a reduction in their punishment. Don't give in even one time. A basic understanding of operant conditioning principles, variable schedules of reinforcement in particular, tells us that even occasionally giving in strongly encourages students' future attempts to argue or negotiate themselves out of receiving their punishment. Las Vegas casinos help create compulsive gamblers by giving in every once in a while and letting the customer win.

So do not listen to students' arguments and negotiating attempts. To listen is to give some possible hope. Why lead students on with false hope? Further, don't let a student's good behavior influence your responsibility for disciplining bad behavior. Some teachers let students off the hook for misbehavior that occurred during the morning because the students behaved themselves all afternoon. All this does is encourage children to misbehave in the earlier hours of the day.

Stand by your discipline policy. Burns (1985, p. 3) recommends that teachers make sure students "know there is a certainty that violations will be caught and dealt with." When students misbehave, they must pay the piper. Get rid of your sense of fair play that makes you want to orally warn a student several times before you enforce the discipline policy (Morgan, 1984). Once the punishment is administered, the slate is clean. If you have a discipline policy, enforce it. If you don't have a discipline policy, get one and enforce it.

"E" for Eye Messages

This suggestion deals with teachers using nonverbal, in most cases less disrupting, methods of classroom management. A person's eyes can be very communicative. A glance across the classroom at a misbehaving child, followed by momentary eye contact, can stop the misbehavior in its tracks—all without any disturbance to the rest of the class. Eye messages are equally capable of sending messages of approval, acceptance, and empathy.

Wolfgang and Glickman (1980, p. 21) offer "silently looking on" as one of seven typical techniques teachers use in dealing with misbehavior. Silently looking on is their equivalent to sending eye messages. In practice, teachers might (1) simply look over at the offender as if to say, "I see what you're doing, but I know that you can take care of yourself"; (2) observe the behavior and collect information on the entire situation before acting; or (3) gaze directly at the student with a penetrating frown.

Silently looking on is just as appropriate a tool for teachers who believe in intervention as it is for teachers who practice nonintervention. It all depends upon how one goes about sending eye messages.

Although some teachers send eye messages better than others do, it is a skill that can be practiced and perfected. You might invite a fellow teacher to observe your class and report upon how effectively you use eye messages. Do you favor one side of the room or direct your attention to just the front or back? Do you stare more or less directly ahead, perhaps over the heads of your students? Although this may be a successful, anxiety-reducing suggestion offered in the past by speech teachers, it is not a successful technique for showing who is in charge.

When eye messages are combined with other nonverbal gestures such as an index finger raised to the lips signaling "quiet," an open hand moving up and down signaling "settle down," or a raised eyebrow signaling "disapproval," they can be very effective in maintaining classroom discipline.

The use of eye messages (contact) can also increase the effectiveness of delivered consequences. Mendler and Curwin (1983, p. 143) suggest that when you repeat a rule or deliver a consequence to a student, "look directly into the eyes of the student and capture his eyes with yours. After you have finished delivering your message, maintain eye contact for a second or two and continue to maintain it as you slowly move away."

Eye messages, with or without words, can be very powerful. Practice sending them. Get good at it! Having said this, I should add that one must also be conscious of the cultural diversity that exists in many of today's classrooms. Certain Eastern cultures, such as Laotian, Korean, and Chinese, view direct eye contact as a expression of disrespect to adults. Be sensitive to such cultural diversity.

"F" for Friendly versus Friends

There is a difference between being friendly and being friends. I recommend that you be friendly with your students but not be friends with them. Keep a "professional distance" between you (the teacher) and them (the students). This is especially important for new teachers—those without a reputation already established. Students do not have a crystal ball; they have only your behaviors from which to infer your motives. Don't provide them with behaviors from which they might infer the wrong motives.

Students already have friends. In most cases, they do not need you as still one more friend—at least not in the same sense that they view their other friends. Their friends, usually their peers, are very special to them and serve a unique support function in their lives now and in the future. Parents (guardians), too, are unique and serve a special support role. Teachers have a role to play in a student's life, and it is one that is different from the student's peers or parents. Blurring this distinction can cause problems for teachers when they are called upon to establish and maintain classroom discipline.

Teachers must keep in mind the primary reason for which they have been hired—to keep the learning act afloat. This is what teachers, as professionals, should do best. Otherwise, why hire them? Part of the job of teaching is establishing and maintaining classroom management. This can be made more difficult if students perceive you as their friend, for, in most instances, friends do not have to manage others. Friends do not have to tell other friends to sit down and get to work. Friends do not normally assign other friends homework. Friends do not normally formally evaluate other friends' work.

Student teachers, and sometimes even new teachers, are tempted to be the students' friend. The student teacher might see the students as a welcome refuge in a world dominated by university supervisors and cooperating teachers who in the end must submit a letter grade evaluating his or her performance. Avoid the temptation to become the students' friend.

Dress professionally. Act professionally. Have in mind your objectives for the day and how you plan to accomplish them. Do not permit students to call you by your first name. You may wish to return the courtesy by calling them by "Mr." or "Miss." Do not go to student parties. Do not drive students to or from school. Be mindful of telling or listening to student jokes—especially if they are off-color or of an ethic or racial nature. Too often, jokes stress little else. Do not continue to engage in conversations that appear to treat you as one of them and other teachers as belonging to some other group. That is not how it is. Don't mislead students into thinking otherwise.

Students should be mindful that things they tell their friends might stop right there; things they tell you may, in fact, be passed along. Teachers, unlike friends, often have a responsibility under the law to forward certain kinds of information (child abuse, drugs) to the proper authorities. If students think of you as their friend and they tell you things they think will be held in confidence, your "betrayal" (in their minds) will seriously undermine the teacher-student relationship necessary for effective learning to occur.

When given an assignment to read the suggestions in this chapter and to identify two that they would like to work on, my sophomore-level students, who are just about to start their semester-long field experience in a local school, repeatedly single out this suggestion. Many students recall how previous teaching and counseling experiences, at church or at camp, have led to disaster when they became so much of a friend that their ability to lead was compromised.

Be friendly! But do not try to be a student's friend.

"G" for Don't Hold a Grudge

If a student misbehaves, deal with that misbehavior in a calm, confident, and fair manner. Discipline the child according to the offense committed. Supply your logical consequences. That should be—that *must* be—the end of it, however. The slate should be wiped clean. "The more your past mistakes are held against you, the harder it is to summon up the energy to do well now" (Glasser, 1986, pp. 35–36). Whether referring to one's previous academic failures or to one's previous behavior patterns, the past is the past. Now is now.

We all hear of the trouble people experience when they have served a jail sentence and paid their debt to society. No one ever lets them forget the fact that they have misbehaved. Unlike ex-prisoners, students can't so readily move to a different city or state, change their name, and start again. You can't do a whole lot about society's reactions to ex-prisoners, but you can do much about how you treat a student offender once he has paid his "debt to society."

Bartosh and Barilla (1985) make the same point but use slightly different language. They tell educators to avoid the once-a-thief-always-a-thief syndrome. Avoid holding a grudge!

"I" for Identify Specific Misbehaviors

Before any classroom management strategy can be successful in changing a student's behavior, that behavior must first be identified. This is the only way it can work. Specific behaviors must be targeted, for it is only specific behaviors, not general characteristics, that one can hope to change.

Saying that a student is "uncooperative," "a troublemaker," "undepend-able," or "immature" doesn't tell you a thing. These terms mean different things to different people. A child's refusing to follow directions could be seen by one teacher as "uncooperative" and by another teacher as "indepen-dent." What matters here is not which teacher is correct, but what *specific behaviors* of the student led both teachers to their general conclusion. It is only these specific behaviors that may be increased, maintained at the pre-sent level, or decreased. This is really your goal. Therefore, make specific observable behaviors your focus.

If Johnny is labeled a troublemaker as a result of regularly striking fellow students when out on the playground for recess, then the targeted behavior in need of correction is his striking fellow students, not the summary label of being a troublemaker. Ask yourself, "What is the student doing that leads you [and perhaps others] to label him as a troublemaker?" In this case, it is hitting other students. Once you are successful in getting him to stop strik-ing fellow students (targeted behavior), then the label of troublemaker will no longer apply. No matter what classroom management techniques you decide to use, they must be directed at increasing, maintaining at the present level, or decreasing specific behaviors.

One other thing that happens when you label students is that the labels never seem to go away—even when the behaviors that caused the labeling have ceased. Once called a troublemaker, will Johnny forever be saddled with that label even when your classroom management strategies are successful in getting him to stop striking fellow students? Unfortunately, the answer is often yes. Avoid dealing in vague labels when describing misbehaving stu-dents. It does absolutely no good whatsoever! Instead, clearly identify the specific misbehavior, and then set about using appropriate management strategies to change that behavior. Period. Do it; it works.

"J" for Judge and Jury

What students look for in a classroom is justice, equity, and fairness. When they perceive that justice does not exist, one can expect them to act— maybe even act out. They expect no less than we as citizens demand—even in a less than ideal world. In the world outside of the classroom, we have a court system with, among other designated personnel, a judge and a jury. Except in rare cases, the two roles are separated to better serve justice.

What about the situation in a classroom? Teachers commonly find them-selves in the role of both judge and jury when it comes to classroom man-agement. In fact, teachers not only may be the judge and jury, but often they are also the accuser. How would you feel going before a judge who is also both your accuser and your jury? If it appears to be a little bit rigged, it is. This stacking of the deck does not go unnoticed by students.

Take, for instance, the student who is accused of something by his or her teacher. How prepared is the teacher, now playing the role of judge, to ensure procedural fairness? Although one would expect the teacher, now playing the role of prosecuting attorney, to do so with spirit and determination, who will act as the student's defense attorney? The teacher? I hope not. The student? As the saying goes, "A person who acts as his own attorney has a fool for a client." Finally, how able is the teacher, now asked to play a role of jury, to render a fair and impartial decision?

Although I do not expect that all classroom discipline problems are destined to turn into Perry Mason courtroom episodes, the point is that teachers are asked to assume several roles related to ensuring that justice is served. Further, the courts of our nation have traditionally had a hands-off attitude toward a school's disposition of run-of-the-mill discipline problems. This means that educators have a good deal more leeway in their decision making when it comes to what to discipline and how to discipline.

I would ask teachers to be aware of what to discipline and to keep the power that goes with this responsibility in check. Be the judge, be the jury, but govern your actions by sound judgment.

"M" for Mr. or Miss

Do children act any differently when they are dressed in their Sunday-go-to-meeting clothes than when they are in their jeans? Often, the answer is yes. Wearing good clothes signals a special event that warrants special behavior. An expectation is established that is, more often than not, lived up to.

Addressing students by "Mr." or "Miss" can form similar expectations that can also be lived up to by one's behaviors. When students are addressed as Mr. or Miss, a feeling of being more "grown up" is generated. What child does not want to be perceived as grown up? But being treated as a grown-up doesn't come free. Students can understand that. It carries with it responsibilities that did not need to be shouldered when one was addressed simply as "Johnny," "Wendy," or "Bobby." The title Mr. or Miss conveys a trust on the part of a teacher that one is deserving of that salutation. Once again, more often than not, students will make an attempt to live up to that trust. They will act more grown up; they will misbehave less often.

Chances are other teachers have not addressed students as Mr. or Miss. You, then, are doing something different, something special. This action will not go unnoticed by the children. Students like to "get even," "set the score-card straight," "put things back in balance." How can they do this? Most likely, they will reciprocate the respect you have shown them.

There is one caution to keep in mind when using this suggestion. Be careful of the tone of your voice. In the past, some teachers reserve calling students Mr. or Miss for those times when they wanted to use the title as a put-down. For example, "Well, Miss Butler, let's hear what you might have to say on the subject!" If you call students by Mr. or Miss, do so only out of respect. After all, that is how you would prefer they use your title.

"N" for Learn Their Names

Learn the student's names as quickly as possible. This is a must! Many classroom management techniques, as well as teaching techniques, are enhanced by knowing a student's name. It allows you to direct your comments to specific students regardless of whether or not you have eye contact with them. We all know the ease with which a misbehaving student (possibly sitting in the back of the room whispering to a neighbor) can be brought back into the mainstream of a class discussion simply by directing a question in his direction. Because he is apparently paying no attention to the class discussion, you will obviously need to address him by name.

Do not take more than two days to learn students' names. You simply cannot afford to have many incidents occur where you have to say, "Hey you, quiet down," or "Hey, what's-your-name, what do you think the author meant by . . . ?" The kind of "testing" answer you may very well receive, and one you don't want, is one such as "Who, me?" or " Are you talking to me?" This challenging situation is easily avoided by calling a student by name. Then there is no question who your comment was directed toward. How you handle yourself in the first few days, and how much or how little students find they can get away with, are crucial to establishing discipline for the rest of the year.

Consider having students place 4" X 6" name card "tents" on their desks. Or have students complete some sort of background information form or nongraded pretest that keeps them occupied while you move up and down the rows learning their names. Little is more impressive to students than when, at the end of a period, you ask them to look up at you while you identify each of them by name. Seating charts can be a big help. Practice associating student's features with their names. Who has a Scottish name and has red hair? Does Linda over there look a lot like someone you know named Linda? However you learn their names, do it as soon as possible. The students will be in awe. They will wonder, if you know this much about them already, what else do you know about them? It keeps them guessing.

Consider the story of the college student taking a final exam in a room with three hundred other students. The professor saw the student cheating. When the student went to turn in his exam, the professor said, "I can't acccept that exam, you cheated." The student looked at the pile of over two hundred exams that had already been submitted, and asked the professor, "Do you know my name?" The professor said "No," and the student quickly slid his exam into the pile of already submitted tests and quickly exited stage left. What could the professor do? Nothing.

"N" for Personal Needs: Yours and Theirs

When you prepare for that Saturday garage sale by pricing all of those "treasures," it is important to consider what's the least money you will accept—your bottom line. You can really be taken advantage of, and more importantly, *feel* taken advantage of, if you don't think about the least amount you will be satisfied with until it is too late. It is no different in education.

Teachers should decide ahead of time what are their minimum needs— those student behaviors that must be present before they can get on with effective teaching. These needs should be kept to a minimum, clearly communicated to students, defended as with a cause-and-effect argument, and consistently enforced. Whether you consider yourself to be assertive or not, it is important to identify your minimum prerequisite needs.

Do you have a need for students to arrive at class on time, to have pencils ready and books open when the bell rings, to complete assigned homework, to raise their hands before speaking, to keep books properly covered, to . . . ? What student behaviors are really, really important to you? Think about the answer to this question now.

Don't assume students know what is important to you, what bugs you. Your minimum prerequisite needs may be similar to or different from those of other teachers. It makes no difference. Determine, convey, defend, and enforce your minimum needs.

Listen to your kids. Listen to them as they express their needs. When possible, respond. Like you, children cannot meet their own deficiency needs— safety, love and belonging, and esteem. They need help—often your help. You too need help. Often, given the nature of your job, that help can come from students. Students and teachers are in a position to help each other meet respective needs.

Keep in mind that listening to students does not mean that you agree with what they say. Listening should be just that—listening. Often a student's (and teacher's) needs can be met, or at least brought under control, simply by having someone listen to them. Try it; it works!

"O" for Organized

One of the most common characteristics of a successful teacher is that of being organized. Teachers must organize people, materials, time, activities, and lessons. Organizing any one of these things could be a full-time job. Trying to organize all of them at once, especially when there is an interaction among them, takes superhuman effort. Yet, most successful teachers make it look easy.

Feedback from more than a thousand of my sophomore educational psychology students who took part in a semester-long field experience in local schools offers firsthand acknowledgment of the necessity for requisite organizational skills. These preservice teachers never ceased to be amazed at how things went like clockwork in their cooperating teachers' classrooms. Students were where they were supposed to be, and they were on time; materials were available and distributed with little or no fuss; time was allocated effectively; activities were precisely coordinated; and lessons for individuals, as well as groups, were designed and delivered. Added to this were all the unexpected events that had to be handled without disturbing the established organization.

I was in a classroom recently where the children were celebrating a Scandinavian holiday. Tradition has it that the oldest "daughter" (oldest female in class) and the youngest "son" (youngest male in class) serve the food and drink to the "family" (classmates). Drink had to be poured and passed out. Food had to be placed on trays and distributed. Two cups of drink spilled and had to be wiped up. Three girls working on a computer in the back of the room asked for assistance. The principal made an announcement over the public address system. And, finally, I was there for a short visit with the teacher. The teacher needed overlapping skills!

The more organization a teacher has, the fewer discipline problems that teacher will have. Even if you are not an organized person by nature, work at giving every outward appearance that you are organized. Take the time to plan what is going to happen in your classroom with people, material, time, activities, and lessons. Play a "what if" game with yourself. Ask yourself, "What if I have this group doing such and such, what is likely to happen with the rest of the children?" "What if we are able to get the Thanksgiving turkeys only partially cut out and glued before we run out of time?" "What if I prepared individual student folders to make it easier for students to locate their work?" Explore the pros and cons of the answers to these questions.

Appear organized. Be organized. Plan, plan, plan. Accept the reality of overlapping events; they will not go away. Learn how to handle them.

"O" for Overprepare

When do students misbehave? Often, says Tenoschok (1985, p. 30), "it is when students are bored or do not have a specific task to perform." You can make students have something constructive to do by overpreparing for your lessons. As a rule, it is far better to have more planned to do than you are able to do. To underprepare would be just asking for problems to occur.

Beginning teachers are often asked to overprepare their teaching assignments, at least until they have taught a lesson several times so that they can better predict just how much can and should be taught in a given period of time. Even now, after twenty years' teaching experience, I occasionally get caught at the end of a period.

Overpreparing not only applies to the quantity of material you plan to deliver but also the minimum and maximum limits of what you can effectively do with the material. Say that you glance at the clock and there are ten more minutes left in the class period. You now have several options. Can the discussion of the present material last for ten minutes? Should you ask for one or two more open-ended questions to extend the discussion? Can you wrap up the present material in a minute or so and effectively use the remaining eight minutes to get started on new material? Should you plan to complete the present discussion a minute or two before the end of the period and then provide two minutes of low-volume talk time as a reward for their eager participation?

I don't know which of these paths you would follow. By overpreparing and thinking of alternative ways you can present, shorten, or extend presentations, you will more effectively use instructional time. You will keep students on task. Fewer discipline problems are likely to occur.

There is a positive correlation between overpreparing and presenter confidence—and it shows. Teachers who know what they want to get done and who have designed relevant and interesting instructional strategies step into the classroom ready to move forward with recognizable goals in mind. They exude confidence. Confident teachers have fewer discipline problems.

Overpreparing does not equate with knowing all there is to know about any given subject. No one can be that prepared. It is okay not to have all the answers.

"P" for Don't Take It Personally

As hard as it might sound, don't take student misbehaviors personally.

Except for the most extreme set of circumstances, students do not plot just to make your life more miserable. Therefore, deal with the specific misbehavior problem, the specific rule that has been broken, the specific discipline problem. Deal with it impartially.

It is all right for a teacher to behave in a manner showing concern, caring, and respect. It is *not* all right, nor it is helpful in establishing and maintaining classroom discipline, to act in a disrespectful or vengeful manner.

Students who are discouraged, who feel they don't belong, who have their own personal, or family, problems may very well engage in behaviors that are deemed unacceptable. In plain terms, they may misbehave. Certainly do not overlook the misbehavior. It must be dealt with. At the same time, though, don't take it personally.

"P" for Premack Principle (Grandma's Rule)

"Hey, Dad, just let me watch this television program, and then I will do my homework." "Right after I go play some tennis, I will complete that report." "Sure, I'll get the garage cleaned up, right after I get back from an afternoon at the beach." Promises, promises, promises—often unkept!

What do these at-home examples have to do with being a teacher? Well, they are presented as a frame of reference. If you can identify with these examples and realize how often we end up not doing the homework, completing the report, or cleaning the garage, then you can begin to understand why such statements lead to problems. Doing what you want to do first and promising to do what you would rather not do after doesn't often work. Any grandma knows this when she states the proposition, "First eat all of your dinner, and then you may have ice cream." No amount of grandchild urging will persuade her otherwise.

The Premack Principle states that one should use high-frequency behaviors as a reward for low-frequency behaviors. High-frequency behaviors are those things the person really wants to do—watch television, play tennis, go to the beach. Low-frequency behaviors are those things the person really does not want to do—do homework, complete reports, clean the garage.

No matter how good children's intentions are to live up to their word, allowing people (even yourself) to engage in the more desired high-frequency behaviors first, with the promise that they will then engage in less desired low-frequency behaviors, rarely works well. As the teacher or parent, you end up having to remind, nag, and generally pester the child into living up to his or her end of the bargain. This strains the relationship.

Make access to the more desired high-frequency behaviors contingent upon the completion of the less desired low-frequency behaviors. This way works. Tell students who would rather chat with their neighbor, "If you correctly complete the ten assigned math problems, then you will be able to chat with your neighbor for five minutes." Tell students who would rather just sit and draw pictures, "If you correctly complete the remaining three pages of your skill pack, you may have five uninterrupted minutes to draw your pictures." Tell students who just love to daydream, "If you correctly identify 90 percent of the capital cities in your map exercise, you may have ten minutes to just sit there and daydream."

Connecting the low-frequency behaviors to the high-frequency behaviors increases the odds that students will do the math, their skill pack, and their map. Try rewording the statements by allowing the high-frequency behaviors first. The odds that students will fail to complete the low-frequency behaviors will be significantly reduced!

Note that in each of the three correctly worded statements I specifically defined what was expected of them when engaging in the low-frequency behaviors. In each case, the low-frequency behaviors must be done correctly—no rushing through in a slipshod manner. Further, exactly how much of each low-frequency behavior to be done has been defined: ten math problems, three pages of skill pack, 90 percent identification of capital cities. This is crucial. Do not simply say, "If you work on your mathematics problems for a while, then you may talk with your neighbor."

How long is for a while—ten problems, one week, a full semester? Who knows? How long will I be able to talk with my neighbor? Fifteen seconds, one class period? Put yourself in the place of a child who is asked to do a chore. The parent says, "Work on these leaves for a while, and I'll let you play on the computer." You would like more specific definitions of what "work on" and "for a while" mean. You would also want to know how much time you will get to "play on the computer." Real discipline problems can occur if the two of you have different definitions for these terms. Don't let this happen.

How do you know what are high-frequency behaviors for each of your students? You could simply ask them ahead of time to identify their *expressed* interests. Another way to identify these behaviors is to schedule some "free time" in the students' day, sit back, and observe their *manifested* interests— what they decide to do during this free time. Record your observations for future use in forming Premack Principle contingency statements.

The Premack Principle works. It works best when the low-frequency behaviors and the high-frequency behaviors are clearly specified.

"P" for Punctuality

"Neither rain nor snow nor last-minute copier needs nor unfinished cups

of coffee shall keep me from my appointed duties." This slightly altered let-
ter-carrier oath applies just as well to teachers. You expect your students to
be dependable, accountable, where they are supposed to be when they are
supposed to be there. Can you expect anything less of yourself? RHIP (rank
has its privileges), as a reason (excuse) for not being on time, ought to be
used sparingly. Don't be a hypocrite. If you demand behaviors of others, be
willing to model them yourself. It is a poor leader who does not hold himself up to the same standards as those he leads.

Enough preaching. The fact is that when students are left unsupervised,
you are just asking for trouble. It is during this time that students are more
prone to act out, act up, act differently than when they are at task under the
supervision of an appropriate adult. For every discipline problem that does
not occur because you are where you are supposed to be when you are supposed to be there, that is one less time you will have to use classroom management strategies.

Is this to say that students are incapable of self-supervision? Of course not.
In fact, more and more self-supervision (self-discipline) is just what we would
hope would emerge over a student's years in school. The difference, though, is
that self-supervision is something that should be planned. For instance, students could be told ahead of time that you will be late for a class and asked to
get on with their assigned tasks. Here it may be fair to hold them accountable.

This is very different from simply not showing up on time and expecting
students to go on as if you were there. The popular television public service
spot that says "It's ten o'clock. Do you know where your children are?"
speaks to teachers as well. It is the start of second period. Do you know
where your students are and what they are doing? If you are where you are
supposed to be—on time—you can answer, "Yes!"

This reminds me of a story. A new teacher showed up late to her third-
floor classroom only to see a student sitting on the window ledge with his
legs dangling outside! The teacher screamed at him, "Get back in here immediately!" She followed with a discourse on how he could have been killed had
he fallen to the cement pavement below. Later, in the teacher's room she confessed to a fellow teacher that what really worried her was how she would
explain to the principal and the child's parents just how the student had had
the time and opportunity to be out on the ledge in the first place. What possible excuse could she have, had an accident happened, for not being at her
assigned post. None!

Be where you are supposed to be, and be there on time. Don't be caught
in a position of having to defend undefendable behaviors. Besides, the more
you are where you are supposed to be, the more constructive learning should
take place. That's the bottom line.

"R" for Return Assignments and Tests Quickly

What does this have to do with classroom management? Educational psychologists suggest that learners will not continue to learn unless they receive "knowledge of results," or more appropriate, "knowledge of correct results." If learners are not continuing to learn, because of a lack of prompt corrective feedback from you, what are they doing? They may be inclined to misbehave. Let them know how they are doing; let them know right away. Create the conditions that enhance student's continued learning. Give them prompt feedback.

Learners want to know how they are doing. Presumably, the many assignments and tests required of students are designed to provide just this information—to us and to them. We want students to be prepared, to be ready, to complete this work. We are prone to "get on their case" if they are late in submitting required work. Are students not entitled to be equally disturbed when we delay returning their work? How will they show this discontent? How would you show it? Misbehaving seems a likely student response.

If we don't act in a fashion that tells students that we think our assignments and tests are important, how can we expect students to take them seriously? Returning student work as quickly as possible and doing as accurate a job scoring it as you can sends students the right message: this work is important. Failing to return the work on time or within a reasonable time sends an entirely different message: this work really wasn't that important anyhow. Students start to think that if the work they submitted is not seen as being that important to the teacher, then future work is not that important either. This attitude could lead to disinterested students—the basis for misbehavior.

Don't let this happen. Go out of your way to return student work quickly. Through your behavior, model the same importance your words convey.

"S" for Secure Their Attention—First!

Before you start, get everyone's attention. Common sense? Apparently not for everyone. McDaniel (1986, p. 63) points out that "beginning teachers often make the mistake of trying to teach over the chatter of inattentive students." He states further that some teachers "assume that, if they begin the lesson (and there are *many* beginning points within each lesson), students will notice and quiet down." How long should you wait until students notice? Two minutes? Five minutes? What if some students never notice? Eventually you will need to secure their attention if any effective teaching is going to take place. Because you are going to demand their attention at some point, why not make that point before starting to teach?

If a student does not hear what you have said, sure enough he will talk across the aisle or across the room trying to get the information he missed. You will see this as a misbehavior, and we are off and running with a discipline problem that did not need to exist in the first place. What may happen instead is that the student will interrupt the class to ask for the missing information. You will get upset that he did not pay attention in the first place, maybe tell him so verbally or nonverbally, and once again we are off and running with a possible discipline problem that did not need to exist.

Practice different strategies for securing students' attention. Some are rather straightforward. You could simply tell them, "Okay, let's begin. Put everything but your math book away. It is time to start the math lesson for today." Other common ways of securing students' attention might be simply to stand in front of the class and say nothing. Silence is often the loudest message. You could play a chord or two on the piano, blink the lights, ring a bell, cough, or tap the pointer on the board. When using any of the nonverbal methods for securing attention, be sure to first teach them what those messages mean. Lights being turned off could mean a power failure; a cough could mean a lingering cold; a tap of a pointer stick could be a nervous habit.

Parr and Peterson (1985, p. 40) offer an interesting variation for getting students to focus upon the lesson at hand. They suggest you embed an assumption or presupposition in what you say to them. For example, "While you quiet down and get settled in your seat, open your text to page 50" or "I don't know which part of this chapter will interest you the most, but . . . " The first statement assumes they will "quiet down and get settled." The second statement presupposes something "will" interest them in the chapter. Secure their attention before proceeding with your lesson.

"S" for Surprise Them, or "How Did You Know That?"

Go out of your way to learn things about your students—their work in other classes, efforts and accomplishments in sports, part-time job experiences, home life, youth organizations, and so on. Actually, this is not difficult or time consuming to do. Just keep your eyes and ears open.

This is not an exercise in gossip gathering. It is an exercise in collecting information on students and their lives that you can surprise them with when they least expect it. At the beginning of class you say, "Mary, how is the slinging of hamburgers going at McDonald's?" or "Larry, that was an interesting collage you did in art class" or "Sam, what's this I hear about you earning another merit badge in Scouts?" Don't dwell on any one item. That's not the point. Don't give the students time to think about why you know what you know. Just drop the surprise information and go on with your scheduled lesson.

The effects of your delivering this nice information are several. It certainly conveys to your students that you are tuned into their lives beyond simply how they are doing in your class. It shows that you recognize other accomplishments of theirs, whether it is winning an award, scoring a touchdown, or simply being persistent enough to show up night after night slinging hamburgers at a local fast-food joint. This effort on your part cannot help but strengthen the relationship between you and your students.

But surprising students with information you have about their lives does something else. It keeps students on their toes a little more. It keeps them wondering how you seem to know so much about them. They start to think that if you know this nice information about them, perhaps you are also in a position to know when they might try to get away with something—by misbehaving. The effect of delivering this information is that students begin to think that you have eyes and ears everywhere.

A local principal readily admits to dropping this nice information on his students as well as on his teachers. While they like to receive evidence that the principal is tuned in to what they are doing, at the same time they too are sure he has eyes and ears everywhere. He doesn't; they just think so. But their perception that he does is enough. The result is that students (and, at times, teachers) exhibit more self-discipline—the *very best* classroom management technique.

Take the time to establish the "eyes and ears everywhere" image. After it is established, it takes only an occasional demonstration to maintain that image. Do it; it works!

"T" for Say "Thank You"

When students do something for you, say "Thank you" and mean it. If they have been cooperative, if they have done anything at all that has made your job even a little bit easier and more pleasant, show your appreciation. Thank them. Try saying "Thank you" when students turn in homework, head their paper correctly, carry something for you, pick something up off the floor, help another student, hold open a door for you, quietly take their place in line, or get quickly into their reading groups.

Why do they deserve your thanks for doing no more than what they should be doing anyhow? Well, for one thing, it is the polite thing to say. For another thing, "Thank you" is said, especially to students and children, far too infrequently. Because no damage can be done by saying it, why not err on the side of saying it too often rather than not enough.

If you want to catch students really off guard (in a positive sense), say "Thank you" (implying, "Thank you for all the time and effort you put into this exam") as they individually hand in tests or quizzes. If you think about it, most students taking the test have sat through your lectures, completed your assignments, read the chapters you have assigned, studied for your test, and now have just devoted an hour or so of their lives to taking your test. A "Thank you" is in order. Without students, there would be no need for teachers. Besides, the "Thank you" helps temper what may have otherwise been a pretty anxiety-ridden experience.

When possible, identify the specific behavior for which you are thanking them. This results in a cause-and-effect relationship between a deed and a "Thank you." At other times, such as when they have labored over your test, just a simple "Thank you" without further explanation is sufficient.

Saying "Thank you" lets them know *you* know they are there, they are being noticed, they are being appreciated. It shows them that they are pleasant. After all, we are all too ready to point out to them when they make our life unpleasant, aren't we? Saying "Thank you" also models for students the appropriate way to respond when others make your life just a little bit easier. Who knows, students may end up saying "Thank you" to you as well as to classmates. It really could happen. Make a habit of saying "Thank you."

"T" for Threats and Warnings

Don't threaten to take action. Take action. If you have a discipline plan, then the plan dictates that either action is warranted or it is not warranted. There can be no other choice! Your discipline plan, the agreed-upon rules, should be clear enough to all concerned so that teachers and students alike understand what triggers the plan and what does not.

Threats can undermine an otherwise successful discipline plan. They make discipline personal when it need not be—should not be. Even worse, some teachers use their threats as their discipline plan—forming it "on the run." Students are forced to interpret or extrapolate from threats just what the teacher's discipline plan is. Woe to the student who does not figure out the plan in time!

What usually happens when teachers threaten is that students try to figure out just how far they can go before the teacher will actually carry out the threat. "When teachers finally decide to impose consequences, hostility and ill feelings are likely to result for everyone" (Charles, 1985, p. 136). A discipline plan based or formed on a series of teacher threats is often heavily influenced by a teacher's feelings. If a teacher feels great one day, students can get away with more. If a teacher feels lousy another day, students can get away with less. Too much precious student time and energy are wasted playing this decoding game.

Another trouble with threats is that, after a while, they are ineffective unless they are carried out. How many teachers have you heard threaten to throw kids out of class, suspend them, or expel them? Obviously, far more teachers are going to carry out their threats of throwing a student out of class than expelling him or her. Which threats are the students to believe? What happens to classroom discipline when threats are made and found to be unenforceable? Teachers should never paint themselves into a corner by promising (threatening) what they can't deliver!

Nothing is to be gained by threats. Avoid them. When tempted to threaten a student, refer to your thought-out discipline plan. Let your plan dictate your actions. Don't let your threats dictate your actions.

Is there any place in a teacher's discipline plan for issuing warnings? Charles (1985, p. 137) feels that a warning should be given only once, if at all. Even that warning might take form of the teacher's saying, "The next time you do such and such, I must enforce the consequence (penalty) you seem to be choosing."

"U" for Be Up

Wouldn't it be wonderful if the advice, "Don't worry, be happy," displayed on millions of smiley-face T-shirts, could be followed? But reality often dictates otherwise. Nevertheless, when you enter school, try your best to leave your worries outside. They can be retrieved after school when you leave. No one will take them.

Carrying personal problems into the classroom can interfere with your teaching and with students' learning. Problems unrelated to health, such as insurance bills that are due, a fight with your spouse, or a recent fender-bender, can put a real damper on your day. I understand that. But you need to deal with these problems on your own time, not the students' time.

If a student says, "Good morning, Mrs. Knouse. How are you?" you don't have to lie and say, "I'm doing great." Besides, the emphasis you would place on these words and your accompanying body language would probably send a mixed message. You could just say, "Not bad, how about you?" Often a "How are you?" whether initiated by you, a student, or a fellow teacher, is just a polite way of acknowledging one another. While on the run, most people do not want to listen to your problems anyhow. On the other hand, during a planning period where you and a valued friend or colleague have some private time, you might bend his or her ear for a while. Once the bell rings, put the problem away and get on with devoting your full attention to being a teacher.

There are problems of a health nature that are sometimes difficult to conceal. These cannot be placed on the school's doorstep. If a sprained back suffered in a fall on the ice the night before is impeding your movement about the room, the problem probably ought to be shared with students, using as few details as possible, to let them know what to expect that day. For instance, "Because of a fall I had on the ice, I will like you to help me by coming up, one at a time, to my desk when you need assistance."

In general, "being up" can be contagious spreading throughout the school. What a wonderful epidemic it would be!

"V" for Visibility (and At Times Invisibility)

The bell has rung, and students are changing class. Where are you? The students are called for an assembly. Where are you? Numerous extracurricular events are taking place. Where are you? My suggestion is that you make yourself visible. Let students note your presence.

When classes are changing, consider standing near the doorway so that you can monitor both your classroom *and* the hallway outside of your room. Present the appearance that you are ready to deal with disciplinary infractions when you see them—in or out of your room. Keep in mind that, legally, any and all students in the school are partially your responsibility. Your responsibility for discipline is schoolwide; it does not end with the last person on your homeroom or class roster.

Will the end result of being visible be more discipline work for you? No! In fact, the more visible you as well as fellow teachers are, the less often students will misbehave. Misbehaving students are opportunistic. Don't give them quite so many opportunities. Drivers speed less often when the police are visible. Siblings tend to battle less when parents are visible. Students misbehave less when teachers are visible.

Now, what about being invisible? I recommend that you purchase a pair of softsoled shoes that will enable you to move about the classroom, study hall, assembly, lunchroom, or building while making a minimum of noise. Unlike police who turn on their sirens blocks away for all to hear, teachers should be able to move about without their noisy shoes providing advance notice. In addition to the fact that the noise may be annoying to students who *are* trying to work, it is clear giveaway to students who *are not* working. Vary your path and time schedule so that you are not so predictable. "Good" students perceive that you are available, and "not-so-good" students think you are everywhere (Graff, 1981, p. 3)!

Be visible—at the right times. Be invisible—at the right times.

"W" for Wait-Time

An analysis of teachers' questioning behavior shows that it is not at all uncommon for teachers to wait no more than one second before repeating a question, rephrasing it, or calling upon someone else (Rowe, 1978, p. 207). Further, according to Rowe (p. 207), "Once a student has responded, the teacher typically waits less than one second . . . before commenting on the answer or asking another question."

The net result of this pattern of behavior often is a flurry of questions and answers that leaves, at best, both the teacher and the student exhausted and, at worst, does little "to stimulate a student's thought or quality of explanation" (Rowe, p. 207). When, according to Rowe, teachers extended their wait-time to three seconds or more, several things happened. The length of student responses increased; the number of unsolicited but appropriate responses increased; failures to respond decreased; incidences of speculative thinking increased, contributions by slow learners increased; and, related to the focus of this book, the number of disciplinary moves the teachers had to make dropped dramatically!

The anticipated increase in discipline problems due to the teacher's not keeping "the action going" simply did not materialize. Students did not use this three-second wait-time to act up; they used it to think. Tobin and Capie (1982) support this conclusion showing a significant positive correlation between wait-time and achievement. The message here is that a better way to maintain classroom discipline (as well as to increase learning) is to keep the students busy *thinking*, not necessarily *answering* rapid-paced questions so common in many of today's classrooms.

Perhaps, according to Stahl (1994), the term "think time" would be a more accurate label than "wait-time" because, among other things, it names the primary academic purpose of this period of silence—to allow both the teacher and students to complete on-task thinking.

"W" for "We," Not "You"

We are all in this together with a shared responsibility for the success or the failure of today's class, of this semester, of the school year. A behavioral problem is not just a student's problem, nor is it just a teacher's problem. It is a problem for both. To increase *our* chances of success and reduce *our* chances of failure, cooperation is the name of the game. Preach this message, practice this message. The more the idea of shared responsibility and mutual cooperation is accepted, the less likely it is that there will be behavioral problems.

Consider the hidden message delivered in the following statements—both designed to set the morning's activities. Statement one: "This morning we are going to complete our science write-up during the first half of our morning, and then we will use the remaining time to discuss the selection of books you and I think we should request the library to order." Statement two: "This morning you are going to complete your science write-up during the first half of the (your) period, and then you can use the remaining time to discuss the selection of books (you think) the library should order."

The first statement contains a lot of mutual ownership—*our* write-up, *our* morning, *our* discussion, *our* request. It conveys a message that the teacher will be working just as hard as the students. In fact, this is what will normally occur. The students set about doing the write-up while the teacher circulates among them answering some questions and asking still others, making comments, offering words of encouragement, posing what-if situations, and more. Such assignments are no free ride for a teacher. The "we" in the message suggests that the teacher is asking no more of his or her students than he or she is willing to do. Both are working. It is clear that the teacher and students are in this together.

In the second statement there is little, if any, mutual ownership. It appears that only the students have work to do; only they will work to complete the assignments. The teacher's role seems to be one of simply telling students what they will do (with statements such as "You are going to . . . "). I wonder what the teacher will be doing? "You do this" and "you do that" statements from teachers are often accompanied by finger pointing. Have you ever tried to point your finger at someone and say "we"? It is like trying to shake your head back and forth and say "yes" at the same time.

What is done in a classroom usually involves both the teacher and the student. Together they can make quite a team. They can complete assignments, make plans, and solve problems. Where it applies, use "we" rather than "you" when talking with students.

"X" for Exemplify Desired Behavior; Don't Be a Hypocrite

Most of us have been in the position of hearing someone in authority say, "Don't do as I do, do as I say." Try to remember how you felt when he or she made that statement. Think of how you felt when the person used that authority to enforce his or her demand. You probably felt some resentment. You probably thought to yourself, "Where do you get off telling me to do such and such? You tell me to do it, but don't do it yourself—you hypocrite."

The bottom line is for educators to practice what they preach.

Although there are legitimate times when, as an adult and as a teacher, you will have the right to do things your students are not permitted to do, such instances should be kept to a minimum. RHIP, though steeped in fraternity, military, and societal tradition, can cause discipline problems if abused. When you do things that students are not permitted to do, especially if you flaunt it, it offends their sense of fairness. Children see fairness in simple black-and-white terms. Although maturity helps clarify their view of fairness, until then, what is good for the goose is seen as good for the gander as far as they are concerned.

I understand that you have worked long and hard to become a good teacher—a respected professional in the community. Shouldn't certain privileges accompany the title? Haven't you earned the right to do all the things you saw many of your teachers doing when you were a student? Although the answer may be yes, it would be best to control the temptation to do so from a classroom management viewpoint.

Try to put yourself back into the position of a student. Look at your behavior through your students' eyes. What do you suppose they are thinking when, during your 30–minute, duty-free lunch period, you cut into the lunch line? Are you really any more hungry than the students? Even if you are, does that give you the right to cut in? If you constantly interrupt students when they are speaking and yet criticize them when they do so, where is the fairness? When you tell them that you just bought a radar detector, is it fair in the same breath to chastise them for cheating on a test or for plagiarizing a term paper? After all, what is the radar detector used for other than to cheat on the speed limit—the law? Your actions do speak louder than your words.

Keep in mind that students learn a lot more from observing models or exemplars (teachers) than may be readily evident in their observed performance. The learning has taken place even if students are reluctant to repeat the observed behavior. Study after study has shown that, when enticed (perhaps by peers or by other circumstances) to demonstrate an earlier observed behavior, *most students* are capable of repeating that behavior. Watch what you are doing; others are. Don't let your words and actions make you a hypocrite. Exemplify desired behaviors.

TEST YOURSELF

Given the variety of A through Z suggestions offered in this chapter, no specific TEST YOURSELF questions have been prepared. However you should be prepared to explain each suggestion and then be able to provide an original example of the suggestion as it might apply to your classroom. Further, you should be able to defend whether or not each suggestion "should" be used in your classroom.

CHAPTER 13

Violence in Today's Schools

Coauthored with Dr. James J. Tracy, Ed.D.,
Elementary School Principal

OBJECTIVES

This chapter will help you, among other things, to:

- Understand several reasons for the increase in school violence.
- Identify the characteristics of a safe school.
- List the components of a good prevention program.
- List early warning signs that may indicate students will do violence to themselves or others.
- Understand how a crisis intervention team helps to prevent school violence.
- Understand the role of the teacher in dealing with a potentially violent student.

THE INCREASING PROBLEM OF SCHOOL VIOLENCE

Although most schools are still considered safe places where children can learn, there is a growing concern about the increasing violence reported in our schools. The recent shootings in Jonesboro, Arkansas; Edinboro, Pennsylvania; West Paducah, Kentucky; and Littleton, Colorado, have alarmed teachers, administrators, students, and the public in general. Over a period of fifty years, youth crime has risen and fallen with relatively modest curves demonstrating that youth violence is not something new. However, youth homicide increased 144 percent from 1984 to 1994 (Dohrn, 1997).

Teachers across the nation are increasingly concerned about the violence in schools and on school grounds. A survey administered by the National Center for Educational Statistics found that from 1987 to 1994 there was an increase in the percentage of teachers reporting physical conflicts among the students as a moderate or serious problem (Shen, 1997). This survey also indicated that the percentage of teachers reporting weapons possession in schools as a moderate or serious problem had doubled. During the 1995–1996 school year, the California public schools reported that twenty-two thousand violent crimes occurred in California schools including assault and battery (Remboldt, 1998).

Currently, school violence is perceived as one of the most serious problems facing our schools. Fighting, violence, and gangs were listed as the number one concern facing public schools today in the recent PDK Gallup Poll (Rose & Gallup, 1998). A survey of sixty-five thousand school students conducted by the National Association of Secondary School Principals (NASSP) found that over half of the tenth through twelfth grade students knew of weapons in school and more than one-third of the students sampled felt unsafe in school (Gullat & Long, 1996). According to Buckner and Flannery (1996), one-fourth of all suspensions from school were because of violent incidents committed by elementary school students, and 12 percent of the incidents involving guns were at the elementary level. The violence that we once saw happening on our nightly news, usually in someone else's neighborhood, has made its way into our classrooms—urban, suburban, and rural.

ORIGINS OF SCHOOL VIOLENCE

What are the origins of this increasing violence? Johnson and Johnson (1995) list as one of the factors leading to an increase in school violence the changing patterns of both family and community life. Social and economic changes that have occurred over the past twenty years, such as an increase in divorce, poverty, both parents working, and child abuse, can be found at the root of youth violence.

Images of violence so commonplace in our media have desensitized children to violence, and society's redefining it as normal and acceptable is another source of the increased violence. Some educators have become more tolerant of violent student behaviors, even to the extent of denying that there is a violence problem at all, by minimizing, rationalizing, or justifying it. Administrators, too, have a tendency to avoid or ignore the problem of violence altogether because they don't want to admit that their school has a problem. Schwartz (1996) calls this the Ostrich Syndrome.

The easy access to guns and drugs by children may be another reason violence has increased among youth. Recently, a kindergarten student attending a suburban elementary school decided to bring a gun for "show and tell."

He was able to get his father's hand gun, put it in his back pack, transport it on the school bus, and bring it into the classroom undetected. Luckily, the weapon was not loaded, and the student had no bad intentions.

There is considerable evidence that indicates a link between marijuana and other drug use with juvenile violence (*Youth and Violence,* 1998). The two boys who shot and killed four students and a teacher in Jonesboro, Arkansas, talked to other students about doing "weed," and the young man from Edinboro, Pennsylvania, who wounded three students and killed a teacher, was arrested for gun and drug charges along with criminal homicide and aggravated assault.

WHAT IS THE SCHOOL'S RESPONSIBILITY?

Learning cannot take place in an atmosphere of fear, intimidation, and violence. The federal government's goal of having every school in America free of drugs and violence by the year 2000 seems virtually unattainable. Yet, educators know that a safe, orderly climate is one of the essential components of an effective school. Schools should be safe havens where teachers and students can engage in learning activities without being concerned about personal safety. Students have a right to be educated in a safe environment (*Safer Schools,* 1998).

There are a number of characteristics of a safe school (*Early Warning Timely Response,* 1998). A safe school has a safe physical environment. Access to the building and grounds is supervised, schedules are arranged to reduce time in the halls, and supervision is present during critical transition times like class changes as well as during lunch and dismissal.

It does not have to be costly to provide supervision. A high school successfully reduced discipline problems and vandalism in its restrooms simply by utilizing student restroom monitors. Student monitors would check the condition of the restroom at the beginning of their shift and again at the end of the shift (approximately one period). Any student using the facility had to sign in and out with the monitor. If a monitor found a problem during the inspection at the end of the shift, it was understood that all students who had signed in and used the facility were held accountable until the guilty party was found.

Other characteristics of a safe school include a focus on academic achievement, a clear and relevant curriculum, and clearly communicated high expectations. Safe schools also develop and utilize links to the community (police, outside agencies), encourage student citizenship, value community partnerships, discuss safety issues openly, and provide extended day programs for students (*Early Warning Timely Response,* 1998; Heller, 1996). One of the most critical characteristics is the emphasis on positive relationships between students and staff because it is critical to have a caring adult available to provide support to the student when needed.

School personnel would rather catch the children being good and emphasize positive student behavior and responsibility rather than emphasize consequences for misbehavior (Heller, 1996). Educators need to treat children as children and resist the criminalization of students because their mistakes can be golden opportunities to teach and not merely an occasion for punishment (Dohrn, 1997). Safe schools also have discipline policies that are reviewed at least annually.

PREVENTING SCHOOL VIOLENCE

Prevention programs that focus on get-tough physical measures include the use of metal detectors, weapons checks, and the employment of security guards. Research on the use of high-tech safety measures and these physical prevention methods indicates that they are not very effective and have little long-term success (Halford, 1998; Remboldt, 1998).

Physical adjustments in a school building do not necessarily have to include high-tech safety equipment to promote safety and the feeling of safety. In one elementary school, teachers, students, and parents indicated that they felt their school was much safer after they instituted a simple locked door policy. This same school is also considered to be a friendly and open place where parents are always welcome, yet during the school day there is only one door through which people can enter the building. This door is in full view of the office where all visitors must check in. This locked door policy and mandatory sign-in of all guests was a cost-free program that not only created the feeling of safety, but also increased safety by reducing the risk of undesirable intruders.

A prevention program should include the development and implementation of a code of conduct and a discipline policy. The federally mandated zero tolerance act should be the cornerstone of this policy in order to demonstrate the school's commitment to violence prevention (Schwartz, 1996). After instituting a discipline policy with zero tolerance for violence, not just for guns, a high school in Tacoma, Washington, reported a measurable and dramatic decrease in the number of fights and related incidents (Burke & Herbert, 1996). These codes of conduct should include clear rules and consequences for infractions. It is also essential that these policies be reviewed with students and parents at least once a year.

Monitoring students in the hallways, restrooms, and cafeteria, as well as when they are entering and leaving the building, are strategies that should be included as part of a prevention program. Monitoring of students during these critical times can be done by police, security guards, faculty, staff, parent volunteers, or even by the students themselves. An elementary school drastically reduced the pushing, shoving, bullying, and fighting that had been occurring as students loaded and unloaded the school busses by putting a student safety patrol in place. This patrol stationed trained sixth graders between the school and buses, as well as outside of each bus, at a ratio of about two students per bus.

Reducing violence by encouraging students to be good citizens and by promoting mutual respect among the school community's members is another piece of a comprehensive prevention program. A peer tutoring program at one school trained older students to work with younger students in the building. This same school also encourages students to participate in various community experiences such as an intergenerational program with a nearby senior citizens complex. These kinds of activities help the students feel that they are an important part of the school and community, and they nurture the core values of caring, mutual respect, responsibility, and good citizenship through participation in these activities.

Cooperation with community agencies also can be beneficial in the prevention of violence. For instance, a United Way-funded program in Pennsylvania provided a violence prevention curriculum along with trained instructors to teach this curriculum (i.e., preventing violence, confronting bullies) to all students in grades two, three, and four.

The state police are also working cooperatively with this school by responding immediately if the administrator feels intervention is needed. In addition, the police provide a prevention program where an officer teaches classes, kindergarten through sixth, on topics like gun safety/awareness and smart choices. Officers come to lunch with students to help with student/police officer rapport.

Another component of a prevention program should be the schoolwide instruction and training of teachers and students in anger management, problem solving, peer mediation, and conflict resolution. Because conflicts often do not just disappear by themselves, it is important to manage them constructively. Training students in conflict resolution helps them learn the skills of negotiation, mediation, and arbitration in order to solve problems rather than resort to violence. These skills will be used throughout their lives. Johnson and Johnson (1996) reported an 80 percent drop in student-to-student conflicts that required teacher intervention, and a 95 percent decrease in referrals to the principal after implementing conflict resolution training.

WHAT IS THE TEACHER'S RESPONSIBILITY?

Classroom management skills are a key to violence prevention. Most discipline problems usually begin as relatively minor disruptions in the classroom (Hernandez & Gay, 1996). To prevent these minor disruptions from escalating, classroom teachers must develop and implement effective classroom management strategies. Involving students in the development of classroom rules is one strategy that helps students become part of the classroom community by encouraging citizenship and responsibility (Hill, 1996). These rules need to be clear and have consequences for infractions.

Classroom teachers should model nonviolent discipline techniques. You cannot prevent violence by using violence (Scherer, 1998). The teacher should not be someone to be feared but should be someone who is there to help. In fact, the research shows that a positive relationship with an adult (teacher) who is available to provide support when needed is one of the most critical factors in preventing student violence. Teachers should help students feel safe and comfortable when expressing their feelings, and teachers need to treat all students with respect.

Teachers need to create a positive classroom climate with an emphasis on learning skills and knowledge, student involvement, attendance, trust and mutual respect. There also must be consistency in the treatment of students and clear expectations for all students (Lederhouse, 1998; Scherer, 1998). Many times ineffective teaching can lead to behavior problems. The effective teacher has clear objectives for the lesson, actively involves the students, and maintains the interest of the students throughout the lesson.

Educators need to be able to meet together and discuss the subject of classroom management, in general, and violence prevention, in particular. Teachers need to feel supported by the administration and feel that they can seek help from fellow professionals.

Developing a cooperative community within the class is another of the ways to help prevent violence. A teacher can foster this environment by using cooperative teaching methods that enhance students' abilities to work with other students. A teacher can also promote a cooperative environment at the school level by participating in building-level teams. A school that has developed a cooperative environment may have several building teams. For an example, one elementary school has a building steering committee that deals with the running of the school, a support team that deals with helping the teacher with at-risk students, a crisis management team, and a building-level team that helps the student who is having emotional or acting out problems.

RECOGNIZING WARNING SIGNS

There are early warning signs that may be indicators that a student could do violence to him/herself or to others. It is important to remember not to jump to conclusions; early warning signs are only indicators. Training teachers to recognize early warning signals for possible violence in a student is an essential piece of a good violence prevention program. Research (*Early Warning Timely Response*, 1998; *Safer Schools*, 1998) shows an individual will usually exhibit multiple warning signs such as:

- social withdrawal (depression, a lack of self-confidence)
- excessive feelings of isolation (appears friendless, a loner)
- excessive feelings of rejection; being picked on
- low school interest; poor academic performance (grades falling off)
- expression of violence in writings and drawings
- uncontrolled anger (shortened temper, sudden outbursts of anger)
- intimidating and bullying behaviors
- history of discipline problems (persistent refusal to follow rules, disregard for rules)
- drug and alcohol use
- gang affiliation
- inappropriate access to or possession of firearms
- serious threats of violence (to others or to self)
- change in friends
- cruelty to animals
- sudden change in dress

A TEAM APPROACH TO INTERVENTION

The use of problem study teams or support teams offers the opportunity for a teacher to intervene by accessing the help of other teachers, counselors, parents, and other professionals. Together they can develop a game plan for any student who is exhibiting warning signals. One school system's elementary and middle school's Instructional Support Team (IST) and high school Student Assistance Programs (SAP) have been successful in helping students at risk for violence. For instance, the IST process allows the classroom teacher to examine the roots of the student's problem with other teachers, the child's parents, and other professionals from within the school or from outside agencies. After identifying the problem, these teams help the teacher put into place mechanisms to ensure the success of the child.

If a student exhibits imminent warning signs, safety is always the first and foremost concern. Some examples of imminent warning signs are serious physical fighting, severe destruction of property, severe rage for minor reasons, possession of a weapon, and threats of violence to himself/herself or to others. When a student is close to acting in a dangerous way, the teacher needs to take quick action. Either the teacher needs to be trained in how to deal with exceptionally disruptive students or the school needs to put a crisis response team in place to help the teacher in these dangerous or potentially dangerous situations. Having both responses in place would be preferable.

When the building principal and the faculty talk about discipline and violence prevention, they should also discuss crisis situations and the need for a crisis response team. Faculty and staff who either have been enlisted or have volunteered to serve as crisis team members should develop a plan to manage possible crises in the building. This plan should include the prevention of violence and not just the control of it (Gullat & Long, 1996). These plans also should include all kinds of crisis situations including natural disasters. But the handling of potentially violent situations needs to be specifically addressed.

USING A CAT

All team members, as well as those teachers who may call upon the team, need to know what their role and responsibility is in a crisis. Any good crisis response plan should delineate these roles and responsibilities and address the necessary ongoing training needed for team members to be able to handle a potentially violent crisis situation. The key to managing crisis in a school, as well as responding to the aftermath of an incident, is a trained Crisis Intervention Team (Gullat & Long, 1996).

One Crisis Intervention Team, known as the Crisis Action Team, CAT for short, that was developed and implemented in a public elementary school has been effective in preventing and controlling violent situations in the classroom. For example, a kindergarten teacher began to notice that one of her students demonstrated multiple warning signs for possible violence. The teacher enlisted the help of the Instructional Support Team, a team composed of other teachers, a parent, a guidance counselor, and a behavioral specialist. The team identified problems and helped the teacher put a behavior plan into place for the student in order to improve his behavior. Usually this takes care of the problem.

However, in this case, the teacher recognized that the kindergartner was close to acting in a dangerous manner and that a violent situation was developing. She accessed her Crisis Action Team by sending a CAT card (actually a picture of a kitty cat) with her room designation on it to the office with another student. These CAT cards are kept on the doors of each and every room and area (playground, cafeteria) in the building. When the CAT card reached the office, an "all call" went out over the public address system simply stating "CAT-KC." (This meant Crisis Action Team—Kindergarten, Miss Carolyn's room.) This alerted those CAT members whose jobs were to go immediately to the kindergarten room. In this case, the team members arrived in less than a minute and successfully removed the child who was yelling and throwing things.

Because of the quick action of the CAT, no one was hurt, and a violent situation was prevented. This school's CAT team members have been extensively trained in passive restraint and in methods to transport a violent child out of the classroom to a setting where he or she can de-escalate and be worked with in private. Without the assistance of the team, the teacher felt that the situation would have become violently dangerous and someone would have been hurt.

AN INDIVIDUAL APPROACH TO INTERVENTION

Teachers should insist that they receive training in violence prevention, early warning signs, and crisis management. Preservice, as well as in-service, teachers report that they have little to no training in these areas. If a teacher has been trained to recognize the early warning signs, many potentially violent situations can be averted.

At a minimum, Crisis Intervention Team members must be trained in the application of safe and effective techniques to manage a potentially combative student. If the situation causes the Crisis Team member to decide to use force to control a student, this training will provide the teacher with nonviolent methods to manage the student while using reasonable force. Without training, the teacher might use an improper level of force, thus opening the possibility of criminal or civil liability (Frisby & Beckhan, 1993).

Teachers need to be cautious when reading about holds and moves to handle violent students. If a teacher were to read these types of materials, often accompanied by diagrams, and then attempt to use them in a violent situation without training or practice, either the teacher or the student might be seriously hurt. The National Crisis Prevention Institute, which trains both trainers and individuals in nonviolent crisis prevention, has strongly recommended that the training in these techniques be presented in not less than a twelve-hour block of time to class sizes no larger than forty, with refresher sessions at least every year! To further illustrate the importance of training to learn these skills, the National Crisis Prevention Institute has placed the following disclaimer on each page of its workbook where a hold or move diagram is located.

> *Caution*: These techniques should only be learned and practiced under the supervision of a qualified Crisis Prevention Instructor. Attempting to learn the techniques from the diagrams may result in injury.

CONCLUSION

The grim conclusion is that it is not *if* a school will experience violence, but *when* it will experience violence and if it will be ready (Armstead, 1996). Almost every piece of literature dealing with violence prevention in schools seems to say the same thing: teachers need to be provided with information, information, and more information; training, training, and more training!

SELECTED INTERNET RESOURCES

The reader may use ERIC (described in the next chapter) to locate still more information on the breadth of school violence, how to prevent it, and how to handle it if and when it occurs. In the meantime, several of the Internet resources listed below can be of help.

http://www.ncsu.edu/cpsv/CtrPreSchVio.html

Information and research available from the Center for the Prevention of School Violence.

http://www.weprevent.org

National Crime Prevention Council document titled *Safer Schools* which provides strategies for educators to help prevent school violence.

http://education.indiana.edu/cas/tt/v2i3/v2i3toc.html

Tips for the teacher on managing student disruptions and creating a peaceful classroom.

http://www/ed/gov/offices.OSERS/OSEP/earlywrn.html

A U.S. Department of Education guide to safe schools including early warning signs, intervention, and prevention of school violence.

TEST YOURSELF

This is a sampling of the kinds of factual and open-ended questions that you should be able to answer after having read this chapter.

1. Briefly describe the possible causes or origins of violence in the schools.
2. What are some of the characteristics of a safe school?
3. When developing a violence prevention program in a school, what are the components that should be included?
4. List the warning signs that a teacher should recognize as early signals of possible violence.
5. What is the role of the classroom teacher in dealing with the potentially violent student? . . . the violent student?
6. Explain how a crisis intervention team works to prevent violent situations in the classroom setting.

CHAPTER 14

Educational Resources Information Center (ERIC)

OBJECTIVES

This chapter will help you, among other things, to:

- Describe the history of ERIC.
- Identify the services provided by ERIC.
- Compare and contrast the two ERIC resources, *RIE* (*Resources in Education*) and *CIJE* (*Current Index to Journals in Education*).
- Use ERIC to locate information relevant to the subject of "discipline."
- Identify one or more ERIC clearinghouse that may best provide resources for you as a teacher.
- Suggest how you could use ERIC in your day-to-day teaching.
- Describe how ERIC may be accessed via the Internet.

INTRODUCTION

Do you own a copy of Balson's (1992) *Understanding Classroom Behaviour*, a 248–page, down-to-earth book full of classroom management suggestions published by the Australian Council for Educational Research? Probably not. Have you had the opportunity personally to hear the lecture on "Disciplinary Techniques Reported by Parents of Gifted Children" recently delivered at the Western Psychological Association Conference in San Jose, California? Couldn't get the time off? No money in the travel budget? Did you read the 1993 article "Transforming Schools Through Total Quality Education" in *Phi Delta Kappan*, which highlights William Glasser's application of Deming's ideas to schools? No? That journal isn't in your school's professional library? Have you or your colleagues reviewed Gaffney's (1997) provocative paper titled, "A Study of Preservice Teachers' Beliefs about Various Issues and Myths Regarding the Use of Scholastic Corporal Punishment?" No? This paper didn't come across your desk? Too bad. All four of these resources, and tens of thousands more, can be a real help in establishing and maintaining classroom discipline.

The reality is that most faculty, busy with teaching responsibilities and on limited travel budgets, do not have the time or resources to attend as many professional meetings as they would like. Further, even the best of reports, conference proceedings, and curriculum guides generally have a rather limited distribution—often only to participants. Busy educators have limited time to skim the literature, even the limited publications available to them, looking for just the right article to help them. Yet, for classroom teachers, information gained through such sources could serve as the basis for establishing, maintaining, and improving their classroom management.

DISCIPLINE TOPICS OF INTEREST TO TEACHERS

What kinds of topics related to classroom management might teachers have a need to know more about? Just for starters, how about delinquency, suspensions, due process, child abuse, academic versus nonacademic penalties for misconduct, legal issues, gifted children, handicapped children, school size and school disorder, discipline in foreign countries, beginning teachers' guides to discipline, managing classroom conflict, assessment of classroom problems, influence of families, change strategies, assertiveness training, behavior modification, first-year-teacher survival, punishment, medicine and discipline, disciplinary hearings, knowledge of legally sanctioned discipline procedures, and gender and corporal punishment? The topics are almost endless, each demanding quality information before precious time, effort, and resources are committed.

Wouldn't it be great if it were possible to quickly and easily access, at minimal cost, conference proceedings, curriculum or instructor guides, opinion papers, bibliographies, descriptive or research reports, program evaluations, journal articles, speeches, and tests/questionnaires in education? You might be thinking that while you are wishing, you may as well wish for a brand new lab, more motivated students, and a forty-five-foot sailing yacht! Send in the bottle with the genie!

All of these sources of information are in fact currently available through a system called ERIC—"the most widely used educational database in the world" (Smith, 1990, p. 79). It is even better than a bottle with a genie in it. A genie grants only three wishes; ERIC is able to grant an unlimited number of requests for information. ERIC's database, the world's largest, contains approximately 850,000 journal articles and documents. Yet, for some reason ERIC has too often been kept a secret from practitioners.

WHAT IS ERIC?

ERIC, an acronym for Educational Resources Information Center, is an almost thirty-year-old information system available worldwide. It is sponsored by the National Institute of Education within the U.S. Department of Education. ERIC is "one of the most important, if not the most important resource that has helped educators bridge the gap between practice and theory" (Barron, 1990, p. 47).

ERIC is dedicated to the progress of education through the dissemination of education research results, practitioner-related materials, and other resource information that can be used in developing more effective educational programs. Being decentralized, it is composed of sixteen clearinghouses, each responsible for obtaining, evaluating, abstracting, and disseminating information in a specific field of education. The sixteen clearinghouses are listed at the end of this chapter.

ACCESS TO ERIC

Access to ERIC materials can be made through one of two paper indexes, *Resources in Education* (*RIE*) and *Current Index to Journals in Education* (*CIJE*), as well as through on-line computer-retrieval systems. The indexes and the on-line computer-retrieval systems are available in most college or university libraries, state departments of education, larger school districts, and some public libraries.

RESOURCES IN EDUCATION

As with the "R" in ERIC, the "R" in *RIE* stands for "Resources," not "Research." This is an especially important point for those who might dismiss ERIC as being useful only for researchers, not practitioners. *RIE* is a monthly journal that abstracts, indexes, announces, and provides a procedure to access "fugitive," or hard-to-find, documents. These nonjournal documents, such as conference proceedings, speeches, curriculum guides, and project reports, are not normally available through library channels. Before *RIE*, the only way one was aware of such documents was to have personally attended the conference, heard the speech, or known someone who had an extra copy of the desired curriculum guide or report. This hit-or-miss process severely limited one's access to information in the past. Not so now!

To use *RIE*, first look up the topic in the subject index or the author in the author index. Once an appropriate title is identified (for example, "A Study of Assertive Discipline and Recommendations for Effective Classroom Management Methods"), make note of the accompanying six-digit identifying ED (ERIC Document) number. In this instance, the number would be ED 379207. Documents are also catalogued by institution and publication type. As titles can often be misleading, the second step is to turn to the Resume portion of the same index and use the six-digit ED number to locate the appropriate Resume (detailed abstract).

An *RIE* Document Resume provides much information, including:

- author,
- origin of document,
- publication type,
- descriptive note,
- key descriptors, and,
- most important, a lengthy informative abstract.

Content experts at ERIC clearinghouses read each document to prepare these abstracts. This saves users a lot of time, effort, and possible disappointment in ordering something that ends up being nothing like what it was thought to be. Often the detailed abstracts alone contain enough information to help make decisions.

If an identified document appears to be just what you are looking for, follow the simple directions provided in the *RIE* index to secure a microfiche (or paper) copy of the entire document. These can be obtained directly from ERIC at a minimal cost for a microfiche, each of which can hold up to ninety-six pages of print. A more common method of getting a desired document on microfiche is to obtain it from a government-sponsored ERIC microfiche collection depository (usually based, or at least available, through college libraries). These microfiche collections ensure that a document will never go out of print.

RIE documents go through a quality-screening process by reviewers who typically have terminal degrees in their field and have a decade or more experience with ERIC. They apply selection standards similar to those used for refereed journals to decide what is worth announcing in *RIE*. The fact that ERIC's *RIE* is used by approximately 190,000 people per week and that three out of every four educators cite what they receive as being "very useful" testifies to the success of the screening process (*How to Use ERIC*, 1979).

CURRENT INDEX TO JOURNALS IN EDUCATION

CIJE includes articles from more than eight hundred education periodicals ranging from the most popular U.S. practitioner-oriented journals to British, Canadian, and Australian journals. ERIC clearinghouses abstract, index, announce, and provide access to these journal articles. You have an enormous library right at your fingertips!

To use *CIJE*, first look up the topic in the Subject Index. Upon identifying an appropriate article, note its title, the journal in which it appears (name, volume, number, page), and the six-digit EJ (ERIC Journal) number. The same information can be located by scanning *CIJE*'s Author Index or Journal Contents Index. Using the latter is like walking up and down the aisles of a very large library, opening desired journals to examine their tables of contents.

As with the titles of *RIE* documents, the titles of journal articles do not always convey the real content of the articles. Why waste your time requesting and securing articles that may not be of use? Instead, note the six-digit EJ number and turn to the Main Entry section to locate the corresponding abstract.

CIJE entries include key information such as:

- article title,
- journal name, volume, number, and pages,
- author,
- key descriptors, and
- a one- or two-sentence abstract.

This one- or two-sentence abstract, although considerably less than what is included in *RIE* abstracts, often clarifies whether or not an article is worth obtaining. Selected articles are usually accessible from college libraries. If not, by using the EJ number and the Article Copy Service address in the *CIJE* index, you can obtain them directly from ERIC. No resource is beyond your reach!

The quality of articles identified and accessed through *CIJE* is ensured by the referee process inherent in most journal selection procedures. Users apparently agree; approximately 140,000 people use *CIJE* each week, with three out of every five reporting success in finding sought-after information (*How to Use ERIC*, 1979).

THESAURUS OF ERIC DESCRIPTORS

One difficulty some busy practitioners have when looking up information is that they call what they are looking for by one name, but the index they are using calls it something else. To alleviate this problem, ERIC publishes a *Thesaurus of ERIC Descriptors*. It is normally found on the reference shelf with the *RIE* and *CIJE* indexes. The ERIC Thesaurus is a controlled vocabulary of educational terms called descriptors. They are used to index and enter documents into the ERIC system and to assist users in searching the system. A user might look up "discipline" only to find descriptors including "disciplinary actions," "discipline," "discipline policy," and "discipline problems."

Most often, each of the descriptors will list related terms. For instance, "discipline" refers the reader to, among other descriptors, "behavior problems," "classroom techniques," "corporal punishment," "obedience," "punishment," "sanctions," and "self-control." In turn, each of these related terms would refer the user to the descriptor "discipline." A couple of minutes work with the Thesaurus pays great dividends when undertaking a search for information.

COMPUTER-SEARCH CAPABILITY

Thus far, what has been described is a hand search of the two ERIC indexes, a process available to all educators. Today's CD-ROM (Read Only Menu) technology (for example, DIALOG and SilverPlatter) now enables educators to conduct an online (on-screen, menu-driven) computer search of ERIC, entering key descriptors and allowing the computer to do the clerical work of sorting through documents. DIALOG, for instance, supplies ERIC on two CD-ROMs. One covers the time period 1966 to 1982 and one (updated periodically) covers the period from 1983 to the present.

A computer's potential is evident when doing a Boolean-type search using the AND, OR, and NOT logic functions. The AND narrows a search, the OR broadens a search, and the NOT reduces a group of titles (Purcell, 1989). If a topic under investigation has several aspects—for example, "discipline," "special education," and "secondary school"—all three can be combined with the AND function so that only bibliographic citations with all three descriptors will be highlighted.

ERIC ON THE INTERNET

More and more, educators are accessing information of all kinds on the Internet. You can access ERIC on the World Wide Web (www) by using the nearest computer with Internet applications. From there, it is simply a matter of point and click.

- Log onto Netscape Navigator or whatever software your machine uses.
- In the address box, type in: http://www.search.com
- Choose the "A-Z list." (It is located in the green box.) You will be immediately rewarded with a very long alphabetical list of databases that you may wish to explore at a later date.
- When this screen appears, scroll down to the "E's." Choose "ERIC Database."
- At this point you will be greeted by ERIC.
- Type in the term(s) that you are investigating, for example, corporal punishment, and then hit the enter button. Up will come a variety of citations.

You can also access ERIC by typing in the specific Internet address for each of the sixteen individual clearinghouses. These Internet addresses, along with phone and FAX numbers, are included with the list of clearinghouses that appear at the end of this chapter.

The end result of an on-line search is a bibliography of sources for your perusal. Most on-line computer-search technology also makes available a printer so that a hard copy of desired resources can be produced quickly. The ERIC system is a valuable resource for any educator, and on-line searching simply makes it even more accessible.

Currently, ERIC is a bibliographic database only. Plans are in the works for full-text access to selected educational materials (Stonehill & Brandhorst, 1992). The future for ERIC looks bright indeed.

WARNING! PREPARE A "SHOPPING LIST"

Most people know what happens when they are hungry and go grocery shopping without a list. They come home with a lot more than they went for. The same is true when an information-hungry person uses ERIC's *RIE* or *CIJE*. As you scan an ERIC Subject Index, you end up spotting interesting and useful resources outside your primary area of investigation. If you want to avoid this situation, prepare an investigation "shopping list" beforehand. Then again, why not let your imagination and your newfound information retrieval system run wild?

PUBLISH, WHO ME?

Who are these people who publish in ERIC, especially in *RIE*? Who designs the curriculum guides, tests, and follow-up questionnaires listed in *RIE*? Who conducts and then writes up the successful projects that are reported? Moreover, who describes the workings of the general advisory committees? People just like you publish in ERIC. In most schools, exciting things are happening that really ought to be shared. ERIC's *RIE* is just the vehicle for that sharing. The simple guidelines for doing this are described in *Submitting Documents to ERIC*, which is listed below.

CONCLUSION

There is simply not enough space to describe fully the workings of ERIC and its potential to serve educators. The goal of this chapter is to spark your interest in using ERIC as a tool to acquire the information so often requisite to successful problem solving. Quite bluntly, no other single information cataloging, indexing, and retrieval source exists that can match ERIC. Just as students are taught how important it is to possess the proper tools of the trade before tackling a job, it is equally important for educators to do the same. For educators facing problem situations, this means being able to access useful information quickly.

As a concerned educator, consider scheduling (or asking to have scheduled) an in-service program on ERIC. Acquire copies of the following resource publications, identify the closest library having the *RIE* and *CIJE* indexes, and clarify the specific process faculty would use to acquire microfiche or paper copies of requested information. Pick out a problem in education, and put ERIC, the information genie, to work for you. (Most ERIC clearinghouses have toll-free phone numbers.)

ERIC CLEARINGHOUSES

Feel free to contact any of these clearinghouses. My experience has been that they love to help educators locate and secure information in their respective specialties. Often, because other educators have made the same request, the clearinghouse will have already conducted a search on the very topic you are investigating. Some topics are requested so often that the clearinghouse has prepared a two-page *DIGEST* on the subject that can be supplied immediately. Don't be shy in using ERIC. Note that the information below was accurate at the time of printing.

- Adult, Career, and Vocational Education

  Ohio State University
  Center on Education and Training for Employment
  1900 Kenny Road
  Columbus, OH 43210–1090
  Phone: (614) 292–4353; (800) 848–4815
  FAX: (614) 292–1260

E-mail:ericacve@magnus.acs.ohio-state.edu
Web: http://coe.ohio-state.edu/cete/ericacve/index.htm

* Assessment and Evaluation

  Catholic University of America
  210 O'Boyle Hall
  Washington, DC 20064–4035
  Phone: (202) 319–5120; (800) 464–3742
  FAX: (202) 319–6692
  E-mail: eric_ae@cua.edu
  Web: http://ericae2.educ.cua.edu

* Community Colleges

  University of California at Los Angeles (UCLA)
  Math-Sciences Building, Room 8118
  405 Hilgard Avenue
  Los Angeles, CA 90024–1564
  Phone: (310) 825–3931; (800) 832–8256
  FAX: (310) 206–8095
  E-mail: ericcc@ucla.edu
  Web: http://www.gseis.ucla.edu/ERIC/eric.html

* Counseling and Student Services

  University of North Carolina at Greensboro
  School of Education
  Greensboro, NC 27412–5001
  Phone: (336) 334–4114; (800) 414–9769
  FAX: (336) 334–4116
  E-mail: ericcas2@dewey.uncg.edu
  Web: http://www.uncg.edu/~ericcas2

* Disabilities and Gifted Children

  Council for Exceptional Children (CEC)
  1920 Association Drive
  Reston, VA 22091–1589
  Phone: (703) 264–9474; (800) 328–0272
  FAX: (703) 264–9494
  E-mail: ericec@cec.sped.org
  Web: http://www.cec.sped.org/ericec.htm

* Educational Management

  University of Oregon

1787 Agate Street
Eugene, OR 97403–5207
Phone: (503) 346–5043; (800) 438–8841
FAX: (503) 346–2334
E-mail: ppiele@oregon.uoregon.edu
Web: http://darkwing.uoregon.edu/~ericcem

- Elementary and Early Childhood Education

  University of Illinois
  805 West Pennsylvania Avenue
  Urbana, IL 61801–4897
  Phone: (217) 333–1386; (800) 583–4135
  FAX: (217) 333–3767
  E-mail: ericeece@uiuc.edu
  Web: http://npin.org (National Parent Information
  Network)

- Higher Education

  George Washington University
  One Dupont Circle, N.W., Suite 630
  Washington, DC 20036–1183
  Phone: (202) 296–2597; (800) 773–3742
  FAX: (202) 296–8379
  E-mail: eriche@eric-he.edu
  Web: http://www.gwu.edu/~eriche/

- Information and Technology

  Syracuse University
  Center for Science and Technology, 4th Floor, Room 194
  Syracuse, NY 13244–4100
  Phone: (315) 443–3640; (800) 464–9107
  FAX: (315) 443–5448
  E-mail: eric@ericir.syr.edu
  Web: http://ericir.syr.edu/ithome

- Languages and Linguistics

  Center for Applied Linguistics
  1118 22nd Street, N.W.
  Washington, DC 20037–0037
  Phone: (202) 429–9292; no 800 number available
  FAX: (202) 659–5641
  E-mail: eric@cal.org

Web: http://www.cal.org/ericcll

- Reading, English, and Communication

  Indiana University
  Smith Research Center, Suite 150
  2805 East 10th Street
  Bloomington, IN 47408–2698
  Phone: (812) 855–5847; (800) 759–4723
  FAX: (812) 855–4220
  E-mail: ericcs@indiana.edu
  Web: http://www.indiana.edu/~eric_rec

- Rural Education and Small Schools

  Appalachia Educational Laboratory (AEL)
  1031 Quarrier Street, P.O. Box 1348
  Charleston, WV 25325–1348
  Phone: (304) 347–0465; (800) 624–9120
  FAX: (304) 347–0487
  E-mail: lanhamb@ael.org
  Web: http//aelvira.ael.org/erichp.htm

- Science, Mathematics, and Environmental Education

  Ohio State University
  1929 Kenny Road
  Columbus, OH 43210–1080
  Phone: (614) 292–6717; (800) 276–0462
  FAX: (614) 292–0263
  E-mail: ericse@osu.edu
  Web: http://www.ericse.org

- Social Studies/Social Science Education

  Indiana University
  Social Studies Development Center
  2805 East 10th Street, Suite 120
  Bloomington, IN 47408–2698
  Phone: (812) 855–3838; (800) 266–3815
  FAX: (812) 855–0455
  E-mail: ericso@indiana.edu
  Web: http://www.indiana.edu/~ssdc/eric_chess.htm

- Teaching and Teacher Education

  American Association of Colleges for Teacher Education

One Dupont Circle, N.W., Suite 610
Washington, DC 20036–1186
Phone: (202) 293–2450; (800) 822–9229
FAX: (202) 457–8095
E-mail: ericsp@inet.ed.gov
Web: http://www.ericsp.org

- Urban Education

    Teachers College, Columbia University
    Institute for Urban and Minority Education
    Main Hall, Room 303, Box 40
    525 West 120th Street
    New York, NY 10027–9998
    Phone: (212) 678–3433; (800) 601–4868
    FAX: (212) 678–4048
    E-mail: eric-cue@columbia.edu
    Web: http://eric-web.tc.columbia.edu

TEST YOURSELF

This is a sampling of the kinds of factual and open-ended questions that you should be able to answer after having read this chapter.

1. What do the letters ERIC stand for?
2. Why is it important for teachers to realize that the "R" in ERIC stands for "resources," not "research"?
3. ERIC could best be described as which, a centralized or decentralized system? Why?
4. Which part of ERIC, *RIE* or *CIJE*, was established first?
5. What does ERIC mean by the term "fugitive literature"?
6. If you had a six-digit ED number, you would know that the ERIC source must be which—*RIE* or *CIJE*?
7. Which one or more ERIC clearinghouses might best apply to your specific teaching interests and responsibilities?
8. Describe what ERIC clearinghouses do.
9. Why would one use a *Thesaurus of ERIC Descriptors*?
10. Describe how ERIC may be accessed on-line.

References

Abrami, P. C., Leventhal, L., & Perry, R. P. (1982). Educational seduction. *Review of Educational Research, 52*:446–464.

Albert, L. (1996a). *Cooperative discipline.* Circle Pines, MN: American Guidance Services.

Albert, L. (1996b). *A teacher's guide to cooperative discipline.* Circle Pines, MN: American Guidance Service.

Albert, L. (1989). *Cooperative discipline: How to manage your classroom and promote self-esteem.* Circle Pines, MN: American Guidance Service.

Alonzo, T. M., LaCagnina, G. R., & Olsen, B. C. (1977). Behaviorism vs. humanism: Two contrasting approaches to learning theory. *Southern Journal of Educational Research, 11*(3):135–151.

Aquayo, R. (1990). *Dr. Deming, the American who taught the Japanese about quality.* Secaucus, NJ: Carol Publishing Group.

Armistead, L. (1996). What to do before the violence happens: Designing the crisis communication plan. *NASSP Bulletin, 80*(579):31–37.

Armstrong, P. (1984). Let teachers spank unruly students? *U.S. News & World Report, 97*(24):79.

Ashton, P., & Urquhart, C. (1988). *Detrimental effects of mandated models of discipline on the practice of reflective teaching.* Florida. Project Description. ERIC Document Reproduction Service No. ED 307 267.

Ausubel, D. (1980). Schemata, cognitive structure, and advance organizers: A reply to Anderson, Spiro, and Anderson. *American Educational Research Journal, 17*(3):400–404.

Ausubel, D. (1968). *Educational psychology; A cognitive view.* New York: Holt, Rinehart & Winston, pp. 315–319.

Axelrod, S. (1977). *Behavior modification for the classroom teacher.* New York: McGraw-Hill.

Bailis, P., & Hunter, M. (1985). Do your words get them to think? *Learning*, *14*(1):43.

Baker, J. N. (1987). Paddling: Still a sore point. *Newsweek*, *109*(25):61.

Ball, J. (1989). Where PTA stands on corporal punishment. *PTA Today*, *14*(4):15–17.

Balson, M. (1992*). Understanding classroom behaviour.* 3d ed. Hawthorne, Victoria: The Australian Council for Educational Research Limited.

Balson, M. (1985). Discipline: An old problem in a new world. *SET: Research information for teachers, 2.*

Balson, M. (1982*). Understanding classroom behaviour.* 2d ed. Hawthorne, Victoria: The Australian Council for Educational Research Limited.

Barnard, H., & Thornburg, K. (1989*). Corporal punishment: Correction or retribution?* Paper presented at the annual meeting of the National Association of Teacher Educators, St. Louis, MO.

Barrett, E. R., & Curtis, K. F. (1986). The effect of assertive discipline training on student teachers. *Teacher Education and Practice, 3*(1):53–56.

Barron, D. D. (1990). ERIC, research and online update. *School Library Media Activities Monthly, 7*(3):46–50.

Bartosh, F., Jr., & Barilla, J. (1985). Discipline—Still number one on the administrator's list of problems. *NASSP Bulletin, 69*(479):6–10.

Bauer, G. F., Dubanoski, R., Yamauchi, L. A., & Honbo, K.A.M. (1990). Corporal punishment and the schools. *Education and Urban Society, 22*(3):285–299.

Baughman, M. D. (1979). Teaching with humor: A performing art. *Contemporary Education, 51*(1):26–30.

Bear, G. C. (1983). Usefulness of Y.E.T. and Kohlberg's approach to guidance. *Elementary School Guidance and Counseling, 17*(3):221–225.

Bettencourt, E., Gillett, M., & Hull, J. (1983). Effects of teacher enthusiasm training on student on-task behavior and achievement. *American Educational Research Journal, 20*(3):435–450.

Bettencourt, M. (1982). The present in the past: The Concord public schools. *The Educational Forum, 47*(1):47–57.

Blumenfeld-Jones, D. (1996). Conventional systems of classroom discipline (The Patriarchy speaks). *Journal of Educational Thought. 30*(1):5–21.

Bobgan, M., & Bobgan, D. (1990*). Profits of psychoHeresy II: Critiquing Dr. James C. Dobson.* Santa Barbara, CA: EastGate.

Boonin, T. (1979). The benighted status of U.S. school corporal punishment practice. *Phi Delta Kappan, 60*(5):395–396.

Bordin, E. S. (1981). Landmarks in the literature: Two views of human nature. *New York University Education Quarterly, 12*(2):29–32.

Bower, B. (1986). Skinner boxing. *Science News, 129*(6):92–94.

Brandt, R. (1988). On students' needs and team learning: A conversation with William Glasser. *Educational Leadership, 45*(6):38–45.

Brandt, R. (1985). On teaching and supervising: A conversation with Madeline Hunter. *Educational Leadership, 42*(5):61–66.

Brophy, J. (1981). On praising effectively. *The Elementary School Journal, 81*(5):269–277.

Brophy, J., & Good, T. (1986). Teacher behavior and student achievement. In *Handbook of research on teaching,* ed. M. Wittrock. (pp. 328–375). New York: Macmillan.

Brown, E. J. (1949). Punishment: 14 rules for handing it out. *The Clearing House, 23*:345–347.

Browne, M. N., & Keeley, S. M. (1985). Achieving excellence: Advice to new teachers. *College Teaching, 33*(2):78–83.

Buckner, K. G., & Flanary, R. A. (1996). Protecting your school and students: *The Safe Schools* Handbook. *NASSP Bulletin, 80*(579):44–48.

Burka, A. A., & Jones, F. H. (1979). Procedures for increasing appropriate verbal participation in special elementary classrooms. *Behavior Modification, 3*(1):27–48.

Burke, E., & Herbert, D. (1996). Zero tolerance policy: Combating violence in schools. *NASSP Bulletin, 80*(579):49–54.

Burns, J. (1985). Discipline: Why does it continue to be a problem? Solution is in changing school culture. *NASSP Bulletin, 69*(479):1–5.

Burts, C. C. et al. (1985). Effects of teacher enthusiasm on three- and four-year-old children's acquisition of four concepts. *Theory and Research in Social Education, 13*(1):19–29.

Campbell, C. P. (1981). Characteristics of effective vocational instructors. *Canadian Vocational Journal, 16*(4):24–28.

Campbell, R. (1977). *How to really love your child.* Wheaton, IL: Victor Books.

Cangelosi, J. S. (1988). *Classroom management strategies.* White Plains, NY: Longman.

Canter, L. (1996). Discipline alternatives. First, the rapport—Then, the rules. *Learning, 24*(5):12, 14.

Canter, L. (1996). *The high performing teacher.* Santa Monica, CA: Lee Canter & Associates.

Canter, L. (1994). *Scared or prepared.* Santa Monica, CA: Lee Canter & Associates.

Canter, L. (1989). Assertive Discipline: More than names on the board and marbles in a jar. *Phi Delta Kappan, 71*(1):57–61.

Canter, L. (1988). Let the educator beware: A response to Curwin and Mendler. *Educational Leadership, 46*(2):71–73.

Canter, L., & Canter, M. (1997). *Assertive discipline: Positive behavior management for today's classrooms.* Santa Monica, CA: Lee Canter & Associates.

Canter, L., & Canter, M. (1993). *Succeeding with difficult students.* Santa Monica, CA: Canter & Associates.

Canter, L., & Canter, M. (1976, 1992). *Assertive discipline*. Santa Monica, CA: Canter & Associates.

Chance, P. (1993). Sticking up for rewards. *Phi Delta Kappan*, 74(10):787–790.

Chanow-Gruen, K. J., & Doyle, R. (1983). The counselor's consultative role with teachers, using the TET model. *Humanistic Education and Development*, 22(1):16–24.

Charles, C. M. (1996). *Building classroom discipline*. 5th ed. White Plains, NY: Longman.

Charles, C. M. (1985). *Building classroom discipline*. 2d ed. White Plains, New York: Longman.

Charles, C. M. (1981). *Building classroom discipline*. White Plains, New York: Longman.

Christenson, L. (1970). *The Christian family*. Minneapolis, MN: Bethany Fellowship.

Clarizio, H. (1980*). Toward positive classroom discipline*. New York: John Wiley & Sons.

Cockrum, J. R. (1989). Reality therapy: Interviews with Dr. William Glasser. *Psychology: A Journal of Human Behavior*, 26(1):13–16.

Cornell, A. W. (1993). Turning abstractions into teachable skills. *Perspective*, May/June:26–27.

Cowen, R. J., Jones, F. H., & Bellack, A. S. (1979). Grandma's rule with group contingencies: A cost-effective means of classroom management. *Behavior Modification*, 3(3):397–418.

Crockenberg, V. (1982). Assertive discipline: A dissent. *California Journal of Teacher Education*, 9(4):59–74.

Cryan, J. R. (1987). The banning of corporal punishment: In child care, school, and other educative settings in the United States. *Childhood Education*, 63(3):146–153.

Curwin, R., & Mendler, A. (1989). We repeat, let the buyer beware: A response to Canter. *Educational Leadership*, 46(6):83.

Curwin, R., & Mendler, A. (1988a). *Discipline with dignity*. Alexandria, VA: Association for Supervision and Curriculum Development.

Curwin, R., & Mendler, A. (1988b). Packaged discipline programs: Let the buyer beware. *Educational Leadership*, 46(2):68–71.

Curwin, R., & Mendler, A. (1987). *Discipline with dignity: Resource handbook*. Bellevue, WA: Bureau of Education & Research.

Davidman, L., & Davidman, P. (1984). Logical assertion: A rationale and strategy. *Educational Forum*, 48(2):165–176.

Dembo, M. H., Sweitzer, M., & Lauritzen, P. (1985). An evaluation of group parent education: Behavioral, PET, and Alderian programs. *Review of Educational Research*, 55(2):155–200.

Dinkmeyer, D., & Eckstein, D. (1996). *Leadership by encouragement*. Boca Raton, FL: St. Lucie Press.

Dinkmeyer, D., & Losoncy, L. (1996). *The skills of encouragement: Bringing out the best in yourself and others.* Boca Raton, FL: St. Lucie Press.

Dinkmeyer, D., McKay, G. D., & Dinkmeyer, D., Jr. (1980). *Systematic training for effective teaching: Teacher's handbook.* Circle Pines, MN: American Guidance Service.

Dinkmeyer, D., & Dinkmeyer, D., Jr. (1976). Logical consequences: A key to the reduction of disciplinary problems. *Phi Delta Kappan,* 57(10):664–666.

Dinkmeyer, D., & Dreikurs, R. (1963). *Encouraging children to learn: The encouragement process.* Englewood Cliffs, NJ: Prentice-Hall.

Discipline in Schools: Report of the committee of enquiry. (1989). London: Department of Education and Science and the Welsh Office.

Dobson, J. (1996). Our schools must have enough structure to require certain behavior from students, says Dr. Dobson because one of the purposes is to prepare our children for life. *Focus on the Family: With Dr. James Dobson.* Colorado Springs, CO: Focus on the Family.

Dobson, J. (1992). *The new dare to discipline.* Wheaton, IL: Tyndale House.

Dobson, J. (1978). *Preparing for adolescence.* Wheaton, IL: Tyndale House.

Dobson, J. (1978). *The strong-willed child.* Wheaton, IL: Tyndale House.

Dobson, J. (1970). *Dare to discipline.* Wheaton, IL: Tyndale House.

Dohrn, B. (1997). Youth violence: False fears and hard truths. *Educational Leadership,* 55(2):45–47.

Dollar, B. (1972). *Humanizing classroom discipline: A behavioral approach.* New York: Harper & Row.

Dr. Discipline. (1998). *NEA Today,* 17(1):6.

Dreikurs, R. (1977). Holistic medicine and the function of neuroses. *Journal of Individual Psychology,* 55:171–192.

Dreikurs, R. (1968). *Psychology in the classroom.* New York: Harper & Row.

Dreikurs, R. (1964). *Children: The challenge.* New York: Penguin.

Dreikurs, R. (1950). *Fundamentals of Adlerian psychology.* New York: Alfred Adler Institute.

Dreikurs, R., & Cassel, P. (1972). *Discipline without tears.* New York: Hawthorne.

Dreikurs, R., & Dinkmeyer, D. (1963). *Encouraging children to learn: The encouragement process.* Englewood Cliffs, NJ: Prentice-Hall.

Dreikurs, R., & Grey, L. (1968*). A new approach to discipline: Logical consequences.* New York: Hawthorne Books.

Dreikurs, R., Grunwald, B. B., & Pepper, F. C. (1982). *Maintaining sanity in the classroom: Classroom management techniques.* 2d ed. New York: Harper & Row.

Dreikurs, R., Grunwald, B. B., & Pepper, F. C. (1971). *Maintaining sanity in the classroom: Illustrating teaching techniques.* New York: HarperCollins.

Duke, D., & Jones, V. (1984). Two decades of discipline. Assessing the development of an educational specialization. *Journal of Research and Development in Education,* 17(4):25–35.

Early warning timely response: A guide to safe schools. (1998). Washington, DC: U.S. Department of Education.

Eison, J. (1990). Confidence in the classroom. *College Teaching,* 38(1):21–25.

Ellison, C. G., & Sherkat, D. E. (1993). Conservative Protestantism and support for corporal punishment. *American Sociological Review,* 58(1):131–144.

Emmer, E. T., & Aussiker, A. (1990). School and classroom discipline programs: How well do they work? *Student discipline strategies: Research and practice,* ed. O. C. Moles. Albany, NY: State University of New York Press.

Erie Daily Times. (1996). Man pleads guilty to shocking sons with dog collar. May 29, p. 9A.

Erie Morning News. (1993). Corporal punishment study done: Some school districts more likely to use method. October 7, 4A.

Essex, N. L. (1989). Corporal punishment: Ten costly mistakes and how to avoid them. *Principal,* 68(5):42–44.

Evans, T. D. (1996). Encouragement: The key to reforming classrooms. *Educational Leadership,* 54(1):81–85.

Farson, R. (1963). Praise reappraised. *Harvard Business Review,* 41(5):61–66

Ferguson, E., & Houghton, S. (1992). The effects of contingent teacher praise, as specified by Canter's assertive discipline programme, on children's on-task behavior. *Educational Studies,* 18(1):83–93.

Ferre, V. (1991). Effectiveness of assertive discipline in rural settings. *Rural Educator,* 12(2):6–8.

Focus on Teachers. Colorado Springs, CO: Focus on the Family.

Focus on the Family. Colorado Springs, CO: Focus on the Family.

Freiberg, H. J. (1997). From tourists to citizens in the classroom: An interview with H. Jerome Freiberg. *Mid-Western Educational Researcher,* 10(2):35–38.

French, J., Jr., & Raven, B. (1960). The bases for social power. *Group dynamics: Research and theory,* ed. D. Cartwirght & A. Sander. New York: Harper & Row.

Frisby, D., & Beckham, J. (1993). Dealing with violence and threats of violence in the school. *NASSP Bulletin,* 47(552):10–15.

Gaffney, P. V. (1997*). A study of preservice teachers' beliefs about various issues and myths regarding the use of scholastic corporal punishment.* ERIC Reproduction Service No. ED 409 315.

Gartrell, D. (1987). Assertive Discipline: Unhealthy for children and other living things. *Young Children,* 42(2):10–11.

Gaskins, J. (1987). Teaching as parenting, or "More die of heartbreak." *Freshman English News,* 16(3): 16–19.

Gathercoal, F. (1997). *Judicious discipline.* 4th ed. San Francisco: Caddo Gap Press.

Gathercoal, F. (1996). *A judicious philosophy for school support personnel.* San Francisco: Caddo Gap Press.

Gathercoal, F. (1991). *Judicious leadership for residence hall living.* San Francisco: Caddo Gap Press.

Gazda, G. M., Asbury, F. R., Balzer, F. J., Childers, W. C., Phelps, R. E., & Walters, R. P. (1995). *Human relations development: A manual for educators.* Boston: Allyn and Bacon.

Gerson, M. J. (1998). A righteous indignation. *U.S. News & World Report,* 124(17):20–25.

Gillett, M. (1980). *The effects of teacher enthusiasm on the at-task behavior of students in elementary grades.* ERIC Reproduction Service No. ED 202 823.

Ginott, H. (1971). *Teacher and child.* New York: Macmillan.

Ginott, H. (1969). *Between parent and teenager.* New York: Macmillan.

Ginott, H. (1965). *Between parent and child.* New York: Avon.

Glasser, W. (1998). *Choice theory: A new psychology of personal freedom.* New York: HarperCollins.

Glasser, W. (1997). A new look at school failure and school success. *Phi Delta Kappan,* 78(8):597–602.

Glasser, W. (1996). The theory of choice. *Learning,* 25(3):20–22.

Glasser, W. (1994). *The control theory manager.* New York: HarperCollins.

Glasser, W. (1992). The quality school curriculum. *Phi Delta Kappan,* 73(9):690–694.

Glasser, W. (1991). The quality school. *Principal Matters,* 3(3):17–27.

Glasser, W. (1990). *The quality school: Managing students without coercion.* New York: Harper & Row.

Glasser, W. (1989). Quality: The key to discipline. *Phi Kappa Phi Journal,* 69(1):36–38.

Glasser, W. (1986). *Control theory in the classroom.* New York: HarperCollins.

Glasser, W. (1977). 10 steps to good discipline. *Today's Education,* 66(4): 61–63.

Glasser, W. (1969). *Schools without failure.* New York: Harper & Row.

Glasser, W. (1965). *Reality therapy: A new approach to psychiatry.* New York: Harper & Row.

Goldberg, J., & Wilgosh, L. (1990). Comparing and evaluating classroom discipline models. *Education Canada,* 30(2):36–42.

Good, T. L., & Brophy, J. E. (1978). *Looking in classrooms.* 2d ed. New York: Harper & Row.

Gordon, T. (1988). The case against disciplining children at home or in school. *Person-Centered Review,* 3(1):59–85.

Gordon, T. (1981). Problem solving: How to help others do their own. *Nursing Life,* 1(1):57–64.

Gordon, T. (1981). Problem solving: When you need to confront other people. *Nursing Life, 1*(2):57–63.

Gordon, T. (1981). Crippling our children with discipline. *Journal of Education, 163*(3):228–243.

Gordon, T. (1977). *L.E.T.: Leader effectiveness training.* New York: Peter H. Wyden.

Gordon, T. (1976). *Parent effectiveness training workbook.* Solana Beach, CA: Effectiveness Training.

Gordon, T. (1974). *T.E.T.: Teacher effectiveness training.* New York: Peter H. Wyden.

Gordon, T. (1970). *P.E.T.: Parent effectiveness training.* New York: Peter H. Wyden.

Gough, P. (1987). The key to improving schools: An interview with William Glasser. *Phi Delta Kappan, 68*(9):656–662.

Goulden, N. R. (1991). *Improving instructors' speaking skills. IDEA PAPER NO. 24,* Center for Faculty Evaluation and Development, Kansas State University, Manhattan, KS.

Graff, P. (1981). Student discipline—Is there a bag of tricks? Or is organization the solution? *NASSP Bulletin, 65*(441):1–5.

Gregory, J. F. (1995). The crime of punishment: Racial and gender disparities in the use of corporal punishment in U.S. public schools. *Journal of Negro Education, 64*(4):454–462.

Greven, P. (1991). *Spare the child.* New York: Alfred A. Knopf.

Grossman, H. (1995). *Classroom behavior management in a diverse society.* Mountain View, CA: Mayfield.

Grossman, H. (1991). Trouble-free teaching: Solutions to behavior problems in the classroom. *Adolescence, 26*(102):495–496.

Grossman, H. (1990). *Trouble-free teaching: Solutions to behavior problems in the classroom.* Mountain View, CA: Mayfield.

Grossman, H. (1984). *Educating Hispanic students: Cultural implications for instruction, classroom management, counseling and assessment.* Springfield, IL: Thomas.

Gullatt, D. E., & Long, D. (1996). What are the attributes and duties of the school crisis intervention team? *NASSP Bulletin, 80*(580):104–113.

Halford, J. M. (1998). Toward peaceable schools. *Educational Leadership, 56*(1):103.

Hanko, G. (1994). Discouraged children: When praise does not help. *British Journal of Special Education, 21*(4):166–168.

Hanning, R. W. (1984). The classroom as theater of self: Some observations for beginning teachers. *ADE Bulletin, 77*(spring):33–37.

Hansen, J. (1979). Discipline and classroom management: Different strokes for different folks. *NASSP Bulletin, 63*(428):40–47.

Heller, G. S. (1996). Changing the school to reduce student violence: What works. *NASSP Bulletin, 80*(579):1–8.

Henle, M. (1957). Some problems with eclecticism. *Psychological Review*, 64(5):196–205.

Hernandez, R., & Gay, G. (1996). Students' perceptions of disciplinary conflict in ethnically diverse classrooms. *NASSP Bulletin*, 80(580):84–94.

Hill, D. (1990). Order in the classroom. *Teacher Magazine*, 1(7):70–77.

Hill, M. S. (1996). Making students part of the safe schools solution. *NASSP Bulletin*, 80(579):24–30.

Hitz, R., & Driscoll, A. (1988). Praise *or* encouragement? New insights into praise: Implications for early childhood teachers. *Young Children*, 43(5):6–13.

Hogan, M. P. (1985). Writing as punishment. *English Journal*, 74(5):40–42.

How to use ERIC. (1979). December. U.S. Government Printing Office.

Hunter, M. (1994). *Mastery teaching.* Thousand Oaks, CA: Corwin Press.

Hunter, M. (1977). Humanism vs. behaviorism. *Instructor*, 86(8):98, 100.

Hunter, M., & Barker, G. (1987). "If at first . . . ": Attribution theory in the classroom. *Educational Leadership*, 45(2):50–53.

Hyman, I. A. (1997). *The case against spanking: How to discipline your child without hitting.* San Francisco: Jossey-Bass.

Hyman, I. A. (1996). *School discipline and school violence: The teacher variance.* Needham Heights, MA: Allyn & Bacon.

Hyman, I. A. (1990). *Reading, writing and the hickory stick: The appalling story of physical and psychological abuse in American schools.* Lexington, MA: Lexington Books.

Hyman, I. A. (1989). The make-believe world of "Lean on me." *Education Digest*, 5(3):20–22.

Hyman, I. A. (1988). Should children ever be hit?: A contemporary answer to an historical question. *Journal of Interpersonal Violence*, 3(2):227–230.

Hyman, I. A. (1982). Discipline in the 1980's: Some alternatives to corporal punishment. *Children Today*, 11(1):10–13.

Hyman, I. A. (1978). Is the hickory stick out of tune? *Today's Education*, 67(2):30–32.

Hyman, I. A., & Dahbany, A. (1997). School discipline and school violence: The teacher variance approach. Boston: Allyn & Bacon.

Hyman, I. A., & D'Alessandro, J. (1984). Good, old-fashioned discipline: The politics of punitiveness. *Educational Leadership*, 66(1):39–45.

Hyman, I. A., & Wise, J. H. (1979). *Corporal punishment in American education: Readings in history, alternatives.* Philadelphia: Temple-Press.

Johnson, D. W., & Johnson, R. T. (1996). Reducing school violence through conflict resolution training. *NASSP Bulletin*, 80(579):11–18.

Johnson, D. W., & Johnson, R. T. (1995). *Reducing school violence through conflict resolution.* Alexandria, VA: ASCD.

Johnson, D. W., Johnson, R. T., Stevahn, L., & Hodne, P. (1997). The three C's of safe schools. *Educational Leadership*, 55(2):8–13.

Jones, F. H. (1997). Discipline alternatives. Did not! Did too! *Learning*, *24*(6):24, 26.

Jones, F. H. (1987a). *Positive classroom discipline*. New York: McGraw-Hill.

Jones, F. H. (1987b). *Positive classroom instruction*. New York: McGraw-Hill.

Jones, F. H. (1979). The gentle art of classroom discipline. *National Elementary Principal*, *58*(4):26–32.

Jones, F. H., Fremouw, W., & Carples, S. (1977). Pyramid training of elementary school teachers to use a classroom management "Skill Package." *Journal of Applied Behavior Analysis*, *10*(2):239–253.

Jones, V. (1984). An administrator's guide to developing and evaluating a building discipline program. *NASSP Bulletin*, *68*(471):60–73.

Jordan, J. R. (1982). The professor as communicator. *Improving College and University Teaching*, *30*(3):120–124.

Kessler, G. (1985). Spanking in school: Deterrent or barbarism? *Childhood Education*, *61*(3):175–176.

Kilpatrick, W. K. (1985, November). Carl Rogers' quiet revolution: Therapy for the masses. *Christianity Today*, pp. 21–24.

Kirschenbaum, H. (1991). Denigrating Carl Rogers: William Coulson's last crusade. *Journal of Counseling and Development*, *69*(5):411–413.

Kizer, B. (1988). *Adlerian therapy with aggressive children*. ERIC Document Reproduction Service No. ED 302 790.

Kohn, A. (1996). *Beyond discipline: From compliance to community*. Alexandria, VA: ASCD.

Kohn, A. (1996). By all available means: Cameron and Pierce's defense of extrinsic motivators. *Review of Educational Research*, *66*(1):1–4.

Kohn, A. (1996). Should we pay kids to learn? *Learning*, *24*(5):6–7.

Kohn, A. (1994). Bribes for behaving: Why behaviorism doesn't help children become good people. *NAMTA Journal*, *19*(2):71–94.

Kohn, A. (1993). *Punished by rewards: The trouble with gold stars, incentive plans, A's, praise, and other bribes*. New York: Houghton Mifflin.

Kohn, A. (1993). Rewards versus learning: A response to Paul Chance. *Phi Delta Kappan*, *74*(10):783–787.

Kohn, A. (1991). Caring kids: The role of the schools. *Phi Delta Kappan*, *72*(7):496–506.

Kounin, J. S. (1983). *Classrooms: Individuals or behavior settings? Monographs in teaching and learning*. Bloomington, IN: Indiana University.

Kounin, J. S. (1977). *Discipline and group management in classrooms*. New York: Holt, Rinehart & Winston.

Kounin, J. S. (1970). Observing and delineating technique of managing behavior in classrooms. *Journal of Research and Development in Education*, *4*(1):62–72.

Kramlinger, T. & Huberty, T. (1990). Behaviorism versus humanism. *Training & Development Journal*, *44*(12):41–45.

Krasner, L. (1978). The future and the past in the behaviorism-humanism dialogue. *American Psychologist, 33*(9):799–804.

Lasley, T. (1981). Helping teachers who have problems with discipline—A model and instrument. *NASSP Bulletin, 65*(441):6–15.

Lederhouse, J. N. (1998). You will be safe here. *Educational Leadership, 56*(1):51–54.

Lehman, B. (1989). Making a case against spanking. *The Washington Post.* Thursday, March 23, p. D5.

Lessen, R. (1979). *Spanking: Why, when, how?* Minneapolis, MN: Bethany Fellowship Inc.

Lewis, R. (1997). *The discipline dilemma: Control, management, influence.* Melbourne, Australia: Australian Council for Educational Research.

Lewis, R. (1991). *The discipline dilemma.* Hawthorn, Victoria: Australian Council for Educational Research.

Lewis, R., & Lovegrove, M. (1984). Teachers' classroom control procedures: Are student preferences being met? *Journal of Research for Teaching, 10*(2):97–105.

Lowman, J. (1984). *Mastering the techniques of teaching.* San Francisco: Jossey-Bass Publications.

Mager, R. (1968). *Developing attitude toward learning.* Palo Alto, CA: Fearon.

Maslow, A. (1968). *Toward a psychology of being.* New York: Van Nostrand.

McConnell, J. V. (1990). Negative reinforcement and positive reinforcement. *Teaching of Psychology, 17*(4):247–249.

McCormack, S. (1989). Response to Render, Padilla, and Krank: But practitioners say it works. *Educational Leadership, 46*(6):77–79.

McCormack, S. (1986). Students' off-task behavior and assertive discipline (time-on-task, classroom management, educational interventions). *Dissertation Abstracts International Online,* 46/07–A, 1880. (Order No. AAC 8520723)

McDaniel, T. R. (1986). A primer on classroom discipline: Principles old and new. *Phi Delta Kappan, 68*(1):63–67.

McDaniel, T. R. (1984). Developing the skills of humanistic discipline. *Educational Leadership, 41*(8):71–74.

McDaniel, T. R. (1980). Corporal punishment and teacher liability: Questions teachers ask. *The Clearing House, 54*(1):10–13.

McEwan, B. (1994). *Practicing judicious discipline.* San Francisco: Caddo Gap Press.

McEwan, B. (1991). *Practicing judicious discipline: An educator's guide to a democratic classroom.* San Francisco: Caddo Gap Press.

McKeachie, W. J. (1986). *Teaching tips: A guidebook for the beginning teacher.* Lexington, MA: D. C. Heath.

Mendler, A. N., & Curwin, R. L. (1983). *Taking charge in the classroom.* Reston, VA: Reston.

Merton, R. K. (1948). The self-fulfilling prophecy. *Antioch Review, 8*:193–210.

Milhollan, F., & Forisha, B. E. (1972). *From Skinner to Rogers: Contrasting approaches to education.* Lincoln, NE: Professional Educators Publications.

Miller, A. T., & Hom, H. L. (1997). Conceptions of ability and the interpretation of praise, blame, and material rewards. *The Journal of Experimental Education, 65*(2):163–177.

Morgan, K. (1984). Calm discipline. *Phi Delta Kappan, 66*(1):53–54.

Morris, R. C. (1996). Contrasting disciplinary models in education. *Thresholds in Education, 22*(4):7–13.

Murray, H. (1938). *Explorations in personality: A clinical and experimental study of fifty men of college age.* New York: Oxford University Press.

National Commission on Educational Excellence. (1983). *A nation at risk: The imperative for education reform.* Washington, D.C.: U.S. Government Printing Office.

Nazzal, A. (1996). Book Review. Acting lessons for teachers: Using performance skills in the classroom. *Social Education,* January: 62.

Neill, A. S. (1968). *Summerhill.* Harmondsworth, England: Penguin Books.

Nelsen, J. (1996). *Positive discipline.* New York: Ballantine.

Nelsen, J. (1987). *Positive discipline.* New York: Ballantine Books.

Nelsen, J., Dufy, R., Escobar, L., Ortolano, K., and Owen-Sohocki, R. (1996). *Positive discipline: A teacher's A-Z guide.* Orem, UT: Empowering People.

Nelsen, J., & Glenn, H. S. (1992). *Time out: Abuses and effective uses.* Orem, UT: Empowering People.

Nelsen, J., Lott, L., & Glenn, H. S. (1997). *Positive discipline in the classroom.* Rocklin, CA: Prima.

Orentlicher, D. (1992). Corporal punishment in the schools. *JAMA, 267*(23):3205.

Overman, W. (1979). Effective communication: The key to student management. *NASSP Bulletin, 63*(428):34–39.

Page, E. B. (1958). Teacher comments and student perfomance. A seventy-four classroom experiment in school motivation. *Journal of Educational Psychology, 49*:173–181.

Painter, G., & Corsini, R. J. (1990). *Effective discipline in the home and school.* Muncie, IN: Accelerated Development.

Palardy, J. (1996). Taking another look at behavior modification and assertive discipline. *NASSP Bulletin, 80*(581):66–70.

Parr, G., & Peterson, A. (1985). Friendly persuasion. *The Science Teacher, 52*(1):39–40.

Perry, R. P. (1985). Instructor expressiveness: Implications for improving teaching. In *Using research to improve teaching,* ed. J. G. Donald and A. M. Sullivan. San Francisco: Jossey-Bass.

Plax, T., Kearney, P., & Tucker, L. (1986). Prospective teachers' use of behavior alteration techniques on common student misbehaviors.

Communication Education, 35(1):32–41.

Pruess, N. (1997). Compelling whys in athletics. *The Heart of Teaching,* April(59):1–8.

Purcell, R. (1989). Electronic ERIC. *Small Computers in Libraries, 8*(2):18–21.

Radin, N. (1988). Alternatives to suspension and corporal punishment. *Urban Education, 22*(4):476–495.

Radin, R. (1978). Classroom management made easy. *Virginia Journal of Education,* September:14–17.

Raffini, J. (1980). *Discipline: Negotiating conflicts with today's kids.* Englewood Cliffs, NJ: Prentice-Hall.

Reimer, C. (1967). Some words of encouragement. In *Study group leaders' manual,* ed. V. Soltz. Chicago: Alfred Adler Institute.

Remboldt, C. (1998). Making violence unacceptable. *Educational Leadership, 56*(1):32–38.

Render, G. F., Padilla, J.N.M., & Krank, H. M. (1989a). What research really shows about assertive discipline. *Educational Leadership, 46*(6):72–75.

Render, G. F., Padilla, J.N.M., & Krank, H. M. (1989b). Assertive discipline: A critical review and analysis. *Teachers College Record, 90*(4):607–630.

Rich, J. M. (1991). Should students be punished? *Contemporary Education, 62*(3):180–184.

Richardson, M. (1985). Perceptions of principals and teachers of effective management of student behavior. *SPECTRUM, 3*(3):25–30.

Rogers, B. (1998). *You know the fair rule: And much more.* Hawthorn, Victoria: The Australian Council for Educational Research.

Rogers, B. (1997). *Cracking the hard class: Strategies for managing the harder than average class.* Gosford, New South Wales: Scholastic Australia.

Rogers, B. (1995). *Behaviour management.* Gosford, New South Wales: Scholastic Australia.

Rogers, B. (1989). *Making a discipline plan.* Melbourne, Australia: Thomas Nelson.

Rogers, C. (1977). Forget you are a teacher. *Instructor, 81*:65–66.

Rogers, C. (1969). *Freedom to learn.* Columbus, OH: Charles E. Merrill.

Rogers, C. (1961). *On becoming a person: A therapist's view of psychotherapy.* Boston: Houghton Mifflin.

Rogers, C. (1953). *Client-centered therapy.* New York: Free Press.

Rogers, C. (1951). *Client-centered therapy: Its current practices, implications and theory.* Boston: Houghton Mifflin.

Rogers, W. A. (1993). *The language of discipline: A practical approach to effective classroom management.* Plymouth, England: Northcoate House.

Rose, L. C., & Gallup, A. M. (1998). The 30th annual Phi Delta Kappa/Gallup Poll of the public's attitude toward the public schools. *Phi Delta Kappan, 80*(1):41–56.

Rosenthal, R., & Jacobson, L. (1968). *Pygmalion in the classroom.* New York: Holt, Rinehart and Winston.

Rosenthal, R. (1973). The mediation of Pygmalion effects: A four-factor "theory." *Papua New Guinea Journal of Education, 9*(1):1–12.

Rowe, M. (1978). Wait, wait, wait. . . . *School Science and Mathematics. 68*(685):207–216.

Rubin, L. J. (1985). *Artistry in teaching.* New York: Random House.

Rutter, M., Maughan, B., Mortimer, P., Ouston, J., & Smith, A. (1979). *Fifteen thousand hours.* Cambridge. MA: Harvard University Press.

Safer schools. (1998). Washington, D.C.: The National Crime Prevention Council.

Scherer, M. (1998). The discipline of hope: A conversation with Herb Kohl. *Educational Leadership, 56*(1):8–13.

Schmoker, M., & Wilson, B. W. (1993). Transforming school through total quality education. *Phi Delta Kappan, 74*(5):389–395.

Schmuck, R., & Schmuck, P. (1979). *Group processes in the classroom.* Dubuque, IA: William C. Brown.

Schubert, D. G. (1954). Discipline without disruption. *Journal of Education, 136:*112–113.

Schwartz, L. L. (1980). Criteria for effective university teaching. *Improving College and University Teaching, 28*(3):120–123.

Schwartz, W. (1996). *An overview of strategies to reduce school violence.* ERIC Clearinghouse on Urban Education. ERIC Document Reproduction Service No. ED 410 321.

Sendor, B. (1987). Kids gain new protection from corporal punishment. *American School Board Journal, 174*(11):32, 53.

Shen, J. (1997). The evolution of violence in schools. *Educational Leadership, 55*(2):18–20.

Shrigley, R. (1985). Curbing student disruption in the classroom: Teachers need intervention skills. *NASSP Bulletin, 69*(479):26–32.

Skiba, R. J., & Deno, S. L. (1991). Terminology and behavior reduction: The case against "punishment." *Exceptional Children, 57*(4):298–313.

Skinner, B. F. (1986). Programmed instruction revisited. *Phi Delta Kappan, 68*(2):103–110.

Skinner, B. F. (1980). Reward or punishment: Which works better? *U.S. News & World Report, 89*(18):79–80.

Skinner, B. F. (1973). The free and happy student. *Phi Delta Kappan, 55*(1):13–16.

Skinner, B. F. (1972). *Cumulative record: A selection of papers.* 3d ed. New York: Appleton-Century-Crofts.

Skinner, B. F. (1971). *Beyond freedom and dignity.* New York: Alfred A. Knopf.

Skinner, B. F. (1957). *Verbal behavior.* New York: Appleton.

Skinner, B. F. (1954). The science of learning and the art of teaching. *Harvard Educational Review, 24*(2):86–97.

Skinner, B. F. (1953). *Science and human behavior.* Boston: Houghton Mifflin.

Skinner, B. F. (1948). *Walden II.* New York: Macmillan.

Slavin, R., & Hunter, M. (1987). The Hunterization of America's schools. *Instructor, 96*(8):56–58, 60.

Smith, C. (1990). Answer your questions with ERIC. *The Reading Teacher, 44*(1):78–79.

Soenksen, R. (1992). *Confessions of a professor, nee actor.* Paper presented at the Speech Communication National Convention, Chicago, IL.

Stahl, R. J. (1994*).* Using "think-time" and "wait-time" skillfully in the classroom. *ERIC Digest,* ERIC Reproduction Service No. ED 370 885.

Stefanich, G., & Bell, L. (1985). A dynamic model of classroom discipline. *NASSP Bulletin, 69*(479):19–25.

Stonehill, R. M., & Brandhorst, T. (1992). The three phases of ERIC. *Educational Researcher, 21*(3):18–22.

Straus, M. A., Gelles, R. J., & Steinmetz, S. K. (1980). *Behind closed doors: Violence in the American family.* New York: Doubleday/Anchor.

Sussman, S. (1976). *A critical examination of disciplinary theories and practices.* Toronto: York Board of Education.

Swaim, E. E. (1974). B. F. Skinner and Carl R. Rogers on behavior and education. *Oregon ASCD Curriculum Bulletin, 28*(324):48 pages.

Sylwester, R. (1970). B. F. Skinner: Education's efficiency expert. *Instructor, 79*(7):72–73.

Tauber, R. T. (1992). Those who can't teach: Dispelling the myth. *NASSP Bulletin, 76*(541):97–102.

Tauber, R. T. (1991). Praise "strikes" out as a classroom management tool. *Contemporary Education, 62*(3):194–198.

Tauber, R. T. (1990). Changing teachers' attitudes toward punishment. *Principal, 69*(4):28, 30.

Tauber, R. T. (1988). Overcoming misunderstanding about the concept of negative reinforcement. *Teaching of Psychology,* 15(3):152–153.

Tauber, R. T. (1986a). Head teachers: Subjective and objective examinations of their social bases of power. *Secondary Heads Review, 80*(248):1028–1034.

Tauber, R. T. (1986b). French and Raven's power bases: A focus for educational researchers and practitioners. *The Australian Journal of Education, 30*(3):256–265.

Tauber, R. T., & Mester, C. S. (1994). *Acting lessons for teachers: Using performance skills in the classroom.* Westport, CT: Praeger.

Tenoschok, M. (1985). Handling discipline problems. *Journal of Physical Education, Recreation, and Dance, 56*(2):29–30.

Thomas, N. (1928). *The child in America.* New York: Knopf.

Thompson, T. (1997). Do we need to train teachers how to administer praise? Self-worth theory says we do. *Learning and Instruction*, 7(1):49–63.

Tjosuold, D. (1996, April). The issue of control: A critical review of the literature. Paper presented at the annual meeting of the American Educational Research Association, San Francisco, CA.

Tobin, K., & Capie, W. (1982). The relationship between classroom process variables and middle-school science achievement. *Journal of Educational Psychology*, 74(3):441–454.

Toffler, A. (1996). *Powershift*. New York: Bantam Books.

Trumbel, L. D., & Thurston, P. (1976). Improving classroom management: A systematic application of Dreikurs' theory of misbehavior in the elementary school. *Planning and Changing*, 7(2):29–34.

Trumbull, D. A. (1998, April p. 4). *Parent guide: Guidelines for disciplinary spanking*. Colorado Springs, CO: Focus on the Family.

U.S. Department of Education. (1997). *Our Ten Worst States*. Office of Civil Rights, 1994 Elementary and Secondary School Civil Rights Compliance Report.

U.S. News & World Report. (1996). The moral child, June 8, p. 52.

Valentine, M. (1988). *Difficult discipline problems: A family systems approach*. Dubuque, IA: Kendall-Hunt.

Valentine, M. (1987). *How to deal with discipline problems in the schools: A practical guide for educators*. Dubuque, IA: Kendall-Hunt.

Vockell, E. L. (1991). Corporal punishment: The pros and cons. *The Clearing House*, 64(4):278–283.

Wade, R. K. (1997). Lifting a school's spirit. *Educational Leadership*, 54(8):34–36.

Wagar, W. W. (1963). *The city of man, prophecies of a modern civilization in twentieth-century thought*. Boston: Houghton Mifflin.

Walters, G. C., & Grusec, J. E. (1977). *Punishment*. San Francisco: W. H. Freeman & Company.

Wang, M. C., Haertel, G. D., & Walberg, H. J. (1994). What helps students learn? *Educational Leadership*, 51(4):74–79.

Watson, J. J., & Remer, R. (1984). The effects of interpersonal confrontation on females. *The Personnel and Guidance Journal*, 62(10):607–611.

Webster, L., Wood, R. W., & Eicher, C. (1988). Attitudes of rural administrators toward corporal punishment. *Journal of Rural and Small Schools*, 3(1):19–20.

Weimer, M. (1993). *Improving your classroom teaching, Survival skills for scholars series*. Newbury Park, CA: SAGE.

Weiner, B. (1980). The role of affect in rational (attributional) approaches to human motivation. *Educational Researcher*, 9(7):4–11.

Weinstein, R. (1991). Expectations and high school change: Teacher-researcher collaboration to prevent school failure. *American Journal of Community Psychology*, 19(3):333–363.

Wolfgang, C., & Brudenell, G. (1982). The many faces of praise. *Early Child Development and Care, 9*(3):237–243.

Wolfgang, C., & Glickman, C. (1986). *Solving discipline problems.* 2d ed. Boston: Allyn & Bacon.

Wolfgang, C., & Glickman. C. (1980). *Solving discipline problems.* Boston: Allyn & Bacon.

Wubbolding, R. E. (1986). *Using reality therapy.* New York: HarperCollins.

Youth and violence: Is there a drug connection? Erie, PA: The Chemical People of Erie County, Inc. (Newsletter).

Zaiss, C., & Gordon, T. (1993). *Sales effectiveness training.* New York: Penguin.

Zirkel, P. A., & Gluckman, I. B. (1988). Constitutionalizing corporal punishment. *NASSP Bulletin, 72*(506):105–109.

Author Index

Abrami, P. C., 229
Albert, L., 109, 124, 130, 181–184, 210
Alonzo, T. M., 28
Aquayo, R., 148
Armstrong, P., 50
Asbury, F. R., 166
Ashton, P., 81
Aussiker, A., 41
Ausubel, D., 18, 239
Axelrod, S., 19, 237

Bailis, P., 195, 196
Baker, J. N., 57
Ball, J., 57
Balson, M., 7, 21, 112, 118, 121, 123, 239, 299
Balzer, F. J., 166
Barilla, J., 267
Barker, G., 238
Barkley, S., 182, 184
Barnard, H., 223
Barrett, E. R., 80
Barron, D. D., 301
Bartosh, F., Jr., 267
Bauer, G. F., 50
Baughman, M. D., 228
Bear, G. C., 174

Bell, L., 260
Bellack, A., 105
Beckman, J., 295
Bettencourt, E., 225
Bettencourt, M., 6
Blumenfeld-Jones, D., 38
Bobgan, D., 62
Bobgan, M., 62
Boonin, T., 57
Bordin, E. S., 31, 35
Bower, B., 29
Brandhorst, T., 305
Brandt, R., 136, 145, 150–151, 196
Brophy, J., 214, 224, 234
Brown, E. J., 4
Browne, M. N., 225
Brudenell, G., 241
Buckner, K. G., 288
Burka, A. A., 105
Burke, E., 290
Burns, J., 264
Burts, C. C., 225

Campbell, C. P., 226
Campbell, R., 55
Cangelosi, J. S., 7
Canter, L., 20, 67–70, 76, 79–80, 84–85, 87, 158, 170–171, 271

Capie, W., 283
Carples, S., 105
Cassel, P., 127
Chance, P., 85–86
Chanow-Gruen, K. J., 174
Charles, C. M., 4, 7, 8, 28, 114, 175,
    280–281
Childers, W. C., 166
Christenson, L., 47
Clarizio, H., 237
Cockrum, J. R., 151
Cornell, A. W., 174
Corsini, R. J., 129
Cowen, R. J., 105
Crockenberg, V., 80
Cryan, J. R., 47
Curtis, K. F., 80
Curwin, R. L., 9, 68, 84–88, 182,
    186–188, 210, 265

Dahbany, A., 63
D'Alessandro, J., 11
Davidman, L., 70, 77
Davidman, P., 70, 77
Dembo, M. H., 174
Deno, S. L., 50
Dinkmeyer, D., 109, 111, 122, 125,
    127–128, 248
Dobson, J., 20, 29, 41, 43–49, 52–53,
    58, 60–65, 154, 191
Dohrn, B., 287, 290
Dollar, B., 39
Doyle, R., 174
Dr. Discipline, 18
Dreikurs, R., 7, 21, 28, 34, 39, 41, 61,
    109–112, 114, 116, 119–121, 123,
    125, 127–131, 181–182, 190,
    200–201, 205, 210, 236, 247
Driscoll, A., 123
Dubanoski, R., 50
Dufy, R., 201
Duke, D., 13

Eckstein, D., 127

Eicher, C., 47
Eison, J., 226
Ellison, C. G., 46, 49, 57
Emmer, E. T., 41
Escobar, L., 201
Essex, N. L., 51
Evans, T. D., 128

Farson, R., 235–236
Ferguson, E., 69
Ferre, V., 80
Flanary, R. A., 288
Forisha, B. E., 28, 54
Freiberg, H. J., 39
Fremouw, W., 105
French, J., Jr., 17–19, 21–22, 25, 28,
    30, 39, 44, 68, 90, 110, 134–135,
    158–159, 250–251
Frisby, D., 295

Gaffney, P. V., 300
Gallup, A. M., 3, 288
Gartrell, D., 74
Gaskins, J., 174
Gathercoal, F., 182, 188, 190, 210
Gay, G., 292
Gazda, G. M., 166
Gelles, R. J., 51
Gerson, M. J., 43, 47
Gillett, M., 225
Ginott, H., 139, 182, 190–191, 241
Glasser, W., 7, 10, 21, 28, 37, 41,
    61–62, 114, 117, 133–146,
    148–155, 181, 190, 205, 238, 247,
    252, 267, 299
Glenn, H. S., 201
Glickman, C., 7, 17, 19, 21, 30, 39,
    44, 68, 90, 110, 134–135,
    158–159, 265
Gluckman, I. B., 45
Goldberg, J., 38–39, 128
Good, T. L., 48, 74, 97, 211, 214, 224,
    231, 237, 254–255, 281–282
Gordon, T., 7–8, 21, 25–26, 31, 37,

41–42, 49, 61–62, 79, 88,
157–161, 164, 167, 169, 170–176,
181, 190–191, 239–240
Gough, P., 136, 143, 145
Goulden, N. R., 224
Graff, P., 282
Gregory, J. F., 57
Greven, P., 55
Grey, L., 119, 121, 127
Grossman, H., 182, 191, 194
Grunwald, B. B., 127, 128
Grusec, J. E., 46, 49
Gullatt, D. E., 288, 294

Haertel, G. D., 4
Halford, J. M., 290
Hanko, G., 123
Hanning, R. W., 227–228
Hansen, J., 9, 12
Heller, G. S., 289, 290
Henle, M., 37
Herbert, D., 194, 290
Hernandez, R., 292
Hill, D., 80, 85
Hill, M. S., 292
Hitz, R., 123
Hogan, M. P., 120
Hom, H. L., 81
Houghton, S., 69
Huberty, T., 31
Hull, J., 225
Hunter, M., 39, 182, 194, 195, 196,
210, 238
Hyman, I. A., 11, 45, 58, 59, 63,
64

Jacobson, L., 25, 213
Johnson, D. W., 134, 150, 152–154,
288, 291
Johnson, R. T., 134, 150, 152–154,
288, 291
Jones, F. H., 10–11, 15, 29, 37–38, 61,
89–90, 92–96, 98–99, 102–107,
130, 182, 186, 200

Jones, V., 12–13
Jordan, J. R., 224–225

Kearney, P., 12
Keeley, S. M., 225
Kessler, G., 55
Kilpatrick, W. K., 30
Kirschenbaum, H., 30
Kizer, B., 129
Koenig, L., 182, 196
Kohn, A., 55, 68, 81–83, 85–87, 234
Kounin, J. S., 182, 197–200
Kramlinger, T., 31
Krank, H. M., 69, 86
Krasner, L., 28

LaCagnina, G. R., 28
Lasley, T., 261–262
Lauritzen, P., 174
Lederhouse, J. N., 292
Lehman, B., 51
Lessen, R., 46, 49
Leventhal, L., 229
Lewis, R., 17–19, 35, 44, 68, 90, 110,
134–135, 158–159, 198, 260
Long, D., 288, 294
Losoncy, L., 125, 128
Lott, L., 201
Lovegrove, M., 260
Lowman, J., 226–227

Mager, R., 222–223, 244
Maslow, A., 30, 113, 143–144
Maughan, B., 50
McConnell, J. V., 244
McCormack, S., 69, 80, 86
McDaniel, T. R., 7, 11, 51, 80, 277
McEwan, B., 190
McKay, G. D., 122, 127
McKeachie, W., J. 226
Mendler, A. N., 9, 68, 84–85, 182,
186–188, 210, 265
Merton, R. K., 213
Mester, C. S., 231

Milhollan, F., 28, 54
Miller, A. T., 81
Morgan, K., 45, 264
Morris, R. C., 36
Mortimer, P., 50
Murray, H., 219

Nazzal, A., 231
Neill, A. S., 45
Nelsen, J., 109, 119–122, 130,
    181–182, 200–201, 210

Olsen, B. C., 28
Orentlicher, D., 45, 54, 57
Ortolano, K., 201
Ouston, J., 50
Overman, W., 7
Owen-Sohocki,, 201

Padilla, J.N.M., 69, 86
Page, E. B., 239
Painter, G., 129
Palardy, J., 80, 86
Parr, G., 278
Pepper, F. C., 127–128
Perry, R. P., 229, 269
Peterson, A., 278
Phelps, R. E., 166
Plax, T., 12
Pruess, N., 145
Purcell, R., 304

Quale, D., 50

Radin, N., 57
Radin, R., 106
Raffini, J., 140
Raven, B., 17–19, 21–22, 25, 28, 30,
    39, 44, 68, 90, 110, 134–135,
    158–159, 250–251
Reimer, C., 122
Remboldt, C., 288, 290
Remer, 169
Render, G. F., 69, 86

Rich, J. M., 50
Richardson, M., 12
Rogers, C. R., 17–19, 21, 28, 30–31,
    33–35, 39–40, 44, 61, 68, 90, 110,
    134–135, 157–159, 164, 174, 176,
    254
Rogers, W., 202–205, 210
Rose, L. C., 288
Rosenthal, R., 25, 213, 216, 231
Rowe, M., 283
Rubin, L. J., 227–228
Rutter, M., 50

Scherer, M., 292
Schmoker, M., 152
Schmuck, P., 248
Schmuck, R., 248
Schubert, D. G., 4
Schwartz, W., 288, 290
Sendor, B., 45
Shen, J., 288
Sherkat, D. E., 47, 49, 57
Shrigley, R., 120, 253, 262
Skiba, R. J., 50
Skinner, B. F., 17–20, 28–31, 33–35,
    39–40, 44, 53, 54–55, 61, 65, 68,
    81, 90, 110, 134–135, 153,
    158–159, 254
Slavin, R., 196
Smith, A., 50
Smith, C., 300, 309
Soenksen, R., 224
Stahl, R. J., 283
Stefanich, G., 260
Steinmetz, 51
Stonehill, R. M., 305
Straus, M. A., 51
Sussman, S., 129
Swaim, E. E., 39
Sweitzer, M., 174
Sylwester, R., 53

Tauber, R. T., 25, 27, 36–37, 46, 72,
    124, 218, 226, 236

Tenoschok, M., 73
Thomas, N., 213
Thompson, T., 219–221, 235
Thornburg, K., 223
Thurston, P., 19, 129
Tjosvold, D., 248
Tobin, K., 283
Toffler, A., 54
Tracy, J. J., 287
Trumble, L. D., 19, 129
Trumbull, D. A., 52
Tucker, L., 12

Urquhart, C., 81

Valentine, M., 182, 205, 208, 210
Vockell, E. L., 50–51

Wade, R. K., 80, 152
Wagar, W. W., 214
Walberg, H. J., 4
Walters, G. C., 46, 49

Walters, R. P., 166
Wang, M. C., 4
Watson, J. J., 169
Webster, L., 47
Weimer, M., 226
Weiner, B., 238
Weinstein, R., 217
Wilgosh, L., 38–39, 128
Wilson, B. W., 152, 186
Wise, J. H., 59
Wolfgang, C., 7, 17, 19, 21, 30, 39, 44, 68, 90, 110, 134, 135, 158, 159, 241, 265
Wong, H., 182, 208
Wood, R. W., 47
Wubbolding, R. E., 152

Yamauchi, L. A., 50

Zaiss, C., 157
Zirkel, P. A., 45

Subject Index

"A" for Act: Don't Just React, 256
"A" for Assign Responsibility, 257
Accountability, 102, 199
Acting Lessons for Teachers: Using Performance Skills in the Classroom (Tauber and Mester), 224, 226, 231
Active listening (Gordon), 26, 158, 164–166, 169–173, 175, 190, 240
Adler School of Professional Psychology, 129
Alpha male, 69, 70, 87
The American Family (Quale), 50
American Guidance Service, 130, 131, 184
Appearance, 222, 272, 282
Assertive discipline (Canter), 20, 29, 41, 42, 67–70, 75, 80, 81, 83–88, 152, 170, 302
Attribution theory, 238
Authority, 24, 46–49, 70, 112, 130, 248, 250–251, 284

"B" for Back Away, 258–259
Backup systems, 104, 107
Behavior modification, 54, 76–77, 80–81, 86, 102, 144, 154, 235, 242, 244–245, 247, 300
Beyond Freedom and Dignity (Skinner), 28

Bids for attention (Dreikurs), 112
Body language, 73, 78, 91, 93, 95, 97, 99, 105, 185, 187, 202, 204, 230, 281
Boredom, 97–98, 222, 244
Boss-managing (Glasser), 147, 152
Broken-record technique, 77, 87, 139
Building Classroom Discipline (Charles), 7

"C" for Calm and Businesslike, 259–260
"C" for Catch Students Being Good, 260
"C" for Individual or Private Correction, 261
Calm and businesslike, 70, 259–260
Choice Theory (Glasser), 134, 153
Classroom structure, 90, 92–93, 101
Client-Centered Therapy (Rogers), 28, 30
Climate, 30, 191, 216–217, 289, 292
Coercive power, 22, 23, 30
Common sense, 14, 62
Communication, 25, 91, 93, 105, 158–159, 161, 162, 164, 166–167, 173–176, 184, 191, 206–208, 210, 225, 237, 240, 258
Communication Discipline (Ginott), 182, 190

Conflict resolution, 25–26, 171–175, 291

Consequence grid, 233, 252

Consequences, 29–30, 50, 52, 55, 65, 70, 73–77, 79–80, 84, 110, 118–121, 127, 130, 131, 142, 186–187, 189, 201, 203, 205, 213, 222, 233, 235, 243, 260, 262, 265, 267, 280, 290, 292

Control theory, 151, 153

Control Theory in the Classroom (Glasser), 135, 205

Cooperative Discipline (Albert), 130, 182–184, 210

Corporal punishment, 44–46, 50–59, 61, 63, 65, 223, 300, 304, 305

Corporal Punishment in American Education (Hyman), 59

"D" for Make a Deal with a Fellow Teacher, 262

Dare to Discipline (Dobson), 20, 29, 43, 46

Decisive Discipline (Rogers, W.), 182, 202, 210

Delivering praise, 233, 235

Demographics of discipline, 44, 57

Dignity, 26, 186–188, 204, 210

The Discipline Dilemma: Control, Manage, and Influence (Lewis), 35

Discipline in Schools: Report of the Committee of Enquiry, 4

Discipline with Dignity (Curwin and Mendler), 182, 186–188, 210

Discouragement, 113, 122, 169, 183, 200, 247, 248

Diversity, 193, 265

Door-openers, 164, 240

"E" for Enforce; Don't Negotiate, 264

"E" for Eye Messages, 265

"E" for Prepare an Emergency Plan, 263

Early Warning Timely Response: A Guide to Safe Schools, 293

Eclecticism, 17, 36–38, 40

Educational Resources Information Center (ERIC), 10, 46, 299

Effective teaching, 5, 9–10, 224, 226, 254, 271, 277

Encouragement, 34, 40, 110, 118, 122–128, 131, 183–184, 187, 201, 239, 284

Enthusiasm, 84, 224–228, 231–232

Excuses, 76, 136, 139, 141, 201, 206

Expectations, 25, 27, 70, 81, 184, 207, 209, 212–219, 231, 236, 269, 289, 292

Expert power, 22, 25, 27

"F" for Friendly versus Friends, 266

Fear, 22, 45, 53, 73, 140, 169, 222–223, 240, 244, 248, 289

Feedback, 103–104, 126, 216–217, 234, 239, 277

Feelings, 22, 65, 71, 88, 107, 112, 114, 116, 127, 131, 146, 155, 161, 164–167, 169, 176, 183, 185, 191, 201, 237–241, 248, 251, 261, 280, 292, 293

The First Days of School (Wong), 182, 208–209

Focus on the Family (Dobson), 63

Four-factor theory (Rosenthal), 216, 231

Frameworks, 17–19, 28, 30, 44, 64, 68, 87, 89, 106, 109, 130, 134, 154, 158, 181

Freedom to Learn (Rogers), 21, 30

Fun, 48, 82, 144–145, 147–148, 153

Fundamentals of Adlerian Psychology (Dreikurs), 128

"G" for Don't Hold a Grudge, 267

Gallup Poll, 5, 288

Giving in, 113, 116, 233–234, 248–250, 252, 264

Giving solutions, 162

Glasser's hierarchy of needs, 143–145
Goals of misbehavior (Dreikurs), 61,
    109, 114–115, 129–130, 247
Grandma's rule, 105

Hostile, 70–71, 87, 114, 203–204, 207
Humor, 191, 227–228, 231

"I" for Identify Specific Behaviors, 267
I-messages, 26, 79, 88, 167–173,
    175–176, 190–191, 239
Incentives, 83, 88, 91, 101
Influence, 4, 10, 17–18, 23–25, 28,
    35, 41, 47, 49, 80, 134, 144–145,
    147, 157–159, 183, 218, 238, 253,
    264, 300
Input, 127, 149, 187, 216–217
In-school suspension, 136
Interactionalists, 19, 21
Interventionists, 19, 21

"J" for Judge and Jury, 268
Johnson City, 134, 150, 152–154
Judicious discipline (Gathercoal), 182,
    188–190, 210

Layer cake (Jones), 61, 90
Lead-managing (Glasser), 149, 152
Lean on Me, 45
Legitimate power, 24, 39, 251
L.E.T.: Leader Effectiveness Training
    (Gordon), 25, 159
Limit setting, 73, 98, 104
Logical consequences, 55, 119–120,
    121, 127, 130, 142, 201, 205, 260,
    267
Lord of the Flies, 48
Luck, 238

"M" for Mr. or Miss, 269
*Maintaining Sanity in the Classroom:
    Classroom Management Techniques*
    (Dreikurs), 127
Making a discipline plan, 205

Marbles in a jar (Canters), 74–75, 84
Maslow's hierarchy of needs, 143
Modeling, 72, 93, 172
Motivation, 20, 31, 82–83, 85, 86,
    103, 105, 116, 118, 122, 136, 145,
    149, 150, 237–238, 247
Multicultural discipline (Grossman),
    182, 191

"N" for Learn Their Names, 270
"N" for Personal Needs: Yours and
    Theirs, 271
NASSP Bulletin, 7, 86
National Center for the Study of
    Corporal Punishment and
    Alternatives in Schools (Hyman),
    58, 61, 63
Natural consequences, 118–119, 121,
    130
Negative reinforcement, 193, 233–235,
    241, 242–247, 252, 262
*A New Approach to Discipline: Logical
    Consequences* (Dreikurs and Grey),
    127
No-lose method (Gordon), 175
Nonassertive, 70–72, 87
Noninterventionists, 19–20

"O" for Organized, 272
"O" for Overprepare, 273
Omission training (Jones), 102, 104,
    107
Operant conditioning, 29, 52, 249,
    262, 264
Output, 216–217
Overlapping, 198, 272–273

"P" for Don't Take it Personally,
    273
"P" for Premack Principle (Grandma's
    Rule), 274
"P" for Punctuality, 275
Palms (Jones), 98
Pastoral care, 217

P.E.T.: Parent Effectiveness Training
(Gordon), 157
Phi Delta Kappan, 5, 69, 84–86, 151–
152, 299
Philosophy, 4–5, 13, 18–19, 21,
33–36, 38, 172, 190
Positive Classroom Discipline (Jones),
10, 29, 89, 101, 103–104
Positive Classroom Instruction (Jones),
10, 89, 103
Positive recognition, 68, 83
Positive reinforcement, 46, 84, 204,
234–235, 242–246, 252, 262
Power struggles (Dreikurs), 105, 112,
116, 130, 187, 233–234, 247, 249,
250–252
Praise, 14, 33–34, 40, 69, 80-81, 110,
118, 122–127, 131, 166, 190, 193,
216, 233–241, 252
Praise-prompt-leave (Jones), 104, 107
Praising, 104, 162, 201, 237
Preferred Activity Time (PAT) (Jones),
99–102, 104, 107
Project T.E.A.C.H. (Barkley), 182,
184–186, 210
Props, 230
Proverbs, 46
Proximity control, 106, 187, 259, 262
Psychology in the Classroom (Dreikurs),
128
Punished by Rewards (Kohn), 88
Punishment, 22, 44–47, 49–65, 79,
120–121, 127, 136–137, 142, 149,
172, 174, 182, 187, 191, 201, 204,
205, 210, 211, 221–224, 231–232,
235–236, 243–244, 246, 252,
262–264, 290, 300, 304, 305
Pygmalion, 212–213, 218, 231

*The Quality School: Managing Students
without Coercion* (Glasser), 135

"R" for Return Assignments and Tests
Quickly, 277

*Reading, Writing and the Hickory Stick:
The Appalling Story of Physical and
Psychological Abuse in American
Schools* (Hyman), 59
Reality therapy, 61, 117, 133–136,
138–139, 140–142, 145, 150–155
*Reality Therapy: A New Approach to
Psychiatry* (Glasser), 133, 135
Referent power, 24–27, 39
Reinforcement, 13, 23, 29, 46, 50,
54–55, 76, 84, 193, 204, 233–235,
241–247, 252, 262, 264
Respect, 5, 7, 24–26, 31, 41, 48, 50,
61, 71, 85, 109, 119, 126, 164,
171, 187, 198, 201, 204, 215–216,
218, 230, 251, 259, 270, 274, 291–
292
Response styles (Canter), 68, 70, 83,
87
Responsibilities, 117, 184, 188, 190,
269, 294, 300, 310
Responsibility training (Jones), 90
Revenge seeking (Dreikurs), 112
Rewarding, 75, 82, 136, 147
Rights, 24, 38, 45, 70, 74, 85, 188,
190, 204
Roadblocks to communication
(Gordon), 158, 161–162, 164,
166–167, 173, 176, 240
Rod, 46, 55, 65, 223
Routines, 92–93, 101, 104
Rules, 9, 29, 48, 50, 55, 68, 72–76,
78, 80, 84, 91–92, 94, 98, 104,
116, 134, 136–138, 142, 154, 187,
189, 204–205, 209, 248, 280, 290,
292–293

"S" for Secure Their Attentions—First!,
277
"S" for Surprise Them, or "How Did
You Know That?," 278
Safer Schools, 289, 293
Sales Effectiveness Training (Gordon),
157

Schedules of reinforcement, 23, 264

Schools of thought (Wolfgang and Glickman), 5, 19, 21, 44, 68, 110, 134, 158

Schools without Failure (Glasser), 133–135, 205

Science and Human Behavior (Skinner), 28

Seating patterns, 106

Self-actualization, 143

Self-discipline, 5, 30–31, 80, 82, 86, 109, 123, 173, 276, 279

Self-fulfilling prophecy, 25, 70, 211–214, 218, 231

Signals, 91, 96, 161, 262, 269, 293, 297

Smart Discipline (Koenig), 182, 196–197

Social bases of power (French and Raven), 17–18, 27

Solving Discipline Problems (Wolfgang and Glickman), 7

Spanking, 44, 50–51, 53, 63

Strategies, 5, 10, 13, 37, 49, 76, 84, 136, 181, 186, 190, 197, 217, 228, 241–242, 253–255, 257, 268, 273, 276, 278, 290, 292, 296, 300

The Strong-Willed Child (Dobson), 49

Succeeding with Difficult Students (Canter), 20

Summerhill (Neill), 45

Systematic Training for Effective Parenting (STEP), 130

Systematic Training for Effective Teaching (STET), 127, 130

"T" for Say "Thank You," 279

"T" for Threats and Warnings, 280

Task difficulty, 238

Teachers in Focus, 64

Teams, 145, 147, 150–151, 183, 292–294

T.E.T.: Teacher Effectiveness Training (Gordon), 8, 25, 31, 42, 159, 173

Time-out, 55, 136, 141, 185, 204, 235, 243–244, 246, 262–263

Toward a Psychology of Being (Maslow), 30

"U" for Be Up, 281

Understanding Classroom Behaviour (Balson), 7, 21, 299

Use of space, 230

"V" for Visibility (and at Times Invisibility), 282

Violence, 54, 59, 84, 287–297

Vocational education, 306

"W" for Wait-Time, 283

"W" for "We," Not "You," 283

Walden II (Skinner), 28

Withitness (Kounin), 182, 197, 198

Working the crowd (Jones), 91–92, 98–99, 101, 103–104

"X" for Exemplify Desired Behavior; Don't Be a Hypocrite, 284

You-messages (Gordon), 167–169, 170, 173

About the Author

ROBERT T. TAUBER is Professor Emeritus at the Behrend College of The Pennsylvania State University. His more than thirty years' experience includes teaching at an inner-city junior high, counseling at a vocational-technical high school, and teaching courses in educational psychology and foundations of education. He is the author of six books, among them *Acting Lessons for Teachers* (Praeger, 1994) and *Self-Fulfilling Prophecy* (Praeger, 1997).

ISBN 0-89789-618-1

HARDCOVER BAR CODE